Tales from My First
90 Years

Tales from My First
90 Years

Alpha C Chiang

Professor Emeritus of Economics

University of Connecticut, USA

World Scientific

NEW JERSEY • LONDON • SINGAPORE • BEIJING • SHANGHAI • HONG KONG • TAIPEI • CHENNAI • TOKYO

Published by

World Scientific Publishing Co. Pte. Ltd.
5 Toh Tuck Link, Singapore 596224
USA office: 27 Warren Street, Suite 401-402, Hackensack, NJ 07601
UK office: 57 Shelton Street, Covent Garden, London WC2H 9HE

Library of Congress Cataloging-in-Publication Data
Names: Chiang, Alpha C., 1927– author.
Title: Tales from my first 90 years / Alpha C. Chiang.
Other titles: Tales from my first ninety years
Description: Hackensack : World Scientific, 2021.
Identifiers: LCCN 2020039766 | ISBN 9789811220999 (hardcover) |
ISBN 9789811221002 (ebook) | ISBN 9789811221019 (ebook other)
Subjects: LCSH: Chiang, Alpha C., 1927– | Economists--United States--Biography.
Classification: LCC HB119.C49225 C45 2021 | DDC 330.092 [B]--dc23
LC record available at https://lccn.loc.gov/2020039766

British Library Cataloguing-in-Publication Data
A catalogue record for this book is available from the British Library.

For any available supplementary material, please visit
https://www.worldscientific.com/worldscibooks/10.1142/11850#t=suppl

Desk Editor: Sia Geng Jie

Typeset by Diacritech Technologies Pvt. Ltd.
Chennai - 600106, India

Printed in Singapore

To the loving memory of my extraordinary parents:
Rev. and Mrs. P. S. Chiang

my beloved wife and friend:
Emily Chiang

the cherished family of my dear son:
Darryl Chiang, Andrea Jue, and Julian Chiang

and the cherised family of my dear daughter:
Tracey Chiang, Jonathan McGrath,
Emmett McGrath, and Kieran McGrath

Table of Contents

Preface

Some people write memoirs about the pains they have taken to achieve earth-shaking scientific discoveries. Some others write about the tough struggles they had had to go through to overcome daunting obstacles and attain ultimate success, freedom, or riches. Yet some others write about how they have survived challenging man-made or natural disasters.

I do not have such big stories to tell. So, why am I writing this book? The answer is that when I had occasions to relate some of my life experiences—some of them extraordinary, and some of them not that out of the ordinary—at dinner conversations, my friends often showed substantial interest. Some friends even asked for sequels or other related stories. That led me to think that it might be worthwhile to put such stories in writing for the entertainment of my other friends, and beyond.

At first, I just wrote anecdotal essays at random and even had some of them published. But when I participated in a Memoirs Group at Cedar Crest, a retirement community I moved to in 2012, I began to consider seriously the possibility of a book project. Ms. Helene Zablocki, the lady who has led the Memoirs Group for many years even though she does not live at Cedar Crest, provided the initial impetus via her encouragement.

Publisher

In that incipient stage, I did not even think of the problem of finding a publisher. That would likely be a difficult, time-consuming job, which I was not yet ready to face. Fortuitously, however, an unexpected suggestion from Professor Y. Y. Kueh (郭益耀教授), a former student of mine who later became my "boss," kindly introduced me to a suitable publishing company. Professor Kueh had just published his own memoirs with World Scientific Publishing Co. (WSPC) in Singapore, and offered to introduce me to its Founder and Editor-in-Chief, Dr. K. K. Phua (潘國駒博士). Since WSPC publishes books in both English and Chinese, I immediately submitted sample chapters for both the English and the Chinese versions of my memoirs. Gratifyingly to me, Dr. Phua expressed interest in both versions, with the English one as the first project. With a contract in hand, I then became earnest.

Book Title

Choosing a title for my project proved to be more difficult than I envisaged. Since my book would cover many aspects of my life, rather than focus on a single theme, the title has to be general in nature. The original working title I selected, without too much thought, was simply: *Tales from My First 90 Years.* I liked the word "first" for the humor in it, and quite a few friends consider it a good, catchy title. But some others deemed it too vague, revealing nothing at all about the exact nature of the tales. That forced me to do some more thinking.

Trying to be less vague, I first altered the original title to: *A Multifaceted Life: My First 90 Years.* The reaction I got was "still too vague." To be really specific, however, I would have to refer to my profession, teaching economics and writing papers and books, as well as the many side interests and hobby pursuits that I had ventured into. Then the book title could read something like: *Tales from a Professor-Author-Chinese Classical Style Painter and Calligrapher-Chinese Opera Instrumentalist-Photographer-Ballroom Dancer-Pianist-Composer-and Playwright: His First 90 Years.* Patently awkward and unwieldy, such a title had to be discarded, even though it effectively catalogs both the WORK and PLAY aspects of my "first 90 years."

A simplified version of the work–play theme then came to mind: *Rocky Road to Academe and Enchanted Detours to the Land of the Muses: My First 90 Years.* Or, to make it less wordy: *Halls of Academe and the Land of the Muses: Tales from My First 90 Years.* My son Darryl's reaction made me hesitate: "The words Academe and Muses are too opaque, and not conducive to reader interest."

So, what could I do next? I tried the categorization of the types of tales I include in the book. The resulting title was: *The Cheery, Scary, Ludicrous, and Surreal: Tales from My First 90 Years.* Again, too wordy! Thinking about the book's contents, I realize that I have devoted quite a lot of pages to many uncanny, incredible stories that happened to me or to my family. So, setting my mind on the word "surreal," I was tempted to choose the title *The Real and the Surreal: Tales from My First 90 Years.* But, still, it does not properly characterize the book.

At long last, I decided to revert to the original title.

So, was the above report on the title choice a waste of time? Not really, for by going over the title-choice process, I have actually (somewhat sneakily) given you a sketchy indication of what the book is about.

Regardless of the title, I hope my tales inside will give you some enjoyable moments of reading.

Photos

The book will be adorned with photographs. Again, the selection process is no easy job; I have had to sift through several decades' worth of photographs, and meticulously decide "yes" or "no" for each one. Why? Because I only have space for 32 pages of colored photos in the front part of the volume, and a limited number of other photos to be printed in black-and-white within the text. The photos in the color section are numbered 1, 2, 3, . . . The black-and-white ones contain decimal points, for example, the number 1.2 indicates Chapter 1, Photo 2.

The photos taken in my early years, in Shanghai, China, and in Colorado and New York City, originally in black and white, are of course relegated to the text—including my wedding pictures. Some photos, originally in color but without too much color in them, are also printed within the text. Some pictures appear smaller than I intended, on account of space limitations. Some friends and relatives, an integral part of my life, do not even appear in any pictures in the book, because I either do not possess any or have exhausted the photo quota. My sincere apologies for all of these omissions.

Appreciation

Many people should be thanked for their help in bringing this book into being. Ms. Helene Zablocki gave me the initial spark and offered suggestions on a few chapters she read. Professor Y. Y. Kueh introduced me to Dr. K. K. Phua, and Dr. Phua kindly agreed to publish this volume. Sincere thanks go to them. Ms. Deborah Greenberg and Ms. Therese Murray Faesller read parts of the manuscript and made suggestions. My wife Emily (何欽翠) read all of the chapters and made a critical impact on its final form. And I consulted my son Darryl (蔣澹如) several times on the book title.

But my deepest debt was to Ms. Ruth Hsiao (蕭俞毓慶)—see Photo 38—a longtime friend from whom I learned a great deal about writing. Every year her eagerly awaited Christmas letter came as a showcase of excellent English writing, with the best choice of words and phrases, plus the right touch of humor. I was overjoyed when she consented to be a reader and mentor for my memoirs. And I felt honored when she asked me to be a reader for her own memoirs. Unfortunately, Ruth passed away before I finished the draft, so that the later chapters of this book had no opportunity to benefit from her valuable critique.

For their help in locating for me a copy of *Who's Who in Economics: A Biographical Dictionary of Major Economists 1700-1986,* second edition, I am indebted to the efficient librarians Ms. Lois Fletcher (University of Connecticut, Storrs campus), Ms. Phara Bayonne (University of Connecticut, Stanford campus), as well as Ms. Lori Stethers (Wesleyan University).

Lastly, I am grateful to Mr. Sia Geng Jie (盛耿捷) of WSPC, my editor, for his unsparing efforts and patient cooperation, to Dr. Zhai Yubing (翟宇冰) of the US office of WSPC for helping with the transmission of photo prints, and to Ms. Pauline Tan (陳寶凌) for creating as many as 4 elegant cover designs for this book, from which I made the final, happy choice with the advice of my daughter Tracey (蔣粹似).

Alpha C. Chiang (蔣中一)

Memories in Color

1. My parents on their Golden (50th) Anniversary, Hong Kong, 1976.

2. My father became an ordained minister at age 61.

3. Celebrating my parents' Diamond (60th) Anniversary in Hong Kong, 1986.

4. My favorite teacher of English, Mr. I-shin Cheng (鄭逸欣老師) at age 93, China, 1996.

5. Professor William Vickrey, who directed my PhD dissertation at Columbia University, won the Nobel Prize in 1996.

6. Visiting my wife Emily's parents in Taipei, Taiwan, 1974.

7. My home on Beech Mountain Road (別趣山居) in Mansfield Center, Connecticut, 1971–93.

8. In the foyer of the house, 1986. The seal on the wall shows the name of the house.

9. In our living room, with Emily, Darryl (son) and Tracey (daughter), 1989.

10. My late-coming son, Darryl, at age 2 in a custom-made Chinese outfit, 1970.

11. My late-coming daughter, Tracey, in an affectionate pose at age 3, 1973.

12. I photographed Darryl (6) and Tracey (4) in the backyard, 1974.

13. Emily as my photographic model, 1978.

14. Emily in 1987.

15. Tom and Jane Tang were instrumental in bringing Emily and me together. (2002 photo)

16. A painting by Darryl, done when he was three-and-half years old, 1972.

17. A painting by Tracey, done at Brown University, circa 1990.

18. Halloween: Tracey (9) as a lion, 1979.

19. Halloween: Darryl (10) as a hobo, 1978.

20. Opera: "The Duan Bridge (斷橋)," with Emily (in blue), Julia Ho, and Chia-dann Chi, 1965.

21. Opera: Emily in "Han Yu Niang (生死恨)," 1991. (She made the spinning-wheel prop herself.)

22. Opera: "The Tragic Tale of the Bride (販馬記寫狀)," with Emily (left) and Chia-dann Chi, 2002.

23. Opera: Emily in "Su-san on Trial (玉堂春會審)," 2005.

24. All four members of our family were on stage in the same show, 1981.

25. The Chinese-opera orchestra, with Roger Yeu on the right, and me in the middle, 1999.

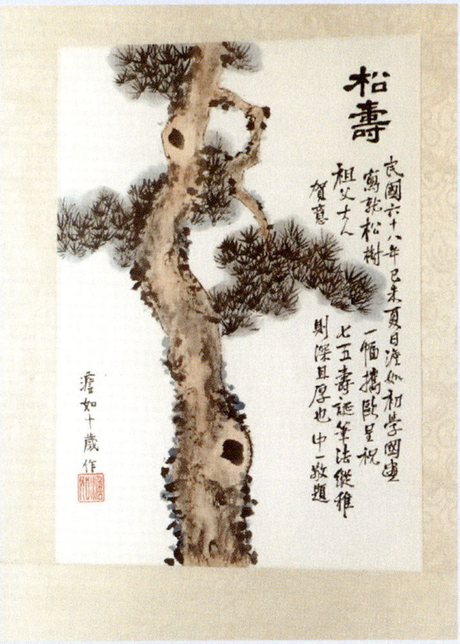

26. Darryl did this painting (at age 10) for Grandpa's 75th birthday, 1979.

27. I did this painting for Father's 80th birthday, 1985.

28. Four scenes of Huang Shan (黄山) as seen by my camera, 2002.

29. The red IBM Selectric typewriter in my UConn office was the state-of-the-art writing instrument in the pre-computer 1960's.

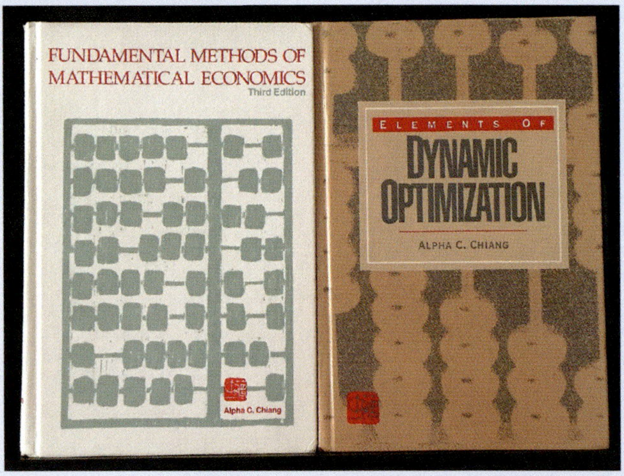

30. Both of these books I wrote feature abacus-themed cover designs.

31. Some of the different editions and translations of my books.

32. Christmas Eve, 1976, with Emily's brother John and his wife Pearl (middle), and sister Chinyee and her husband H. Y. Sung (left).

33. Emily's Aunt Helen Hsiung (熊毛彦文) visiting us in Connecticut, 1979.

34. Visiting us when we lived in Holland, 1989: Emily's brother James and his wife Belinda (left), and Emily's sister Chin-ling (right).

35. With Shu-Tung and Alice Li (Emily's cousin) and my parents in our dining room, 1975.

36. In our dining room with Duo-liang and Sharon Lin.

37. The horrendous Storm Larry descended on Connecticut on February 7, 1978 (Chinese New Year's Day).

38. Ruth Hsiao (my writing mentor) and her husband Professor William Hsiao (in red) and their family. (Undated photo)

39. Arthur and Jenny Yu (Emily's college mate), 1975.

40. Dicky Cheng (my high-school classmate) and his wife Deanna and sons Patrick (right) and Andrew (in white), 1991.

41. Three Christmas-card cover designs by Darryl, 1975, 1979, and 1983.

42. Three Christmas-card cover designs by Tracey, 1978, 1982, and 1991.

43. Anne Lien (a former Miss China) receiving her MA degree from UConn, here with her husband Professor Chan Lien (left), and me (right), 1968.

44. Three generations in my family touring Paris together, 1979.

45. Our whole family in Rome, 1979.

46. A stroll along the West Lake, Hangzhou (杭州西湖), 1993.

47. Climbing the Great Wall (長城), 2001.

48. Acting – a silly moment in our family life, 1980.

49. Darryl graduating from Princeton University, 1990.

50. At the Graduation Ball, Princeton, 1990.

51. Darryl graduating from Harvard Law School, 1994.

52. From the right: Opera friends Herbert and Mary Chu, Catarina Chi, and me, 1991.

53. Tracey presenting flowers to me at her Brown University commencement, 1992.

54. Tracey graduated from Brown University, 1992.

55. My home on Cottonwood Lane in White Plains, New York, 1995–2012.

56. In our White Plains home. Front (from left): Chinyee Sung, Alice Fei. Middle: John Fei, H. Y. Sung, Emily. Rear: Roger and Lilian Yeu.

57. My cousin Kuo Tao Yui, his wife Kung Juan, and their daughters Jane (right) and Julia (left), became naturalized Canadians in 1997.

58. A reunion with (from left) Stephen Li and Kang Yao, in Hong Kong, 1993.

59. At dinner with Chan Lien (連戰), Vice President of the Republic of China in Taiwan, and his wife Anne Lien (連方瑀) in New York, 1996.

60. My Aunt Yun-hsien with her two daughters Ellen Pan (left), and Eva Tien (right) and Rex Tien, 1992.

61. Professor Y. Y. Kueh (in red) and his wife Hsiao-hu (sitting left), with their children, Hong Kong, 1993. Sitting in the middle was my father.

62. George Yan, Lisa Lu, and me at a singing party in 1999.

63. A reunion with George Hsu (middle) and Kang Yao in Beijing, 2001.

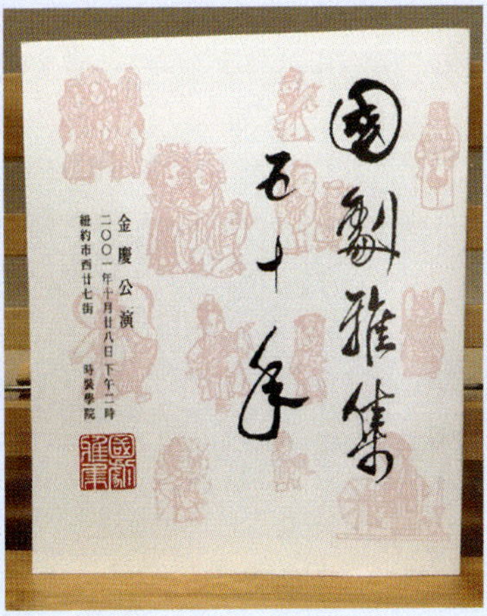

64. The commemorative booklet I produced for the 50th-anniversary performance of our Chinese Opera Association of New York, 2001.

65. Emily secretly published the two stage plays I wrote, and Tracey designed the book.

66. Tracey married Jonathan McGrath in New York City on August 2, 2003.

67. From right: Professor Della Lien, and Professor Cheng Sing Lien, 2002.

68. Some of my cousins. Front (from left): Zhongquan Jiang, Clark and Julia Chiang, Diane and James Chow. Hidden: Shufen Li. Rear: Eva and Rex Tien, Emily and me.

69. At a party. From right: Catarina and Chia-dann Chi, Roger and Lilian Yeu, Emily and me.

70. On our Silver (25th) Anniversary, 1979.

71. On our Golden (50th) Anniversary, 2004.

72. Cutting the Golden-Anniversary cake at a dance party, 2004.

73. Emily and I performed a waltz to Nat King Cole's "Fascination," choreographed by John Nyemchek, at our Golden-Anniversary dance party, 2004. (Photo by Roger Yeu)

74. Celebrating my 80th birthday at two parties: a dance party with a fairy-tale show, plus a Chinese-opera singing party, 2007. (See Chapter 36.)

75. The finale of my magic show at a dance party, 2009. (See Chapter 37.)

76. A family portrait for the cover of my 2010 Christmas card.

77. Tammy Lum, my second piano teacher, released a new CD in 2015, with my composition "Opus 1" included in it.

78. Dr. Andrea Jue married our son Darryl in New York City on September 10, 2016.

79. Joseph and Olympia Jue, Andrea's parents, joined the Chiangs in a photo on the day of the wedding.

80. My portrait at age 90, 2017.

81. My Aunt Lizhen celebrated her 100th birthday in 2002 in Shanghai. This photo shows her at 98, attended by her daughter Yilian Jiang.

82. Some of our dancing friends. From left front: Ming-nan and Angel Sheng, Emily, Steve and Nancy Kuo, Michael and Rita Ting, and me.

83. Joan Ludwig (my playwriting teacher) and her husband Jay, at Cedar Crest.

84. Our grandson, Julian Chiang, at 6 months, 2019.

85. Andrea, Julian (9 months), and Darryl in New York City, 2019. (Photo by Audrey Lee)

86. Our three grandsons. From left: Kieran McGrath (12), Julian Chiang (10 months), and Emmett McGrath (15), 2019.

87. Pianist Elaine Thomas and her husband Leo Thomas at Cedar Crest.

88. David and Margaret Vowles became friends with us on a cruise when Margaret and Emily expressed their admiration for each other's hairdo.

89. Distant scenic view from our Cedar Crest apartment.

1

Alpha

When I was born, in July 1927 near Shanghai, China, my father naturally only gave me a Chinese name, 蔣中一. By the Wade–Giles system of transliteration prevalent at the time, this would be Anglicized to the English name: *Chiang Chung-i* (the last letter *i* is pronounced “ee”).

The first part of that three-word name, *Chiang*, denotes the family name, which happens to be the same as that of Chiang Kai-shek, the national hero of the Republic of China against Japanese aggression during World War II (WWII). The second word, *Chung* (before the hyphen), meaning “middle,” represents a generational indicator shared by every male sibling of the same generation in my extended family. Thus, only the last word, *i* (after the hyphen), is what uniquely differentiates me as an individual. This word means “one” or “first,” which befits my status as the first son of a first son.

But now I have become known as Alpha C. Chiang. What happened?

Behind a Name

The short answer I usually give is that I went to a missionary high school in Shanghai, where it was customary for students to adopt English names, and I simply followed that custom. The opportunity to name myself, a privilege normally reserved for Popes, Kings, and Queens, was a luxury I treasured, so I put much thought into it. My first principle was to avoid popular names like John and James, because too many people would answer to a call of such names. I also ruled out peculiar names that could become laughingstocks. (One of my fellow students, a lanky boy, ridiculously called himself Colossus!) After quite a few tentative choices, I settled on *Alpha*, the first letter of the Greek alphabet, for its simplicity, uniqueness, and the ostensible connection to the "one/first" connotation of my Chinese name. The Chinese given name, *Chung-i*, was then condensed into the middle initial "C." I became Alpha C. Chiang—now following the Western tradition of listing the family name last, instead of the Chinese custom of listing it first.

What I have rarely shared with friends is a deeper reason behind the name *Alpha*. My hesitation to reveal it was because it may sound boastful, as it involves a horrendous obstacle encountered at the missionary school that I had to fight with all my might to overcome.

The missionary school in question was St. John's Middle School (聖約翰大學附屬高中), run by the prestigious St. John's University in Shanghai (聖約翰大學, now defunct), a cradle for a long list of illustrious alumni. My father sent me there despite its high tuition fees and (for him) its unfortunate Christian affiliation, partly because of its excellent reputation, but also because he liked its big campus with tennis courts. He hoped that I, a nonathlete by nature, would not only train my mind there, but also strengthen my body by learning to play tennis. "Do use the tennis courts," he said, and then added solemnly and repeatedly, "but promise me never to become a Christian!"

I enrolled at St. John's Middle School in the fall of 1941. At that time, Japan was already engaged in a ferocious war of aggression against China. But living in the French Concession in Shanghai, free from Japanese influence, I did not quite feel the danger of war. Soon thereafter, however, after Japan attacked Pearl Harbor in December, 1941, and engaged in warfare against all the Allied Countries, even the foreign-leased districts within Shanghai were no longer safe from the Japanese invaders, and I began to live under Japanese occupation until the end of WWII in 1945. Life under enemy occupation was hard and humiliating, to say the least, but for some reason, my academic work was able to go on without interruption, except for the addition of a compulsory Japanese language class into the curriculum.

St. John's was radically different from my previous schools. It used English as the language of instruction for its entire curriculum, except in two courses: Chinese Literature and Chinese History. Even Chinese Geography was taught in English. For me, a graduate of a public school, where English was taught as a peripheral foreign language, learning just a few new words per week, this systemic change posed a daunting challenge. When I opened up the book for the first semester English class, *The Vicar of Wakefield*, an 18th-century novel by Oliver Goldsmith, I could count on the first two pages nearly 100 words I did not know. Worse, we had to explain those words in class not in Chinese, but in English, which required the learning of even more new English words for the explanations. Looking at those pages was therefore like facing a firing squad, with each new English word coming at me as a well-aimed bullet. I felt destined to bleed to death from those bullets. But now, so soon after graduating from junior high at the top of the class, how could I accept the shame of failure? How could I ever face my parents whose expectations for me were as high as their love for me was deep?

In the face of such a threatening situation, I vowed to fight, to survive. I decided to forgo all personal entertainment and social activities in the following months, and literally allowed myself to become a desperate swimmer struggling in an ocean of English words. You cannot possibly imagine how hard it was. But, to my much-needed relief, I could sense some steady progress every day. In fact, learning a large number of new words all at once, and in context, enabled me to discover quickly how prefixes and suffixes work, how to choose between the articles "*a*" and "*the*," and how to distinguish between the various tricky prepositions (look at, look for, look in, look on, look up). The words I learned day by day steadily expanded my vocabulary, and, strangely, English soon became my favorite subject.

My fascination with the English language was inspired by my growing awareness of its logical structure. But I also found excitement in the discovery of some quirks in English. When comparing pairs of words like possible/impossible, valid/invalid, legal/illegal, or reversible/irreversible, I deduced the general rule that the attachment of a prefix such as *im-, in-, il-, ir-* to an adjective will negate it. But look what happens when the prefix *in-* is added to the word *valuable*! It results in a new word, *invaluable*, which not only does not mean "valueless," but means "extremely valuable." Very interesting, but very strange. No?

Another quirk I have found concerns the work *luck.* When something fortunate befalls someone, he or she may say, "I was in luck." An alternative, using the verb form of the word, is "I lucked out." Looking back at the phrase "in luck," I would have said, "I lucked *in.*" But the normally used phrase is "lucked *out.*" Bizarre or not?

I won't even go into the seemingly illogical pronunciations assigned to certain words here, such as *cough, rough, ought,* or even the word *one.* And why is the letter "o" pronounced differently in the words *love* and *dove* on the one hand, and *move* and *cove* on the other?

Some classmates came to St. John's with good prior English training. But there were plenty of others who, like me, were struggling. With poor English, they occasionally became laughingstocks. One widely told story concerned a student who needed to go to the washroom while in class. Having not learned the proper English to ask the teacher's permission to leave the room, he raised his hand, and courageously improvised a roundabout request: "Teacher, I have some water in my body which is useless. May I go out to get it out?" Funny. After hearing that story, I quickly learned to say: "Sir, may I go to the W.C.?" The abbreviation W. C., for "water closet," was the term we used for the washroom then. In America, today, we often hear people ask in public places, "Where is the bathroom?" I have always wondered why a washroom, without a bathtub, is called a "bathroom," but more people say "bathroom" than "washroom" or "restroom."

On the basis of my intense efforts, I dared to hope that, by the end of the first semester, I might emerge in the top quartile of the class. To my surprise, at the end of the first semester, the Registrar officially declared me to be the "first best" in the freshman class. That result taught me, a 14-year-old boy with zero initial hope, a vital lesson about hard work and perseverance! I decided to name myself Alpha—not so much for celebrating my unexpected success, as to remind me of the arduous road to that honor, and what I need to do to remain in the forefront. I did manage to stay at the top of the "Class of 1943," winning the St. George's Cup upon graduation. No, I did not get to keep the silver cup, but was allowed to take it home for a few days for picture-taking. My name would be inscribed on the cup along with the early winners. But now that the school has become defunct, I doubt that the cup still exists.

1.1 St. George's Cup, St. John's Middle School, Shanghai, 1943.

I did not fulfill my father's earnest wish about tennis. But I did faithfully heed his emphatic admonition against Christianity.

Albie

There are several other stories related to my name.

After the WWII, I came to the United States for graduate studies. During the early years of my doctoral program at Columbia University, I rented a room from a Mrs. Fisher on W. 124th Street in Manhattan. When introducing myself to her, I distinctly said "Alpha," but she heard it as Albert and, to be affectionate, called me "Albie." Successive efforts to correct her all proved futile. Thus I lived under that nickname for quite a number of years.

Dear Mrs. Fisher was actually able to bring the story of mistaken name to a higher level of error later. One day, my friend Patrick Chen (陳禾嘉) came to see me in my absence, and he wanted my landlady to tell me on my return that he, Patrick, came to visit. Mrs. Fisher was conscientious about her mission. When I returned that evening, she hurried out of her room, and called out loudly, "Albie, Albie, what's-his-name *Murphy* was here!"

Patrick left New York for China via Europe in March, 1952, after earning his MA degree. Several classmates in the Economics Department went on board his ship to see him off. But upon his father's advice not to return to China, then already under Communist rule, he settled in Paris. A similar advice from my father led me to settle in the United States. Far apart in two different countries, we gradually lost track of each other. But I would see Patrick again, under surreal circumstances after almost four decades.

The Alpha Serenade

In 1954, I started my full-time teaching career as Assistant Professor of Economics at Denison University in Ohio. But 10 years later, I had an opportunity to join the University of Connecticut (UConn) at the full rank of Professor of Economics, to help them launch their new PhD program. And I remained in that post until I retired. As soon as I began

1.2 Some economics graduate students at Columbia University, New York, circa 1951. From left: Me, Chi-ming Hou (侯繼明), Helen Chang and Richard Yin (張萬宏殷一昌伉儷), Patrick Chen (陳禾嘉).

my appointment at UConn, I initiated a long-planned project, writing the textbook titled *Fundamental Methods of Mathematical Economics* (McGraw-Hill). And I taught a required graduate course nicknamed "Math Econ" based on my own fresh-off-the-typewriter manuscript, which I wrote on a specially requisitioned, bright-red IBM Selectric typewriter. This typewriter, the state-of-the-art writing instrument before the advent of the personal computer, and the envy of my colleagues, played an important role in my writing project, because it featured interchangeable font balls that allowed the typing of mathematical symbols and Greek letters needed for my mathematical manuscript (see Photo 29).

Mathematics is always perceived to be a difficult subject. In spite of my persistent efforts to give patient and lucid explanations, some students would still find the material puzzling, and constantly lived under the dark shadow of math phobia. At that time, the movie

"Alfie," starring Michael Caine, was being shown in cinemas. It features a catchy theme song with the first line, "What's it all about, Alfie?" That song provided the basis for one of the more amusing episodes in my teaching career. One day, I heard singing voices, in high decibels, coming from the graduate student lounge located directly across the hall from my office. It was the Alfie tune! But my name had replaced Alfie: "What's it all about, *Alpha*?"

Was I being blamed for their nightmarish frustration in mathematics learning? Or, was I being thanked for my valiant teaching efforts? I heartily smiled at the chorus with great admiration for their imaginative adaptation of a popular song. Regardless of their true intent, I decided to take the song as a fond "Alpha Serenade" from my hardworking graduate students.

Alpha and Beta

Whenever I introduce myself by saying "Alpha, as in Alpha, Beta," people would often ask, "Do you have a brother, Beta?" Being an only child, I would naturally answer in the negative.

The question is: Am I really an only child? This question never arose before I was 19, but soon after that, my mother unexpectedly became pregnant for the second time after almost two decades. What followed was a serious disaster for her, involving the rupture of a fallopian tube, surgery, complications after complications, and a near death. Fortunately, all ended well with a miraculous healing (see Chapter 6).

I saw the fetus which my father brought home. It was male. So, yes, I had a brother (Beta?). But no, he was never born.

Alpha and Omega

Since Alpha is not a standard name, many people would, as Mrs. Fisher did, mistake it to be "Albert" when I introduce myself. Others would guess "Alfred" or "Arthur." But after the name is clarified, they would often follow up with, "Oh, Alpha and Omega." Since I am not only the first child, but an only child, both Alpha and Omega are consistent with my status. Yet, into my life, "Omega" also entered in other ways.

First, for more than two decades, a gold Omega watch adorned my wrist. It was such an expensive watch that I would never have purchased it myself. But my father bought it, even though he was unaware of the Alpha–Omega linkage, as a gift to me to commemorate our reunion in 1960, after a 13-year separation. The reunion was noteworthy, because my parents had to endure the tumultuous life in China for eight years before they were able, in 1957, to migrate to Hong Kong, then a British colony. That watch was also a gift to congratulate me on the completion of my studies, for I left Shanghai in 1947 as a graduate student, but was now bringing a lovely wife, Emily Ho (何欽翠), to visit my parents in Hong Kong as an assistant professor on sabbatical leave. To my father, with his lifelong concern for my education, the progress to date brought him much pride and gratification.

That Omega watch, a beautifully designed Swiss creation with the self-winding feature, a major novelty at the time, is an elegant work of art. I treasured it and intended to keep it forever. But some years ago my son Darryl (蔣澹如) started to collect old watches, and fancied my Omega as a suitable candidate for his collection. I was of course only too happy to pass the watch on as a transgenerational gift, from father to son, to grandson.

Another Omega in my life was a car, an Opel Omega. In contrast to the Omega watch, a gift to me bought without regard to the Alpha–Omega link, this Omega was a car I bought for myself expressly on account of its Omega name. It gave me, Alpha, a special personal delight to be wearing an Omega watch while driving an Omega automobile.

The Opel Omega unfortunately displayed a serious flaw. Soon after taking possession of the car, I noticed a hissing noise through the side window whenever the car was in motion. Such a flaw would have bothered any buyer of a new car, but, for a person with perfectionist tendency like me, it was truly unbearable. When I complained about it to the car salesman, a green hand at the job, however, he had no answer for me and had to consult his manager. Ten minutes later, he came back with this gem: "Believe it or not, Mr. Chiang, it is a new feature called 'flow-through ventilation.'" The prefatory remark "Believe it or not" led me to suspect that this was just a fabricated explanation. But despite my endless efforts at finding a remedy for the situation, nothing satisfactory emerged. Finally, concluding that further negotiation would be unproductive, I grudgingly accepted defeat, and decided to "grin and bear it."

The hissing continued to bother me a lot but, strangely, after a month or so, it started to become less and less audible to my ears. The sudden realization that a flaw has a way of automatically fading with the passing of time, set in motion a slow process of alleviating my longtime perfectionist propensity. Imperfections of daily life used to lock me in agony or regret for three or four weeks; now, they would often release me in just a day or two. For this improvement in my personality, I have to thank the defective Opel Omega.

But the most striking encounter with "Omega" did not occur until after I retired from UConn and moved to White Plains, New York, so that my wife Emily could be closer to her sister Chinyee Sung (宋何青意). In the Lutheran Church we attended (oh yes, we had converted to Christianity by then), I was asked one day in April 1998 to do the Scripture Reading, without prior notice. Things went smoothly at first as I read from the open Bible, but my jaw suddenly became locked as I approached the verse "I am the Alpha and Omega, the first and the last, the beginning and the end." What an amazing coincidence that I, Alpha, should be the one assigned to read that particular verse!

Or, was it a coincidence?

I checked with the lady who assigned me the reading job; she assured me that there was no preplanning. And as I reflect upon it now, I realize that this coincidence is even more remarkable: that Sunday was the *first* and the *last* time I ever did Scripture Reading in church.

A Surprise from the New York Times

One of the reasons I chose the name Alpha was its uniqueness. Once in a while, I would read about somebody also with the name Alpha, but such occurrences were extremely rare. But I got a definite jolt from reading about a wedding in which both the bride and the groom are named Alpha! As reported in the "SundayStyle" section of the New York Times (May 22, 2016, p. ST-13), the bride, an Ethiopian with an MBA from Harvard University, is named Alpha Mengistu, and the groom, an Ethiopian with a degree from James Madison University, is named Alpha Kiflu.

The name is obviously unisex. I have known that for a long time, since many advertisement mails have come to my mailbox for *Ms.* Alpha C. Chiang, largely because most names ending with the letter "a" (such as Anna, Cecilia, Julia) are feminine.

For this family of newlyweds, though, there is an inevitable complication: How do the two Alphas address each other? And how their relatives and friends distinguish between the two? I suppose at least one of them will have to adopt a nickname.

Could they possibly choose "Albie?" Ha! Ha!

2

A Family of Three

The most popular phrase used by well-wishers in the traditional Chinese culture is "*duo fu duo shou duo zi sun* (多福多壽多子孫)," meaning "lots of blessings, lots of years of life, and lots of children." The first two, a blessed life and longevity, require no explanation. The third, regarding progeny, is perhaps a legacy from the agricultural country mentality. Children are a source of domestic labor power in the rice field, and, as the years go by, a source of support after the parents become old and frail.

The norm for Chinese families during the 1920s was, in my impression, to have anywhere from 2 to 10 children. My father was the elder of two sons. My mother had two sisters and seven brothers. But my parents produced only a single child, me. Of course, my family was not in agriculture. Even so, having an only son was not up to par. At the time of my birth, there was no governmental regulation on the number of children a family could have. So, why was I an only child?

Why Indeed?

As a weak attempt at humor, I offered to my high-school friends this explanation: At my birth, my parents took a long look at me, and, seeing such a good-looking son with facial features portending infinite wisdom, said to each other: "This baby is pure perfection, the very best, and we cannot possibly hope to top this. So, we'd better stop and have no more!"

Not willing to accept my explanation, Stephen Li (李永寬), one of my best friends in high school and a quick wit, immediately came back with this repartee: "No, no, you got it all wrong! When your parents saw you at birth, they jointly uttered a heavy sigh, and said to each other, 'Sorry. If this is the kind of baby we'd get, then let's just forget it, and try no more!' And, my dear Alpha, that's why you are an only child. Ha!"

The truth: I almost had a younger brother. But he was not meant to be, as I mentioned in Chapter 1.

A Triangle of Deference

Until I was 5, my mother and I lived in the native village of Baoshan (寶山) with my grandfather and his second wife, while my father stayed in the nearby city of Shanghai where he worked. Since he came home only on weekends, there was little bond between us. In fact, his bright and authoritative eyes carried a faint threat of potential disciplinary actions, and I felt it best to avoid him. Whenever his arrival was imminent, I would habitually escape to our neighbor's home to play with my same-aged young buddy, Huai-jiang Chu (朱懷江).

2.1 Mom and me (at age 5), Shanghai, 1932.

The bond with my father began only after my mother and I moved to Shanghai, to form a family of three. Mother was most happy to move to Shanghai, because my step-grandmother, yet with no children at the time, was jealous of my grandfather's great affection for me, his first grandson, and she often made life difficult for my mother. The move to Shanghai represented a major liberation for my mother.

Using the Shanghai dialect, I call my father *Diadia* (爹爹), and my mother *Mma* (m-媽). In this book, however, I will for convenience alternatively refer to them as Father and Mother, or Dad and Mom, respectively.

Named Bo-xi Chiang (蔣伯熙)—which I arbitrarily Anglicized to Peh-shi Chiang early on for his passport—Father received his education from an old-fashioned classical tutor instead of in a modern school. And he left home at a young age to become an apprentice to his uncle, who managed an established firm dealing in grains trade in Shanghai. My father's sharp mind, coupled with his impeccable work ethic and abacus skills, quickly won the approval and trust of his uncle, and soon he was promoted to be the firm's trader at the Shanghai Flour Exchange (上海麵粉交易所). I had numerous occasions to see him at work, standing around the trading pit, shouting out buy and sell orders, often gesturing with hand signs. It was strenuous work. I often wondered how these traders could even hear one another among the loud noises all around, let alone keep the orders straight. He developed a powerful voice as a result. He also possessed a lot of common sense, and was sought after as an adviser, mediator, or arbitrator, when problems of various nature arose among our close circle of relatives.

I was in awe of Father, and naturally always deferred to him.

My mother, née Suo-fen Wang (王鎖芬)—which I arbitrarily Anglicized to Su-feng Wang for her passport—had no modern education either. But she was blessed with many virtues deemed essential for a new household mistress at the time: hard work, frugality, culinary expertise, and a clear sense of what is good for the family. As her predominant virtue, she cared for relatives and friends more than she cared for herself. This became evident during the eight-year Sino-Japanese War, during which we took in and helped many of her relatives. Later, in the famine years in mainland China in the early 1960s, my parents, then already living in Hong Kong, regularly sent food packages to relatives in China, and Mother tried to earn money from her skilled knitting, despite her deteriorating eyesight, to finance her remittances to faraway relatives. Father fully encouraged Mother's kindheartedness, and supported her efforts with generous funding, though he never received as much credit for his generosity as he deserved.

In admiration for her wifely virtues and golden heart, Dad generally deferred to Mom.

I knew that Mother's beneficence over the years made great impact on people. But I did not fully realize the extent of it until I attended a reunion in Shanghai of my cousins from Mom's family, almost a decade after her passing. She had two sisters and seven brothers, who in turn produced a lot of children. Thus, I had many cousins from Mom's side alone. I had not seen some of these cousins for many years, and I had never even met the others. The three-day reunion in October 2004, organized by cousins Frank Wang (王曾冲) and Kuo-tao Yui (余國燾), therefore, promised to be very exciting for me and my wife Emily. The attending cousins came from many parts of China, and some were from Taiwan, Canada, and the United States. To my great surprise, it turned out that in the cousins' reminiscence speeches, they all had a story or two to tell about how much my mother helped them. In particular, one cousin told us that his father, Mom's fifth brother, with no way to feed his family, was secretly planning to end his life by drowning, only to be saved by a remittance from my mother that arrived in the nick of time. In no time, this reunion virtually turned into a memorial for my mother. When Kuo-tao announced that he had purposely chosen my mother's birthday as the opening day of that reunion, my eyes became moist. It was almost 10 years after my mother's death, and yet, amazingly, she still occupied such a dear place in my cousins' hearts! I noticed that Emily was also wiping her eyes.

In her gentle but persuasive way, Mom molded me into a well-mannered boy. On visits to relatives, when candies were offered to me, I would always take one piece only, never trying to pick up several to put in the pocket as some of my contemporaries did. I politely listened to grown-up conversations, eager to learn, never to interrupt. I was often touted by my uncles and aunts as a model for their children to emulate. Feeling that I made her look good as a parent, Mom inevitably doted on me. The label of a "model child" unwittingly imposed a heavy social cost on me through no fault of my own. As one of my cousins belatedly revealed to me when I was already in my 70s, I was the common target of hate among my male cousins! The female ones, fortunately, felt differently; they were friendly, or even affectionate toward me.

My father never gave me monthly allowances, telling me instead: "Whenever you need money, just ask me." Well, I hated to have to "ask," and never actually went to him. But Mom would automatically and regularly offer me spending money. I felt warm appreciation in my heart for her, but, to my deep regret now, I rarely said to her, "Thank you, *Mma!*"

She usually deferred to me on everything.

A close relative gave her astute observation about our family of three thus: "The three of them form a triangle: The son is afraid of the father; the father is afraid of the mother; and the mother is afraid of the son." The phrase "is afraid of," with the connotation of "dread," was obviously an overstatement. But I would admit that there existed in my family a "triangle of deference," one of respect and homage.

Chinese Opera

As Father became more expert about trading, he started to trade for his own account on the side. And our family steadily grew better off. Although I never discussed finances with him, I had the impression that he was quite rich. Otherwise, he would not have been able to fund Mother's largesse over the years without visible strains. Also, he treated Mom and me to various kinds of pleasure of life, more and more often as I grew. We went to all kinds of restaurants, including Western-style ones, where I learned to use the knife and fork—the European way. We went to Chinese opera performances regularly, and patronized movies and stage plays as well, and often.

Even before his marriage, Father had the financial means to venture into various hobbies. He played billiards sometimes, and poker, too. But, more seriously, he learned to sing Chinese opera, known then as Peking opera (now Beijing opera), a most popular form of entertainment in the populous city of Shanghai. Many amateur devotees not only watched shows, but personally pursued this art form, hiring professional actor–singers as tutors, with the aim of putting onstage performances of their own. Father joined the opera association at the Shanghai Flour Exchange early on, and learned to sing the female role, as many famous professional singers did.

He then did something quite unheard of.

A Unique Show

He invited all his friends at his opera association to his wedding in our Baoshan home, and put on a performance for the guests, on a stage specially set up for the occasion. Musicians, makeup artists, and stage hands all came from Shanghai. These were not unusual. What made it unique was that Father, the bridegroom himself, performed two opera excerpts on his own wedding night. And, don't forget, he sang the principal young female roles! In one, "Royal Flirtation (遊龍戲鳳)," he played an innocent young waitress in a country inn with whom an emperor traveling incognito fell in love. In the other, "Death or Matrimony? (二本虹霓關)" the role was that of a maid who had to decide how to deal with her mistress in a dilemmatic situation. The mistress had succeeded in capturing the enemy general who killed her husband, but she now hesitated to kill the handsome captive, with whom she had fallen in love. She intended to offer the captive general a choice: die, or marry her? And she sought the maid's counsel.

The show, a big hit, was undoubtedly the "1926 Event of the Year" in my native town, Baoshan. But Mother, the bride, did not have the opportunity to partake in the enjoyment. As tradition prescribed, the bride was supposed to sit on the bed in the wedding chamber, her head wholly covered up with a red silk kerchief, and to wait patiently for the bridegroom to come, to lift the kerchief. But, busily singing and acting on the stage, the groom did not show up until very late that night.

I understandably inherited the Chinese opera hobby from Father. He taught me to sing and play the stringed instrument for opera accompaniment early on. I chose to sing the female role after the style of Mei Lan-fang (梅蘭芳), whom I have idolized since my childhood as THE greatest performer of all times, and I kept up my fondness for Chinese opera throughout my life. Much later, in my graduate student days in New York, I co-founded The Chinese Opera Association of New York with three other opera friends, and also participated in numerous stage performances we put on over several decades, as a musical accompanist as well as a designer of performance programs.

In chatting with my opera friends, I had occasion to tell this unusual story of my father performing at his own wedding. They all marveled at my father's unconventional decision. To my surprise, one of the listeners responded with this remark: "How lucky you were to be able to see your father's performance! You must have enjoyed it tremendously!" The other listeners all laughed out loud. My father did that unusual show before he even went to the wedding chamber to meet his bride. Even my mother did not see the show. How could I, their not-yet-conceived child, be able to witness that performance?

Years later, though, I did see my father onstage several times when he was in his 30s. He had a good singing voice, and he felt totally comfortable onstage, always keeping pace with the development of the stories. Unfortunately, there were no recordings. And I was not yet into photography then to capture some of the scenes.

Mom never learned to sing, but she was as enthusiastic about going to opera shows as Dad and I.

Grinding the Inkstick

My father also bequeathed to me his love of classical Chinese arts of calligraphy and painting. As a junior high-school student, I practiced ink-brush calligraphy every morning before school, and Father usually kept me company at practice. I did not use ready-made ink, but prepared fresh ink every day by adding water to an inkwell, and then grinding an inkstick in it. Father often ground the inkstick for me, to save time as well as to show me his support. In those days, the typical Chinese father did not bother to develop close relationships with the children, thus my father was atypical. The fact that he ground the inkstick for me almost daily gave me much encouragement, and it remained one of the fondest memories of my relationship with him. But, regrettably, I too often neglected to say, "Thank you, *Diadia*."

He was not an art collector, but he did take me to see many art exhibitions. I can still recall distinctly the calligraphy exhibition–demonstrations of two child prodigies, Hai-long Qian (錢海龍) and Wen Fong (方聞) in Shanghai. My father even arranged for me to visit the former at his home. And the latter, I met in New York when I was at Columbia, and he was studying at Princeton. Easily recognizing him, I told him about attending his calligraphy exhibition–demonstration in Shanghai; he could not believe it. Mr. Fong later became a famous historian of Chinese art, professor at Princeton, and special consultant to the Metropolitan Museum of Art.

Joint Baptism

The most important thing our family of three did together was our joint baptism into the Christian faith.

An anti-Christian, Father emphatically and repeatedly admonished me not to become a Christian when I first enrolled in the missionary high school, St. John's Middle School. Not that he was a Buddhist or a Taoist. Like many other families in China, mine just followed the folk religious practices of that era, worshipping a multitude of deities from whatever religions they came from. The idea was, if one god can benefit us, then more gods would give us more potential benefits. The result was a tolerant and mutually inclusive religious conglomeration.

Even though I honored Father's admonition, I did attend an occasional Christian service just to satisfy my curiosity. And I treated the religion classes as just history classes. But when a miracle occurred in the family, Father had to admit that his admonition to me was a big mistake, and there was no way we could deny the power of Christianity. And all the three of us in the family received baptism together, shortly before I left Shanghai in 1947 for graduate study in the United States.

2.2 A family portrait on the eve of my leaving Shanghai, 1947.

The joint witnessing of the miracle (the subject of Chapter 6), and the subsequent joint baptism, added further cohesiveness to the family of three that's already bonded by the triangle of deference, and our shared love for Chinese opera, varied cuisines, as well as the sundry other pleasures of life.

3

Baoshan

For easier geographical recognition, I always told people that I was born in Shanghai, the best-known city in China. Actually my birthplace is Baoshan (寶山), on the outskirts of Shanghai. Annexed as a district of the metropolis of Shanghai years ago, Baoshan was, at my birth, an independent political entity, with its own "city walls" in spite of its small size.

The Chiang family home, where I lived for the first five years of my life, was located just outside of the West Gate. By following the stone-paved main street of Baoshan toward the other direction, east, one could exit from the East Gate in not much time, and continue on a gradually rising terrain to reach a large plateau. This plateau, ending in a cliff facing the Yangtze River, near where it pours into the South China Sea, was the top of a levee that was built decades ago to guard against threatening tidal waves. Looking eastward from there, we could see an expansive waterscape; looking westward, we could see Baoshan lying low, down below; looking in the northern direction, we could see the Chongming Island (崇明島), near the mouth of the Yangtze River; and looking southward, we could see the far, far tail end of the levee.

I have many fond memories of Baoshan. But this levee was where two of the most memorable events of my life took place, including one that challenges credibility. But those tales will have to wait.

Grandfather's General Store

The Chiang house was a magnificent building I could be proud of. Its stately double doors opened to a formal reception room, a courtyard with a big tree, side rooms, a couple of kitchens, another courtyard, and an immense hall and an extensive garden in the back with various kinds of fruit trees, and a tiny rivulet as its border. The bedrooms upstairs, with a long balcony, could accommodate all the offspring of my grandfather and his younger brother.

Unlike his brother, Lan-sheng Chiang (蔣蘭生) who ran a big grains firm in Shanghai and was my father's mentor, my grandfather, Yan-sheng Chiang (蔣延生), just managed a small general store in Baoshan that sold farm equipment, fertilizers, rice, and housewares at that time. Later, during the Sino-Japanese War, he managed a textile-manufacturing firm in Shanghai. A kind gentleman, he preached frugality all the time. The store was small, but its meager size did not bother me. What I hated was its location. By common sense, the store should have been placed a good distance away from our lovely home, or at least off to its side. But they—whoever made that decision—deserved a good spanking for planting the store right in front of the Chiang family house, thus blocking and hiding its stately double doors! What kind of sense of design, or lack of design, was that?

3.1 My grandfather, Yan-sheng Chiang.

After I moved to Shanghai at age 5, I still visited Baoshan on many occasions in my childhood. I would spend time in the store, watching the customers making their purchases. When my grandfather was not busy, he would teach me to read at his desk. I was able to delight him with my good memory. But it was when my grandfather was out, leaving the store to the care of Big Monk and Little Monk, that my stay at the store became more fun.

Fun Games

Big Monk (大和尚) and Little Monk (小和尚) were two apprentice employees at the general store. I could not understand why they were nicknamed "monks," because neither of them had a shaved head. Big Monk, especially, was a handsome young man with a nice head of hair. Lively and courteous, they enjoyed playing with me. What my parents did not know is that the two Monks secretly taught me forbidden subjects, like poker and twenty-one (blackjack). These games were imported pastimes popular in the city, and Big Monk and Little Monk were eager to show me that they were up-to-date on these. They used Chinese terminologies, of course, so that spades are called "black peaches," and hearts, diamonds, and clubs are referred to, respectively, as "red hearts," "square blocks," and "plum flowers." But the rules of the games are entirely the same. Thus "three-of-a-kind" beats "two pairs"; and "sequence (straight)" beats "three-of-a-kind"; "same pattern (flush)" beats "sequence"; and so on.

Learning blackjack at an early age proved, to my surprise, to be good for my arithmetic practice and mental calculation. You have to add numbers to get the current total points, and you have to subtract that total from 21, to know what cards will safely improve your total, and what cards would cause you to be busted.

Luckily for me, early introduction to such games did not lead me down the path of becoming a gambler. There were occasional games with friends with low stakes, but that's all. On one special occasion, however, I was fired up with a strong desire to study up further on blackjack, for a possible battle in a casino. The Class of 1943 of St. John's Middle School was to hold its 55-year reunion in Las Vegas in April 1998, and we would be staying at Bally's for three days. Doing no gaming at all at the casino would seem unnatural, even impolite. I felt that I should at least try "21," reputedly the least unfair game at the casino. So, after some 60-odd years since my first exposure to "twenty-one" from Big Monk and Little Monk, I decided to refresh my knowledge by studying a book written by a professional gambler, even becoming familiar with the intricacies of "doubling up," and "splitting," etc.

And I had a well-thought-out exit plan: I would stop playing after either winning 300 dollars, or losing 200, whichever occurs first. However, the croupier at the table I sat at had a winning streak that literally ate up all the customer–players. And, after I decisively migrated to another blackjack table, the new croupier also enjoyed a winning streak, again eating up everybody. I finally decided that it was not my day, so I quit after losing 150 dollars.

Fortunately, this failure at the casino was not significant enough to overshadow the pleasures of meeting many of the former classmates, including three former roommates Stanley Chen (陳宣亨), Y. C. Lee (李榮就), and Wellington Lo (羅明開). Although I will have more to tell about these and other friends in Chapter 18, here is a picture of four guys who roomed together almost six decades ago.

3.2 Roommates at St. John's Middle School in 1941, reuniting after 57 years in 1998. From left: Me, Stanley Chen, Y. C. Lee, and Wellington Lo.

Sunrise at the Levee

Learning poker and blackjack was interesting, but hardly a major event. One event that became indelible in my memory was when Big Monk and Little Monk took me to the levee to see a sunrise.

That morning, the three of us walked in darkness from the West Gate through the East Gate to the levee. I do not remember whether they held my young hand while walking on the roughly paved street in the dark. But we arrived at the levee without mishap. The entire levee was totally deserted before dawn. Approaching the cliff, we chose a spot closest to the seascape, and sat on a sheet Big Monk brought. There was a chilly breeze, but we were dressed for that. As Big Monk and Little Monk chatted about some things that I did not quite comprehend, I took the opportunity to look out into the water. In the darkness, not much came into the eyes, but the horizon was vaguely visible as an interminable straight line. It separated, yet also connected, the sky above it and the water below, forming a simple but grand picture. Nothing blocked this awesome wide-angle view of nature—not a tree, not a house, not anything.

At the first moment of the sunrise, a bit of golden-yellow hue suddenly emerged from the horizon. It then quickly expanded into a sheet of splendor that grew ever higher and wider until it became a big, gorgeous tent all over us and all around us, enveloping everything. The vastness of the glorious color display endowed me with a sense of "beauty" never experienced before or after. It also made me feel very small, like an ant. And what the ant felt was warmth, energy, comfort, and hope—especially hope—seeping into every pore of its tiny body.

As it turned out, hope was my greatest need at that time, for I was then mired in a deep slump of my scholastic history, which I will explain in Chapter 4. The inspiration I received from the sunrise at the levee proved to be of immense help to my psyche during this period of gloom, and beyond.

Ghosts and Spirits Galore

On some visits to Baoshan, Mom and I stayed at her old home, the Wang family home, located within the city walls. I had been to weddings and other banquets there, but my most vivid memory was a ghost story session with my sixth *jiujiu* 六舅, my mother's sixth brother, a quiet man usually without much to say on any subject. Though often appearing to be dull, he proved to everyone to be a sparkling ghost story teller.

It was nighttime after dinner. At someone's suggestion, there began a long ghost story fest. In the absence of electric power, only a lone candle reigned in the center of the table as the source of illumination. With about 10 of us adults and children sitting around the table, the flickering flame of the candle ominously cast a multitude of magnified shadows on the four walls. So, even before the ghost stories began, the atmosphere already felt fittingly creepy. Then the air thickened with each tale, and with the appearance of each type of ghost—the drowned ghost (with water dripping all over), the hanging ghost (with the tongue hanging out of the mouth), the beheaded ghost (with the head held in the hand), and so on, enhanced by the varied facial and tonal variations of the lively narrator.

When we retired to our respective bedrooms afterward, hardly anybody was free of dread. I wished that the dark hallway I had to walk through was not so long, and that my bedroom was not the last one at the end of the hall. I gingerly sneaked into the bedding after Mom did, trying to minimize motion, so as not to disturb the spirits that could be around. More importantly, I tried to remain awake, figuring that, if awake, I would have a better chance to run and escape if necessary.

While waiting for a possible appearance of a ghost, however, my young mind began to ponder such questions as: Are there really ghosts and spirits? How should I deal with them if they suddenly appeared? Why should I be afraid of them, if I had not done anything harmful to them? After a long time, I reached some conclusions: (1) I cannot rule out the existence of spirits, even though I had not seen one. (2) Spirits,like humans, can be benevolent as well as malevolent. (3) I need not be afraid of them since I have done nothing to harm them. (4) The world is big enough for humans and spirits to coexist. (5) In any event, I would better behave myself, always, so as to be on the good side of spirits, and not become a potential candidate for recruiting by the evil ones.

After this series of thoughts, I was gradually able to relax into a tranquil slumber.

The Inconceivable at the Levee

Outside the East Gate of Baoshan, lived the Chow family, related to the Chiang family via two marriages. First, one of my grandfather's sisters married into the Chow family as a second wife, following the death of the first. So she immediately had two stepsons and one stepdaughter, who all officially became my father's cousins. Second, the abovementioned stepdaughter, by the name of Lizhen Chow (周麗珍), married my father's younger brother, and became my aunt. So, the Chows and the Chiangs became doubly related. Little did I know in my youth that, several decades later, I would have the rare opportunity of attending Aunt Lizhen's 100th birthday party in Shanghai in 2002. (See Photo 81.)

When I visited Baoshan, I often played with the Chow youngsters, especially one whom I call *Ding-ge* (鼎哥), Fou Tse Chow (周復智), two years my elder. We told stories to each other, and skipped pebbles into ponds, or walked in the woods together. But the most unforgettable excursion was one he and I took, along with some other "cousins," to the levee situated not far to the east of their house.

Our purpose was not only to play on the plateau. We also wanted to climb down the side of the cliff to the ground below, which was totally dry during certain times of the day, strewn with rocks of all sizes. There were "steps" on the sharp, vertical side of the precipice, but each step was only about two inches deep, forming a compressed stairs. We could not just walk down, but had to climb down gingerly while facing the cliff-like rock climbers, trying to find a footing on the narrow steps below for our outward-pointing feet, and with our stretched fingers clinging to the narrow step above. With a bit of practice, climbing proved not so difficult, and I climbed down with some others in the group. A few of them even climbed up and down several times.

At one point, while I was down below, there was big laughter coming from the plateau above. Wanting to join in the fun, I climbed up to join them, but as soon as my eyes could see them, I stopped climbing further up, and, with my body hugging the cliff, used my hands to grab two pieces of grass for anchor. A country boy would perhaps instinctively know that grasses have shallow roots and are not reliable as anchors. But I was a city boy totally ignorant of such things! It only took a few seconds for the two pieces of grass to be uprooted by my weight. And I immediately fell! Back and down!

In the next second, I frankly thought that this would be the end of my life. But, incredibly, I felt no pain as my back hit the ground. No pain at all! In height, my fall was like a fall from a two-story house onto a rocky terrain. But, though hard to believe, the exact spot I fell onto was completely flat, and free from rocks. What a lucky break: not a single rock was there to crush my skull, break my backbone, or injure my arms or legs! Since I had earlier pondered over the matter of spirits, a question naturally arose in my mind: Could there have been some benevolent spirits, maybe ancestral spirits, present by my side either by coincidence or by design, to protect me from peril? Could they have mythically cushioned my fall, or magically removed some rocks out of my way as I fell?

The whole crowd was duly alarmed. They all came to me, some from above. "Are you all right? Do you feel any pain?" they asked, in imperfect unison. "I am all right," I was happy to assure them. In a moment of frivolity, I even added a joking remark: "But I am afraid my buttock is now in two pieces."

I swore my playmates to secrecy, so my parents never learned about this accident.

On our way home, I had time to reflect upon my fall. It was then that I realized how enormous a catastrophe we just avoided. My companions at the levee were merely a bunch of kids; they would not know what to do if I were injured in any way. Even if they could seek adult help, the adults would still face the tough problem of how to lift an injured body from the bottom of the precipice to the top of the levee. And, in fact, Baoshan did not have a hospital.

My inexplicable escape from injury was the first of several inconceivable things that happened in my life. I felt that some unknown force had spared me, and, deservedly or not, maybe I would be blessed with some form of divine intervention, protection or guidance, throughout my life. Deeply indebted to that force, I silently offered thanks, and pledged that, in appreciation, I would try to grow up to be a "good person," although I had no clear idea of what a "good person" should be like.

A Revisit Decades Later

My mother had seven brothers and two sisters, who produced many cousins for me. When the Wang–family cousins held a big reunion in 2004 in Shanghai, I participated with anticipation. Aside from meeting many cousins whom I had not seen for years, I planned to have a nostalgic walking tour in Baoshan in search of the Chiang home (where I spent the first five years of my life and learned poker and blackjack), the Wang home (where, among other things, the ghost story fest was held), and the levee by the sea (where I experienced the grandest sunrise, and had a perilous fall).

But more than 70 years had passed, and the whole landscape had been reconfigured. The economic progress that was initiated by the modernization move of Deng Xiaoping—essentially the adoption of market economy policies—was clearly visible. Old houses have been replaced by tall buildings. The streets are all paved. And there is electricity. Baoshan, now a district of Shanghai, boats a gigantic steel mill.

The levee site has been developed into a seaside park, perched high above the sea. You can still watch sunrise there, but the scene would now be blocked by trees, lamp posts, and other park structures. The wall of the park facing the sea now has a smooth surface, and it is no longer possible for adventurous boys to climb down.

4

Academic Demise and Renaissance

The academic slump I mentioned in Chapter 3 began innocently enough. In fact, it followed directly from my great success in the first grade.

Honor and Prizes

The day I finished the first grade in elementary school, I found out that I was at the top of my class. Elatedly, I ran home from school, eager to show my mother the several prizes I had won, mostly stationery items, plus a ball. She was extremely pleased. Upon coming home from work, Dad was of course equally happy when he heard about my accomplishment.

Then, a few days later, my second *jiujiu* 二舅, my mother's second brother, Wei-fong Wang (王衛丰)—made an off-the-cuff suggestion that, in view of my academic success, I could easily skip a grade and save a year in my academic life. Since this second *jiujiu* had taught school, and written poems and essays, his opinion carried weight with my parents. I myself was too young to have any opinion. Thus, without too much ado, I was enrolled in the third grade the following semester, without the benefit of the second grade. Strangely, nobody at the school tried to warn our family about the possible ill consequences of such a move.

Slump to Demise

The ill-advised decision for me to skip the second grade plunged me forthright into a vast academic wilderness, in which I could not tell east from west, south from north, with no idea of what was going on in class. In every subject, numerous gaps of knowledge conspired to stump me, one after another. Worse, the hope of finding an exit from this wilderness, if any, appeared to dwindle faster and faster as the gaps hit me harder and harder.

Of particular significance was the fact that I missed the fundamental skills of sentence construction taught in the second grade. Without that foundation, how could I now undertake to compose full essays as required in the third grade? I began to feel at a total loss in my classes. And my academic ranking dramatically sank from the very top to the bottom quartile. I used the term "academic slump" above. A more accurate term would be "academic demise." Besides, feeling ashamed and worthless, I even lacked the courage to tell my parents about my frustration and dismay, or to seek help.

The ironic thing was that an easy solution was available then and there: Just hire a tutor to fill the gaps in my learning! But neither my second *jiujiu*, nor my parents, nor I myself thought of the tutor solution. As a result, I had to rely on the sunrise scene in the Baoshan levee for support and for a lift in my spirit, time and again. This struggle lasted over a period of four or five years before I fully caught up, when I had a fresh start in junior high (seventh grade).

Wusong (Ho Chung) Middle School

The precollege education system in China at that time consisted of six years of elementary school, followed by three years of junior middle school (junior high) and three years of senior middle school (senior high). The seventh grade, at Wusong Middle School, was where my academic Renaissance finally began, providing me with a fresh start in a new environment.

Wusong Middle School (吴淞中學) had its start in my native place, Baoshan, but after receiving a donation of land in the nearby town of Wusong, it built its permanent campus there instead. From 1925 on, it soon earned a good reputation. But the outbreak of the Sino-Japanese War in 1937 ravaged its campus, and forced it to move to temporary quarters in Shanghai. Part of the faculty left, leaving a small group of dedicated and persevering teachers to sustain the school under stringent financial circumstances.

During my three years at this school, it operated in classroom space rented from a privately run elementary school in the International Settlement area of Shanghai, under the temporary name of Ho Chung Middle School (和衷中學). With small classrooms, and much noise from the children in the primary school, the physical environment left much to be desired. But at least for the time being, its location in the International Settlement protected it from the Japanese military intrusion. And the education it provided me was outstanding. In every subject in the curriculum, I could now start from square one, and build up from there with no gaps. By proceeding step-by-step, my progress felt effortless.

Just as Ho Chung had moved to the International Settlement to avoid the Japanese military presence in China, my family had moved to the French Concession in Shanghai, an area south of the International Settlement, safe from the Japanese, until 1941. My home was in a housing compound called Mei Lan Fang (梅蘭坊, meaning Plum and Orchid Square), which, to my great delight, sounded just like the name of my Chinese-opera idol (梅蘭芳). Every school day, I walked northward from home on *Rue Amiral Bayle* (貝勒路), crossing the romantic *Avenue Joffre* (霞飛路) with its tramcars, entering into the International Settlement, going around the vast grounds of the Shanghai Race Club, commonly called the Race Course (跑馬廳), to turn into the stately Bubbling Well Road (靜安寺路), with tramcars of its own, and then turning right to the school premises on Cheng Du Road North (成都北路). It was quite a long walk, although I never measured the exact distance. I walked round trips for three years, except for days of inclement weather, when I might call a rickshaw. These long walks could be a contributing factor to my good health, even now.

I described the home-to-school route in detail, because each walk was now filled with anticipation of enjoyable classes, in sharp contrast to the dread that overshadowed the bygone years in elementary school. What a feeling of relief, joy, and triumph!

Mr. Cheng and Grammar

More auspicious than anything else, I found good teachers who took special interest in me because of my rate of progress. That made Ho Chung that much more endearing to me. The teacher with the greatest impact on me was Mr. I-shin Cheng (鄭逸欣老師), the teacher of English. From his patient instruction, I learned all the essentials of English grammar, without which I could not have handled the later, intense English training in senior middle school at St. John's.

The textbook he used, by Lin Yutang (林語堂), a literary figure well-known in both China and the United States, was well-organized, and easy to follow. But it was unambitious about vocabulary building, introducing no more than two or three new words in each lesson. So I quickly became advanced in grammar, but remained woefully anemic in vocabulary.

Mr. Cheng used humor to illustrate the differences between English and Chinese usages. Once he mocked English people as "color blind." What we Chinese see obviously as "red tea," they call "black tea." The English are also "numerically confused." We Chinese count the floors in a building as the "first" floor, "second" floor, and so on; they call it "ground," then "first," and so on, causing a deceptive designation for us. Moreover, Mr. Cheng told us, the English had a serious problem with the "yes/no usage." Let's say someone asks the question "So, you don't like this movie?" A Chinese person who does not like the movie would answer in the affirmative, "*Yes*, I don't like it." But his English counterpart would respond, "*No*, I don't like it." The Chinese "*yes*" indicates *agreement* with the wording as stated in the question ("don't like this movie"). The English "*no*" is, on the other hand, meant to indicate the responder's attitude (not liking the movie). This distinction in the language usage struck me as extremely interesting and significant. Remembering Mr. Cheng's teaching proved very useful whenever I encountered English questions put in the negative form.

I had kept sporadic contact with Mr. Cheng over the years, and he sent me pictures. The last one I received from him was dated 1996, when he was at age 93. With great veneration, I print that picture as Photo 4 in the front of this book.

Mr. Ma and Punctuation

In Chinese language, my impactful teacher was Mr. Chao-kuei Ma (馬兆奎老師). He was full of anecdotes about the celebrated literary figures in Chinese history, as well as examples of clever plays on words. I especially enjoyed a story about the conflicting interpretations of text resulting from the absence of punctuation marks in ancient China. In the story, a friend comes to visit, and shows no sign of leaving at dinner time, as the rain comes. The host writes out a message of 10 words and shows it to the visitor:

下雨天留客天留我不留

Even readers who do not knowing Chinese could appreciate better the humor of the story with Chinese characters as illustrations. As you may know, each Chinese character (word) appears in print as a square entity; here, you should be able to count 10 such squares.

What the host wants to communicate could be made clearer with a comma after the fifth word and a period at the end of the sentence:

下雨天留客, 天留我不留.

which reads: "The rain seems to be inviting the guest to stay, but I am not doing any inviting."

The guest, however, still shows no intention to leave, and explains his action by reading the same message in a different way:

下雨天, 留客天, 留我不? 留.

which now reads: "A rainy day is a day to invite the guest to stay. Invite me or not? Invite!" This, of course completely turned the meaning of the message around.

This story is simple but interesting. Decades later, when I was giving my children private Chinese lessons during their high-school years, I told them this story, and they were duly intrigued, too. And it became even more so when my wife Emily suggested yet another way of repositioning the punctuation marks:

下雨天, 留客天, 留我? 不留.

The new meaning now becomes: "A rainy day is a day to invite the guest to stay. Invite me? Not invite." The meaning of the 10-word message is completely turned around again.

At a later point in Chinese history, a small circle mark (。) was introduced to facilitate the proper phrasing of texts. And nowadays, the use of the modern punctuation marks has become universal. But the above story about punctuation remains an interesting one to tell.

Other Subjects

Mr. Cheng and Mr. Ma sparked my interest in languages, but other teachers' instructions also made lasting influences on me. The music teacher introduced me to the western way of writing musical notations, which helped me in my venture into music composition decades later (Chapter 35). The geometry teacher inspired me in the step-by-step process of logical thinking. I believe that this training helped me in my writing of a textbook in mathematical economics, also decades later (Chapter 17).

Scholarship Award

At the end of the seventh grade, I was at the top of the class again since the first grade. Despite the tight finances of the school, they awarded me a scholarship. The word "scholarship" meant a monetary award for excellence, with no connotation of financial aid. It consisted of a certificate and a sum of money. My father was pleased by my new academic status, but instructed me to accept the certificate only, and request the school to give the award money to some deserving but needier student. I, too, thought that this was the right thing to do. I did the same thing in eighth and ninth grades.

St. John's Middle School

My academic renaissance continued at St. John's. Even though Ho Chung and St. John's shared the designation "middle school," the former was a junior middle school, and the latter, a senior middle school.

As I mentioned earlier in Chapter 1, the total emphasis on English at St. John's overwhelmed me. Once again I was thrust into an academic wilderness, seemingly impossible to escape from. My anemic English vocabulary was, well, too anemic for St. John's. And it was only because of my fear of sinking again from the top of the class to the bottom, that I vowed to work hard, harder, and hardest, to overcome the "mission impossible" lying ahead of me day in, day out — everyday!

Incredulously, I earned "first best" in the first semester at St. John's. Even with the sweat I put in, I could only hope to end up in the 75th percentile. How do I explain the higher result?

Mr. Wong the Quizzer

The answer is: I was lucky. I had Mr. W. P. Wong (黃文斌老師) as my first semester English teacher. At St. John's, the entering class of about 120 students was divided into five sections alphabetically for the first semester. Thereafter, academic achievement determined the section assignment. My name, Chiang, starting with a C, placed me from the outset in Section A, which had the best teachers. And I was lucky enough to remain in Section A in the remaining semesters as well.

Mr. Wong, a most strict and conscientious teacher, gave a quiz in every class. The papers were always graded and returned to the students in the next class. One time, I misspelled "antique" as "antigue," but he did not take points off. After he read out the correct answer, I went to him after class to tell him that he should adjust my grade downward. He praised my honesty, and kept the original grade. The second time a similar thing happened, I went to him again, and he again retained the original grade, but took a long look at me. I never went to him again for any misgrading. Mr. Wong was one of the most pivotal teachers in my life. I wish I had a photo of him to print in this book.

The first semester we studied *The Vicar of Wakefield*, followed by short stories and essays in the second semester. I loved the stories by O. Henry for their surprise endings. When, later in college, I wrote two short stories (in Chinese) that were successively published in a magazine and the literary supplement of a newspaper, the endings were imitations of O. Henry. It was hard to believe that after so many years of English emphasis at St. John's Middle School, and then at St. John's University, I retained strong enough an interest in the Chinese language to become a published author of stories and essays.

Novel, Novel, Novel

For the higher class English Literature books, we studied *Hans Brinker: or the Silver Skates, A Tale of Two Cities, Les Misérables*, and *The Three Musketeers*, all taught by different teachers. These books brought me engrossing entertainment while stealthily enriching my vocabulary day by day.

Hans Brinker did not excite me that much at the time. But, later in my life, when I had an opportunity to take a group of students from the University of Connecticut to a "Study Abroad" semester in the Netherlands, where the story of *Hans Brinker* was set, I recalled that novel with warm feelings.

The Dickens novel, *A Tale of Two Cities*, was one that won a lot of tears from me at the end. What a great act of sacrifice Sydney Carton undertook, to die in place of Charles Darnay, the husband of Lucie whom Sydney adored! I dared not ask myself whether I would have made the same decision under the same circumstance.

The interesting thing about Victor Hugo's novel was that it was taught by a new part-time teacher who happened to be the manager of a movie theater in Shanghai. His name I can no longer recall, but I remember clearly that, upon finishing this book in class, he arranged for us a special showing of the movie "*Les Misérables*," starring Fredric March as Jean Valjean, and Charles Laughton as Javert. That was the only time I had the privilege of seeing a movie specifically shown for a small, exclusive audience. A "command performance," so to speak.

But for political intrigue, fighting action, forbidden love, and breathless suspense, Alexandre Dumas' *The Three Musketeers* reigned supreme in my literary estimation throughout the years at St. John's Middle School. The names d'Artagnan, Athos, Porthos, Aramis, and Milady will remain with me forever.

The Japanese Influence

Shortly after I went to St. John's Middle School in the fall of 1941, Japan attacked Pearl Harbor, and the war expanded. From then on, Japan no longer respected the special status of the foreign settlements in Shanghai, and the entirety of Shanghai went under Japanese control.

Life became more traumatic. Air raids made it necessary to enforce frequent blackout orders—no lights, or at least no lights that could be detected from outside. Food shortages, including unavailability of rice, the staple food of the Chinese, caused widespread difficulties. Greedy merchants put sand and even granular pebbles into the rice they sold, and people had to pay for those inedible add-ons and then had the additional chore of sifting them out before cooking. The currency issued by the puppet government had an unstable value. And, one time, when there was an inexplicable shortage of coins, people just used postage stamps in place of them.

Japanese invaders or their underlings, not in military garb, also came to individual houses to force-sell subscriptions to propaganda publications. I happened to be home when they came, so I took the responsibility to deal with them. They did not speak Chinese, but their gestures were clear: they wanted to make people pay for their propaganda. I of course refused to subscribe, and in a rare upsurge of anger after some heated argument, I slammed the door hard on them. They responded with anger as well, kicking the door with their boots, and cursing for at least 10 minutes before leaving to pester the next family. Fortunately, they never came back.

Surprisingly, though, my school was allowed to operate as usual, without too much interference. The only two things that I recall as distastefully authoritarian are: (1) All of us had to study Japanese, and (2) some of us were drafted to represent our school in a citywide political rally under the auspices of the puppet Chinese government under Japanese sponsorship.

I originally held no objection against learning a new language, even an enemy country's language. But, to my consternation, the teacher of the Japanese class, a Chinese national with a Japanese wife, would start each class by extolling Japan and disparaging China. His insensitivity naturally enraged us students, and made the whole idea of language teaching unworkable. In the end, I did not learn that much Japanese, thanks to that terrible teacher. I wonder what happened to him after Japan surrendered to China at the end of the war.

The political rally I participated in took place in the expansive Race Course. As one of the students selected to join, I had to wear paramilitary garb specially made for the occasion. It was two or three hours of totally wasted time, during which we followed instructions to stand up and yell political slogans. I recalled that, just a couple of years earlier, when I passed by the Race Course on my way home from Ho Chung Middle School, I always enjoyed the bagpipe music played by the Scottish regiment in the British barracks nearby. But now, I was sitting inside the Race Course, as an extra in a silly vanity show, listening to political speeches. What a change, and what disgrace!

The Class of 1943

St. John's offered summer sessions, and many of the students took advantage of this and were able to complete three years of studies in two. Thus we began in 1941, and graduated as the Class of 1943.

I was lucky to keep my top status, and won the St. George's Cup (see Photo 1.1), which was not meant for me to keep. I did see later that my name was inscribed on it along with those of the earlier winners, for posterity to see. But now that the school is long extinct, posterity certainly means nothing anymore.

5

The Three Musketeers

It's a testimonial to Dumas' novel, *The Three Musketeers*, that whenever a trio of friends, colleagues, or relatives displays a special bond and maintains close contact with one another, they will automatically be nicknamed "The Three Musketeers." I have been a member of such a trio. From high-school days, through college and graduate studies in the United States for our Master's degrees, the three of us were inseparable.

The Beginning

It is not easy to pinpoint the exact beginning of our affiliation. Most likely, I met Stephen Li (李永寬) and George Hsu (徐克繼, later spelled Xu Keji) in the second semester at St. John's Middle School (10th to 12th grades). Our freshman class was divided into five sections, initially by alphabet, but later by academic achievement. I was assigned to Section A from the beginning, because my family name, Chiang, starts with C, an early letter. But Stephen Li and George Hsu were probably in Section C, so I did not meet them then. Besides, I was too busy struggling with my English in the first semester even to befriend my roommates, let alone others. Starting from the second semester, however, by dint of achievement the two of them came to join me in Section A, which had the best teachers for the 20-odd best students. I had also become less shackled by academic work, and found more time to socialize.

Since we three met, we took the same classes in Section A. Taking advantage of the summer session offerings, we all compressed three years of academic work into two. Thus, entering St. John's Middle School in 1941 at the time of Pearl Harbor, we were able to graduate in the high-school Class of 1943. Once enrolled in St. John's University, we still took the same classes in the same major, economics. And, by taking summer courses, we together hastened our graduation to become part of the college Class of 1946. That already meant five years of close attachment.

Singing and Dancing

What factors bound us to each other?

One reason was our common interest in Chinese opera (Peking opera, now Beijing opera). Not only did we like opera, but we all sang. Stephen sang the principal male role with a tenor-like voice, known as *laosheng* (老生); George sang the hero–rogue role with a broad voice, called *hualian* (花臉); and I sang the principal female role, with a falsetto voice, known as *qingyi* (青衣, pronounced *chingyi*). In addition, I played the stringed instrument, *jinghu* (京胡), for musical accompaniment. So, we complemented one another. There was a loose group of Chinese opera singers that met occasionally after classes. Stephen and George probably met me at those meetings. But the fact that they were day students, and I, a boarding student, meant that we became really close only after we entered college when we all became day students.

Stephen Li, a sharp wit with a great sense of humor, was always fun to be with. Both born in 1927, a year of the rabbit, he and I were the same age. George Hsu, one year older, born in a year of the tiger, struck people as more of the down-to-earth type, straightforward, not so talkative, but totally trustworthy. I, the bookworm of the group, could have been a dull person, but I happened to be blessed with several fun hobbies in addition to Chinese opera, plus an adequate sense of humor. I guess I might be considered as (Stephen Li + George Hsu) divided by two.

Ballroom dancing, one of my other hobbies, proved to be another source of affinity for Stephen, George, and me. They were equally passionate about this foreign-inspired pastime that was especially popular at St. John's. We loved to learn new steps in waltz, foxtrot, rumba, tango, and other dances from each other and from other fellow students. It was a real boon that Stephen Li's two younger sisters, Vivien and Dora, were also fond of dancing, and could be called upon to join us for our practice parties along with some of their classmates. Besides the Li sisters, there were the petite Chen twin sisters, who could follow so well. And, Josephine Yu, the best dancer in the group, was at one time my "girlfriend," although I was not her only "boyfriend."

We took substantial pride in our dancing, and unashamedly considered ourselves good dancers. It was not until when I started formal lessons in professional dance studios in the United States, several decades later, that I realized that we, as young dancers, were doing our steps wrong, wrong, wrong! For example, we used to do all the three steps in each bar of waltz music—1, 2, 3—with "toe-toe-toe" footwork. But the correct footwork pattern is: (1) heel-toe, (2) toe, (3) toe-heel. In the first step, for the man's left foot, the "heel-toe" movement requires his body first to be lowered and then heightened. In the second step, for his right foot, the word "toe" means that he is supposed to stay high. And, in the third step, for his left foot again, the "toe-heel" pattern implies a downward movement of the body on the second half of the beat while he closes his two feet. Waltz normally involves a left turn during these three steps. But more importantly, there is a mandatory rise-and-fall motion in the body, which is the hallmark of a waltz. Our erroneous "toe-toe-toe" footwork could never produce the wave-like body motion, an essential characteristic of the waltz.

But ignorance is truly a blessing; our mistakes never spoiled our fun.

Language, Language, and Language

We three musketeers were not only good for fun and frivolity. There was also a serious side.

Inasmuch as we were already planted in a school with a heavy emphasis on English, I proposed to Stephen and George that we should push ourselves further up the ladder of mastery, with regular practices of extemporaneous speaking in English. We set up study sessions in which each of us would select an article or story from the *Reader's Digest* each week, learn its vocabulary and literary structure, then report on it orally to the group, with no written notes allowed. The oral reports themselves were not hard, because they could be pre-rehearsed. But the question-and-answer period following each report always loomed as a dreaded killer. It demanded an ability to think on one's feet. It was often tempting for us to decide that "It's too much work; let's just quit and disband." But a rare, shared self-discipline made us persist in holding these practice sessions throughout our college years, sometimes joined by another classmate Otis Shao (邵鴻義), who, incidentally, also joined us as a dancer.

Even though our major interest was in English, we ventured into other languages as well, including Japanese, Russian, and French.

The study of Japanese was forced upon us after Japan occupied Shanghai after Pearl Harbor. St. John's Middle School, like other schools in Shanghai, was ordered to set up mandatory Japanese class, taught in the big Assembly Hall to accommodate a large number of students. I was never against language studies, not even an enemy's language. But the teacher hired for this course, a Chinese with a Japanese wife, soured the class by unpatriotic remarks that made the students' blood boil. "Japan is far superior to China, and that's why their troops are winning against our inferior forces. . . . Blah- blah- blah!" he would frequently remind us. We, all Chinese students humbly living under Japanese occupation, found it impossible to swallow such degrading remarks about our own country, especially from a fellow Chinese. No wonder shrill "boos!" exploded out from every corner of the Assembly Hall! Sadly, the teacher, with inexplicable insensitivity, would just carry on unmoved. From such a class, we ended up learning very little Japanese. When, in our college years, Japanese became an elective course, the three of us unanimously chose not to take it.

Instead, we all took three years of French in college. Two gracious French ladies trained us with authentic accents. But classroom contacts gave us only three hours per week, not nearly enough for effective language learning. I cannot claim that I could ever carry on a real-life conversation in French, but on one occasion, I did deploy my meager French, and saved a few francs. While touring in Paris with Emily, I saw at a box office a notice of over-60 senior discount, and was able to blurt out our age qualification: "*Nous sommes plus de soixante ans.*" Now, with advancing age, my vocabulary has shrunk a lot. But I can still recite two sentences all young men would proudly brandish if the opportunity ever arose: "*Tu es très belle.* (You are very beautiful.)" and "*Je t'aime.* (I love you.)" *Voilà!*

The funniest experience about language studies occurred in the French classes. Certain French words, innocent in themselves, could be assigned pornographic meanings when interpreted in the Shanghai dialect. Thus, when words like *le garçon* (boy); *le carton* (box); *le parapluie* (umbrella) were read in class, the boys would break out in loud laughter. The girls in class, on the other hand, all remained silent and expressionless. They either did not know, or pretended not to know the sexual implications. The lady teacher, with a surprised look, would fix her quizzical eyes on the boys, hoping for a clue for this sudden hilarity. But, of course, none of us boys would volunteer to tell her that the word "*le*" sounds like the word for the male sex organ in the Shanghai dialect, with the word that follows "*le*" indicating explicitly what happens to the "*le.*"

Our venture into Russian, a brief one, was initiated by another high-school classmate, Kang Yao (姚剛). More politically oriented than we musketeers, he was of the opinion that the Soviet Union would become a major international force after WWII. It might, therefore, be worthwhile to know its language. He soon lined up a private tutor, a Russian immigrant in Shanghai, and persuaded three of us to join him in taking private lessons. Those lessons, held in the teacher's home near *Avenue Joffre*, were instructive and enjoyable, and we learned authentic pronunciation. The only thing that I found difficult to adjust to was the Russian alphabet, which is based on the Greek. Thus, in Russian, the letter P (the Greek rho) is pronounced as "R," and, similarly, the letter "B" is pronounced as "V." (In America, the Greek letter B is pronounced as "beta," but my graduate students from Greece have corrected me to pronounce it as "veeta.")

Although we gradually conquered the Russian alphabet, it was not as easy to deal with the heavy odor of cabbage cooking that permeated the apartment and constantly assaulted our Chinese nostrils. For that reason, when Kang Yao decided, after a few months, to leave St. John's University in Shanghai for Yenching University in the interior province of Szechwan (now spelled Sichuan), we just let the Russian class die off. It is a pity that the only Russian words and phrases I still remember are not much more than: "How are you?" "I understand." "I don't know." "Thank you." "Goodbye." As in French, though, I still retain excellent memory of the Russian version of the two poetic sentences: "You are very beautiful"; and "I love you." In the Anglicized equivalent of the Russian alphabet, they are *"Vy ochen' krasivya"; and "Ya lyublyu vas."*

Stephen, George, and I took all those language classes together. In fact, we took every single college course together, year after year, totally living up to the title "The Three Musketeers."

In those years, textbooks in English were scarce in Shanghai, and we relied heavily on professors' lectures. Shanghai was under Japanese occupation for much of this period, but there was little interruption in our educational progress to speak of. By the time we graduated together in the Class of 1946, it was already one year after China won the war against Japan.

The Bund

As fresh college graduates with a major in economics, we each found a job in Shanghai. George Hsu, as he was known then, tried out a career in aviation, and obtained a position at the China National Aviation Corporation (CNAC), an airline. Stephen, whose father was a high official in the Central Bank of China, started a banking career with the Bank of China. I, on the other hand, was drafted by my second *jiujiu* (mother's brother) to work as his assistant in an accounting position. He was the Chief Accountant for the newly established consolidated Shanghai office for the various government-run industrial corporations in Taiwan, an island province ceded to Japan during the Qing Dynasty and newly returned to China at the end of WWII. He had to staff his new office, and was eager to recruit me. This *jiujiu* was the same one that caused my long academic slump by misdirecting me to skip the second grade. But I held no grudge against him, and agreed to work for him. That consolidated Shanghai office did not last long, though, and its Head, Mr. Cohen Pao (包可閎), asked me to be the accountant for a new import–export company he was founding with a German business partner. I was picked for this job, because English was required, which my *jiujiu* could not handle.

It turned out that, the offices of the three of us were all located near The Bund (外灘). The Bund, an area of Shanghai by the Huangpu River (黃浦江), had a high concentration of offices of the major banks, corporations, insurance companies, and government agencies. The proximity of our respective offices made possible frequent luncheon meetings among us three.

We regularly compared notes on our work routines, mostly boring stuff. But George was able to provide some exciting fun. One of his jobs at the airline was to apply for passports for the newly recruited stewardess. So he often had temporary custody of the passport photos of lovely young ladies to show off to Stephen Li and me. The photo-sharing added great fun to the lunches, although we had to handle the pictures gingerly among food dishes. Careful as we were, we might have caused a couple of the new stewardesses to wonder why the photos on their passports were decorated with soup stains.

Other topics for lunch conversations were, inevitably, girlfriends. Past, present, and future. More and more, however, the topic of girlfriends was supplanted by the questions of graduate studies abroad.

Going Abroad

Before WWII, most of the youngsters intent on advanced studies abroad would choose Britain, France, or Germany as their destinations, depending on their majors. But by the end of WWII, the favorite place to go had switched to the United States. I do not remember which one of us started thinking about going abroad first. But we were of the same mind. The big impetus came when a giant poster appeared on the college bulletin board, advertising the graduate school at the University of Colorado (CU). We had no knowledge about the education scene in the United States, and lacked the sophistication to go to the American consulate in Shanghai to seek information. Thus, that lone poster on the bulletin board decided for us where to apply for admissions. We were excited when we were all accepted by the CU into its MA program in economics.

Further excitement befell when we learned that the National Government in Nanking planned to offer a nationwide examination for students intending to study abroad. Passing the examination would automatically guarantee a passport, plus the right to purchase a set amount of U.S. dollars at the low, official exchange rate. With academic background like ours, we were sure to pass the examination. So, we only had to attend the examination on the set date, and everything should fall into place.

But leave it to stupid me—the bookworm of the group with a perfectionist propensity—to want to "prepare" for the examination! I decided to undertake a thorough review of all the college work I had done. The intensive review made me extremely well-prepared, but it also made me sick on the very day of the examination. As expected, Stephen and George both passed the examination. But I missed it altogether!

Not willing to wait for next year's examination, I was determined to try whatever means available to get a passport, and go together with Stephen and George to the United States. My father, bless him, did finally succeed in securing for me a ray of hope. Through several indirect introductions, I heard from Dr. Liwu Hang (杭立武), the Vice Minister of Education, who kindly consented to grant me a special interview–examination in his office in the capital city of Nanking. Ecstatic about such a rare favor, I made sure to go to Nanking by train, and arrive at his office on time. Surprisingly, he was punctual to the nanosecond, and let me into his office at the exact appointed time. After interviewing me in English for 15 minutes, he graciously told me that he would immediately notify the Ministry of Foreign Affairs to issue me a passport, but, sorry, regulations would not permit me to qualify for the official-rate purchase of U.S. dollars.

I thanked Dr. Hang with a few brief words, and hurriedly left because I knew he had a busy schedule. But, once out of his office, I realized that my expression of appreciation was hardly in proportion to the huge, huge favor he did me. Sincerely, I wished that I would be given a second opportunity to thank him more properly. As time went by, such an opportunity did eventually come, but I had to wait as many as 27 years for it.

It was at a banquet in August, 1974, in Taipei, that I met Dr. Hang again. During my short stay in Taipei for the National Reconstruction Conference (國家建設研究會), Emily and I were invited to a dinner by Dr. Chan Lien and Mrs. Anne Lien (連戰、連方瑀伉儷), where Dr. Hang was also a guest. After 27 years, I could not recognize him, but when the hosts introduced us, I excitedly addressed him as "My Venerable Benefactor" (恩公), and knelt to him to express my utmost respect. He did not quite remember the special examination he granted me, but said "I am glad I could help a good student." Later, I found out that Dr. Hang, PhD (University of London), had later served China in many high government posts, including Minister of Education and Ambassador to various countries. He also played a pivotal role in safeguarding and transporting the national treasures in the Palace Museum to Chungking (during WWII), and subsequently to Taiwan (after the Nationalist Government left the mainland).

Dr. Lien, the host, was at the time the Premier (行政院長) of the Republic of China, and I was a plain professor with no political connections. Why would the Premier invite me and my wife to dinner? The reason: Dr. Lien had taught at the University of Connecticut (UConn) before returning to Taiwan to begin his political career, and he had thus been my colleague at UConn, where he taught Political Science for two years. Since I was away at Cornell University as a Visiting Professor during his first year, we became colleagues and good friends only in the year 1968–1969. After that, the Liens returned to Taiwan, but we always got together when they visited the United States, and when we visited Taiwan.

While Chan taught political science, Anne studied for an MA degree in biochemistry at UConn. One day, near the end of the semester, I saw the two of them coming into the cafeteria, and we had lunch together. Anne, fully dressed up, showed no appetite at all, and I became somewhat concerned. "Are you okay, Anne? You are hardly eating," I said. Anne did not reply, but her husband offered the explanation: "She is just a bit nervous before her MA oral examination this afternoon." As expected, she passed the oral with flying colors. I heard later that, as many as seven professors were present at her examination instead of the usual three. There was a good reason for the high professorial attendance record: that oral examination was not for an ordinary graduate student; it was for Anne Lien, a former Miss China!

Anne received her MA degree at UConn in June, 1968. Since her husband, Professor Chan Lien, and I both attended the commencement, we took a picture together afterward in full academic regalia (Photo 43).

As a follow-up to this story, some years later, on a return visit to UConn, Anne made a casual comment at our home: "MA degrees at UConn are pretty easy to get." I felt obliged to respond: "Yes, Anne, they are indeed pretty easy. But I actually know of people who lost their appetite before taking their oral examinations." She gave out a hearty laugh.

The Liens had their first child, Arlene (連惠心), in Connecticut. At that time, Emily and I, after 14 years of marriage, still did not have a child. One day, Anne left a pair of Arlene's booties at our home on purpose, hoping for some magical effect. And, lo and behold, Emily did obligingly become pregnant soon thereafter. Anne of course claimed full credit for Emily's pregnancy! And when leaving Connecticut for Taiwan, they left all the baby-care stuff, such as diaper-changing table and baby bathtub, to us.

But I digress.

Crossing the Pacific

The years 1947–1949 saw a big wave of Chinese students going to American colleges and universities, many studying engineering, chemistry, physics, and medicine, but others pursuing literature, economics, and political science. Due to political circumstances back in China, many decided to stay on in the United States after the civil war, and they made significant professional contributions to America. This new group of Chinese professionals painted an image of Chinese immigrants totally different from the old one of railroad workers and others of the laboring class. Some won awards and prizes, including the Nobel.

Like most students in those years, The Three Musketeers came to America by steam ship. Our vessel, the Marine Adder, sailed on September 7, 1947, from the Bund. Stephen's father had kindly arranged for a big bank bus to carry the relatives and friends of the three families to see us off. With our early arrival at the wharf, we had plenty of time for goodbyes with our families.

My mother, already in tears, gave me last-minute instructions on how to take care of myself—since her only child was going away from home for the first time. It was not much consolation for her to hear me say, "Don't worry, *Mma*, I am already 20 years old. Besides, my best friends Stephen and George are with me; together we can handle everything." Dad, with a happy face, reminded my mother that "This is a happy occasion. You should smile, not cry. Besides, our son will be coming home soon enough." I immediately echoed with "Yes, yes, I will be home real soon." As the events turned out, though, it would be 13 years before I saw my *Diadia* and *Mma* again, in Hong Kong instead of Shanghai.

The ocean voyage was meant to be pure transportation, not luxurious pleasure. With close friends by my side, I felt no loneliness, and the days went smoothly. Only two onboard events stayed indelibly in my memory.

At the Bow

The first event occurred one day when we took an after-dinner stroll on the deck, ending up at the bow of the ship. The distant horizon, where the water and sky joined, naturally inspired us three youngsters on a lone ship amid waves upon waves, to contemplate our respective future. We were going for advanced education in a foreign land, while a civil war was raging in our homeland. What would happen to our country during our sojourn abroad? What would happen to us, still young, in the years to come? Would we find suitable positions in society when we returned? Would we be able to make worthwhile contributions to society?

Having already experienced two academic upsets—the unwise step of skipping a grade, and the shock of the immersive English in a missionary school—I could not help but see the waves around us as foreboding ups and downs in life. "I hope the waves in our lives will prove to be gentle and mild, not violent and devastating," I said. Stephen expressed the same hope, and added, "See how far the horizon is? We are young, and our opportunities are limitless." George and I agreed on the potentially bright hope of the future, but when he saw some dark clouds in the bare, empty scene in the distance, George said in a somber voice, "I just wish that there won't be too much uncertainty clouding our future."

A Ceremony at the International Date Line

The second event occurred at the International Date Line (IDL). At the exact time the ship was going to cross the IDL, George wanted me to be on deck with him "to bear witness" to a private ceremony he was to perform. His request, patently mysterious, was made even more so when he added, "Please don't tell Stephen." Exclude Stephen? Why?

At the exact moment, George's ceremony began. He solemnly took out from his pocket a dainty pink handkerchief and a small photo of a young girl, whom I recognized to be Stephen's little sister Dora. After carefully wrapping the photo with the handkerchief, he threw both into the ocean. As I learned later, Stephen had stolen both items from

Dora, and given to George when the latter's affection for her became known. Unfortunately, things did not turn out the way George had hoped, and the ceremony was to mark his decision to end it all. No wonder he did not want Stephen to join us.

I felt George's agony. But, aside from giving him a long hug, I knew not how to provide effective consolation.

The University of Colorado

The University of Colorado (CU), located in Boulder, has a campus much more beautiful than I could imagine. The buildings at the University, mostly made of pink stones, provide a harmonious big picture, and the walking paths around the campus were neatly placed among shapely trees and clean-shaven lawns. With Flat Iron, a part of the Rocky Mountain Range, as the backdrop, lovely Boulder was a superb town to get our first taste of American living. The people in town, shopkeepers, restaurant personnel, and the professors, staff, and fellow students at the university were uniformly friendly. Even the climate was genial—not too hot, and not too cold. Unbelievably, even after a big snow, we could walk on streets wearing nothing more than a sweater. Could it be divine guidance that landed me at such an idyllic place? In fact, Boulder impressed me so much that, when the sensational homicide case of the young beauty queen JonBenét Ramsey exploded into the news in 1996, I could hardly accept the fact that such a horrid thing could ever happen in Boulder.

We arrived at CU a few days after the fall quarter had already started, to find the classrooms bulging with students. Many of them were G.I.s (WWII veterans) taking advantage of the education subsidies offered by the Servicemen's Readjustment Act of 1944, commonly known as the G.I. Bill. There being no vacancies in the dormitories, we three had to stay in a hotel for the first quarter. The next quarter, we moved into dorm rooms, but, in order to experience American home living, I soon moved into a rented room by myself. On the campus, however, since we all took the same courses, we quickly lost our individual identities, and became known collectively as The Three Musketeers of the Department of Economics.

5.1 The University of Colorado campus. (Photos by Steve Ying)

To our surprise, we soon found three other alumni of St. John's University studying at the CU: Steve Ying (應道宸), Robin Chen (陳鵬卿), and Thomas Koo (顧正邦). Pleased about discovering this small "alumni association," we had a group picture taken at a photo

5.2 The Three Musketeers in our hotel residence in Boulder, Colorado, 1948. From left: Stephen Li, me, and George Hsu.

5.3 Six St. John's alumni studying at the University of Colorado. From left, front row: Me, George Hsu, Steve Ying; back row: Stephen Li, Robin Chen, Thomas Koo.

studio as a souvenir. The photo has faded a lot, but facial features are still visible.

Since my rented room did not include cooking privileges, and since I did not know how to cook anyway, I frequently went out for dinner with Steve Ying and Robin Chen. We often ate at Wayne's Restaurant in Boulder, where we found an excellent waitress, Virginia, the wife of a G.I. student at CU, who very quickly learned about our eating habits, likes and dislikes. For her efficient and courteous service, each of us used to tip her a silver quarter (25 cents), considered as a generous gratuity for a dinner check of a little over a dollar. Robin, who was into photography, especially special-effect photo techniques, arranged a photo session for double images. Among the many pictures he produced was one of Virginia serving dinner to herself. I reproduce this interesting picture here, to show that there did exist a fun side of life at the CU.

Picnics were something totally new to us city boys from Shanghai. At the first picnic we were invited to, not knowing any better, we actually wore jackets and ties, and walked on grass in well-polished

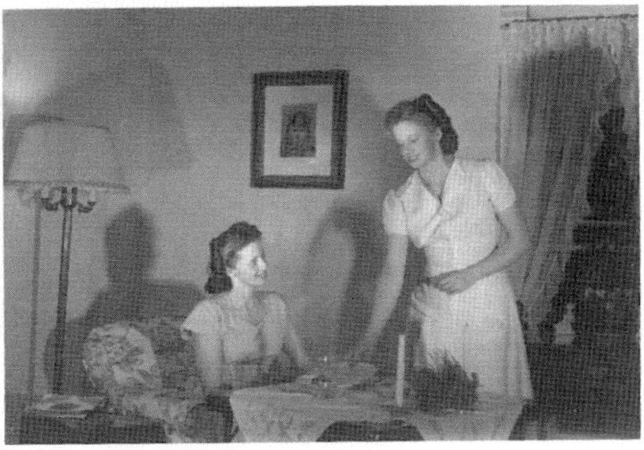

5.4 Virginia, a favorite waitress, pictured as serving dinner to herself. (Photo by Robin Chen)

dressy shoes as though going to a dance! But we quickly learned how to swim in the mainstream.

We befriended American as well as Chinese students. We also had contacts with Chinese students at other colleges nearby. There was CU Day, as well as Homecoming Day with a parade of floats and a Homecoming Queen. We were also introduced to Halloween. Listening to popular songs on the radio, I somehow fell in love with "*To Each His Own*" by the Ink Spots. Often, while munching a hamburger or hot dog at lunch, I found myself feeding a nickel into the jukebox to hear "A rose must remain, with the sun and the rain, or its lovely promise won't come true. To each his own, to each his own, and my own is you. . . ." What a spendthrift I was, squandering five cents just to listen to a single play of a single song!

But mostly, we studied, very hard. At the end of the first quarter, our good grades prompted Dean Worcester of the Graduate School to award us each a tuition scholarship for the whole academic year (three quarters), saving each of us a substantial sum of money. We naturally hurried to complete all the requirements for the MA degree, including a Master's Thesis, within those three tuition-free quarters.

MA Thesis

Even though we took the same courses, we each had a different thesis supervisor. My thesis, *A Postwar Export Policy for China*, 141 pages long, was written under the supervision of Professor Carl McGuire, my

5.5 On an outing with Professor Carl McGuire (at right).

mentor in International Economics. I wrote it on a portable typewriter I bought in Denver. But since the thesis must be submitted in four copies (plus one copy for my own file), it must, before the advent of the computer, be typed on a heavy-duty typewriter to accommodate five sheets of white bond paper, separated by four pieces of black carbon paper inserted in between. If, heaven forbid, a mistake were made, the typist must erase the original error plus the carbon images left on each of the other pieces of white paper, and then retype. Thus, only highly competent typists could handle the job of preparing theses for submission. Since all the MA and PhD candidates had theses and dissertations to submit near the end of the academic year, good typists were in hot demand at that time of the year, like tax accountants in March to April 15. My typist, the wife of a graduate student, had to work overtime, and typed into the late hours for days, while I proofread with red eyes by her side as each typed page rolled off the typewriter. What a relief when she did finish the job before the deadline!

Stephen and George finished their respective theses in time, too. As the summer season approached, the Three Musketeers became The Three Masters of Arts. Our jobs at the CU were done, well-done. That was in the summer of 1948.

5.6 The Three Musketeers became The Three MAs, 1948.

Separate Ways

From there on, we Three Musketeers would go our separate ways to pursue our different careers.

But we first went to New York together. I was moving to the big city to continue my doctoral studies at Columbia University. Stephen simply wanted to spend some vacation time in New York before answering his father's call for him to return home to Shanghai. And George decided to take some summer courses at Columbia before going back, to have a little taste of another American university.

Parting after so many years of day-in day-out closeness was somewhat jarring. We promised to keep communications open. Except when government restrictions prevented us from keeping each other posted, I knew most of what happened to Stephen and George. I even had occasions to see them in person again, later.

6

The Healing

In telling the story of The Three Musketeers' academic togetherness, I disregarded the limitations of both time and space. I went over a span of about six academic years from 1941–1942 to 1947–1948, and covered a space of thousands of miles, from Shanghai to Boulder, Colorado, and then to New York City.

Now, I must back track to a special event that occurred in Shanghai in 1946, that rocked the Chiang family.

A Late Pregnancy

I was 19 at the time, just out of college and starting to earn an income of my own, though still staying with my parents. I normally went home for dinner after work. One afternoon, however, my father called me at my office to ask me to go directly to the XXX Hospital after work, "Your mother is going to have an operation." This hospital, whose name I no longer recall, was located on Yu Yuan Road (愚園路) near the Bubbling Well Temple (靜安寺), in the western part of Shanghai, quite far away from my office. I arrived there at dusk, with a heavy heart.

I found out that my mother had fainted that morning with internal bleeding shortly after I left home for office. Since my father, the principal of his business firm, normally went to office late, he was, luckily, still at home when my mother fell to the floor. The diagnosis was quite simple: My mother had a tubal pregnancy, followed by the rupture of the fallopian tube. That was certainly a late pregnancy, and an unexpected one, since I, hitherto an only child, was already 19.

The operation went without complication and, had it been a normal pregnancy, the baby would have been a boy. I almost had a brother!

With smooth recuperation, indications were clear that the patient could be discharged in a few days. Then, a little something—my mother's wish to try a tasty snack—wreaked havoc.

Bean Curd Drop Soup

Tired of the hospital food, and uncomfortable in her sickbed, Mom earnestly pleaded with Dad one afternoon to buy for her some bean curd drop soup, a snack item she loved. That request was rather sudden and strange. She must have heard the sales calls from the street vendors outside the hospital. Even though my father did not think it was a good idea, he did not have the heart to deny his dear wife's seemingly innocuous request. He gladly went out to procure a bowl of the soup, and watched with pleasure her enjoyment of it.

Soon after ingestion, she got violently sick! We never determined whether it was because the soup was bacteria-laden, or the soup bowl was contaminated, or the soup had a bad interaction with the medicine she was taking. Mom had dysentery at first. That era was pre-penicillin, but sulfur drugs were certainly available. Nevertheless, all medications were to no avail, and mother's illness got worse and worse. Incredibly, the original ailment successively developed into other diseases: pneumonia, pleurisy, and peritonitis, and some others. Her stay in the hospital was extended to more than two months.

Under the circumstances, my father just lived in the hospital throughout that period, sleeping on a cot beside her sickbed. He could do this because he could direct his business transactions over the phone. As for me, I had to commute every day in a triangular route from home (south) to office (east) to hospital (west), and home again at night. Spending so much time in the hospital and on the road, I learned to go without all entertainment, including my favorite radio shows of Shanghai-style comedy (上海滑稽), Soochow ping-tan (蘇州評彈), and light Western music on the French radio station (法國電台輕音樂).

Our long presence at the hospital made my father and me popularly known there. At Christmas time, I was even invited by the friendly young doctors and nurses to join their Christmas party. Some high-spirited junior doctors put on funny sketches, and one irrepressible male doctor did a comedic hula dance. The evening of gaiety stayed long in my mind, because it contrasted sharply with the gloom that usually permeated Mom's sickroom.

The Prayer Group

As the patient's condition steadily showed deterioration instead of improvement, with pains growing and extending, there came a Christian prayer group, offering to pray for my mother. Father's polite declines, day after day, did not surprise me. I could still recall clearly how he made me promise "never to become a Christian" when I enrolled at St. John's Middle School.

After several days, I felt obliged to say to him, "*Diadia*, you should allow them to pray for *Mma*. The prayers may help, and at any rate they cannot possibly do any harm." And Nurse Tai (戴彩雪), a devout Christian, who had faithfully and effectively served as Mom's special nurse at night, also added her plea to allow the prayer group into the room. I cited to Dad the old Chinese saying: "Always treat a dying horse as a live one!" Try everything! Incidentally, Mom was born in 1906, a year of the horse, which made that saying especially pertinent.

Father finally relented. He even agreed to kneel while the prayers were being said or sung out loud. But a couple of days of fervent prayers produced little beneficial effect. And on one day, it seemed that, with multiple inflammations in her body, Mom was ready to succumb.

In desperation, Dad consulted successively with 10 well-known physicians about my mother's condition. The consensus was: No hope. The vote was: 9–1. The dissenting vote was cast by a doctor (his name has escaped me) who was busy with many civic projects, but was willing to perform a final surgery on Mom, promising no more than 1% chance of success. He would be willing to do it that very night at 11:00 p.m., after finishing a couple of important civic meetings. Father nodded agreement, but Nurse Tai showed great concern that at such a late hour, especially after several meetings, the doctor would be too tired to operate. She suggested, sensibly, to have the operation postponed to the next morning. Everybody agreed, including the doctor.

A Dream

That night, my mother had a dream. A white-robed man, with a face so shiny as to render his facial features unrecognizable, was performing surgery on someone lying on a table. As she witnessed the operation not too far from the operating table, she felt a stream of warmth entering her own body. So comfortable did she feel that she easily slipped into a deep sleep—a long, peaceful slumber.

When the doctor came into her room early the next morning, he habitually tried to press on her body to test her reaction. Normally, she would yell loudly in pain, "Oyo, Oyo!" But that morning, she showed no reaction at all. Surprised at the change, the doctor ordered an X-ray taken. He could not believe what the new X-ray showed: Her inside was totally clear, totally normal!

"A miracle has occurred to your family; there is no need for surgery now," the doctor, also a Christian, declared in a congratulatory tone.

My father, obviously awed, said to me when I got to the hospital, "Take me to a Christian church at the first possible opportunity." With apology, he formally released me from my earlier promise "never to become a Christian." And as soon as my mother gained sufficient physical strength after a few days, our family of three arranged to receive our respective baptism from Rev. Timothy S. K. Dzao (趙世光牧師), a well-known Christian evangelist, at his church (靈糧堂).

Religious Pursuits

By the time Mom returned home from the hospital, I was busily involved in preparing for my impending trip to the United States. Miracle or not, religion was not the uppermost thought on my mind. I became a good Christian, trying to be consistent and persistent in doing my prayers and living a righteous life. When living in Connecticut, Emily and I regularly attended the Storrs Community Church. We even hosted a Bible study group at our home on Beech Mountain Road in Mansfield Center. Rev. Dennis Reiter, then the pastor of the said church, was our mentor along with his wife Judy. A very learned scholar with a doctoral degree, Dennis and I had many enlightening discussions, even debates on religious questions. But I never developed a knack for evangelizing.

My parents, on the other hand, became more and more serious in their religious lives. From our regular correspondences, I learned from Dad that they found a suitable church near home in Shanghai, and they were devoting a lot of their energy to church activities. Evangelizing widely among their acquaintances, they succeeded in converting many of their friends and relatives to Christianity. Conversion wrought big changes in people. My step-grandmother, for example, soon repented

6.1 Rev. Dennis Reiter, Judy, and their children (1989 photo).

and formally sought my mother's forgiveness for her earlier mean behavior in Baoshan, before Mother and I moved to Shanghai.

Dad soon learned to become a lay preacher, was elected a Deacon at the church, and, to my amazement, he even received the gift of healing by prayer during a certain period of time.

But political changes brought in a new regime in China in 1949, and religious activities were not looked upon with favor by the new government. Ten years after I left Shanghai, my parents took advantage of a rare opportunity that unexpectedly opened up, and moved to Hong Kong, where they could pursue religion free of restrictions. When my wife Emily and I visited them in 1960–1961, they took us to the church they belonged to. It was located on a dirty street lined with food stalls, and the inside of the church was shabby and minimalist. But they were happy. I secretly prayed that their church would move to a better location in Hong Kong.

In 1962, news came that their church had found a better place, large enough to seat 150 people, and would officially carry the name Shanghai Christian Church, Hong Kong (香港基督教上海禮拜堂, also abbr. as 上海禮拜堂). The move was made possible by a successful major fundraising undertaking. Dad played an important role in it. The geographical area, known as North Point, has a great concentration of immigrants to Hong Kong from Shanghai, and the use of the Shanghai dialect, as against the Cantonese dialect (the norm in Hong Kong), is prevalent there. One feature that distinguishes the Shanghai Christian Church from other churches is its use of the Shanghai dialect as the principal means of communication. Sometimes, guest sermons might be rendered in Mandarin. But my father preached only in the Shanghai dialect.

A Second Career as Rev. Chiang

A more significant development was that my father had decided to study theology with a view to becoming an ordained minister. He was almost 60 years of age, perhaps with a deteriorating memory. It must have taken extraordinary perseverance to pursue such an undertaking. I had no doubt that Mom did her best to encourage and support him.

He was ordained on March 5, 1966, starting his second career as Rev. Chiang (蔣牧師) at age 61, and led the church for 31 years until his death on July 9, 1997. (It was little wonder that when I retired from teaching at age 65, Dad's comment was: "Why do you retire so early?".

Acting as the central force of the church, he would oversee yet another move of the church to a more spacious location, complete with wooden pews, a baptismal basin, office, lounge, a grand piano, and a modern sound system. As a result of arduous but successful efforts at fundraising, they relocated in November, 1974.

We attended Dad's church in the new location every time we went to Hong Kong to visit, almost every summer. As I expected, he was a remarkable minister. With good voice training in his early days as a trader, and with careful preparation through concentrated prayers, his sermons were invariably substantive and effectively delivered. He was caring about his flock, and frequently helped them resolve family

6.2 Father's ordination at age 61 (left), Hong Kong, March 5, 1966.

conflicts, and in these and other church matters, Mom was his important right hand (and left hand). To serve the illiterate, Rev. Chiang wrote letters for them. And, on account of his connections with restaurants and flower shops, he was always able to arrange banquet events like weddings, celebrations, and funerals for church members at reduced cost. He also managed church finances well because of his business acumen. For his contributions to the church, its Board of Directors voted to increase Father's salary on several occasions. But each time, he would either decline, or agree to accept a reduced raise, saying that he was just honored to be doing God's work.

But what impressed me the most about Dad was what happened on one Sunday, when a guest preacher gave a sermon so lengthy, unfocused, and hardly audible that I, sitting in a back pew, almost fell asleep. Then, at the end of that sermon, Dad walked to the pulpit, thanked the guest preacher, and rendered a succinct, well-organized, one-minute summary of that sermon in a sonorous voice. And he did not even take notes during the sermon. I was totally awed by this amazing feat of his. Photo 2 in the front of the book shows Dad giving a sermon at his church in Hong Kong.

A Changed Priority

Dad was the one that baptized Emily, and later also our children Darryl and Tracey. That pleased him, because he was strongly family oriented. But over the years, he embraced more and more a "church first, family second" philosophy. Despite Mom's innate desire to join us in their later years, Dad could never fully accept our invitations to come to live in the United States. Twice, we arranged permanent residency for them, but twice they decided to give that up. They did visit us several times, and we took those opportunities to take them to see the sights in Washington, DC, including the White House, and the Niagara Falls from both the American and Canadian sides. But each visit never lasted more than three months. Mails from church members would earnestly plead for them to return to Hong Kong, and Dad would go back without fail.

Dad never intended to retire. From the time he was ordained in March 1966, to the time he collapsed at age 92 on a Hong Kong street in July, 1997, on his way to a scheduled medical checkup, his second career as a Christian minister lasted more than three decades. At the time of his death, about two years after Mom passed away in a hospital after a brief illness in March 1995 after she had already suffered from Alzheimer's disease, Dad was still a devoted minister on active duty at his beloved Shanghai Christian Church, in North Point, Hong Kong.

Eventually, though, both Mom and Dad did permanently immigrate to the United States, but not as live persons. As they wished, I had their remains shipped over. It was necessary to apply for visas for their remains to enter into the United States, but the American Consulate in Hong Kong issued the necessary documents with little fuss. In two somber ceremonies with relatives and friends attending, they were interred at Kensico Cemetery in Valhalla, New York, near White Plains where we were residing at the time.

6.3 My parents' resting place, Kensico Cemetery, Valhalla, New York.

7

Vive les Cultural Differences!

In my first year or two in the United States, I marveled at the large number of cultural differences between the two countries. Some aspects of American ways inspired my admiration and respect. Others impressed me as puzzling, disillusioning, eccentric, or beyond reason. Of course, in the decades I have been in the United States, things have changed tremendously, but my first impressions are still fresh in my mind.

Cars on the Streets

On my voyage from Shanghai to San Francisco, our ship Marine Adder had a brief stopover in Honolulu, for unloading cargo or fueling, or both. Walking on the sidewalk of a busy thoroughfare in that tropical city, I could not believe the quietness—bordering on total silence—that saturated my ears. The street was full of automobiles going in two directions, but the atmosphere was absolutely calm. Nobody was honking the horn as the drivers in Shanghai would, to herald their approaching and to scare the pedestrians away. The orderliness I noticed in Honolulu won my admiration as my first impression of the United States! The street scenes I found in New York later were a different matter, but even to this day I clearly remember the awe that came over me in Honolulu.

I was also favorably impressed by the pervasive use of stop signs on street corners to maintain traffic order in less busy areas. With rare exceptions, drivers do stop at the stop signs. The right of way accorded to pedestrians vis-à-vis motorists was also in sharp contrast to Shanghai, giving me a refreshing impression.

From Hollywood movies shown in the cinemas in Shanghai, I noted something I could not believe: Everybody in America—young or old, male or female—could drive a car! In Shanghai, cars were driven only by chauffeurs. First of all, automobiles were luxury items only owned by rich families. Any family that owned an automobile would as a matter of course hire a professional chauffeur, to take the family members out at all hours of the day, and also to keep the car clean, properly maintained, and adequately fueled. Even a small car, such as a British-made Austin, might have a chauffeur in the front seat, with the owner occupying the tiny space in the back. Only after I came to the United States did I realize that indeed everybody could drive here. Hollywood movies do sometimes depict the truth.

I must add that things are drastically different in China now, decades since I left there. In Chinese movies and TV shows of recent vintage, almost all of the young characters, male or female, can get into a car and drive on, just as in Hollywood movies.

Attire

But other impressions from Hollywood movies remain unconfirmed. It is not true that, every night, gentlemen in black ties escort ladies in flowing gowns down a marble staircase to dinner. Nevertheless, because of the movie illusion, some Chinese students did include in their luggage custom-made tuxedos. I did not bring tuxedoes, only suits. When, laughably, I went to the first picnic in Boulder in suit and tie, it was partly because of my ignorance about picnics, but mainly because I did not even own any casual wear.

There was no need for a tuxedo in Boulder anyway, because all dance events were semiformal. But in New York, I had to buy one when a fellow graduate student at Columbia, Herman Yueh (岳毓衡), kindly invited me to a formal dance sponsored by his fraternity, Alpha Lambda. He had to find a dance partner for me, too, since I had none then. For such dances, I learned how to tie a bow tie, and quickly developed a preference for bow ties to four-in-hands. A bow tie never flaps around. Moreover, it can never get into the soup by accident (Ha! Ha!). Soon, I collected a sizable collection of bow ties, and I wore them more and more as a matter of habit. After I started teaching, I became known as "the professor with the bow tie." (Some astute readers may have noticed that I wore a bow tie even at age 5, in Photo 2.1. But that was a fake one, not the self-tied kind.)

Why This Name?

Everything has a given name. But not all given names are reasonable or logical.

Soon after I arrived in Boulder, Colorado, I was introduced to American football in a game of Colorado versus Nebraska. When the National Anthem was played and the Stars and Stripes raised, everybody in attendance stood at attention. The patriotic feeling that permeated the entire stadium called forth tears in my eyes. What a great country with a national pride! That was, of course, just a couple of years after the end of WWII. Things are way different now, to my dismay.

7.1 Goody Wong, circa 1947 (photographer unknown).

It was Goody Wong, the lovely and genteel American-born Chinese girl whom I dated during my nine-month stay in Boulder, who introduced me to the football game. Her name struck me as strange and funny, but she got this nickname simply because one of the two words in her Chinese name is pronounced in Cantonese dialect like "good." Goody was supposed to be introducing me to an American sport, but she was either unable or unwilling to explain the rules of the game to me, leaving me to figure out the difference between a "first down" and a "touchdown." The question uppermost in my mind, however, was something else: Why in the world is this game called "football" when the "foot" gets in touch with the "ball" only in the kickoff and punt? Nobody, except me, was ever bothered by such a flagrant misnomer?

In China, incidentally, the word "football" means soccer. For proper distinction, American football is referred to as "olive ball," in view of the shape of the ball.

Another big misnomer in America is "drugstore." To me, "drugstore" is a synonym for "pharmacy." But in Boulder, the pharmacy I saw occupied no more than a counter in the back section of the store. In the front, all kinds of wares were available: toothpaste, toothbrushes, shampoo, cosmetics, greeting cards, candies, and magazines. At one time or another, I had also ordered from the soda fountain in the drugstore all sorts of soft drinks, ice cream soda, banana splits, and even simple lunches. Sitting on the round high stools at the counter, and sipping a soda, was inexpensive fun. But eating a banana split was a royal treat. Soda fountains now seem extinct. They probably do not belong in a drugstore in the first place. But I miss them.

Local Expressions

To my "Thank you," I normally expected the answer "You are welcome." But, in Boulder, I often got the response "You bet." I soon learned to use that response myself, although I never understood how "betting" can ever have a place in an expression of welcome. Anyway, "You bet" is not popularly used in New York, so I quickly dropped it in favor of "You are welcome." The currently popular response, "No problem," has never gained entry into my vocabulary.

The greeting "Howdy?" is another expression I learned in Colorado, but later dropped in New York in favor of the more mundane "Hi."

By the way, have you ever heard of the expression "two bits" as a monetary figure? Once, trying to make a payment in Boulder, I heard the saleslady saying, "That would be two bits." I did not know how much to give her until she added, "twenty-five cents." So, a "bit" is equal to twelve and half cents. As far as I know, no coin of that value has ever been minted. Actually, I also heard the expressions "four bits" and "six bits" used during transactions. They qualify as good mathematical puzzles.

At the Dining Table

Eating utensils in China consist of chopsticks for solid food and spoons for soup. There is no place on the dining table for knives, because all the foods served are supposed to be properly precut before coming onto the table. Similarly, no condiments appear on the table, because all the seasoning is supposed to have been done, optimally, during the cooking process.

At my first introduction to a Western meal in a Shanghai restaurant, the sight of salt and pepper shakers surprised me as redundant. A greater surprise was the knife. Why would they place a "weapon" on the table? As to the fork, I had intuitively viewed its four prongs as two pairs of short chopsticks put together, but unfortunately in a rigid, stationary position, thus affording no maneuverability that one could enjoy with a pair of chopsticks. But since the food is placed on a flat plate, instead of a round bowl for Chinese cuisine, the use of a fork makes good sense, and I heartily approved the fork–plate combination. Chopsticks, meant to be used by digging into a bowl, do not really go well with a flat plate. I always sigh when I see people trying the patently illogical and almost impossible task of picking up grains of rice with chopsticks from a plate. This is a clear case of an unwise juxtaposition of the East (chopsticks) and the West (dinner place).

Another case of unwise juxtaposition relates to the use of stemmed wine glasses at the Chinese banquet table. In my youth in China, we always used low cups (like the tea cups provided in Chinese restaurants in the United States) for the rice wine served to guests. When the guests extended their arms to partake the food in the middle of the table, the low wine cups allow plenty of air space for their arms to go forward. With the stemmed wine glasses at the table, however, their height invaded into the air space, and acted as an unwelcome barriers to the food dishes in the middle. It becomes worse if, aside from the glasses for wine, there are also stemmed glasses for water, doubling the barrier around the food, and halving the joy of dining.

My father taught me the European way of fork-and-knife use in Shanghai. When I first saw the American way, it surprised me: The fork, originally held in the left hand during cutting, has to be passed to the right hand for eating. Then it has to be transferred again to the left hand for the next round of cutting. There was already a lot of cutting work in the European way. Now, with the constant shifting of the fork from hand to hand, there is even more hand work added to the dining experience. Why should the diner be required to do that much?

I tried many times to inquire into the origin of the practice of handing the fork from left to right, and right to left. But never have I received a satisfactory explanation. Once, though, my friend John Foord told me in a confident tone during dinner, that this practice was first used in France during the reign of Louis XIV, and soon became fashionable in America. When it was later discarded there, though, the practice persisted here. His explanation came out very readily, without any noticeable hesitation or thinking. Either he was extremely knowledgeable about this matter, and able to give me his answer right off the tip of his tongue, or he just made the whole story up, right on the spot. I believe he is correct.

Talking about France made me think of Germany. And then I think of war. And then I think of a particular war movie. I no longer remember the name of that movie, but the story centered on an American young man sent to Germany as a spy. Since he spoke German fluently just like a native, and knew all the German idioms and customs, he made a fool-proof spy, and accomplished many important missions of espionage. But, alas, he was finally found out. Guess how? He was seen eating with the fork in his right hand!

I have sounded like I am against forks and knives, and especially against the American way of fork-and-knife wielding. In fact, I have been an adherent of the American way for 70 years, ever since I got acclimated to the United States. I am not afraid of being found out either; I have never been a spy.

Chop Suey and Chow Mein

My first impression of Chinese restaurants in America was that they serve something I had never eaten in China, called "chop suey" and "chow mein." In the 1940s and 1950s, these two terms appeared in bright neon signs in the windows of all Chinese restaurants. By an educated guess, I figured that "chow mein" means fried noodles. But I could not quite understand the meaning of "chop suey" until somebody told me that it means "a mixture of different ingredients (雜碎 in Cantonese dialect)." Many Americans mistakenly took these to represent authentic Chinese cuisine. In truth, these dishes were invented in America, as were fortune cookies.

Over time, as a concomitant of waves of Chinese immigrants into the United States, chop suey and chow mein have faded into history, with the void gradually filled by different styles of genuine Chinese cuisine, including Szechuan (or Sichuan), Hunan, Shanghai, Beijing, besides Cantonese. They are available at least in the big cities, and many Americans have become accustomed, or even addicted, to them. Over the decades, I have seen more and more Americans becoming dexterous with the use of chopsticks.

Communalism versus Individualism

Cultural differences can be found even in these Chinese restaurants here in the United States. A Chinese family would normally order dishes and place them in the middle of the table, with or without a Lazy Susan. With every diner having equal access to the dishes, each can enjoy a varied meal. Americans, on the other hand, tend to order individual dishes, to each his own. The idea, I suppose, is that each will order whatever suits his/her specific taste. As an economist, I can see this as a proper way to maximize satisfaction. But it leaves out the consideration of variety, not to say the opportunity to test–taste something others have ordered that you are not venturesome enough to order on your own.

One time, I saw an American gentleman order a whole fish for himself, not realizing that the whole fish is usually a big dish meant to be shared by several people. Another time, in a Chinese restaurant in Chinatown in Manhattan, one of four American guests told the waiter after carefully studying the menu, "I think I'll have a Peking duck." The second one said, "I guess I'll have one, too." And the other two quickly echoed the order. They probably did not realize that a whole duck is, like a whole fish, meant to be shared, and accompanied by other dishes. At that moment, I seriously thought of doing a good deed by offering these four gentlemen advices on ordering, but, since such a move would embarrass them—not only one person, but four people at once—I decided against it. The waiter did not say anything to them either, probably for the same reason, but perhaps more because four ducks meant better business than four normal orders. But the chefs and the serving staff must have had a big laugh at this unheard-of order of four ducks with nothing else.

Even when dishes are shared communally, American and Chinese habits differ. The Chinese tend to bring their individual plates to the communal dishes to pick up what they want. Americans, on the other hand, tend to take the communal dish to their individual plates for serving. I have no explanation for this diverse behavior. From an economic point of view, though, to do the task with less energy, it would make more sense to bring the lighter object to the heavier one. Since the individual plate usually has less food on it than the communal dish—unless that communal dish is near its point of exhaustion—it is generally more economical to take one's own plate to the communal dishes on the Lazy Susan. But, economics is not the only consideration in life, and I admit that the difference in energy consumption here is way too trivial to warrant invoking economic principles into the decision-making process.

Slangs from Sports and Games

Over the years, I have learned to use many American slangs. One interesting discovery of mine is that quite a few slangs have their origin in various sports and games terminology. I am mentioning them here because, surprisingly, even many American friends had no clues until I told them.

A very easy one is "Three strikes, and you are out." The most rudimentary familiarity with baseball would explain this slang.

A more difficult one is "I had a bad break." The sense of this expression is clear enough: I had bad luck, and I did not get what I wished for. But where does the word "break" come from? I know the phrase "to take a break," but this phrase does not fit into the notion of "bad break." Only after I tried to learn pocket billiards, did it dawn on me that the term "bad break" refers to a poor opening shot of the game. A "bad break" occurs when a billiard player's opening shot fails to drop even a single ball into the pockets. He is then not allowed to continue to play, and must yield the turn to the opponent.

"Losing one's shirt" is also a phrase with a fairly obvious meaning. But why pick on the "shirt" rather than anything else? The answer came to me one day, when I noticed that Darryl, my son at Princeton, possessed a shirt bearing the name "University of Pennsylvania." Why would he buy the shirt of another university? "I didn't buy it; I won it." He explained to me that at the collegial boat races, everyone on the losing crew must by tradition take off his shirt and give (lose) it to his counterpart on the winning team. And, as another tradition, the winning crew will then throw their own coxswain into the water in celebration. In the Spring of 1987, Darryl coxed the Princeton Freshman Lightweight Crew (second boat) to victory against the University of Pennsylvania. So he should get the opposing coxswain's shirt. However, the opposing coxswain happened to be a woman! She did not take off the shirt she was wearing, but just gave Darryl another one she brought. The other tradition was observed, too; he was thrown into the Schuylkill River in Philadelphia. Even though that was the only official race he entered, he participated in the sports banquet at the end of the term, where he received two humorous gifts: a map of Princeton and a compass. For me, I was glad that he led me to the origin of the phrase "losing one's shirt."

For me, the most challenging slang phrase is "no holds barred." Again, the general meaning is quite simple: there will be no restriction whatsoever. But where does the word "holds" come from? Like the word "break" in "I had a bad break," the word "holds" is a noun. But I was only used to its use as a verb. The solution to my puzzle came many years later, when I happened to watch a (rather repugnant) wrestling game. Each wrestler, I found out, uses various "holds" with his arms to lock the opponent into a vanquished position. But certain dangerous holds are illegal, and "barred" from use. When "no holds are barred," then all holds are permissible. It's that simple.

Shirt Collar, Facial Tissue, and Back Page

In my youth days in China, labor was cheap and materials expensive. Unlike in America, we tended to value "machine-made" merchandise, because handmade things were commonplace and thus cheap. And we tended to have things mended or repaired, instead of discarding them in favor of new ones.

In a city like Shanghai, many men wore Western-style shirts. When the shirt collar and cuffs were frayed, it was a common practice to have a new collar and new cuffs made by a tailor, using the extra fabric from the shirttail. The labor cost was low, and the workmanship of the Chinese tailors was such that the custom-made new collar and cuffs could not be told apart from the originals. In my first days in New York, when a need for shirt repair arose, I automatically searched for a tailor in the Yellow Pages for a new collar and new cuffs. To my big disappointment, from the extensive listing of tailors in New York City, all tailors said that they did not make collars. When I finally went to see a rare one that said yes, he looked at the shirt, and cast a puzzled look at me ("Why do you need a custom-made collar for such an old shirt?"), and I reciprocated with a puzzled look of my own ("Isn't this what everyone does to a frayed shirt?")! He agreed to do it, but charged me dearly. It was only after I saw the price tag for a new shirt later, that I learned the economic truth: Never mend an old item in America, just discard it and purchase a new one!

In China, we used handkerchiefs. They were washed and reused. In America, facial tissues have long supplanted handkerchiefs. When facial tissues invaded into my life, they caused a loving reaction in me. These tissues are so well made, clean and neat, conveniently proportioned, and gentle to the touch. I found it hard to discard such a beautiful thing after a single use, even though I knew it was not meant to be reused. That was not a matter of frugality either; it was my reluctance to abandon anything so lovely. It took me a long, long time to overcome this emotional block, and adopt the American culture of guiltless discarding.

The discarding culture in American extends especially into the use of paper. Paper was one of the early inventions of China, and I hold great respect for it. I often saw people throw into the waste basket a nice piece of bond paper with only one or two lines of words on it, simply because of a minor mistake. How could anyone be so heartless? I would feel uncomfortable even to throw away a letter or document whose back side is blank and clean. A clean back page should at least be good for writing the draft of a note, or doing some rough calculations, or making a shopping list, . . ., before being consigned to a waste basket. But, hey, this is a discarding economy.

After so many years in the United States, I can now discard facial tissues without feeling guilty. But paper, I still cannot in good conscience discard without finding a use for its clean back side. I figure that the total effect of my lifetime saving of paper may have easily amounted to the equivalent of having spared the life of a small tree. Perhaps I am worthy of a medal or two from some environmental groups.

8

The Loan

As someone who grew up in a big metropolis like Shanghai, where pickpockets, thieves, and swindlers abounded, I should have enough street smarts to deal with life in New York City. Already a mature man of age 21 when I enrolled at Columbia University in the fall of 1948, I should know better than to lend money to a total stranger without getting his name, checking his ID, or requiring an IOU. But that was precisely what I did. What made me do such a dumb thing?

The Boulder Effect

It was all because of the nine months I spent at the University of Colorado (CU) in Boulder, Colorado, which caused a sea change in my attitude toward humanity in general, and toward Americans in particular. I found universal friendliness and courtesy in the people I encountered there, from professors, university staff, fellow students, townspeople, shopkeepers, restaurant owners, to waiters and waitresses alike. The extent of the kindness and generosity I received in my Boulder days was overwhelming enough to make me eager to reciprocate and repay it in kind when possible.

One particular event was especially powerful in relaxing my "always on guard" habit developed in Shanghai. When I rented a room from a Mrs. Vaniman on 11th Street, and asked her for door keys, her answer astonished me, "Sorry, I have no keys; we never lock our doors." Sure enough, throughout my stay there, with two other lodgers, nobody ever intruded, and nothing was ever stolen. This almost unreal experience of living in a keyless house for several months imbued me with a new, high level of trust in my fellow human beings.

Encounter of the First Kind

Transferring to Columbia University for my doctoral studies put me back into a metropolis, requiring me to resume the "always on guard" attitude. But the dominant thought in my mind was still a strong urge to reciprocate the kindness I found in Boulder.

This was why when a self-acclaimed fellow Columbian approached me one late afternoon on my way home from the library, and asked for a loan because he lost his wallet, I immediately took it as a God-given opportunity to "repay" American kindness. Still, remembering that this was New York, I first applied what I had learned in Shanghai about physiognomy, and examined his facial features to decipher his character. Triangular eyes would be a no-no; he did not show those. His eyes did not shift as he talked to me. His ears, and other features, all showed no obvious character flaws, as was his general deportment. I took out my wallet without hesitation.

What he asked for was two dollars. But, feeling that my first act of reciprocity should not be tainted with miserliness, I offered him five. Five dollars, by today's standard, is a paltry sum. But back in 1948, that was indeed a respectable amount; it could buy you a hundred cups of coffee, or a hundred subway rides. Visibly touched by my offer, he thanked me profusely, and promised to return the money the next day, same time, same place. On my part, I was quite gratified with my act of kindness; so, it never occurred to me to ask for his name and address, let alone an IOU. In fact, I exultantly stood at the spot for a few seconds, just to savor the moment, before striding home with a light heart.

The next day, I was at the corner of Broadway and 120th Street around 5:20, ahead of the appointed time. As the minutes went by, with no sign of him, however, a small grain of doubt started to sprout in my mind: Oh, no; maybe he was not going to show up? When, after half an hour, that little doubt had grown up to a big certainty, a mixture of emotions came over me. I was sad to lose five dollars. Worse, I was ashamed to be proven patently stupid: my application of physiognomy turned out to be a fiasco. But worst of all, I felt crushed because my beautiful view of humanity, tenderly incubated in Boulder over nine months by a whole host of kind people, was now crushed in New York in one day by a single wretched soul. I continued to stand at that street corner for another 10 minutes—just in case he was merely late. Then, finally giving up, I trudged home with heavy feet.

That could be the end of the story. But, by destiny, I was to see that person again, about six months later.

Encounter of the Second Kind

In New York, as in Boulder before, I often had dinner with Steve Ying and Robin Chen, who now held civil engineering jobs in Manhattan. One day, on our way home after dinner in Steve's car, during a stop at a red light on Broadway, I happened to glance out the window and see two men talking on the sidewalk beside the flickering neon light of a restaurant. I immediately recognized one of them as the swindler! I clearly remembered him because I had analyzed his face before. Anger suddenly surged in me, and I hurriedly pushed open the car door, and sprinted toward him. With a ferocity I did not know I was capable of, I grabbed his lapels and yelled, "You, despicable scoundrel! Give me back my money!"

In retrospect, what I did was totally reckless; I had no proof that he owed me money, and he could have called the police and charged me with unprovoked assault. But, luckily for me, his guilty conscience made him psychologically weak. His face became red, and he could only mutter: "Okay, okay, I'm sorry." Then, taking out a bunch of crumpled bills from his right coat pocket, he pleaded with me, "Take these. That's all I have with me." I would have liked to give him a stern lecture, but the red traffic light had already changed to green, and I had to rush back to Steve's car.

Steve and Robin were naturally curious, and anxiously asked, "What happened? What happened?" Needing a couple of minutes to catch my breath, I did not immediately reply. I just counted the money in my hand. One, two, three, four, . . ., wow, it came to nine dollars! On a loan of $5, I had earned an interest of $4. For half a year, the $4 interest on a loan of $5 implied an interest rate of (as I calculated out later) 160% per annum. What an extraordinary rate of return!

My friends were still asking me about my strange sortie from the car. With a sigh of relief and delight, I finally told them, "It's a story of poetic justice. I was at first a victim of a premeditated swindle, but now, the swindler has made me an unintentional loan shark!"

9

Inches from Hollywood Glamour

The first paycheck I ever received in the United States was not an ordinary one. It was not for office work, or for manual labor, but for a performance on television (TV), in 1952.

True, the University of Colorado waived my tuition charges, which was just like giving me a substantial sum of money. But that was an award, not earnings. And I later received usurious interest from a loan swindler. But, again, that was a gratuitous income, not earnings in the true sense of the word. The paycheck from TV work was, on the other hand, truly earnings for my work. But, in those early days in the history of Television, TV work was far from a regular type of employment. How did I get mixed up in it?

Sea Monster

It all started with a phone call from one of my Chinese opera friends, Ren-ying Yen (嚴仁穎) in late 1951. Known by his nickname, "Sea Monster" (海怪), he was a many-faceted man, working not only for the China Institute in American, a cultural institution in New York, but also as a photojournalist for a Chinese magazine in New York. More unusually, he was a professional actor on television, playing occasional roles as Chinese warlords or peasants, Japanese generals or soldiers, and the like. By his Northern Chinese habit of addressing friends by their family names, but prefixed with "Little" or "Old" depending on age, he called me "Little Chiang" (小蔣) since I was only 24 then.

"Little Chiang, this is Sea Monster. My theatrical agent wants me to find some people to play Oriental musicians in a TV drama. I was thinking about a trio, with you playing the erhu (二胡), S. W. Hsiang, his bamboo flute (笛子), and me, the moon guitar (月琴). Would you be willing to do it?"

Television was still relatively new and exotic at the time, and here, freely falling into my lap, was an opportunity to perform on TV! The timing was great, too: Since I had already finished my coursework at Columbia, my time schedule was flexible. Without asking for further details, I immediately said, "It sounds great. I wouldn't miss such an opportunity."

Sea Monster supplied further details: The drama was called "Ceylon Treasure," on Lux Video Theater, to be done on January 14, 1952, at CBS Studio 41. There would be one rehearsal before the show. Edmund O'Brien and Maria Riva (daughter of Marlene Dietrich) were the main actors. We musicians would be accompanying Audrey Meadows as a Ceylonese nightclub singer. Last, but not least, Sea Monster added: "I almost forgot: For the performance, you will be paid $100."

A hundred dollars! That was a very handsome payment, when you could enjoy a cup of coffee for five cents, or ride the subway from one end of Manhattan to the other for a nickel.

At the Rehearsal

At the rehearsal, we, the Oriental trio, were given the music we were to play. The song was written by an American composer who obviously had never been exposed to Oriental music. But he composed it specifically for the show, so it was our job to play it. The good thing was that the tune was simple enough for us to learn in just 10 minutes. The bamboo flute of Mr. Hsiang, an insurance executive, had a set pitch, so Sea Monster and I simply tuned our respective stringed instruments to go with the flute. Then we were introduced to Audrey Meadows, the singer, a most sweet young lady and a rising star. We tried out the song together, even though there were no lyrics written. She told us not to worry; she could easily extemporize. As it turned out, Audrey Meadows lived for many years in China as a child of missionary parents. That was one reason why we got along especially well, and we had a good time chatting with each other. As for her extemporaneous lyrics, I felt she just cleverly uttered a few random Chinese words she knew. As you may know, Audrey would become very famous later for her role in the "Honeymooners" with Jackie Gleason. But, in 1952, she was only a rising star.

Just as we settled on the musical end of our job, some assistant to the producer came over with bad news: "Sorry. Two of you musicians cannot participate in the show. You are not union members." Uh-oh! Fired at the rehearsal? Of course, S. W. Hsiang and I, the nonmembers, could join the union then and there, but the union due would be much more than our $100 pay! Fortunately, the producer negotiated with the union, and we got a temporary exemption from the union member requirement, because we were "one-time performers for difficult-to-fill roles."

We also saw Edmund O'Brien, Maria Riva, and the other actors. But they had no interactions with us in the show, so we never interacted in private either.

"Ceylon Treasure" and Another Treasure

The show was aired on the appointed date, live. We played the same piece of music whenever the director signaled to us. But, following strict instruction, we stayed stationary at one spot in the studio, remaining absolutely quiet except when we were supposed to play the music. The actors roam from area to area as the story line developed, so we could not follow all the actions or learn the whole story.

When the last nightclub scene was finished, we retired to an off spot. But, suddenly I felt a strong presence beside me to my right. I turned my head to check, and—OH, MY GOD!—what did I see? Within inches of me, stood the glamour star Marlene Dietrich in the flesh! She was there obviously because her daughter, Maria Riva, was in the show. Totally stunned, I almost started to talk to her, but, remembering the vow of silence, I kept my lips shut. We looked at each other for a few seconds, until I felt that it would be impolite to stare at her any longer. Her stare was gently piercing, and her unique "sleepy" eyelids were sweetly captivating.

She wore a simple but elegant dress, and had minimal makeup. Her blond hair flowed down naturally with just a soft wave on the side. The simplicity of her appearance made her look much more attractive than her images in some films, where she was often too heavily made up, with complicated hairdos, and in tight costumes. Without thinking twice, I promoted her from sixth place to third place on my "Favorite Glamour Stars List," only after Hedy Lamarr and Gene Tierney. (This list was, of course, pre-Marilyn Monroe.)

When I tried to look at her once more, she was gone. This brief encounter with Marlene was the main reason I will never forget "Ceylon Treasure."

Four or five weeks later, while I was sitting in a barber's chair on Broadway, the barber handed me a magazine to read. And the first article I laid my eyes on happened to be a write-up on Audrey Meadows, which immediately aroused my interest. It mentioned her life in China, her sister Jayne Meadows, and her break into show business, and some other things she herself had told me. Then the author of the article sang praise of her many talents, and specially noted that she wrote the lyrics, in a foreign language, for a song she sang in the drama "Ceylon Treasure." I almost laughed out aloud.

"Royal Showcase"

For my job in "Ceylon Treasure," I was exempted from the union membership requirement, on grounds that I was a "one-time performer." But, in fact, just a little over three months later, Sea Monster asked me to join him in another TV show, making me a "two-time performer." This time around, I still played a musician, but it was not in a drama, but on a variety show called "Royal Showcase," hosted by George Abbott, and aired on WNBT on April 6, 1952.

The reason they needed Chinese musicians was Frankie Laine's song "Rose, Rose, I Love You," which was an adaptation from a Chinese song by the same name. The plan on the show was to have a Chinese girl singing the Chinese version of the song as a lead-in to Frankie Laine's English version. I was to play the erhu again, with Sea Monster on the moon guitar, and his wife playing bells. The singer Sea Monster invited for this show was not trained in singing, but she wore a Chinese costume for effect. Anyway the "lead-in" would be short, so it mattered little.

Our rehearsal took place just before the show. The studio was full of people because there were many segments to the show. I was surprised to see Audrey Meadows there, too. Even more surprising was that she enthusiastically waved to me as if we were old friends, and even came from the opposite corner of the room to chat with me. That made me feel, for a moment, that I was an old-timer in show business. Audrey was there in a skit with Paul Douglas, who soon arrived with his gorgeous blond wife, Jan Sterling. George Abbott, the show's host, a most gracious old gentleman, came over to talk to the Chinese singer, as well as us musicians. It impressed me that he would take the time to say hello to us minor bit players and wish us well.

At the time, I had no idea who George Abbott was. But, now that "googling" is possible, I felt that I had to research "George Abbott" for this book. To my great astonishment, I found out that he was the winner of many Tony Awards as actor, producer, director, and playwright. He was the Director of such Broadway shows as "Pal Joey," "On the Town," "Call Me Madam," and wrote the books for "Where's Charley?" "The Pajama Game," "Damn Yankees," and others. He even won a Pulitzer Prize. I should have shown him much more respect than I did when he came over to talk to me that day in 1952.

Frankie Laine then also came over to say hello to the "lead-in" team. A heavyset guy, he was courteous and friendly. "Don't worry about anything," he said to us, "before you know it, it'll be over for you, and I'll take over." His statement was prophetic. I thought at first that the Chinese "lead-in" would last five or six seconds; in reality the director of the show switched to Frankie in just two or three seconds.

For that, I was again paid $100. In 1952, that amount could take care quite a few months of my room rent!

Those two $100 checks comprised my first earnings in the United States. I did not do any more TV shows; if I did, I might have to join the union. Anyway, in about two years' time, I completed my dissertation, and moved to Ohio to teach, far away from the show business world of New York.

A Lesson in Economics

My TV experience got featured in my teaching of Economics 101 at Denison University. On the subject of minimum wage, and labor union's bargaining for higher wage rate, it is easy for people uninitiated in economics to equate the two distinct concepts of "wage rate" and "wage income." Wage rate is the amount of pay per unit of time, such as $15 per hour. Wage income, on the other hand, is a dollar amount, equal to the wage rate times the number of hours worked:

Wage income ($) = Wage rate ($ per hour) × Hours worked

Politicians and labor leaders tend to argue, or imply, that a higher wage rate results in higher wage income for workers. But this is true only if, after the increase in wage rate, the number of hours worked either (a) rises, or (b) stays the same, or (c) decreases to a proportionately small amount. Scenario (a) is unlikely. Scenario (b) describes those workers who keep the job with unchanged amount of work. Scenario (c) pertains to workers who are assigned slightly less hours of work than before. But what about the workers who are laid off by the employer after the wage increase? In spite of the high wage rate, their wage income is reduced to zero, because they have no work at all.

The correct inference from a higher minimum wage rate is that some workers will receive higher income as a result, but some others will suffer because they will be laid off. The latter is especially relevant to marginal unskilled workers whose labor productivity now falls below what the higher wage demands. They get laid off.

How does my TV experience fit into this discussion? Well, it perfectly illustrates the distinction between wage rate and wage income. My wage *rate* on TV was very high, $100 for a few seconds or a few minutes on each show. Even if I counted rehearsal time, the wage rate was still a high amount per hour. But my wage *income* was not, because I did not have that much work time offered to me.

As soon as I started to recount my TV escapade in class, all the students' ears perked up and their eyes opened wide. I could feel my popularity shooting up to new heights. Hey, here was a professor who had performed on television before, not once but twice, and he even rubbed shoulders with a big star like Marlene Dietrich!

Follow-Up Stories

I had always wondered why my friend Sea Monster took on so many different jobs, almost beyond his energy capacity. The reason, a touching story, did not come to light until after he died. Upon discovering that he had a terminal disease, which he kept from his family, he tried every means available to earn extra money to provide for his wife and children that he was soon to leave behind. Sea Monster was not a monster at all. He was a thoughtful husband and father, and a kind human being.

Edmund O'Brien and I never talked to each other. But ever since we were in a show together, I developed an interest in his career. I was happy to see him win an Oscar and a Golden Globe for his supporting role in the movie "The Barefoot Contessa" in 1954.

Maria Riva won Emmy nominations for best actress in 1952 and 1953, but became semiretired from acting soon after that. She published a biography of her mother, *Marlene Dietrich*, in 1992, the year of Marlene's death, reportedly not complimentary.

Audrey Meadows, whom I deemed a special friend, went on to achieve great fame as Alice Kramden, to Jackie Gleason's Ralph Kramden, on the popular comedy series "The Honeymooners," during 1952–1957, and in several "The Honeymooners" specials in the 1970s. She also accumulated innumerable other acting credits. Even though we only met briefly twice, I fervently followed her career, and was saddened by the news of her death from lung cancer in 1996.

10

The Girl I Wanted to Marry

In May 2000, I took Emily to the Rainbow Room at Rockefeller Center in Manhattan for dinner to celebrate a special occasion. This fancy place boasted a round, revolving dance floor, and two alternating live bands. As we entered the ornate dining room, we saw about ten of our Chinese dancing friends sitting at a round table, all in cheerful mood.

"It looks like a big celebration here. What's the occasion?" I asked after greeting them.

"Michael Tong is celebrating his birthday," one of the ladies replied, "and the two of you, are you celebrating something, too?"

"Oh, just an anniversary," I said.

One of them thought for a second, and said, "But I thought your anniversary is in the fall. This is only May."

"Wow, I admire your good memory. But we are not celebrating our wedding anniversary; we're celebrating the anniversary of our first meeting."

The whole table looked at me with surprise, and one of them said, "No, don't tell me you still remember the date you two first met!"

"Yes, I sure do. It was May 19, 1951."

"China Night" at Fordham University

May 19, 1951 was the day the Chinese students at Fordham University in the Bronx put on a variety show featuring Chinese folk dances, fairy-tale performances, singing, sword dance, Chinese opera excerpt and instrumental duet, costume show, . . ., all performed by the young talents the organizing team could draft from the widening circle of Chinese students studying in the various colleges and universities in the Greater New York area.

I was asked to do some instrumental operatic music with a friend Old Tung (老董, 董彦曾). The piece we rehearsed for the show was called "夜深沉," which may be translated as "Nocturne," with Old Tung on the *jinghu*, me on the *erhu*, two stringed instruments. For this piece, an expert tong-drum (堂鼓) player was needed to accent the music, and we recruited another friend of mine, Rosana Hsu (徐文緗), who was not only an accomplished male-part singer, but also an expert on the tong-drum. Our performance went over smoothly. The rest of the time, I just watched the other performances from backstage.

For this "China Night," the organizing team, headed by Thomas Ho, a graduate student at Fordham, presented performers with surprisingly high standards, and I especially liked the sword dance done by a petite girl. She wore a red costume with a white silk band around her waist, its ends hanging down her right side. Her movements were dynamic but graceful, diverse but clean. Near the end of the dance, she was positioned near the footlights, close to the audience, but the curtain was prematurely starting to come down in back of her. I feared for her, because her exit might be blocked by the curtain as she was bowing on the wrong side of the curtain. But I didn't have to worry. As if she could sense the curtain descending, she began to back up about a foot each time she bowed, and was able to reach inside the curtain in the nick of time! I did not know the girl, but I was relieved that she could gracefully rescue herself from a potentially embarrassing situation.

Just about the time, Thomas Ho approached me with a request. "Mr. Chiang, this is a rather unusual request, but could you possibly do another number, accompanying a girl performing an aria from a Chinese opera?"

"What?! Thomas!" I replied with an undisguised annoyance. "Are you seriously asking me to accompany on stage someone I have never rehearsed with, and never even met?"

Thomas was apologetic, but he wouldn't give in. Normally, I would have flatly refused him; I most assuredly had set standards about performances. But, on that day, at that moment, my heart somehow softened and, instead of saying "No, no, no," I replied much more diplomatically than normal, "Maybe you can bring the singer over, and we'll have a tryout." Rather pleased at this outcome, Thomas found a backroom and brought the girl to meet me. It turned out to be the girl in red, the sword dancer who escaped from the curtain mishap. She was petite, but gorgeous! Her attractive facial features, partly hidden behind stage makeup, were matched by her elegant movements. I found her beauty overpowering. I managed, awkwardly, to compliment her on her sword dance, and told her of my relief upon her success in avoiding the falling curtain. She smiled with charm.

I closed the door, and quickly tuned my instrument to a pitch I guessed would fit her voice, and asked her, "What opera do you plan to perform?" She said, "Only the opening aria of 遊龍戲鳳 (Royal Flirtation), which Hsiao Ming (蕭明) taught me a few days ago." I noted the amazing coincidence: The opera "Royal Flirtation" was precisely one of the two that my father performed on his own wedding night. Hsiao Ming was one of my opera friends whom I had often accompanied, and who was originally scheduled to perform at the "China Night" show, but later backed out.

The tryout revealed the girl to be a total novice as a singer. But her stage movements were passable, a credit to Hsiao Ming's coaching. And her bravery and courage to go onstage with so little preparation was admirable in itself. More weightily, she was lovely. I nodded to Thomas, and said, "Okay, I'll accompany her." Only then did I realize that I made the decision on my own, having not consulted Old Tung, my fellow accompanist. Fortunately, Old Tung readily agreed to go along with me.

I finally remembered to ask the girl her name. She said, "My name is 何欽翠, Emily Ho." And I said, "My name is 蔣中一, Alpha Chiang."

Only a few minutes later, it was our turn to do "Royal Flirtation." She made her entrance on cue in a simple costume, looking very lovely and innocent as the role called for as the young sister of the owner of a country inn. Old Tung and I accompanied her singing with sufficient rapport to leave the impression that we had rehearsed before. No mishap of any kind occurred, and the audience applauded loud and long.

10.1 Emily performing "Royal Flirtation," May 19, 1951.

Since I was onstage as an accompanist, I could not applaud her, but my heart was pounding with pride. She struck me as not only beautiful, but graceful, artistic, brave, and endowed with a rare stage presence. Then a thought suddenly crystalized in my mind, or in my heart, or in both: Some day, I want to ask her to change her name from Emily Ho to Emily Chiang.

A Birthday Party

After the show was over, and curtain calls were made, Rosana, the drummer for the "Nocturne," rushed over and handed me a piece of paper. "Alpha, here it is. I got her telephone number for you," she said with a smile. I was totally unprepared for this curious "gift" from her. "Rosana! How in the world did you guess that I want her phone number?" She shrugged her shoulder, and gave me a knowing look, and said matter-of-factly, "Oh, simple. I noticed that your eyeballs were devouring her throughout the whole aria."

That precious telephone number did not achieve the intended effect. She said "No," not once, but many times. Rosana then intervened to find out why. She found out that Emily had a problem with my age. Emily was just graduating from St. Mary's Academy, a high school in Maryland, and I was already working on my doctoral dissertation. It was natural for her to think that I was too old. In fact, I was only five years older; my faster-than-usual academic progress resulted only from skipping a grade and taking summer courses.

I kept trying to call her and, finally, Emily agreed to come to my 24th birthday party. In an exhilarated mood, I took her to the Hawaiian Room, a night club in the Hotel Lexington on Lexington Avenue in Manhattan. As we got seated at a table for two in the fancy dining room, she asked, "Where are your guests?" I had to tell her the truth, "You are my only honored guest."

Under the romantic lighting in the club, we had a nice dinner. And we also danced to the soft music of a small band: foxtrot, rumba, waltz, and some other dances. I did my steps in light-hearted rhythm, and she followed effortlessly. With our well-matched heights, clean-cut looks, and natural movements, we won admiring glances from the other diners.

The Three Strikes against Me

Our conversation during dinner went smoothly, but I discovered at least three possible "strikes" against me as far as our backgrounds were concerned. First, her father being a government official, she was actively concerned with political developments in China, whereas I, with a commercial family background, was apolitical. Thus, we lacked a common outlook. Second, she had grown up in the interior province Sichuan, the seat of the national government during the Sino-Japanese War, whereas I had stayed in Shanghai throughout those eight war years. Thus, we did not share a common wartime experience. Third, and most seriously, she seemed to hold a misconception that everyone from Shanghai is a cunning "city slicker." Thus, from the very beginning, I was saddled with a fictitious "original guilt" that I had to absolve: Three strikes! Fortunately, unlike in baseball, "three strikes" in the present situation did not mean I was automatically "out." But it did mean that I had a lot of salvage work to do.

I asked her whether she had been to Shanghai, and she said that she had lived there for a few months after China won the War. This subject gave me a chance to explain away the common misconception. Shanghai being a complex metropolis under international influences, I explained, residents there need to develop skills of self-preservation. They have to learn to recognize dangers quickly, to adapt readily to unexpected changes, to talk their way diplomatically out of awkward situations, and, in short, they have to be "clever" in their daily dealings with people. All of these self-protective traits can easily give rise to the wrong impression that Shanghai residents are cunning, or tricky. She half-conceded.

We conversed in Mandarin, the official dialect based on Northern-Chinese accents. Emily could speak only the Sichuan dialect and Mandarin. Had I not learned Mandarin from my Northerner Chinese-opera friends since coming to New York, I would not, as an exclusive Shanghai dialect speaker, have been able to communicate with her in Chinese. I felt fortunate.

My natural inclination was to have our date last long, but, not wanting to over-stretch it, I offered to take her home right after the floor show featuring a breathtaking bamboo dance (wherein the dancers had to step between constantly shifting bamboo poles), was over at the Hawaiian Room. I drove my new gray Plymouth with extra care, and dropped her off at 500 West End Avenue, where she was living with her elder sister and elder brother, in an apartment temporarily leased from a Columbia professor away for the summer.

The "Send-Her-Off-to-College" Picnic

At the end of the summer, Emily started college at Georgian Court College (now University) in Lakewood, New Jersey. And Tom and

Jane Tang (湯永謙, 姚文琴) organized a party to send her off to New Jersey, with a picnic on the Georgian Court campus.

Tom was a graduate student in chemical engineering at Columbia, and Jane was working on her degree at the Teachers College. I got to know them through Leonard Tong (湯祖望), also a chemical engineering graduate student, who came to the United States on the same ship as I. Tom was one of the earliest among our friends to receive formal training at a dance studio. Leonard and I used to go to his apartment in the evening to ask Tom and Jane to show us fancy tango steps that he had learned at an Arthur Murray Dance Studio. That was in the late 1940s. (Photo 15 shows Tom and Jane in their Florida home in a later year.)

Tom and Jane knew Emily's elder sister Catherine Ho (何欽翼, later known by the name Chinyee Sung, 宋何青意), and they wanted, through the picnic, to introduce Leonard and Catherine to each other. Actually, that match-making effort did not pan out, but that picnic did afford an excellent opportunity for me to get closer to Emily.

Around a dozen people went on this picnic in three cars, also including Emily's elder brother James Ho (何欽羽), and her aunt Helen Hsiung (熊毛彥文), plus Allan Chiang (姜義隆) and his *fiancée*, Rio Liu, mutual friends of Tom and me. Emily decided to sit in my car, in the front beside me. To me, that was a promising sign.

We ate, sang, and joked around, and had a good time. Emily, the star of the send-off party, was sociable to everybody. The party came to an end only at the sign of dusk, when we all thanked Tom and Jane, and headed home to Manhattan. In comparison to the morning trip, the return trip turned out especially lonely, not only because Emily was now missing, but also because my passengers were all tired out and fell asleep, leaving me entirely alone by myself at the wheel.

From Postcard to Letters and Phone Calls

I wrote a letter to Emily as soon as I arrived home, and she promptly responded with a cordial postcard. That was followed by a regular stream of letters. These were not perfunctory hello-saying routine messages, but letters exposing our respective inner selves, our hopes, and ambitions. They sometimes provided laughs, but they often also inspired thinking and revisions of personal views on various subjects.

Trying to impress her, I sent her the two short stories I had earlier published in a Chinese newspaper and a Chinese magazine, both of which had O. Henry type of surprise endings. But, instead of some compliments that I was hoping for, she came back with the critique that "Your stories have no social message!" My Lord, I wrote those stories when I was only 18 or 19, aiming at nothing more than the fun of creating a surprise ending. Since I had not even really "lived" a real life, what social message could I have ever offered to the world? Upon later discussion, I learned that her political orientation played a part in her social awareness. More relevantly, she had read many Russian novels in Chinese translation, which deal with human problems and sufferings, and do carry social messages. Fortunately, she did not count my message-less stories as a "strike" against me. She even hinted that she gave me "points" for having written and published those at a young age.

I frequently called her "long distance" on the phone. Her dormitory only had one communal phone, and whoever answered the phone would then yell, "Emily, your boyfriend is calling!" She would have to rush down from her room, a rather inconvenient matter. But incoming calls were a status symbol, so I did not think she minded. In general, I preferred letters. Written words could be read and reread, often with subtle feelings of increasing preciousness on each reading, whereas phone conversations were gone forever once the receiver was hung up.

I also drove to Lakewood to see her. And we always got together on her visits to New York. Sometimes she came to New York by bus, and I would then drive her back to Lakewood, usually barely beating the curfew time. One time, because of heavy traffic, we arrived at Georgian Court about 10 minutes after curfew. When we ran across a nun, I tried to camouflage the time by saying, "Good afternoon, Sister." Her reply was a stern "Good EVENING!"

Priceless Dinners

For a period of time, Emily's siblings lived in an apartment in Forest Hills in Queens. She would invite me to have dinner with her family. Those dinners gave me priceless opportunities to get to know her elder brother James, who had graduated from the University of Dayton in Dayton, Ohio, and her second elder brother John (何欽翔), who was studying at Manhattan College, and her elder sister Catherine who had graduated from the College of Mount St. Vincent in Riverdale, New York. Their parents, Mr. Tze-yuen Ho (何芝園) and Tung-wen Mao Ho (何毛同文), lived in Taiwan, but Mrs. Ho visited the United States several times. Photo 6 in the front of this book shows our visit to them in 1974.

I also got to know Emily's famous *ahyee* (mother's sister), Madame Helen Mao Hsiung (熊毛彥文), who was living with them at the time. This *ahyee* became widely known in her youth as the object of undying (but unrequited) love of a Professor Mi Wu (吴宓), who published numerous poems written for "Helen," her English name. Later, she made even more sensational news in 1935 when she, at age 33 and with a Master's degree in Education from the University of Michigan, married a 66-year-old former Prime Minister of China, Hsi-ling Hsiung (熊希齡), in Shanghai. This widely reported "33-66 match" was actually a myth created for effect. *Ahyee* was actually 38 years old at that time. But to call it a "38-66 match" would not sound nearly as interesting; hence, the journalistic creation of the myth of "33-66." Unfortunately, she became widowed in less than three years. But she did lead a productive life on her own, which included teaching in colleges, being the head of an orphanage (香山慈幼院) established by her husband in Beijing, and later serving as a legislator in Taiwan. She died in 1999 at age 102–103.

For most of our dinners, though, Emily and I patronized Chinese restaurants. There was Old Shanghai (老上海) on West 125th Street near Broadway, and Tientsin (天津樓) across the street, and later, Lucky (鴻運摟) on Amsterdam Avenue near West 122nd Street, Great Shanghai (大上海) on Broadway, where Emily worked briefly as a hostess.

10.2 The Ho family, Christmas Eve, 1951. From left: Catherine, John, Aunt Helen Hsiung, James, and Emily.

The above mentioned restaurants were all on the upper West Side, but the one dining experience that stood out above all others was a literally "priceless" dinner at Imperial Dynasty, an upscale Chinese restaurant on the East Side. I don't remember why we chose to go there, but once we entered its elegantly appointed dining room, we were greeted by the uniformed waiting staff. We first ordered drinks, and then I opened the menu. My body immediately froze! The menu listed all their lovely sounding dishes, but no prices were listed anywhere! In those days before the invention of credit cards, payment was always in cash, and I was not at all sure that the money in my wallet was enough to pay my way out of this restaurant!

There were only two options: (1) back out; or (2) take it in stride, order, eat, and just wait to see what would happen. Since the first option would be too embarrassing, I resolved to stay on, uncomfortably, but doing my best to feign nonchalance. Emily showed little uneasiness, but wisely said to me, "I'll leave the ordering to you." I ordered conservatively, but never felt able to savor the dishes served, because my mind was focused on the financial rather than the culinary aspect of the meal.

When the check finally came, though, it brought a big smile to my tense face as quickly as the menu had made my body freeze. Whew! The total cost of this "priceless" dinner, including tax, turned out to be a lot more "reasonable" than what my "great expectations" had built it up to be an hour ago. My wallet even could allow a respectable tip.

The Betrothal

One day, Emily sent me a special gift. It was a tan-colored, black-trimmed leather wallet she made by her own hand, in which there was a cutout of a photo I took of her on our way to the picnic in Lakewood. A more important enclosure was an inscription that says, "To my dearest Alpha: All my love, Emily." To me, that little message marked our betrothal.

10.3 Emily, my (unofficial) *fiancée*, 1953.

We never went through a formal engagement ceremony, but everything was mutually understood. We did decide between us that we would delay our marriage until after she graduated from college. By taking extra credits each semester, as well as summer courses at New York University, she planned to finish her BS degree in three years.

Meanwhile, the political changes in China disrupted my father's financial support for me, and forced me to take on full-time employment toward the end of 1952. My friend Rosana—the one who gave me Emily's telephone number—alerted me to a vacancy in the office where she worked, and I was able to get an accounting job at the Chinese Government Procurement and Services Mission in New York. It was interesting that my very first job after graduating from college had to do with a government agency related to Taiwan, and now, my first full-time job in America again had to do with a government agency related to Taiwan. My direct boss was Major K. C. Shah (夏功權少校) of the Air Force, a capable leader and perfect English speaker, who later served as the ambassador to the United States from Taiwan (but with an altered title). As my boss, he was later replaced by Col. Shih (石兆騫上校), a capable but more relaxed administrator.

In early 1953, I also had an opportunity to teach evening classes at the University of Bridgeport in Bridgeport, Connecticut. To do these two jobs at the same time, I needed to leave my daytime job 10 minutes early, in order to catch a train from Grand Central Station to Bridgeport in time for the class. Col. Shih was kind enough to grant me permission to leave office early twice a week, even though that technically violated regulations.

Double jobs were taxing. Luckily, the bulk of my research work was already done. When the writing was finished, the dissertation, titled *Income Taxation in the Federal State: A Study of jurisdictional Conflict,* came to a total of 370 pages. Emily volunteered to type the final copy of the manuscript, despite her own heavy class work, and despite the difficult nature of the typing. The typing job involved multiple copies of bond paper, with carbon papers inserted between each adjacent pair of bond papers. So, a heavy-duty typewriter must be used, and each keystroke must be extra forceful. Her help was a great contribution to my degree.

The Wedding

Submitting the dissertation Emily typed for me completed the requirements for the PhD degree, which I received from Columbia on June 1, 1954. She came for the ceremony. Four days later, Emily received her BS degree from Georgian Court College, in three years as planned. I of course went to her ceremony in return.

Then, on September 4, 1954, we were married at the Cathedral of St. John the Divine on Amsterdam Avenue in Manhattan. The

10.4 Our wedding, New York, September 4, 1954.

Cathedral is extremely large. Our ceremony, officiated by Canon West, took place in one of its small chapels, the Chapel of St. Columba. Emily wanted an intimate wedding, with a sit-down dinner for a few guests only. Thus we only invited Emily's sister Catherine (Matron of Honor) and her husband at the time George Chen, her brothers James and John; my three roommates at 640 Riverside Drive, Chris Wu (吳肇勳, Best Man), James Yu (尤紹新), and S. C. Siao (蕭孫祺); Tom and Jane Tang (湯永謙、姚文琴) who arranged the picnic at Georgian Court; Emily's three Georgian Court schoolmates May Lee (李沅薇), Jenny Chen (陳澤容), and Kathleen Lee (李幼幼); my old friends from Colorado Steve Ying (應道宸) and his wife Mildred (I was Best Man at their wedding); Columbia schoolmates Leonard Tong (湯祖望) and his then-wife Patsy, Herman Yueh (岳毓衡) and his wife Grace (I was Best Man at their wedding, too); and my Chinese opera friend Henry Kuan (管德綱).

Emily's Matron of Honor, her sister Catherine, can be seen in Photo 10.5. My Best Man, Chris Wu, is shown in Photo 10.6 with his wife Marlies whom he married later.

The ceremony was brief, but the drive to the banquet was long. Leighton's Woodland Restaurant was located in Ardsley, New York, some 20 miles from Manhattan. The setting was rustic. We sat at a long, well-decorated table, al fresco. There was even an outdoor space for dancing. As time passed, the September air turned a little chilly. The

10.5 Cutting the wedding cake.

staff were accommodating enough to move us indoors for desserts, and the rest of the evening.

It was a momentous day for me: Emily Ho had now become Emily Chiang.

My parents would have loved to be at our wedding, but there was no way they could come to New York. The best they could do was to give a banquet in our honor in Shanghai. Similarly, Emily's parents gave a banquet in Taipei, Taiwan in celebration of our wedding.

10.6 Chris and Marlies Wu, 1983.

Ohio Bound

We squeezed into the next couple of days many farewell dinners with our close friends, roommates, and relatives.

Then on September 8, my bride and I packed up all our belongings and drove west to my first full-time teaching post at Denison University in Granville, Ohio—a position that unexpectedly fell into my lap only in late May, less than four months before the wedding.

Alas, on the Pennsylvania Turnpike, our car unceremoniously broke down, and we were stuck in a small town called Bedford, for car repair. I should clarify that this was no longer the car I drove Emily to the Hawaiian Room. That nice gray Plymouth I had sold for financial reasons. For this trip to Ohio, my roommates Chris Wu and James Yu helped me select this car in a New Jersey used-car lot. Instead of choosing the car in the best condition, the three of us, no experts, took a black Ford that looked the cleanest. Was it any wonder it broke down so early? Car repair forced us to stay in Bedford for two days. Upon reading my letter about this mishap, Chris, my best man with a great sense of humor, wrote back to console us, "Stuck in BEDFORD, eh? Sorry that your *FORD* was out of commission, but at least you still had the *BED*!"

I vowed to shop for a new car as soon as we settled in our new home in Granville, Ohio, assuming that our ill-fated black Ford could indeed fulfill the mission of getting us to our destination. We did arrive in Granville, without further trouble, on September 11, a date that, unbeknownst to us then, was destined to acquire the historic, infamous nickname "9/11" decades later.

11

Chinese Opera in New York

Once in New York, my social circle expanded at a fast pace, but most of my new friends happened to belong to one single category: fans of Chinese opera (京劇), my hobby since I was about 6 or 7. During my early years in Shanghai, my operatic activities were all private, not in any club or association. Often, I sang self-taught arias at home, and even accompanied myself on the stringed instruments *jinghu* or *erhu*. I took pride in my ability to accompany my own singing, especially in the difficult situation when I had to play a multi-note interlude on the instrument, yet at the same time vocally sustaining a single, long note. We Three Musketeers sometimes sang together. Even then, it was usually in a small group.

Since 1948, the pursuit of the operatic hobby has mostly been in larger group situations. The number of fellow Chinese opera fans in New York was beyond my expectations. And many of them had even had long stage experiences back in China. The appellation for an amateur Chinese opera singer–actor or musician is "*piaoyu* 票友," and an experienced one is referred to as an "old *piaoyu* 老票友." The few opera friends I have mentioned before, such as S. W. Hsiang, Rosana Hsu, and Hsiao Ming, had all studied Chinese opera for years under famous coaches, and they well qualified for the title old *piaoyus*.

Chinese opera fans seem to be uncannily endowed with a special magnetic force that attracts them to one another. I met many of them through different channels. Some introduced themselves to me after they heard me play my instrument in Chinese student association parties. Some others performed at parties, and I would then seek them out. Others I met at group dinners.

The Circle Grew

During his short stay in New York, my fellow musketeer George Hsu introduced me to a relative of his, Mr. Perry Huang (黄益), who had studied engineering in Paris, but decided to work in New York. Knowing that I was into Chinese opera, Perry excitedly told me that he was soon going back to Paris to get married to a *piaoyu* with extensive stage credits. His bride turned out to be none other than Hsiao Ming (or Minnie Huang), the lady who coached Emily for her Fordham University performance in 1951. I soon became her regular accompanist, in private sessions as well as for several of her stage performances in New York.

C. K. Hsu (徐積鍇) and his wife Julia (張粹文) were also singers that I accompanied in my early years in New York. I met them at a party of Joan Hsu (徐英) for opera fans. C. K. Hsu, the son of the famous poet Chih-mo Hsu (徐志摩, now spelled Xu Zhimo), had a comfortable apartment where some of us often gathered to sing. We always made sure that all the windows were tightly closed so that our singing would not disturb the neighbors. Still, a policeman came one night to knock on the door, asking us to stop the "strange noises" on neighbors' complaints. "Strange noises," indeed!

Both C. K. and Julia sang the female role in the Cheng style (程派), different from my own Mei style (梅派), and I had to learn their arias in order to accompany them. But I was glad to do it. I liked C. K.'s gentlemanliness. Even more, I basked in Julia's kindness toward me. She was the most beautiful woman I have ever laid my eyes on, with a perfectly proportioned face and figure. And she was also a first-class chef. I naturally treasured being invited regularly to their home. They even invited me to join them on a tour of New Hampshire in 1948 together with P. C. Chao (趙培忠) and Homer Shen (沈熙敬). As their interest in Chinese opera waned, however, they gradually withdrew from the opera circle.

In the meantime, I met Frank Cho (卓孚來) in C. K. and Julia's home. An operatic instrumentalist, he was studying for his MBA at Harvard University. The two of us soon became regular musical partners, and remained as an accompanist team for decades, until he

11.1 Touring New Hampshire, 1948. From left: Julia and C. K. Hsu, P. C. Chao, Homer Shen, and me.

left New York City for health reasons. P. C. Chao (趙培忠), whom I also met in C. K. and Julia's home, then studying at the Lowell Textile Institute in Massachusetts, was an excellent singer of the male role. Amazingly, he made his stage debut in Shanghai while he was still in elementary school.

The most pivotal person in the history of Chinese opera in New York I had the pleasure of meeting, was Peter Hao (郝德元), son of a renowned professional singer Shouchen Hao (郝壽臣) of the *hualien* (hero–rogue) role. At the time, Peter was studying at New York University for his EdD degree, but I met him at a Chinese students' party at my school, Columbia. Invited to give a talk on Chinese opera, he could have just sung a *hualien* aria, but he (wisely) chose instead to talk about the traditional *yinzi* (引子), the twin-verse short introduction a character normally recites at the beginning of a scene. He explained how the *yinzi*, recited musically but without instrumental accompaniment, was designed to lay the background of the scene, and set the mood of the action that was to follow. Then he gave examples and demonstrated the way it is done. It was a marvelous, instructive talk, even for those not into Chinese opera.

I introduced myself to him after his talk, and we became good friends. Later, I was inducted into a Chinese fraternity he belonged to, and we became fraternity brothers. This explains why he always addressed me as *didi* (弟弟, younger brother).

Given that Peter Hao was born into a professional opera family, it was not surprising that he was a versatile operatic artist. He could sing the *hualien* role, play the stringed *jinghu*, and play the little drum used by the conductor of the orchestra. To maintain his voice while studying in New York, he needed to sing regularly, but it was impossible to do this in his small rented room. His ingenious solution was to use the subway station as his practice hall. Whenever a train came into the station and made a huge noise, he could practice his singing for a minute or so, without fear of disturbing anyone or appearing crazy.

On his advice, I also tried to practice singing in the subway station, but I lacked the patience to wait for irregular trains in a dirty, stuffy subway environment. More importantly, I had come to a reluctant decision to give up singing and just concentrate on playing the instrument, because good accompanists were scarce in New York, and I found it very strenuous and unenjoyable to sing when the musicians could not follow my singing closely. I would rather just render a much-needed service to the singers with my accompaniment.

To my regret, my voice deteriorated after stopping regular practices, and eventually I lost it altogether. For this reason, I was happy that I had taken advantage of an opportunity to make a two-sided vinyl record of my singing in April 1949. This was made possible by Joan Hsu, who arranged a singing party held at a Cantonese music association in Chinatown, where we got permission from them to use their record-making machine. My selection for this record consisted of "玉堂春 (Su San on Trial)" and "霸王別姬 (Farewell, My Concubine!)." In spite of the unrehearsed, offbeat accompaniment at this recording, people seemed to like my singing at age 22. Decades later, I had occasion to dig out this old record and play it for Lisa Lu (盧燕), the movie and TV star, who visited my home for some Chinese opera singing with Emily and me.

After listening to my record with a nodding head, she gave me an unexpected high compliment: "可以亂真! (It could pass for the genuine singing of Mei!)" Since Lisa not only came from a professional operatic family, being the daughter of the top professional lady singer of the male role of an earlier era, but actually grew up in the family of Mei Lan-fang, her godfather, this comment was the highest compliment any Mei-style amateur singer could hope for. It was an overstatement, for sure. But, thanks from the bottom of my heart, Lisa!

Lisa Lu, an avid singer of Chinese opera, became a friend only after I moved to White Plains, New York, after my retirement. At that time, Mr. George Yan (嚴仁安) had begun to coach Emily's singing as well as my instrument playing. On Lisa's frequent trips from California to New York, she always tried to get together with us for a singing session. Photo 62 shows us together at a singing party in 1999. Not only did we sing together; Lisa also had many stories to tell us about her TV/movie life, and her childhood while living with Mei Lan-Fang.

The Appeal of Chinese Opera

It never ceased to amaze me that I could find so many fellow Chinese opera fans in New York. During the last phase of the Ching Dynasty, which ended in 1911, Chinese opera became the top national pastime because of the royal patronage by the Empress Dowager. But the continued popularity of this art form after the founding of the Republic of China could only be attributed to its own inherent strong appeal. What factors make it so appealing?

For one thing, the stories told are inherently fascinating, depicting historical events involving dark court intrigues, clever military stratagems, or heart-rending love tragedies. The music is pleasing to the ears, and even the dialogues are presented in a musical manner, as if set to music. The body movements on stage are all stylized and dance-like, often accented or punctuated by the use of percussion instruments, led by the small drum, and supported by gongs and cymbals. The strong dance element in them makes the enjoyment of Chinese opera visual as well as auditory. One unique contributing factor to the dance element is the long sleeves on the costumes of the principal characters. Named

"水袖 (water sleeves)," their flowing movements constitute an integral aspect of the action of many of the characters.

Percussion instruments are also used as lead-in for arias accompanied by stringed instruments. Although some operas involve martial arts and acrobatics, many beloved operas are dominantly aria-oriented. In the opera "二進宮 (Revisiting the Queen)," for example, three characters, one *qingyi* (female), one *laosheng* (male), and one *hualien* (hero–rogue), sang continuously in a three-way musical discussion/argument through the opera, for one whole hour.

The Birth of an Association

The loose organization of the opera fans finally gave way to a more formal structure. One autumn day, Peter Hao invited Frank Cho, P. C. Chao, and me to a luncheon meeting at the Lucky Restaurant on Amsterdam Avenue to discuss the founding of an association. And the four of us became the co-founders of the Chinese Opera Club in America, which, when registered later as a not-for-profit organization, was renamed the Chinese Opera Association of New York.

The Lucky Restaurant, no longer in existence, was reputedly the place where the Nobel physicists Chen Ning Yang (楊振寧) and Tsung-Dao Lee (李政道) held the first discussions of their ideas on the parity laws that eventually earned them the Nobel prize in 1957. Our association was also conceived there. Maybe the name "Lucky" was truly auspicious, because our opera association has been able to enjoy a brilliant life, all the way from 1951 to this day.

The inaugural meeting of the association took place on November 11, 1951, at the Kolping House on East 88th Street in New York, where Peter resided. More than 20 people attended, and at the suggestion of S. W. Hsiang (項馨吾), an insurance executive with the Central Trust of China (中央信託局), and an elder statesman of the Kunqu (崑曲) form of opera, we adopted the Chinese name 國劇雅集 (Cultural Gathering for Chinese Opera). For convenience, however, we habitually use the short name 雅集, pronounced Yaji.

11.2 At the inaugural meeting of the Chinese Opera Association of New York, November 11, 1951. From left: Hsiao Ming (half head), Peter Hao (side view), me, Frank Cho, P. C. Chao, and Henry Kuan (standing).

A Historic Stage Presentation

Even with so many experienced performers in our midst, Yaji did not present its first stage performance until December 1953, two years after its founding. Peter Hao, using his Catholic connections, obtained permission from Fordham University for the free use of their auditorium. He served as the General Manager of out inaugural show, with William Cheng (程威廉), a shipping executive with the China Merchants Steam Navigation Co. (招商局), as the Stage Manager, and me, a graduate student at Columbia, as the Business Manager.

As an economist, I naturally thought of the matter of raising revenue from ticket sales to cover the cost of the production. But S. W. Hsiang insisted on the age-old tradition in China that amateur opera performers do not sell tickets, but give them out free. Without revenue, the cost had to be borne by individual members. Costumes and props were all self-made. I, as the Business Manager, only had to have the tickets printed, and handle their distribution. When news of our forthcoming performance went out, it caused a sensation and, all of a sudden, I emerged as a most sought-after person in New York. I was *the* person in charge of all the tickets, and tickets were in heavy demand. Why? Because our show was the first full-scale Chinese opera performance in New York since the grand master Mei Lan-fang toured America in 1930—nearly a quarter of a century earlier. I was naturally unable to satisfy everyone's request for tickets; I must have disappointed and offended many.

This inaugural show started with a concert (plain singing) in which seven members of our association sang the major arias from the opera "四郎探母 (A Clandestine Visit to the Mother)." Then two complete staged operas in full costumes followed.

In the first, "汾河湾 (The Suspicious Slippers)," a general returned home after many years away, and was devastated when he found man's slippers in the wife's bedroom. Actually, the slippers belonged to his now-grown son who was a baby when he left home. There were a lot of comedic dialogue between the general, played by Dr. Ta-chung Liu (劉大中), an economist at the International Monetary Fund who later taught at Cornell University, his alma mater. The wife was played by Julia Ho (何靈琰), a very talented amateur. The son was played by Phillysia Hsiang (項斯鳳), S. W.'s teenage daughter in her debut.

The second one, "奇雙會 (The Double Reunion)," told a more intricate story. An old prisoner's lamentation reached the ears of the new magistrate's wife, and aroused her sympathy and curiosity. In her husband's absence, she went into the prison to interview the prisoner, and found out that the prisoner was none other than her long-lost father. What happened was the father's evil second wife had kicked out his young son and daughter when he went on a long business trip. When, upon his return, the father inquired about the missing children, he was given different stories by different people. And one of the maids, out of fear, committed suicide after severe questioning. Thereupon, the second wife and her lover accused the father of murder, and bribed a corrupt magistrate to sentence him to death. But now the corrupt magistrate had been replaced by the daughter's husband as the new magistrate. Thus, the new magistrate and his wife together arranged an appeal to a roving judge. And, guess what? The roving judge turned out to be the prisoner's missing son. Thus, the father enjoyed in short order a double reunion, first with his daughter, then with his son. In our presentation, the daughter was played by Hsiao Ming, who had studied this particular part in China with the famous amateur expert of Chinese opera, Pu-tong (溥侗, aka 紅豆館主). The new magistrate was played by Shih-hui Chao (趙世輝), a simultaneous interpreter at the United Nations. Son of Er Hsun Chao (趙爾巽) and son-in-law of Tso-lin Chang (張作霖), two big names in the early history of the Republic of China, he had studied this opera with the famous professional singer Jixian Cheng (程繼仙). Julia Wu (伍杜天薌), a postdoctoral scholar on special education at the Teachers College, Columbia University, played the father, and William Cheng played the son. Both of the latter two also had extensive stage experience in China.

All during the performance, I was in the orchestra, teaming up with Frank Cho and P. C. Chao for the first opera, and with S. W. Hsiang on the bamboo flute for the second. For lack of percussion instrumentalists, I also played the big gong, with Peter Hao at the small drum as the conductor. But, concentrated as I was on my own responsibility as an accompanist, I also paid full attention to the performance. In all honesty, I could objectively label the show as superb!

The audience obviously felt the same way, as evidenced by their enthusiastic applauses, and frequent shouts of "*hao* (bravo)!" Many among the audience were from out of town, including Ambassador Wellington Koo (顧維鈞) and other dignitaries from Washington, DC. Quite a few were moved to tears. Many were inquiring, "When will be your next show?"

Then, . . .

Yaji, our association, did offer stage productions regularly in the succeeding years, too numerous to list here. But soon we lost Peter Hao's leadership, because he went back to Beijing to join his family after he received his doctoral degree. Fortunately, William Cheng's office had moved from Washington, DC, to Manhattan, and he, the most enthusiastic Chinese opera fans that I have ever met, cheerfully succeeded Peter as the de facto leader of Yaji, scheduling our meetings and, more importantly, arranging stage presentations. He was an incurable addict to the stage; his slogan was: "The show must go on!"

But a problem soon arose in the arrangement for performances. We happened to have two prima donnas, Julia Ho and Hsiao Ming, which was one too many. Both of them loved to perform, and both wanted to star in the main opera—the last one to go on stage. William was happy about the availability of principal female singers, but was vexed by the impossibility to satisfy them both. To his credit, William found a solution: Have one performance on Saturday night, starring one of the prima donnas, and another performance on Sunday afternoon, starring the other. Under that arrangement, each time we put on a show, it was really two shows. That would involve altogether six or seven different operas, a big undertaking. In those days, there were no professional Chinese opera personnel in New York, and all the roles, even minor ones, had to be performed by amateurs, supported by amateur musicians, amateur makeup artists, and so on. From my own point of view, Frank Cho and I, the basic accompanist team, must learn several operas, and memorize all the music, since traditionally the musicians do not use music sheets on stage. That was double the usual work.

This arrangement worked for a while, but could not fundamentally resolve the conflict. Saturday evening was considered prime time, as the Sunday afternoon was not. So, the prima donnas still had something to fight about.

The eventual solution came when Hsiao Ming, with Shih-hui Chao, left Yaji in 1958 to form a new opera association. Actually, that association suffered two split-ups of its own, resulting in the coexistence of as many as four opera groups in New York at one time. And this propensity to split up was obviously contagious, because Chinese opera groups that later sprang up in other American cities, such as Washington, DC, Los Angeles, and San Francisco, all displayed the same syndrome.

A New Vista

Meanwhile, we were blessed with the arrival of a professional singer–actress in the person of Hung-yen Hu (胡鴻燕), who married Tzen Chen (陳參), an early member of Yaji. Hung-yen not only joined us as an active performer, but also volunteered to coach and direct the others. Her professional background also expanded our range of feasible operas by enabling us to put on operas with martial arts and acrobatic actions. Prima donna problems never arose again, even though we had quite a few female singers, including Leepo Yu (于鄭麗波), a PhD research physicist, Priscilla Kuo (郭呂寶楣), and later, Emily Chiang. They were not billing-centric. And, luckily, singers of non-female roles generally seemed more prone to peace. It was my pleasure to be an accompanist for all of them.

Under William Cheng's watch, we regularly put on two performances each year, in the spring and in the fall. Unfortunately, he died in 1978. Then, fortunately, we soon found yet another capable leader, Chia-dann Chi (齊家旦), an experienced singer of the *xiaosheng* (小生), or adolescent male role, who joined us in 1961, and headed our association for several decades even though he was extremely busy as a Vice President and Senior Portfolio Manager at PNC Bank, and later as the President of his own investment company, CDC Investments.

When Chia-dann resigned as the president of our association, Celine Foung (金茜琳) kindly agreed to serve in that post. But after she resigned after several years, nobody was available as a successor, and I was drafted to serve as president, but I only agreed to do it for one year. I always felt that I am more useful in the position of Secretary. Now the association is headed by Dr. Kuang-min Chang (張光敏), a singer of the hero–rogue role. He is a periodontist and Associate Professor of Periodontics at the School of Dental Medicine, Rutgers University.

Yaji, as our Chinese opera association has been nicknamed, was not only the oldest, but remained the one that put on the most performances over the years. By the time of our Golden (50th year) Anniversary performance in 2001, the official statistics showed that we had put on a total of 81 shows, with 187 operas or excerpts (98 operas if repeat performances were excluded). These numbers became even more impressive 10 years later, on our Diamond (60th year) Anniversary performance in 2011: a total of 87 shows, and 213 operas or excerpts, and more than 100 even if we excluded repeats. These operas were performed by a large number of singer–actors, some of them being long-standing members, and others being short-term members who were in New York for a short number of years, or even just passing by.

I present here a picture, 11.3, taken at the cast party after our gala Golden Anniversary performance in 2001. I, standing, was being recognized as the only co-founder in attendance. I was surrounded by (left of picture) Mr. and Mrs. George Yan and their daughter Karen, and (right) my close friends Chris and Marlies Wu.

The Association still holds regular meetings, but with advancing ages of our members, and with most of us already in retirement, we now lack the energy to plan any more stage presentations. When I try to count the number of years I have been associated with this organization, I cannot quite believe it – all the way from 1951 to the present – almost 70 years!

11.3 At the cast party after the Golden Anniversary performance of the Chinese Opera Association of New York, October, 2001.

Disasters and Fun Episodes

For an organization that has lasted for over six decades, a host of big things—good and bad—was bound to happen to it. The most heinous thing that possibly could befall did befall on November 30, 1968, on the very day of a performance. A phone call came to William Cheng with an ominous message: "Call off the show, or the theater will be blown up!" William immediately consulted his committee in an emergency meeting. Submit to the threat or ignore it? Sadly, the decision reached was to protect the safety of our audience as well as our performers, and cancel the show at the last minute. An audience of around 650, already sitting in their seats in the auditorium at the Fashion Institute of Technology on West 27th Street, had to evacuate in disappointment and dejection. And all our arduous efforts of preparations and rehearsals came to a complete waste! Ironically, the opera we prepared for that day, "八義圖 or 趙氏孤兒 (The Revenge of the Sole Orphan)," extols the virtues of eight loyal people who sacrificed themselves for the protection of an orphan so that he could, when grown up, avenge the murder of his entire family by a sinister political enemy. Here, in real life, our show itself was mercilessly "murdered" by a wretched coward!

Two years later, in 1970, the episode of bomb threat was replayed. We didn't know whether the call came from the same coward. This time, William Cheng was psychologically prepared, and he simply decided on his own to ignore the phone call. Fortunately, it was a mere empty threat. Nothing happened. And we were never threatened again.

The next big disaster of Yaji, which occurred on March 31, 1996, was entirely different in nature. The electrician of the Fashion Institute of Technology failed to show up at the appointed time for our performance. Curtain time came, and passed, and we could not start the show. It being a Sunday, there was nobody we could try to contact to locate the absentee electrician. Finally, a ray of hope emerged when someone somehow found a single movable spotlight standing in the back of the auditorium, and we had to maneuver that lone spotlight to follow the action on the stage as the only source of illumination. Literally, Yaji had its "darkest moment" during that performance!

We were not exempted from natural disaster either. In September, 1999, there was a rainstorm that poured down 15 inches of water in 24 hours in the Greater New York area. Yaji's collection of costumes, purchased over many years, and stored in suitcases in Chia-dann Chi's basement, suffered extensive water damage. Many of us members had to hold a special meeting to go through the whole collection, salvaging what we could and discarding the rest. From then on, we only used plastic containers instead of nonwaterproof suitcases.

What about fun episodes? Well, there was an interesting case of a little boy stealing the show even before our performance began. In March 1974, we were invited to give a performance at Yale University under the sponsorship of the Yale-in-China Association (雅禮學會). This was not the first time we received invitations to do sponsored shows for colleges and universities outside of New York, or alumni associations of Chinese universities in New York. Over the years, we have done them in Connecticut, New Jersey, and once even as far as in Michigan. We refer to them as "外賣 (take-out)" shows. At this show at Yale, I was an orchestral member, as usual, and Emily worked backstage as a makeup artist, so we had to leave our son Darryl (5) and daughter Tracey (3) to the care of friends in the audience. Just before the curtain time, as the members of the orchestra walked onto the stage to their seats at stage left, there was a loud salutation "Hi, Daddy!" from the completely filled auditorium. Following a couple of seconds of silence, a big applause exploded with laughter. It turned out to be my son Darryl hailing me from down there, and the audience appreciated his show of filial affection. The performers backstage all heard the applause, and wondered why applause could have erupted before they even made their entrances.

In the 1970s, William Cheng often asked his colleague James S. C. Chao (趙錫成) to help at the box office on the days of our performances, who not only offered his own help, but brought three of his daughters to serve as ushers. The elder daughter's name is Elaine Chao (趙小蘭), who later served the U.S. federal government as Secretary of Labor under President George W. Bush and as Secretary of Transportation under President Donald Trump. Meanwhile, her father, the founder of Foremost Group, has become a shipping tycoon and entrepreneur, and a major philanthropist. His gift to Harvard Business School alone, where Elaine and her sisters obtained their MBA degrees, amounted to a cool 400 million dollars.

Speaking of donations, Yaji had mostly subsisted on membership fees, and although some ticket sales were made in later years, our performance expenses were allotted to performers—less for the opening operas and more for the main opera. But we also received donations, including a gift of stocks from a member, Mrs. Ling-ta Yang (楊凌令達), worth $13,000. But the largest gift came from Tom Tang—the same Tom who organized the picnic to send Emily to college—who later became a wealthy industrialist. Over the years, I had always sent him tickets to our performances, and Tom and Jane had always shown up to give us moral support. Then, in a letter to me in September 2007, he expressed his support in a different way; he sent me a check for $50,000 payable to our association, on conditions of anonymity. I immediately forwarded the check to our treasurer, but requested our Board of Directors to faithfully keep his name secret. Later, at our Diamond Anniversary performance in 2011, however, I felt an urge to reveal his name and thank him publicly for his generosity. With his permission, I finally revealed his name in our commemorative booklet for that occasion.

Making Programs, and . . .

In my years of teaching in Ohio, I became less active in Yaji. But once I came back to the East Coast, first as a National Science Foundation Fellow at Yale University in 1963–1964, and then as Professor of Economics at the University of Connecticut from 1964–1965 on, I resumed my full status as a member of Yaji, participating in almost every performance. I partnered with Frank Cho for many years in a cordial musical relationship. After Frank left New York for health reasons, I have had several new partners on stage, including C. T. Shen (沈中泰), Thomas Lee (李學博), H. Y. Kuan (官鴻耀), and S. F. Chao (趙聖符). There have been a lot of talented people in our circle.

But my longest musical partnership was with Roger Yeu (樂亦平), a descendant of the famous herbal medical family with a famous shop (同仁堂) that occupied a whole block in the old Peking, and even with a branch within the Forbidden City by order of an emperor of the Qing Dynasty. Roger and I met in 1951. When we teamed up, we quickly developed a rare musical rapport.

He also helped me with my Mandarin pronunciation in many instances, since he speaks perfect Beijing dialect and taught Chinese language at Columbia. Roger, the most courteous person I have ever met, could never engage in any spat with anyone. The only harsh tone I ever heard from him was when, in his company, I pronounced the word "併" in the third tone (correct in the Shanghai dialect, but not in Mandarin) four or five times in a row within a single minute! Patently annoyed by my repeated mispronunciation, he uncharacteristically shouted out the correct Mandarin version of that word in the fourth tone! It rattled me a little. But you can bet that I have not committed the same error ever since.

Later, I mostly played operatic music with George Ren-an Yan (嚴仁安老師), who kindly offered to coach my instrumental skills as well as Emily's singing. In his youth in Shanghai, he had long associations with famous professional opera singers and musicians, hence becoming knowledgeable in many aspects of that art form. His meticulous coaching brought much improvement in me, and I tried to make my *erhu* go as seamlessly as possible with his *jinghu* in our accompaniment for Emily's singing. We met regularly and frequently, and it was always so exhilarating when we played together, in private or on stage. Needless to say, both Emily and I miss him greatly after his passing in January 2018. And so does Lisa Lu.

Aside from the musical side of Yaji performances, I also became the designer of programs, adding calligraphy into them, and printing them in two colors. Since 1972, I made more than 20 such programs. But the major publication I did for Yaji was a commemorative booklet in 2001 for our Golden Anniversary Performance, consisting of 32 pages of photos and 34 pages of text. Since I badly ran over budget on that booklet, I exercise great financial caution when working on the commemorative booklet for our Diamond Anniversary Performance in 2011. It only had 10 pages of photos and 20 pages of text.

In Photo 64 in the front of this book, I show the cover of the commemorative booklet I produced for our Golden Anniversary performance in 2001.

Unexpected Debuts

Emily did not get involved with Yaji activities until almost 10 years after we got married. In the fall of 1963, Hung-yen Hu, the professional singer–actress who later married a member of our association, planned to perform the opera "翠屏山 (The Fatal Affair)." This is a story about an illicit love affair between a wanton woman (潘巧雲) and a lecherous monk (海和尚). When a loyal friend of the husband learned about it, and alerted the husband, the wife accused the friend of seducing her, causing the husband to sever relations with this friend. Eventually, though, the wife and monk were put to death. The casting was readily set for most of the major roles, but there was still need to find someone to play the woman's maid, a role requiring no singing but a lot of dialogue. William Cheng, with his casting director's eyes, took a look at Emily, and declared her a draftee for the role. To everybody's surprise, Emily accepted the draft without hesitation, even though she had never been in any Chinese opera before. She was used to appearing on stage, so at least there was no problem of stage fright. Hung-yen was pleased about the choice, and volunteered to coach Emily for the many scenes in which they interacted together. The result was a great debut for Emily, and she was henceforth forever chained to the opera casting pool, subject to drafts for increasingly bigger roles. Soon after, she even had the opportunity to join Julia Wu in the opera "打魚殺家 (A Fisherman's Tale)" performed at the China Pavilion at the World's Fair in Flushing Meadows, Queens, New York, in August 1964.

Just as the role of the young maid was a debut for Emily, the role of the monk was a debut for John Fei (費景漢), a Professor of Economics at Yale, whom I had earlier met in Ohio when he taught at Antioch College, a sister institution of Denison. When I went to Yale, I naturally looked him up, and then, learning that he also liked Chinese opera, I introduced him to our association. The role for the monk, a clown, called for someone who could speak pure Beijing dialect. John could. In the tradition of Chinese opera, all performers must follow scripted dialogues and lyrics, except that clowns are allowed to *ad-lib*. This tradition had a historical origin. During the Tang Dynasty, an emperor that patronized drama and operas was fond of participating in performances himself, in clown roles. Being the emperor, he of course was not bound by any rules, so he ad-libbed and did unexpected things for comic effects. From that era on, it became a tradition that clowns, but only clowns, could deviate from scripts, and do funny things of their own invention. John Fei could do that, too. In the final scene, just before he was to be killed, he took off his outer garment, and— surprise!—the monk was wearing a white T-shirt with "YALE" inscribed on it in bold letters. Big laugh!

John and I became close opera friends. And, as fellow economists, we also wrote research papers together and later even co-taught a graduate course at Cornell University. He naturally became a frequent

11.4 Opera: "The Fatal Affair," marking the debuts of Emily and John Fei, 1963. From left: Emily, John Fei, and Hung-yen Hu.

visitor to our home; he is the leftmost figure in Photo 56 in the front of this book.

Gradually, Emily went on to singing roles, first coached at home by me. Then, whenever we visited our respective parents in Hong Kong and Taiwan, she would invariably try to arrange lessons from well-known teachers there (郭曉農老師、包幼蝶老師). In the spring of 1973—about 10 years after her debut—she took on for the first time the prime role of a complete opera "鳳還巢 (The Return of the Phoenix)," with Hung-yen as her acting coach, and George Yan and me as singing coaches. That was followed by several major roles in some operas in which she appeared together with Hung-yen Hu and Chia-dann Chi. But her most exacting prime role, had to wait till the fall of 2005. In the opera "玉堂春 (Su-San on Trial)," coached by George Yan (嚴仁安老師) who also accompanied her on the *jinghu* with me on the *erhu*, Emily faced the grueling task of singing for almost 45 minutes straight. That was done mostly in a kneeling position as a prisoner-defendant in a courtroom, with only brief rests during the dialogues among the three judges. To her credit, in her early 70s at the time, Emily was still able to get up from her kneeling position all by herself after the strenuous vocal workout. She, of course, was no longer the novice singer I met for the first time at Fordham University in 1951. She was now an accomplished singer–performer that I could rightly be proud of.

Some of Emily's stage appearances are shown in Photos 20–23 in the front of this book.

Our children usually accompanied us on our fairly regular trips from Connecticut to New York for rehearsals and performances. Actually, for several years, they also debuted as extras on stage along with the children of our opera colleagues. Darryl took on soldier or guard parts, normally in a group of four, with the sons of Hung-yen, Chia-dann, and Peter Lu (盧德先), our *laosheng* singer. And Tracey even had a speaking part as a lady-in-waiting once. Photo 24 in the front of this book shows our whole family involved on stage in a 1981 show. These youngsters were very good helpers. They worked conscientiously, though not paid too generously. We sorely missed them, when they became unavailable as they reached college ages.

Fiasco at McCarter Theater

Sometimes, I make a fool of myself by my own action. Other times, certain circumstances converge to make a fool of me in an uncanny fashion, through no fault of my own.

When a touring professional Chinese opera troupe from Hepei Province in China did a show at Princeton University in April, 1998, our friends Professor of Economics Gregory Chow (鄒至莊) and his wife Paula (鄒陳國瑞) invited Emily and me to give a brief introductory lecture-demonstration before their show. We had done similar introductions before, and accepted without hesitation. Since the restaurant the Chows took us to dinner before the show was extra slow that night, we arrived at the McCarter Theater quite late, and I had to rush onto the stage with no time to go backstage first to meet the performers.

I was given very limited time to explain a few salient features of Chinese opera. As the primary point, I told the audience that Chinese opera is unique for its bare stage, usually with nothing more than a table and a couple of chairs. The bare stage might be a legacy from the early era when traveling troupes could not possibly carry elaborate sets with them, but the bare stage feature was retained even in theaters, because it provides a flexible, movable locale during the evolvement of the story. If an actor opens an (imaginary) door, and steps over an (imaginary) threshold, the audience would know the locale is the inside of a house. But when the character exits the room and walks around the stage in a circle, the audience would know he/she is now outside on the street. There is no set to confine the locale to a single place. Also, the costumes worn by the characters would indicate whether the locale is a palace or the cottage of a destitute person. So, I told the audience, "Expect to see a bare stage, and use your imagination to visualize the door, or street, or mountain that are not there. And, understand that walking around the stage in a circle could signify traveling for several miles."

Then, I explained the stylized body movements, with Emily demonstrating them at my side. Then, . . ., I had to stop, because it was now curtain time.

The curtain slowly opened up. And, lo and behold, instead of the bare stage I told the audience to expect, there was an elaborate, gaudy set for a palace scene! That troupe had brutally made a liar out of me! There obviously had been an "innovation" in China—to use elaborate sets, but for what purpose? To entertain and dazzle the audience's eyes? It only annihilated the "movable locale" advantage of the bare stage!

Now seated in the first row, I felt embarrassed to the extreme. It was a good thing that my back was toward the audience, so they could not see my face. But as the story evolved, I felt a little better, because a character who told the audience he was leaving the palace was still acting and singing within the confines of that immobile set. At least a portion of the audience should now appreciate the validity of my point about the advantage of a bare stage.

The other three opera excerpts they put on that night also had cumbersome sets, producing the same locale-limiting effects. By the time of the fourth opera, though, I felt more embarrassment for the troupe than for myself.

Nevertheless, I learned a great lesson that night: Don't open your mouth about what's behind a curtain, unless you have first opened your eyes to what's behind that curtain.

The Association Now

We have used many different venues for meetings, practice sessions, and rehearsals over the years. These include the China Institute on East 65th Street, and the Sino-American Amity on Riverside Avenue at W. 81st Street in Manhattan. We have also rented spaces from several churches at different times. Now, with many members residing in New Jersey, we are holding monthly practice sessions in a church in Tenafly, New Jersey.

However, since our Diamond Anniversary performance in 2011, our Association has refrained from putting on stage presentations. For our aging membership, it has become too taxing to go through the overwhelming job of selecting a suitable program of operas, arranging a cast and orchestra, contracting a performance venue, scheduling rehearsals, assembling or purchasing costumes, printing tickets and programs, plus the actual performing. This despite the fact that professional opera actors are now available for hire in New York to help with our performances. Regretfully, therefore, we no longer adhere to William Cheng's motto: "The show must go on!" In fact, following the negotiations of Dr. Kuang-min Chang, our president, we have donated all the costumes accumulated over the decades to the Museum of Kunqu at the National Central University (中央大學崑曲博物館) in Taiwan.

12

Confucius Sez

Even though I was spending much time on Chinese opera, the focus of my attention had always been on my studies toward a doctorate in economics. Was my career to be in business, or in public office, or maybe in academia?

As early as at the age of 6 or 7, I had an unflagging career choice: a singer of Chinese opera. But my father, with good reasons, smothered my decision with a single word: "Silly!" His reason was quite valid: Entertainers had the lowest social status in China in that era, and the likelihood of a successful career was extremely slim.

I also had a second career choice, circa age 10: to be a writer. But my intention met no approval either. Dad simply asked, "How could a writer ever hope to support a family?"

By the time I had to select a major in college, I was wise enough to be practical. And economics emerged as the best choice, since it could lead to careers in banking, import–export business, manufacturing companies, which were prevalent in Shanghai where my family resided. But as I progressed in the pursuit of a PhD degree, the career choice seemed to be moving more and more in the direction of college teaching. An academic career is highly respected in the Chinese culture, and it would certainly meet the hearty approval of my father. Besides, I believed (erroneously) that in academia there would not be much politics, something I hated.

By 1949, China had turned communistic, and the prospect of drastic changes under the new regime induced my father to advise against my return to China. Even though I came to the United States with the full intention to go home, now I was being forced to go through a metamorphosis into an immigrant—a "circumstantial immigrant" as I saw it. If I were to go into teaching, it would be pursued in the United States now rather than in China. Fortunately, I was already proficient in English, thanks to my education at a missionary high school and university in Shanghai, eliminating the communication problem. Unfortunately, though, there loomed another, more formidable barrier in my path: the fear of public speaking.

A Prohibitive Stumbling Block

From early childhood, I had been very shy. I could handle private conversations comfortably, but speaking to a large group was torturous, even crippling. Now, if I became a professor, how could I ever lecture to 20–30 students in each class, with their eyes fixed on me? I would probably be like a deer facing car headlights.

I surely had to select an alternative career. I looked hard for business jobs. But all my inquiries yielded no fruits. I was either "overqualified," or "lacking in experience." I did not think then about racial factors, but it could also be because I am Chinese. Eventually, when I was forced to fall back to a teaching career, I must face the need to overcome my shyness somehow!

My first thought was to learn formal speech making. But that had to be ruled out. Where would I have opportunities to practice? Etiquette would not allow me to burst out into a speech at a social gathering. Maybe a better way would be to learn to tell jokes. Jokes are shorter, and always welcomed at parties. Of course, Bob Hope must be the model to emulate. But his rapid-fire delivery was impossible to master. It was obvious that I could never succeed. There emerged an oppressive feeling of doom.

A Sudden Inspiration

Then, one day, at the Radio City Music Hall, a Chinese song-and-joke team gave me an awakening. The "song" part of that team featured a tall Chinese young man who could imitate the unique voices of Bing

Crosby, Frank Sinatra, Perry Como, and others. And the "joke" part featured an older Chinese gentleman telling "Confucius sez" witticisms, all delivered very slowly, yet still capable of reaping resounding laughs. I had encountered jokes delivered at moderate speed before, but usually as part of a skit, exemplified by Jack Benny. What this Chinese comedian proved to me was that they could be equally effective as plain jokes. I became so focused on his delivery style that I missed many of his jokes. I was elated by the inspiration he gave me, and the resolution to learn joke-telling took root in me.

This revelation was given a further boost when, in the theater lounge downstairs after the show, an old lady at the other end of the room rushed over to me, and excitedly said, "Thank you so much; I really enjoyed your show!" I was amazed that she could have mistaken me for one of the performers. I am much shorter than the young singer, and much younger than the middle-aged comedian. (So, maybe there indeed is truth in the saying that "All Chinese look alike.") Should I correct her mistake? No; I decided instead to support her illusion of having talked to a "star." "I'm so glad you liked the show," I said. Being misidentified as a joke-teller accidentally strengthened my joke-telling resolution.

Building a Repertoire

The initial aim had to be modest, working only with short jokes that are easy to remember. Even so, I spent ample time analyzing each joke-telling event after I went home. Did my friends laugh heartily, or perfunctorily? Did I use proper phrasing? Did I project enough? Was there sufficient use of "pauses"?

In a joke about the four most popular subjects in fiction, a teacher of writing asks each student to write a story that incorporates all of the following elements: (1) religion, (2) royalty, (3) sex, and (4) mystery. The first submitted paper goes:

> *"Holy Moses!" said the Queen, "The princess is pregnant again? I wonder whodunit!"*

Short as it is, the joke is clever, succinct, and funny. When it is read out as it is written, however, it sounds flat, and does not reap easy laughs. The reason, in my analysis, is that the four required elements are bunched too closely to one another, not allowing time for the listeners to process in their minds that "religion" has been covered, then the "royalty," and "sex," . . . A more effective way would be to elongate certain words, insert some pauses, and add some emphasis:

"H-o-l-y M-o-s-e-s!" exclaimed Her Majesty the Queen, "The princess has gotten herself p-r-e-g-n-a-n-t again? (Pause.) I wonder (hush) whodunit this time?!"

When, with slowly built-up confidence, I graduated to longer, more complicated jokes, I had to pay attention also to the sequencing of the contents, and the flow, and the crescendo to the punch line. I learned that, if a joke is a play on words, then a foundation must be laid at the beginning for the audience to hear a clear contrast for the word play.

One joke in this category is about a church that badly needed to have its building painted, with a pastor who was stingy about the use of paint. To save money, he unwisely tried to mix paint with water, resulting in a bad painting job. As he started to pour even more water into the can of paint, a rainstorm suddenly developed and washed out all the paint on the wall. This was followed by a thunderous voice from up above, saying, "Repaint, and thin no more!" This quotation—the punch line and a play on words—is clearly patterned after the phrase "Repent, and sin no more!" But, delivered as indicted above, what kind of response can you expect from the audience? Laughter would come from the people who are familiar with the latter phrase, but nothing from those who are unfamiliar with that phrase. The joke thus bombs. In order to assure success, it is necessary to introduce at the beginning that this pastor had the habit of admonishing his congregation at the end of every sermon, "Repent, and sin no more!" With such a foundation laid, the punch line "Repaint, and thin no more!" would be sure to ring a loud bell. If, in addition, the four key words Repent, Repaint, Sin, and Thin are all uttered slowly and distinctly, I can guarantee a rich harvest of the hoped-for laughter.

Happily, I gradually became known as a joke-teller with a good repertoire, with jokes to fit most occasions. I even became the go-to person for jokes at parties, with no fear of opening my mouth to a large group of people. It took me years, but by the time I officially started to teach, as a part-time lecturer in adult evening classes at the University of Bridgeport, I felt reasonably comfortable with the staring eyes of the students. It also helped that I possessed a trove of stories that I could judiciously sprinkle into the class discussion to enliven the lectures.

An Anonymous Benefactor

That Chinese comedian of "Confucius sez" jokes was a great benefactor of mine. But he had to remain anonymous, because, regrettably, I do not remember his name. And since I was devoting my attention to his delivery during his performance, I also missed many of his material. After so many years, I can only recall two of his jokes. It happens that one of these relates to the question of Life versus Death. The other has to do with Holy Matrimony:

1. Confucius sez: "Bad breath is better than no breath at all."
2. Confucius sez: "Marriage is like cafeteria: you first pick out what you like, then you pay for it later."

13

The Uplifting Hand

Often, at a critical point in one's life journey, an external force would intervene to provide an "uplifting hand" to guide the turn of events toward an auspicious end. The fact that I got a passport to study in the United States even though I missed the nationwide examination, is a good example of the uplifting hand that Dr. Hang of the Ministry of Education kindly extended to me.

The First Uplifting Hand in Academia

At the various stages of my teaching career, I have benefited from several uplifting hands, some of them in unusual, unimaginable ways.

Before I got my first teaching post as a part-time instructor for the adult evening classes at the University of Bridgeport, I had been worrying about an important drawback in my *résumé:* I had zero teaching experience. I had mostly overcome my fear of public speaking by that time, but I still lacked classroom experience, which was looming as a critical negative factor in my search for a teaching post.

Then, one day in early 1953, Chi-ming Hou (侯繼明), a fellow doctoral candidate in economics at Columbia (see Photo 1.2), told me that he was leaving a part-time job at the University of Bridgeport in Connecticut to take a full-time job at Lafayette College. Then he added, "Would you be interested in that Bridgeport position?" I emphatically said, "Yes! Very much so!" And by introducing me to Professor Hans Apel, the Chairman of the Economics Department at Bridgeport, Chi-ming Hou gave me the first uplifting hand in my teaching career.

Luckily for me, Professor Apel was willing to disregard my total lack of prior teaching experience. At the end of an interview lasting no more than one hour in February, 1953, he offered me the position right on the spot, extending to me another uplifting hand. When I reported this good news to Chi-Ming, I told him he had no idea how pivotal this job was to me.

As a novice instructor, I taught adult evening classes at Bridgeport for three semesters from February 1953, until I left the East Coast for a full-time assistant professorship in Ohio.

The basic course, Principles of Economics, I could handle without too much problem. But, still, when some silver-haired students in the class raised questions relating to their real business enterprises, I did not have ready answers since I possessed nothing beyond book knowledge. The greatest challenge for me was the course on American Economic History, in which I had zero training, and all I could do was to try to stay precariously ahead of the students one chapter at a time.

I was 25 at the time, and all my students were older than I. To appear older, I started to smoke a pipe. How silly! I fooled no one, of course. As another ploy, I also started to wear glasses although I really did not need to. The things I had to do for my first teaching job!

To arrive at the Bridgeport campus on time, I had to ask permission to leave my day job 5–10 minutes early, to catch the train at the Grand Central Station in Manhattan. Similarly, to catch the last train back to New York, I had to ask the class whether I could end the class five minutes early. The unanimous student response was: "No problem." Besides, one student enthusiastically volunteered to drive me to the Bridgeport train station, at times even risking a speeding ticket, so I wouldn't miss the last train. In fact, a few times when his car got there, the train was already in motion to leave. And, surprisingly enough, I was able to catch up with the train and, holding my attaché case in one hand while using the other to grab the side railing, jump up the side steps onto the moving train, as it started to gather speed. The things I had to do in my first teaching job!

Chi-ming Hou enrolled at Columbia about the same time I did, and we both received our PhDs in 1954. But we took different courses.

I felt honored when he asked me to be his best man when he married Irene Liu (劉似錦) in 1953. But I was into photography at that time, and told him that I could be more useful as a photographer at his wedding. I did come up with a collection of good photos for that occasion. After a few such events, I became more expert at wedding photographing and, later, in Ohio, I even worked as a "professional" wedding photographer once.

He taught at Lafayette College for a while, and ended up later at Colgate University. He authored two books on foreign investment and economic development in China, and became a chaired professor, and also served as the Chairman of the Department at Colgate. For many years, he worked as a senior visiting research fellow at the Chung-Hua Institution for Economic Research in Taiwan (中華經濟研究院), until he died in 1991.

An Anonymous Uplifting Hand

My appointment to the assistant professorship at Denison University in Granville, Ohio, was attributable to another uplifting hand. Strangely, this one was anonymous!

Denison was one of many schools I sent inquiry letters to by the time my doctorate was nearly in hand. But the response I received was: "Sorry, no opening at this time." On May 18, 1954, the day before the third anniversary of my first meeting with Emily, however, a Western Union telegram came from Denison, asking me, if still interested, to fly to Ohio for an interview, pronto—the following day if feasible. Young people today may not have heard of "telegrams," but these were the means of sending urgent written messages across long distance in those days. The sender of the message would submit a written text to Western Union, to be transmitted by telegraph to a Western Union office near the intended recipient. The message will arrive at the latter office in the form of text strips like a ticker tape. The strips will then be pasted together into a printed letter, to be delivered to the recipient. For those who have not seen a telegram before, Photo 13.1 provides an example.

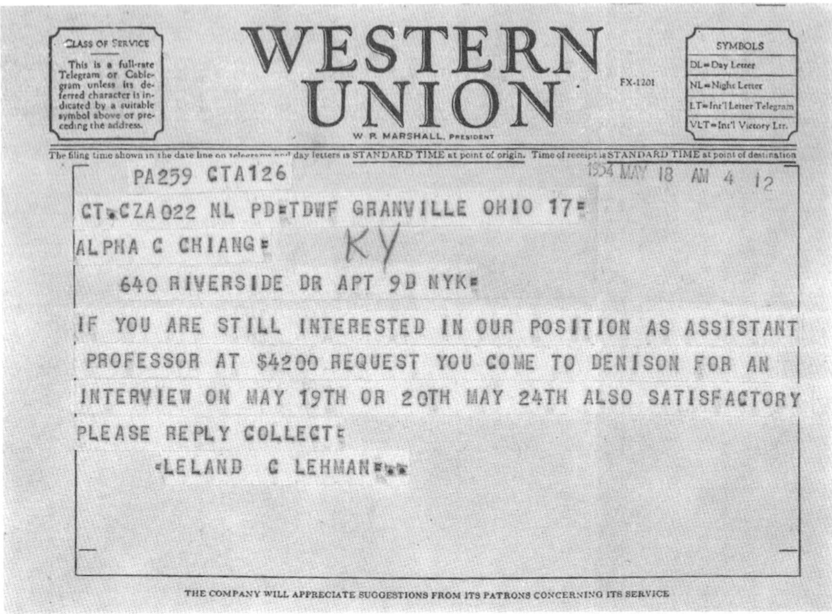

CLASS OF SERVICE

This is a full-rate Telegram or Cablegram unless its deferred character is indicated by a suitable symbol above or preceding the address.

WESTERN UNION

W. R. MARSHALL, PRESIDENT

FX-1201

SYMBOLS

DL = Day Letter

NL = Night Letter

LT = Int'l Letter Telegram

VLT = Int'l Victory Ltr.

The filing time shown in the date line on telegrams and day letters is STANDARD TIME at point of origin. Time of receipt is STANDARD TIME at point of destination

PA259 CTA126 1954 MAY 18 AM 4 12

CT.CZA022 NL PD=TDWF GRANVILLE OHIO 17=

ALPHA C CHIANG= KY

640 RIVERSIDE DR APT 9D NYK=

IF YOU ARE STILL INTERESTED IN OUR POSITION AS ASSISTANT PROFESSOR AT $4200 REQUEST YOU COME TO DENISON FOR AN INTERVIEW ON MAY 19TH OR 20TH MAY 24TH ALSO SATISFACTORY PLEASE REPLY COLLECT=

=LELAND C LEHMAN=

THE COMPANY WILL APPRECIATE SUGGESTIONS FROM ITS PATRONS CONCERNING ITS SERVICE

13.1 The telegram from Denison University, 1954.

What happened was that someone who accepted a job there suddenly withdrew, and Denison must find a replacement in a hurry. I immediately made arrangement to go. The interview on May 20 in Granville went well, first with Professor Lee Lehman, Acting Chairman while Professor Leland Gordon was on leave. I also met the other members of the small Economics Department, and even the President of the University.

Just 10 days later, I happily signed a contract with Denison, thanks to the uplifting hand of an anonymous person. His negative action of withdrawal from a position became a positive force for my appointment. Things really could work out in strange ways, and at the last minute, too.

My first full-time job carried an annual salary of $4,200.00. In 1954, this sum was not considered a laughable wage. Besides, things looked better, when, for satisfactory performance, my salary was raised to $4,500.00, then $4,800.00, respectively, in the next two years.

A Matter of Lifestyle

How could we live on such a low salary? For one thing, living cost was much lower in 1954. We rented a one-bedroom furnished apartment from the university in the College Town House on East Broadway, the main street of the town, for only $65 per month. The furniture was subpar, but utilities were included in the rent, and the university took responsibility for all repairs. They would even send a serviceman to our apartment to replace burnt-out light bulbs for free.

But the main reason for our ability to lead a "comfortable" life was the matter of lifestyle. Emily and I agreed to adopt a basic principle of family finance: Never spend more than what we earn. We often skipped an issue of *Life* magazine, just to save 25 cents. We took advantage of quantity discounts. We never threw away soft drink bottles, but returned them for refunds. Thus, with expenses under control, I never felt the need to cash every paycheck immediately after it got into my hands. Sometimes the check would remain in the letter rack for days.

When Bob Miller, my bachelor neighbor on the second floor of the College Town House, an Associate Professor of Music, came to visit, and saw my uncashed check, he would raise his eyebrows and

13.2 College Town House, our first residence in Granville, Ohio.

yell: "Alpha! What's your paycheck doing here in your letter rack?! Why haven't you cashed it yet?" Bob was earning a higher salary than I, but seemed to be always facing a financial shortfall, saddled with his monthly payments for his nice furniture, his baby grand piano, and his Thunderbird. His baby grand could be considered a legitimate expenditure for a teacher of piano; it was tax-deductible, too. But the Thunderbird?

In contrast, the car I bought to replace the disastrous black Ford was a simple Plymouth. I did decide to splurge on a new car, because after the Bedford incident I vowed never to buy a used car again. But I settled on a plain model—so plain that, to hide its drabness, I felt it absolutely imperative to have a chrome strip added to each side of the car. Through hard bargaining, I got that for free. This enhanced blue Plymouth served us well for several years—until I traded it for a sporty, two-tone Dodge Lancer, with white body and light blue stripes on the sides, and featuring a novel, push-button gearshift.

Before Bob left our apartment that day, he revealed the main purpose of his visit. With some embarrassment, he asked me, "Can I borrow twenty dollars from you?" In the following months, he came with the same request. He always repaid, without fail. He also reborrowed, without fail. As a lower paid colleague with a wife, I ran an interest-free loan operation for a higher paid bachelor neighbor, until he was paid up on one of the installment purchases, and after his salary was raised.

Supplementary Income

I did, of course, think of exploring supplementary sources of income. In academia, the "annual salary" is for two semesters (nine months) of work, leaving the summer free. Some faculty members tried to do summer teaching, though not at Denison which offered no summer courses. Some others tried to earn income in nonacademic jobs, including house-painting. The studious ones, however, studied to finish their degrees, or simply to improve themselves.

In my early encounter with Dr. Leland Gordon, my Department Chairman, he gave me a good piece of advice: "Unless you are really hard up for money, do not teach summer school, or look for non-academic work. Just study, and become a better economist."

I took his wise words to heart. In the summer months of my years at Denison, I read articles in professional journals, studied mathematics, wrote book views and research articles, and got them published in professional journals. And I also wrote an exercise book for my macroeconomics class, *Exercises in Aggregate Economics*, first for my own class use, but later commercially published by Holt, Rinehart & Winston, Inc., in 1964. This last item rewarded me only with a small royalty income, but it would unexpectedly bring about a pivotal turn in my career later.

Wedding Photographer

Once, I worked for supplementary income as a wedding photographer.

It all started with a wedding between Barbara Lee, an Assistant Professor of Art, and a neighbor at the College Town House, with Frank Bachmura, an Assistant Professor of Economics, who joined Denison after I did. I volunteered to take wedding pictures for them, and Frank and Barbara liked my results better than those of the professional photographer they hired. So, when another Denison colleague's sister was getting married, Frank and Barbara recommend me as a photographer. The job was fun, but since the wedding was held in a small house, it was challenging to find suitable places from which to shoot, especially since I had no zoom lens yet at that time. At one point, it was necessary for me to climb up a rickety chair to get a high angle, with flash bulbs jingling in my pockets. The bride and groom were very pleased with the quality of my work, because aside from my own conscientious work, I sent the film out to an excellent laboratory for processing.

I weighed the possibility of continuing to do weddings. But I figured that jobs would be sporadic, and the revenue, meager. So, I decided to dismiss photography as a viable side business.

Meaningful supplementary income came later through Emily. Having had some work experience at the insurance company USF&G

in New York, she tried to find employment at insurance agencies in Newark, Ohio, the county seat. There were only three or four such agencies, and job openings were not plentiful. We also wondered whether, maybe having never seen people of Asian extraction before, they would hire a petite Chinese young woman like Emily. At last, she did find a job at the insurance agency Rankin & Rankin, and commuted from Granville by bus for the seven-mile ride every work day. After she built up a reputation as an efficient worker, other firms tried to bid her away with higher salaries, but in appreciation of Rankin & Rankin's initial confidence in her, Emily declined all other offers.

Chairmanship and Presidency

Returning to the subject of my academic life, I found the early 1960s to be eventful years for me. First of all, I was appointed Chairman of the Department of Economics at Denison for a three-year term, starting on June 1, 1961. By nature, I am an organized person. I can therefore do an effective, orderly job as a chairman. But I do not enjoy dealing with a hundred little problems waiting for my decision and action. With such a personality, I accepted the chairmanship with some reservation. But, I was of opinion that one should take this type of responsibility at least once in a life. I was glad that I discharged my duties conscientiously, with good reviews.

More excitingly, by virtue of another genre of uplifting hand, I was elected Vice President (1962–1963) and President (1963–1964) of the Ohio Association of Economists and Political Scientists (OAEPS). This statewide organization is the conglomeration of two groups, economists and political scientists. One year, an economist is to be elected the new vice president, and he/she will automatically become the president the following year, when the vice presidency will go to a political scientist, and so on.

I had not been that active in OAEPS, but I presented a paper at the annual meeting held in April 1962, which must have impressed the Nomination Committee. I did not personally know any of the members of that committee. Thus, no one was more surprised than I when I heard my name in nomination for Vice President. Thanks to the uplifting hand of the Nomination Committee, I was elected by acclamation. I suppose this gratuitous honor was a good example of my "being at the right place at the right time." It felt rather unreal.

A Year at Yale

Aside from the Chairmanship and the Presidency, I was also lucky in being awarded a National Science Foundation Fellowship in 1963–1964 for advanced studies at Yale University. The time frame, 1963–1964, posed a problem because that was the final year of my three-year term as the Chairman of the Department at Denison. Fortunately, I was granted a special leave at Denison, and my senior colleague Lee Lehman (who, as the Acting Chairman, hired me in 1954) agreed to serve as Acting Chairman in my absence.

There was a more serious problem: 1963–1964 was the year of my presidency of the OAEPS. It was my duty to put together a program for our annual meeting to be held on April 3–4 at the Green Meadows Inn in Worthington, Ohio. And I was also supposed to preside over the proceedings. Fortunately, I was able to gather some interesting papers from colleagues in good time, and found suitable chairmen and discussants for the various scheduled sessions. And my round-trip transportation between Connecticut and Ohio went smoothly without any hitch.

My original plan for my year at Yale was to study econometrics, which involves statistical methods and data manipulation. Because of my declared interest in econometrics, Yale gave me an office at the Cowles Foundation for Research in Economics on Hillside Avenue. It was a spacious room with a large conference-size table, which I shared with another visiting scholar at Yale, Ad Pikkemaat, from the Netherlands. But soon I found that econometrics did not excite me. As a result, I redirected my time and energy to my long-conceived plan to write a book on mathematical economics, tying various mathematical methods to different types of economic analysis. That change in direction produced fruitful results. In addition, at the invitation of Professor John Fei at Yale, he and I collaborated on a research paper, which cemented a close professional relationship between us, besides our common involvement in Chinese opera performances.

Meanwhile, Emily had a job waiting for her in New Haven even before she arrived there. By coincidence, a traveling representative from the Travelers Insurance Company visited Rankin & Rankin shortly before we went to Yale. Upon learning Emily's forthcoming trip, he volunteered to recommend her to fill a vacancy he knew about at an established insurance agency in downtown New Haven. As soon as we settled at the Prince Albert Apartments on Whalley Avenue, she started working at Coan & Bunnell, an insurance agency that had hired her sight unseen.

A Call from the Past

Two shocks marked our year in New Haven. The major one, a shock on a national scale, was the assassination of President Kennedy, which rocked the entire nation, and even the world. It was a dark and gloomy day in history. A minor one, significant only for my personal life, was a surprise call from Paul Weiner, a former colleague at Denison, bringing exciting news.

Paul taught at Denison only for a year, after which he joined the faculty of the University of Connecticut (UConn). I was not close to him, because, frankly, he had some annoying habits. For example, he would come to my office to chat, and when leaving, took my neatly sharpened pencil with him. Pencils were university supplies, and he had a supply of his own. But he would take mine, requiring me to sharpen a new one. He also had a dermatological problem that caused most of his hair to fall off, leaving just 20 or 30 of them straggling sparsely over his head. But I was always courteous to him, and in fact we often lunched together.

His sudden call to me during my temporary year at Yale greatly surprised me. How did he know that I was in New Haven? Who gave him my newly registered phone number? And why would he call me?

The turn of the series of events was uncanny. A couple of sales staff at Holt, Rinehart & Winston had just visited me in New Haven before they called on UConn. Promoting my newly published workbook, *Exercises in Aggregate Economics,* in the Economics Department there, they met Paul Weiner and told him my whereabouts.

Paul's call was not a social call; he had a serious message for me. The Ford Foundation had just given to UConn a big grant, and the President at UConn decided to allot part of it for the launching of a PhD program in Economics. Therefore, in a rare move, the department was recruiting personnel at the senior rank. Hearing that I was living in nearby New Haven, and remembering me favorably, Paul called to ask me whether he could nominate me as a candidate. I did have thoughts of leaving Denison at that time, and in fact already had some leads at other universities. But the location of UConn impressed me as doubly attractive: It is close to New York where I had many friends, including the opera circle, yet it is faraway enough from New York so that I can reasonably decline unwanted invitations from the city without offending people. I thanked Paul for remembering me, and sent him my *résumé* right away.

Things developed at lightning speed. The Holt people visited me in early December, 1963. Then, after Paul's call, I was invited to Storrs for an interview on January 17, 1964. I got a good idea about the University and the Department from perusing the catalog they sent me. And I tried to remember the names of the faculty members, so that I could address them personally. I drove from New Haven to Storrs, about an hour's journey, in my Dodge Lancer, a relatively light car, but I negotiated the icy roads with no problem.

The interview was a most pleasant affair. I had expected them to ask me to present a lecture, to check my teaching ability. But they did not. They did have meaningful questions to ask me, and I also had substantive questions to ask them. Everything was done cordially. I felt that my preparation about faculty names proved worthwhile, for many members of the department seemed to enjoy being addressed by their specific names instead of the generic "sir." Paul Weiner, by the way, had solved his hair problem by shaving his head the Yul Brynner style, making him look a 100 times neater than before.

13.3 Our Dodge Lancer had push-button gearshift.

Only 10 days later, I received a job offer at the Associate Professor level. By that time, however, I already had in my hand two offers at the Full Professor level. After I told Professor Philip Taylor, the Head of the Department of Economics, about that fact, he drove down to New Haven on February 7 to deliver in person a revised offer at the full-professor rank, which I happily accepted within a week. This led to a 28-year affiliation I enjoyed with UConn, thanks to the uplifting hand of Paul Weiner. But what a confluence of events it was—from my publication of my *Exercises in Aggregate Economics,* to my temporary stay at Yale, to the visit of the Holt, Rinehart & Winston salesmen and their subsequent meeting with Paul Weiner, and so on! Things just came together in an uncanny way, temporally and geographically. Could there be some divine intervention again?

Another Uplifting Hand

After I joined the UConn faculty, I learned from an unofficial source that there existed another uplifting hand related to my appointment. According to this source, the Head of the Department preferred a Caucasian candidate to me. But Professor William P. Snavely, a senior member of the faculty, argued strongly in my favor, pointing to my scholarly publications, chairmanship of the department, and presidency of a state association. "If we are hiring only one candidate, then it should be Alpha Chiang who has better qualifications," he insisted, "and you can have the other candidate only if we decide to hire two persons." The final decision of the Department Head was to hire two new people that year.

Unlike many acquaintances of Chinese ancestry, I have always told people, in honesty, that I have not encountered any racially discriminatory acts in the United States. But the story above, if true, could very well count as a case of racial prejudice. I hope it was not true. Otherwise, I must count Professor Snavely as an additional uplifting hand in my academic career, like a strong shield blunting the strike of the sword of discrimination.

14

Two Sides of the Lectern

The lectern in the classroom serves as the demarcation line between the teacher and students. Students, sitting on one side of the lectern, can come to class prepared or unprepared as they wish; the teacher, sitting or standing on the opposite side, is expected to come prepared to impart knowledge, cultivate wisdom, and inspire thinking. As an academic, I spent 20 some years on one side of the lectern from elementary school to doctoral studies, and then switched to the other side of it for almost 40 years as Instructor, Assistant Professor, Associate Professor, to Professor. The switching operation only took a second.

Sounds like a boring life? Actually, not quite.

Teaching Style

For one thing, there was the immense challenge of developing a teaching style. For high-school teachers, their training includes education courses, including courses on how to teach this subject, and how to teach that subject. For college teaching, the doctorate obviates teaching certification. I of course had mentally surveyed the teaching styles of all my teachers I had ever had, trying to adopt their good aspects and avoid the bad.

In the worst style I ever encountered, a teacher sits and reads from a prepared text, without ever looking at the students. The next worst is a teacher who reads in a standing position, rarely glancing at the students. Both cases lack a serious attempt to engage the students in a personal relationship. Leland Gordon, the Chairman of the Department in my first year at Denison, kindly shared with me his lecture notes for the

Principles of Economics course, consisting of 15–20 points that he intended to discuss with the students in a class hour. I tried his method for a week, but had to abandon it, because following a bullet-pointed list made the discussion choppy, and mechanical.

Leland was a very distinguished-looking gentleman. Since he was very disciplined and organized, a story started that he always brought his lunch, and filed it under "L." Then somebody added a little more to it: One day, Dr. Gordon couldn't find his lunch under "L," because he filed it by mistake under "S" for "Sandwich."

The teaching style that I finally decided on is one where I use a very sketchy outline of topics as a rough guide, but the lecture is always done in an extemporaneous fashion. I of course do prepare the detailed points with diligence. But I try to remember them in my mind, and not have them written down in the outline. This way, not bound by a rigidly formatted outline, I can allow myself the freedom to go with the verbal flow at the moment, making the proceedings spontaneous, even sprinkling a joke or two here and there.

I had long cultivated the habit of using the blackboard, because the act of writing on the blackboard (which has been replaced by "greenboard" or even "whiteboard" over the years) affords relief from the tedium of talking and listening. Besides, writing a few keys words on the blackboard can serve to highlight the concepts I want to emphasize. To allow full view of the blackboard, I usually remove the lectern from the table, perhaps also symbolically removing the "demarcation line" between the teacher and the students. A few years into teaching, I introduced the use of colored chalks, making my classroom performance a Technicolor presentation. I intended it to be in CinemaScope, too, since I often write on the blackboard from the extreme left to the extreme right. The colored chalks proved very useful when the analysis in question calls for a graph with three or even more curves, each drawn in a different color to avoid confusion.

At one time, I asked myself whether I should use transparencies as some colleagues do. I decided against it because, projecting an image on the screen gives the students something not different from a "reading," whereas the classroom experience should in my opinion be watching a "performance," with an audio aspect involving pitch and intonation variations, and a visual aspect involving facial and body languages. Even in the study of a complicated graph, I want the students to construct it with me from scratch, one curve at a time, seeing how they're related to another, rather than seeing a finished picture projected onto the screen. This adds a "do it yourself" aspect to the graphical analysis, which, I believe, strengthens the students' understanding.

I have never won any teaching award. Perhaps it was because I mainly taught small classes at the graduate level, but teaching awards often go to teachers who teach large classes in big lecture halls, with many student "voters." But a couple of my graduate students who adopted my teaching style told me that they had won teaching awards at the colleges where they taught. I was happy for them and appreciated their trust in my teaching style.

Embarrassing Moments

In a long academic career, one is bound to have some embarrassing moments. Thinking back to my Bridgeport semesters, I felt embarrassed about the childish use of pipe-smoking to camouflage my young age. In my full-time job at Denison, where the students were mostly youngsters of 18–22, I could easily do without the embarrassing pipe. At age 27, I no longer needed to appear any older than I was.

In my first year at Denison, I had a good student in Econ. 101, named William (Bill) Berger, who, as an economics major in economics, took all the other courses I taught. The year he graduated, he came over to say goodbye after the commencement exercises, and said, "Dr. Chiang, I have never told you this before, but your Econ. 101 was the reason I decided to major in economics." I was much pleased to hear that, and said, "Bill, I am very proud to have had such an outstanding straight-A student like you." Bill hesitated a little, and said, "I am not quite a straight-A student; there is one B+ in my transcript." Showing surprise, I asked, "Really? Which professor gave you a B+?" He hesitated a little again, and replied, "You did." I was lost for words for a while, then took his arms and said, "I am so sorry, Bill." My embarrassment was elevated another notch, when he went on to introduce me to his parents as his favorite teacher.

An even greater embarrassing event occurred at Denison a couple of years later: my alarm clock failed me, and even though I ran all the way from my home on a wintry morning, I arrived at the final examination 15 minutes late. Fortunately, the entire class was still waiting patiently for me. I expressed my appreciation for their courtesy in waiting for me, and tendered my deep apology, and told them that they could disregard Part I of the final examination, for which I would give everyone full credit. I think I graded this set of papers a little more generously than usual, to allay my guilty feeling. From then on, I was never late again for any examination. Once, toward the end of my teaching career at University of Connecticut (UConn), there was a forecast of freezing rain for the morning a final exam in a graduate course of mine was scheduled. Not wanting to risk being late, I reserved lodging on campus for the night before the exam. The extra expense was worth it; I did arrive at the examination room on time the following morning.

In my first years of teaching, I was working under the misconception that a professor should know everything about the subject under discussion. This misconception tricked myself into over-preparation for each lecture. Forcing myself to anticipate all kinds of possible questions that students might raise, and then to answer all those questions to my own satisfaction, the preparatory work made my lectures rich, even impressive. But it cost me a great deal of sleeping time. Only after two or three years, did I come to the realization that a professor does NOT have to know everything, and does not have to feel embarrassed even when making a mistake in class. In spite of such realization, I still could not forgive myself for writing an incorrect term on the blackboard one day in a graduate macroeconomics course. An astute student courageously raised his hand, and said, "Dr. Chiang, could the word you just wrote be an error?" It indeed was. And, despite the realization that professors are human, and it is acceptable for them to make mistakes, I still felt embarrassed about being "caught." Fortunately, quick-thinking led me to turn the situation around, and to create a new teaching device from this experience. I complimented the student and told the class that I value alertness in class, and announced that I always give extra credit to anyone who can spot mistakes I make in class. To implement this teaching device, from that time on, I would deliberately plant one or two mistakes in class, waiting for the students to point them out. If no one did, I would then point them out myself, and reprimand them for not being alert enough. This turned into a regular part of my teaching, although I had to limit its use only to graduate courses, since undergraduates may not possess sufficient critical sophistication and pupillary courage to challenge the professor.

Another embarrassing moment was caused by my careless choice of expression. An undergraduate at UConn, Mary Jo Wilchynsky did well in an undergraduate course I taught, and wanted to challenge herself by trying out my graduate courses. I gave her permission to take my Math Econ, as well as a Macroeconomic Theory course, circa 1980. She did good work at the graduate level, too. In the macro course, specifically, the assignment included an article by a Professor Ghosh that I came across in the Italian journal *Rivista Internazionale di Scienze Economische e Commerciali,* which contained a logical error. I wrote a paper correcting that error, and had it published in a later issue of the same journal. In class, though, I assigned the Ghosh article only, without first telling them about my correction article, and challenged the class to find out the error on their own. Nobody in the class was successful, but Mary Jo was close. I then disclosed the error by giving the students reprints of my article. Because of her work, I formed a good impression of Mary Jo. She obviously liked me, too, for she invited me to be a guest at her induction into an honor society. There, after the induction ceremonies, Mary Jo introduced me to her mother. In a moment of enthusiasm, I said to her, "Mrs. Wilchynskky, I am so glad to meet you. I love your daughter . . ." Before I finished my sentence, she gave me a stern look, and asked, "You LOVE my daughter?!" I hastened, at lightning speed, to finish my sentence: ". . . as a student."

She then relaxed and a smile quickly formed around her lips. Her relief brought me relief, too, and we all had a laugh. It was an embarrassing moment. Fortunately, it was short-lived.

Winning Moments

I had winning moments, too. In fact, I already mentioned two of them in early chapters. One was the episode of "Alpha Serenade" in Chapter 1. Another, in Chapter 9, had to do with the sharing the excitement of my TV performances with the students, which also served as an apropos illustration of the difference between the concepts of wage income and wage rate.

At Denison, I directed an honors paper for Elizabeth Young. It was my first experience directing research, but Elizabeth did an excellent job, and won the first prize, with a cash award. It was a winning moment for her. But I also considered it to be a winning moment for me. She and I maintained a good relationship, and we exchanged Christmas cards for many years after her graduation.

I started writing the book *Fundamental Methods of Mathematical Economics* when I first joined the UConn faculty in September 1964. At the same time, I offered a Math Econ course, using my manuscript as lecture material. My primary objective was to make mathematics easy to understand, thereby liberating students from the pervasive but unwarranted math-phobia. I considered it a winning moment when Carlisle E. Moody, with a serious case of fear of mathematics planted in him by an incompetent math teacher he once had, came to my office after taking my courses, and formally declared that I had convinced him of the manageability of mathematics, and that he now intended to pursue higher mathematics beyond my courses. Later, at the University of Leeds in England, and the College of William and Mary in Virginia, he specifically taught Math Econ among other subjects.

Ming-Jer Wu (吳明哲), a graduate student from Taiwan, served as a Teaching Assistant for me at one time. After receiving his PhD in economics at UConn, he worked for the State of Connecticut in its Office of Policy Management, ending as Principal Budget Specialist. Living in proximity, he and I stayed close. But then I moved away from Connecticut after retirement, and after his retirement, he and his wife ManLi (王曼莉) moved to Georgia, because ManLi, a PhD in Chemistry, had a research director job offer there at Lonza America, Inc. While house-hunting there, they could not agree on where to live. But when they came upon a town called Alpharetta, Ming-Jer announced that he had made a decision, "The name of this town contains Professor Chiang's first name. We'll live here." When he told me this story, I was deeply touched. I don't think he realized how much of an honor he had bestowed on me by this seemingly simple housing decision.

14.1 Ming-Jer and ManLi Wu, 1984.

Ming-Jer and I often talked about nonacademic things. One time he confided in me that he sometimes felt uncomfortable about his shortness. I told him, "I am not tall either. But, so what? You must remember that size is by no means a measure of worth. So, whenever you feel self-conscious about your stature, think of how a dime should feel among nickels." This imaginative dime-nickel analogy is by no means my own invention. I heard it in a speech by General Romulo of the Philippines delivered in a lecture at Denison University. He was very short, but he distinguished himself during WWII as a military legend who worked closely with General Douglas MacArthur of the United States. He made effective use of that analogy in a self-introduction before the speech, and I have remembered it well.

Names and Faces

I have always tried to remember the names of my students and address them by their first names for a personal touch. But because of my seniority in age as well as in the stage of learning, I believe that I should maintain an air of authority. Therefore, I tried to avoid a buddy–buddy relationship with my students, until they are no longer my students. Specifically, when my graduate students attempted to call me "Alpha," I would ask them to call me Professor Chiang, or Dr. Chiang, or Mr. Chiang, until the day they receive their doctorates. Thenceforth, I'd be glad to become "Alpha" to them.

I cannot claim to remember every student I ever had in class. But I still remember a good number of them, even those at Denison decades ago. Those who have kept in touch are of course more often in my mind. Aside from some names I already mentioned above, the following examples easily come to mind. In my first year at Denison, I had a senior student, William (Bill) G. Bowen, who after graduation went to Princeton, earned a doctorate, and then taught there and eventually became Provost and President of Princeton University. He served later as the President of the Andrew W. Mellon Foundation.

John J. Reynolds and his wife Kitty invited Emily and me to dinner the day of his commencement. We appreciated this gesture because it

14.2 John J. Reynolds and Karen.

showed his intention to keep in touch with me after leaving Denison. We brought them two pairs of chopsticks, and he often expressed his love for these chopsticks in his Christmas cards. During one of his trips from his California home to the East Coast, he intended to pay me a personal visit, which would have been a reunion about 40 years after we last met. Unfortunately, a last-minute change in his itinerary upset this visitation plan. After Kitty passed away, he married Karen, and sent me a wedding photo. I appreciated deeply his friendship after so many years out of class.

At New Asia College (新亞書院), where I was a visiting professor in 1960–1961 and which later became a component college of the Chinese University of Hong Kong (香港中文大學), I encountered two outstanding students, Yiyao (Y. Y.) Kueh (郭益耀) and Joseph Chai (蔡俊華). Both of them earned their doctorates in Germany, and both kept in touch with me over the years. At different times, they had driven down from Massachusetts to Connecticut to see me, while they were visiting scholars or fellows at Harvard University. Y. Y. brought his attractive new bride, Hsiao-hu (曉瑚), and Joseph also brought his lovely German wife, Karin, whom he married while working on his doctorate. On my numerous visits to Hong Kong to see my parents, I always called on them, and they never failed to be gracious hosts.

Both of them taught in Hong Kong and Australia. The most interesting thing is that Yiyao later became my boss at Lingnan College (嶺南學院, now Lingnan University), when, as the Dean of Faculty of Social Sciences, he invited me to be a visiting professor there. See Photo 61 in the front of this book for a picture of the Kueh family.

Among UConn alumni, Roberta (Robin) Grower Carey stood out in my mind. I met her in my first year at UConn, and found her so astute that I asked her to be a reader for my manuscript as I wrote each chapter. She offered me useful suggestions, and I acknowledged her contribution in the preface to my book. The last time I heard from her, Robin was teaching at the College of Staten Island in New York.

Warren and Ann Fisher, both PhDs in economics, have always sent me their hand-written Christmas greetings with one or two of their recent photos enclosed. Both of them completed their doctorates decades ago, and Warren was one of my favorite Teaching Assistants. Warren taught at Susquehanna University in Pennsylvania, and Ann taught at Penn State. They are into music, and not only play but also make special stringed instrument. They often perform in a group called "The String Theory".

At UConn, several students wrote their doctoral dissertations under my supervision. But I can only recall five names: Glenn Briercheck, Mary McNally, Enamidem Ubok-Udom, Claude Fongemie, and Ranjit Vohra. Even though it was my tradition to invite each of them to dinner after his/her successful defense of the dissertation, with a request to keep in touch, only Ranjit Vohra did. Ranjit has a great sense of humor, and writes engaging prose. His dissertation was on economic growth, and he penned a funny, catchy opening sentence, which I clearly remember to this day: "Economic growth, like love,

14.3 Warren and Ann Fisher (2000 photo).

is not what it used to be." I made a remark in red on the margin of his manuscript: "Good beginning." The last I heard from him, he was teaching at Bridgewater State College in Massachusetts. He has published a fine book on microeconomics.

Ki Hoon Kim and Ali Zamouri have sent me Christmas cards for decades, though without personal messages.

As a young teacher, remembering names and matching names with faces were not that difficult, even though 50–70 new names would come on the scene every year. As time went by, it took increasingly longer for me to remember names and connect each name to a face. One time, at the start of a new academic year at UConn, I told the new graduate students that "I would need about three weeks to connect your names to your faces." Then I was somehow inspired to add an explanation: "Because all Americans look alike!" The whole class laughed, because I just turned the common saying "All Chinese look alike!" on its head.

Having stumbled on this "joke," I tried it on the new class the following year. But, to my surprise, not many people laughed. "Why?" I wondered. Did I lose my comic touch? I thought not. Most likely, the old students had already broadcast my joke to the new crop of students, so the joke was no longer fresh. I learned from this experience, that a performer—which a professor is, or should be—must not rely on material that has become stale.

Thinking back about this joke now, something somewhat scary occurred to me. I was lucky in that my class awarded me with a laugh. But nowadays, with intensified racial sensitivity, some adherents of "political correctness" might very well have protested and accused me of making a derogatory remark against "all Americans." What kind of penalty would then have been leveled against me, for having made this feeble attempt at humor in class? I have always wondered how "political correctness" could have come into being, and won acceptance in society.

Beyond the Lectern

My affiliation with UConn led me into a side track. In 1968, I was appointed by Connecticut Governor Ella Grasso to the Board of Directors of the Connecticut Product Development Corporation (CPDC), for a six-year term 1968–1976, and again for 1976–1982. The position was a public service appointment without pay.

The corporation was established with public funds for a venture capital type of operation. It was meant to provide seed money for firms developing new products. For funding, these firms would agree to pay royalties to CPDC for their successful products. That work proved quite interesting, witnessing how human ingenuity could create so many new ideas for consumer products. It expanded my view of the production aspect of economics, besides providing an enjoyable diversion from academic work. But I had to resign in 1980, as more and more other activities crowded into my life, and made it difficult for me to attend board meetings held in Hartford.

15

Separate Ways

After a solid six-year span of togetherness, the Three Musketeers, now with their MA degrees in hand, finally faced the need to separate, to pursue their respective career paths. Before separation, however, we still shared a summer in New York City. Stephen Li was thee as a mere vacationer before returning to China in response to his father's call. George Hsu, on the other hand, was a bit more ambitious. He took a couple of summer course at Columbia University—perhaps as a shortcut to qualify as a "Columbia alumnus." Then he returned to China, too.

By the end of the summer in 1948, I was the lone Musketeer still remaining in the United States, a student at Columbia.

Whither Stephen?

The Bank of China in Shanghai, where Stephen worked before studying at Colorado, had a job waiting for him upon his return. A *protégé* of the chief of the Foreign Department there, he was destined for a promising banking career.

Since he and I were both fond of letter-writing, we kept up for years by mail, usually communicating in English. In those days, snail mail was the only way to go, and for economy, we always used low-cost Air Letters. An Air Letter consisted of a single sheet of blue paper that could be folded into the shape of an envelope with a built-in stamp. For full utilization of the paper, we left very little margins on every side, so each Air Letter we receive, filled with typewritten news, would provide much reading pleasure. Writing about romantic developments and other juicy topics, Stephen often penned quotable sentences. After many years, I warned him that "With my collection of the things you wrote in your letters, I can one day blackmail you by threatening to show them to your future wife!"

A little later, we involved George in our correspondence by starting a "circular letter" among us, also adding Kang Yao and Otis Shao to the circle. "A" would first write to "B"; and "B" would add his message and mail it to "C"; and "C" would add his message and mail it to "D," and so on.

After the Communists took over China, the Bank of China moved to Taiwan, and so did Stephen. One year, on the eve of the establishment of a stock exchange in Taiwan, the government there dispatched a group of officials and bankers to New York to observe the working of the New York Stock Exchange. Stephen, a member of that group, found time to look me up in New York. But his official duties demanded his full attention, and allowed only a most brief meeting with me.

After that, I only saw Stephen twice, once in Taipei and once in Hong Kong. In 1960, I took advantage of my first sabbatical from teaching at Denison University to bring Emily to meet my parents who had moved from Shanghai to Hong Kong in 1957. Naturally, Emily also took me to meet her parents in Taipei, Taiwan. While in Taipei, I paid a visit to Stephen and his wife Eileen, and we had long chats about the past, the present, and the future. He had attained a high post in the Foreign Department of the Bank of China, and had the use of an official car. I felt that his future was well-paved at the Bank of China. Afterward, however, I got word that he had left the bank to join a foreign enterprise, named Atlas, first working in Taipei, but later in Singapore, to manage a manufacturing subsidiary of the company. He never volunteered to tell me why he made the move, despite the closeness of our relationship. And I did not feel proper to pry. But I have a suspicion that his leaving might have been prompted by the fact that he was passed over for an important promotion that was rightly his.

I did not see him until 30-some years later. After retiring from the University of Connecticut, I accepted an invitation from Professor Y. Y. Kueh, Dean of the Faculty of Social Sciences at Lingnan College (now University) in Hong Kong to serve as a Visiting Professor in the fall of 1993. Since Hong Kong and Singapore are in close proximity, Stephen was kind enough to make a special trip from Singapore with his wife Eileen, to meet me and Emily in Hong Kong. We chatted to our hearts' content over lunches and dinners, some with mutual friends Kang Yao, and Henry Kuan and his wife Jane joining us.

Kang Yao, with an outstanding career at the British conglomerate Butterfield & Swire (now, Swire, 太古集團) maintained residences in Beijing, London, Washington, DC, Honolulu, as well as in Hong Kong. In Beijing, he visited George Hsu often, thus he could supply us with some details about George's sufferings during the years of the "Cultural Revolution," with extreme political turmoil there. But we of course also reminisced about happier matters in our youthful days. Photo 58 in the front of this book recorded the reunion with Stephen and Kang Yao in Hong Kong in 1993.

When Stephen and I said goodbye a few days later, we did it with the tacit understanding that we would probably never meet again in person. We promised each other to use the telephone often.

On the Phone

International calls used to be prohibitively expensive, and we habitually avoided them. But later, it had become eminently affordable, and we could talk at a leisurely pace with each other, taking pleasure in reliving parts of our earlier lives, including some silly and embarrassing things.

One incident involving "face saving" was a source of our merry reminiscence. We had already graduated from college the year after WWII ended, but were still living at our respective homes. So, free to spend our own earnings, we went night-clubbing a lot. One summer night, we took some girls dancing, including one of Stephen's sisters, Dora, and we all ordered Coca-Cola, a fashionable drink that gained popularity in Shanghai at the end of WWII. Not so expensive in its native country, Coca Cola, with its "imported" status, commanded a much loftier price in Shanghai. When sold in a night club, the price would naturally be further elevated a few notches.

We had a group of six or eight, and after a few rounds of Coca Cola, we sensed the rapid buildup of our bill. So, one of us boys said, casually, "I am tired of drinking the same thing. Coca Cola is too sweet anyway. Maybe we can order iced water instead." Everybody thought that was a good idea, and I told the waiter to bring us iced water. The waiter's response was shocking, to say the least. He said, "Iced water is same charge as Coca Cola." I was going to protest to the waiter, but before I could open my mouth, Stephen, not wanting to "lose face" in front of the girls, abruptly jumped in with a nonchalant "Of course, of course!" As a result, all of us young fools ended up drinking iced water at the price of Coca Cola! Sensing that Stephen might have a cash-flow problem, his wise sister Dora stealthily handed some money to him under the table. From then on, the words "Of course, of course!" became our tease phrase for Stephen, the eager "face-saver." Dora later married Freddie Chang (張甫楠), another classmate of the Class of 1943 of St. John's Middle School.

15.1 Stephen and Eileen Li (on the right, with a grandchild), and Dora and her husband Freddie Chang, Shanghai, 2000.

In another incident involving a dance we recalled together, I performed a gentlemanly act of self-sacrifice, only to be rewarded with mocking comments instead of gratitude. While in Colorado, one weekend The Three Musketeers and another boy arranged a dinner dance in a night club in Denver. We invited Luciana Fan (范國瑾), a student at Loretto Heights College, and asked her to bring three of her schoolmates to our little gathering. Luciana, who earlier went to the Loretto High School in Shanghai, run by a group of American nuns, speaks more fluent English than any other Chinese student, and her outgoing personality made her an object of admiration among the boys. We first met her in the family of Gladys and Yale Parce in Denver. A most warm-hearted couple, the Parces opened their home in Denver to all the Chinese students studying in the various colleges in Colorado in that era.

For our party, we had secret hopes that Luciana would bring three lovely, pleasant young ladies like herself. Not so. One of them, Carey, from Cuba, did meet our expectations: good-looking with soft hair in curls, a good dancer with natural rhythm, and speaking English with a Spanish accent that sounded sweet and charming. And Violet from Hawaii was also positively received by us. But Luciana was evidently out of her mind to invite the heavyset Agnes along, too. From Guam, she could hardly communicate in English, and her dancing was awkward. As might be expected, everybody attempted to dance with Luciana, Carey, or Violet, leaving poor Agnes alone. Thinking chivalrously, I decided to be a gentleman by giving polite, if reluctant, attention to her. Receiving no conversational or dancing enjoyment to speak of, I felt that the evening was interminably long. When the party was over, the relief was commensurably great. Even though I did not expect an outpour of gratitude from the other boys who had a good time, I thought some simple words of appreciation would certainly be in order. But the boys said nothing at all. And Stephen even came up with this beauty: "Alpha, you should be grateful to us. Seeing that you like Agnes so much, we allowed you to monopolize her the whole evening!".

15.2 Luciana and Violet (1948 photo).

Stephen still remembered what happened that night in Denver. I thought my retelling of this story, almost half a century later, could conjure up some remorse in him and even elicit a belated apology from him. No such luck.

Luciana later married Arthur Young (楊漢華), a son of General Sen Yang (楊森). (The name Yang is re-transliterated to Young.) And they both became our friends. Emily and I had visited them in Michigan and California, and they had visited us in Connecticut.

Goody

On the phone, after so many years, Stephen asked me about Goody, the American-born Chinese girl I dated while in Colorado. We never talked about her before, but now he belatedly became curious. "With our tight schedule to finish the MA in nine months," he asked, "why did you burden yourself with a romantic episode?"

"For that," I explained, "I must 'blame' Mrs. Kiang, my professor in American Literature at St. John's University." I admired her as a great teacher, and she liked me as a diligent student. She used to delight me by taking time to chat with me after class. But what really captivated me was her graceful walk! It was so classy, almost royal, and eye-catching, even alluring. Yes, the way she walked was so exquisite that I fell in love with it. And since Mrs. Kiang was an American-born Chinese lady from Hawaii, I somehow subconsciously transferred my admiration for her walk to a blind admiration for American-born Chinese ladies. Then I met Goody in Boulder. She impressed me as a lovely, kind young lady, and I enjoyed being with her.

In reality, though, Goody and I were too different in our backgrounds to suit each other. I was not sufficiently Americanized for her taste. And she was too ignorant of China for mine. Quite naturally, the end of the academic year marked the end of our relationship, amicably.

I did learn a lot from Goody, though. She gave me a better understanding of some basic American customs. More importantly, from her habitual use of the sentence "Everything happens for the best!" I learned to look at things with a more positive attitude. Whenever facing a setback, I now always tell myself: Things could have been worse; do not waste time regretting; accept what happened as the best possible scenario under the circumstances, and be thankful for it. I have Goody to thank for this healthy attitude.

And What about George?

Like Stephen Li, George Hsu returned to his old job in Shanghai. The China National Aviation Corporation (CNAC) seemed to have big things planned for him. They successively sent him to its offices in Taiwan, Canton, and Hong Kong, to broaden his understanding of the inner workings of the organization. But when there was a movement among the personnel to declare their allegiance to the new mainland government in China, he decided to join them. After that, we lost touch with each other. Communications from the United States would cause political problems for the recipients of mail or phone messages in China, and I must cautiously cut off all contacts with him.

Nevertheless, I learned indirectly that he achieved a lot in the aviation field and, after some years, rose to the position of Deputy Director of the Civil Aviation Administration of China (CAAC), International Departure. Obviously, he had moved from an airline to a government agency. Unfortunately, he was unable to escape the misfortune brought to many by the Cultural Revolution. He was humiliated, demoted, and he also suffered in other ways. Later, however, he was rehabilitated, and was sent to more than 20 countries to negotiate air transportation treaties, on account of his command of the English language.

A Familiar Voice from the Past

In May of 1980, there came on the phone a voice that I had not heard for more than 30 years: "Alpha, this is Keji (George's Chinese name). I am in New York, and would like to see you." I was stunned. "George, what brought you to New York? And how did you know my phone number in Connecticut?" I noticed that he identified himself using his Chinese name, because in China it was no longer politically correct to use his English name; but I still followed the old habit of calling him George.

He explained to me that he had been sent to New York as a member of a delegation to negotiate with Pam Am the opening of new air lines between the United States and China. As a guest of Pan Am, he was staying in the Barclay Hotel in Manhattan. He found out my phone number from Kang Yao whom he saw briefly in Hong Kong on the way over.

It was only a three-hour trip from my Connecticut home to Manhattan. Since Emily never met him before, she would not notice the change in him, but for me, he looked like an entirely different person. Languid and white-haired, his appearance spoke volumes about the life he had lived since we separated from each other. I was going to ask him about the happenings of the past decades, but decided not to touch on such topics.

Among other things, I thought of the incident that happened when the ship carrying us to the United States crossed the International Date

Line. In a private ceremony, to which I was invited as a sole "witness," he deliberately threw a handkerchief and a photo of Dora into the Pacific Ocean. I thought he would give a sigh, or a smile, or a laugh when I brought up that incident. To my surprise, he showed little emotion, and, staring blankly at me, he just said, "I don't have any memory of it." I could not believe that he would forget such a significant episode in his youth. This symptom of his deterioration saddened me no end.

George played an important part in international airline negotiations. But the government was very tight-budgeted at the time, and gave him an allowance of only one U.S. dollar per day. Still, he would save his allowance and purchase an inexpensive gift for his wife or his brother after every mission.

From that time on, I tried to chat with him on the phone, too. But he was not in the same league as a conversationalist as Stephen. And, since he was living in Beijing, I had to be more careful about what to talk about with him. Moreover, as a result of multiple unsuccessful operations on his neck and spine, he became very reticent after becoming paralyzed and wheel-chair-bound since 1986.

Reunion in Beijing

Another 20 years later, when Emily and I took our children Darryl and Tracey on a tour of China, with Beijing as our first stop, we of course planned to pay George a visit. Our mutual classmate Kang Yao, then in Beijing but about to return to Hong Kong, was kind enough to postpone his flight by one day, so that he could meet me and accompany me to visit George. That was most helpful, because George had a difficult-to-find address, but Kang Yao's chauffeur knew how to get there quickly.

Upon saying hello to George in his wheelchair, we learned that his wife, our hostess, was in the hospital. Thus, we had to ask Kang Yao's chauffeur to take us to the hospital to meet our absentee hostess. Then we had dinner with George at his home. He was not very talkative, and I was careful not to bring up touchy subjects. I guess we were each thinking of things we did together when we were young, but reluctant to speak out face to face. See Photo 63 in the front of this book, taken

15.3 George HSu and his wife Wen Gengxin (1999 photo).

in Beijing at his home in 2001. Here is an earlier picture of him, with his wife Wen Gengxin (温耕莘) that he sent me in 1999.

When he passed away in July, 2011, our old trio automatically reached its end.

Return to Sender

I still talked to Stephen on the phone after George was gone.

For one thing, in writing this chapter of my memoirs, I needed the name the foreign enterprise Stephen left the Bank of China to work for. I am sure that name contains the word Atlas, but cannot recall the rest. There is no way to check my correspondence files because they were all lost during my downsizing moves after retirement. I called Stephen in Singapore to check. Unfortunately, his disappointing answer was, "I am sorry, Alpha; I no longer remember."

Later, I found him to be much less fluent with words. And conversations became difficult because, with his deteriorating sense of hearing, I had to repeat every sentence several times in slow motion.

I have always sent him my annual Christmas–New-Year greetings, with a personal letter. The last one, for 2018, came back to me from Singapore in April 2019, marked "return to sender, unable to forward."

16

Dutch Treat

I met Ad Pikkemaat, a Dutch economist, in the academic year 1963–1964 at Yale University in New Haven, Connecticut. For two semesters, he and I shared an office at the Cowles Foundation for Research in Economics at Yale, where he was a visiting scholar from the Netherlands (or, less formally, Holland), and I, a National Science Foundation Fellow.

Even though we were each busy with our own study projects, there were lots of opportunities, during lunch or study breaks, to chat about a large variety of topics. Often, we compared the Dutch culture and the Chinese, and also with the American, learning interesting things from each other.

One time, the term "Dutch treat" came up in our conversation and, quite naturally, I asked him about the origin of this phrase, or the related phrase, "go Dutch." To my surprise, he said, "I have never heard of these terms, what do they mean?" After I explained to him that "Dutch treat" refers to a situation where a group of friends go out for dinner or for some other event, and share the expenses, he laughed and said, "Oh, we do that in the Netherlands, too. Only, we call it an American Party!" I found this comment tremendously hilarious! It's a two-way name-calling.

At the end of the academic year, we parted as "old friends." I gave him as a parting gift a cylindrical wooden paper weight with the word "Yale" on top. And he gave me a square crystal paper weight with a map of the Netherlands carved out in its bottom, which has graced my desk ever since. "Come to Holland to see me" were his parting words.

We kept in touch via Christmas messages. But I did not get to see him again until a lapse of 25 years. In the fall semester of 1989, I took a group of undergraduate students from the University of Connecticut to Holland, on a Study Abroad Program. Emily and I spent the semester at Limburg University in the picturesque city of Maastricht, located at the southern tip of the country. Living in Holland for four months brought to life the map encased in the crystal paper weight that Ad gave to me. We enjoyed immensely our exposure to the Dutch culture, and the friendly—really friendly—Dutch people.

Taking advantage of our stay in Maastricht, we toured many places in Holland as well as in other parts of Europe. Among these was a train ride on November 11, 1989, to Amsterdam up north, specifically to look up Ad Pikkemaat and his wife Diny, who lived near that big city. After a quarter of a century, the reunion yielded great nostalgic pleasure. We took a long walk on the streets of Amsterdam, reminisced about our Yale days, caught up with what we were working on professionally, visited some tourist attractions, and had dinner together.

16.1 With Ad and Diny Pikkemaat in Amsterdam, 1989.

When the dinner ended, I tried to grab the check, but Ad insisted on playing host. He did not even allow me to chip in, claiming Amsterdam to be "his territory." In other words, he also forbade an "American party" to occur. Nonetheless, he was powerless to prevent this dinner from being a "Dutch treat" for Emily and me. How else would you call a treat by our Dutch friend, in the land of the Dutch itself?

If Ad ever came to the Greater New York Area again, I would definitely plan to take him to dinner. It would be an American dinner, but not an "American party," because I should also have the right to host it in "my territory."

17

Fundamental Methods of Mathematical Economics

There were two sources of frustration for me at Columbia University. One was the inaccessibility of professors, who, because of their research or consulting activities, kept only a couple of hours of office per week. Students had to queue up to see them, and the usual long lines outside pressured students to limit their visits to the briefest. One time, I was in the office of Professor Frederick Mills for only two minutes, just to point out a typo in the book on statistics he wrote. My sessions with Professor William Vickrey, who supervised my dissertation, were naturally much longer. One time, he even took me to lunch at the Faculty Club. Still, my mind was never free from the pressure of time constraint. But I became resigned to this fact, figuring that a similar situation probably prevailed at all big universities. As a result, I developed an attitude of self-reliance and the goal of self-sufficiency in my studies.

The other source of frustration at Columbia, a more grave one, was the lack of mathematics course(s) to prepare the graduate students in economics to tackle the professional economics journal articles that had become increasingly more mathematical. I often found myself in the unenviable position of being able to read only the "introduction" and the "conclusion" of the article, but not the mathematical analysis in the body of the paper. And that was not only true for one or two articles, but was true for most articles assigned to us. And I suspect that I was not the only one facing this frustration. The option of taking courses in the mathematics department was not open to me; I could not afford the time and expenses. I became more and more resolved to launch a serious study of mathematics on my own.

Preparations

Following the good advice of Professor Leland Gordon, my Chairman at Denison University on my first full-time teaching job, I spent all the summer months on self-study. Learning from mathematics books on my own proved to be much more difficult than I anticipated. Mathematicians as a group seem to me to be overly stingy with words. If a clear explanation of an idea should require 11 words, they would try to use 7. The saving of a few words often introduces a measure of ambiguity into the writing, making it necessary for the reader to wonder and guess what the author meant to say. On many occasions, when encountering a brevity-induced ambiguity, I would first try to figure out the exact meaning of the book statement, and then, to satisfy myself, rewrite the statement for greater clarity. Usually, this involved not much more than adding a few key words. Why save those words?

The phrase in mathematics books that annoyed me the most is: "It is obvious that . . ." Such a phrase is usually only a lame justification for the author to skip a few steps in the explanation. In one story (or joke) I heard, a well-known mathematician paused at one point of his lecture after saying, "It is obvious that . . .," then turned to the blackboard, and mumbled, ". . . just a minute." Then, ignoring the class, he did a series of calculations by himself for 20 minutes, then turned around and continued with a smile of satisfaction: "Yes, it IS obvious!"

The over-conciseness of mathematics books is not alone to blame for the existence of math phobia. Some teachers also do a good job of fear inducement. I only need to cite one example. My son's teacher in the "advanced placement" course of calculus in high school did not explain the subject, but just projected transparencies on a screen, and read from them word by word without any elaboration. How could the student learn anything this way? The night before the final examination, my panic-filled son asked me for help, and I was able to rescue him by giving him a two-hour tutorial. He landed with an A– for the course, the highest in the class, but emphatically said to me afterward, "I'll never take any mathematics class again!" His teacher was an abominable culprit!

It has been said that "Teaching is the best way to learn." I soon offered a seminar on mathematical economics to some seniors at Denison, and learned from discussions with them. The most important thing I learned in such seminars, however, was something negative: No books then available fulfilled my needs. None had a comprehensive coverage that I deemed desirable, and none integrated mathematics with economics in a satisfactory manner.

Gradually, a seed began to sprout in my mind about how an ideal book in this field should be structured. It should integrate various basic branches of mathematics (matrix algebra, differential calculus, integral calculus, differential equations, and difference equations), with the several general categories of economic analysis (statics, comparative statics, and dynamics). The projected book should offer clear, step-by-step explanations of all mathematical concepts, never assuming anything to be "obvious." I then vowed to try to write such a book, with a mission to convince the reader that mathematics is eminently learnable, and whatever fear of mathematics one may have previously acquired is conquerable.

These thoughts became further solidified during my year at Yale.

The State-of-the-Art Writing Instrument

The book project got a quiet but vigorous start as soon as I joined the faculty of the University of Connecticut (UConn). In an ambitious plan, I decided to follow my long-ready outline of the book, and write enough material every week for three hours of lectures in a new math-econ course. To execute such a schedule, I willingly gave up many of my hobbies: no more football game watching on TV, which I enjoyed while living in Ohio, very much a football state, what with Ohio State University's "Buckeyes" and the professional team Cleveland Browns; definitely no more weekend movies, either; in fact, no more evening entertainment of any kind. I became a writing robot.

For time-saving, I asked the Department Head, Professor Philip Taylor, to exempt me from all departmental meetings and committee assignments during my first year. He graciously agreed. That gave me more relief than the mere saving of time; I was also spared the drudgery of having to listen to often-trivial discussions about mundane matters in those meetings.

More importantly for me, the university approved my requisition of an IBM Selectric typewriter, the state-of-the-art writing instrument of that era before the advent of word processors. The revolutionary feature of that electric typewriter was the use of interchangeable font balls that rotate to different angles during typing to strike different keys onto the paper. One ball has its font in roman; it comes in your choice of Times Roman, or Courier, and so on. Another one carries italics, and another one is for bold letters, and there is even one for Greek letters and mathematical symbols (square root, braces, vertical line, superscripts, subscripts, etc.) for mathematical texts. The IBM salesman who came to my office to demonstrate the machine made an interesting suggestion: "Dr. Chiang, be sure to get a RED one." When I hesitated, and said, "A RED typewriter? Wouldn't that be sort of gaudy?" He quickly replied, "Not at all. You'll love it. You have to live a little!"

My red IBM Selectric became the envy of my colleagues. I wrote the entire book on that typewriter, and Emily typed the final manuscript on it, too, around 800 pages of double-spaced texts. The mathematical nature of the manuscript required her to go over every single page twice. The first time around, she took care to leave the Greek letters and mathematical symbols blank, then after the regular text was done, switched to the special ball to fill up those blank spaces. I proudly display my red IBM Selectric in Photo 29 in the front of this book.

Emily made an even more valuable contribution. As she typed, she carefully screened my writing for vague expressions and incomplete explanations. Neither an economist nor a mathematician, she read the text purely from a layman's point of view, looking for statements lacking lucidity or completeness. Whenever she felt that my words did not quite do the job, she would issue a verdict of "Rewrite." I lost count of the number of times I received such a verdict.

A natural thing for an author to do is to think of the quest for a publisher. But I was too busy writing to worry about that. It was a publisher, McGraw-Hill, that actually sought me out, when a book salesman, John Maloney, saw me typing on my red typewriter, and casually asked me, "Is that a textbook you are working on?" I said yes, and explained to him my ideas about what a good textbook should be like. That impressed him enough to set in motion a series of explorations, and a request for my sample chapters. I also contacted Holt, Rinehart & Winston, which earlier published my workbook. In April of 1965, within a few days, Seib Adams, Editor at Holt, Rinehart and Winston came to Storrs with a book contract, and so did Dick Fenton, Editor at McGraw-Hill. I went with McGraw-Hill.

As promised to the publisher, I completed the entire manuscript in exactly two years. Those were two years with no breaks, no rest, in complete isolation from all worldly recreation. It took more perseverance than I thought I could muster at the age of 37–38. As a first in McGraw-Hill history, an author submitted a final manuscript one day before the promised deadline. My deadline was August 31, 1966, and I mailed it in on August 30, 1966—around 800 pages of text plus about 100 sketches for graphs.

Two days after the manuscript was dispatched, Emily and I merrily drove to Ithaca, New York, to start my visiting professorship at Cornell. As soon as we settled in the rented house in Ithaca, however, we took a well-deserved vacation in Bermuda, staying for a week at the Carleton Beach Hotel. Even for us non-water sports people, we enjoyed the hotel's lovely private bay and beach, to celebrate not only the completion of the book, but also our 12th wedding anniversary on September 4.

The Reception

The book, titled *Fundamental Methods of Mathematical Economics*, met with an extra-warm reception after coming off press in the fall of 1967. Many appreciative letters—fan mails—came to me from professors and students at many other schools all over the nation. Most of them were in English, and I derived a lot of consolation from them for the hard work I had put in. One letter from France, written in French, was beyond my French reading ability, and I had to ask a colleague to translate it for me verbally. Fortunately, the content was laudatory; otherwise, it would have been embarrassing. One letter from India referred to me as a "guru." I always thought the term "guru" means a spiritual advisor, unrelated to economics. But who was I to argue about that title?

Some specific comments proved to me that certain efforts I made were not in vain. One reader reported that he found it very "comfortable" to read my book. He showed astuteness. From my own experience, mathematics books that crowd too much material onto every page, especially a lot of symbols and equations, tend to tire the readers even before they peruse the contents. So, I specifically suggested to the book designer to leave enough line space between adjacent rows, to produce an "airy" look on the page. Similarly, I asked the book designer to leave plenty of margin near the spine of the book, for the same "airy" effect.

But no fan mail ever showed that anyone noticed another effort I made to make the book "comfortable" to read. This had to do with the choice of economic illustrations of the mathematical methods. I tried hard to select only economic examples that utilize the mathematics just discussed or already learned before, but not the methods not yet taught. This sounded easy to do, but was in fact very hard to accomplish. Most articles in economics journals employ a whole range of mathematical methods, which extends beyond the stage of mathematical coverage at a particular point of my book. Even though my effort was too subtle to be easily appreciated, I was glad that I spent the efforts.

Another feature I had spent special effort on was the Index section at the end of the volume. Some authors hire professional index preparers to do the job. Often, however, such index people fail to list important concepts and terms, because of their unfamiliarity with the subject of the book. I did the indexing myself, and made sure of adequate cross-referencing.

Some readers found comfort in the positive reinforcement from the exercise problems. I tried to make the problems difficult enough to be mildly challenging, but easy enough to be eminently manageable. My hope was to let the students enjoy the sense of accomplishment and confidence through the successful solution of all the problems, not the feeling of discouragement that might lead to a desire to give up. I chose not to supply the answers to the exercise problems at the end of the book, but in response to popular demand, I included the answers to selected problems in the third edition.

A Replica

My friend and fellow economist, John Fei, returned from a trip to Taiwan in late 1967, and surprised me with a present. "Why a gift?" I said. He gave me a mysterious smile, and said, "Just open the package and see." I tore away the wrapping, expecting some native Taiwan snack items. But what I found was a book that looked exactly like the one I just published, only slightly smaller in size and printed on inferior paper. It had the same cover design with my name on it. I had to utter a surprised "Oh my goodness!" It was a copy of the pirate edition of my *Fundamental Methods of Mathematical Economics*!

Taiwan was not a signatory of international copyright treaties, and it reproduced pirate editions of foreign books at will, cheaply, and with great speed. This replica appeared only a couple of months after my original came off press in the fall of 1967. I asked John how much he paid for it. The figure he quoted was ridiculously low. His answer gave me mixed feelings. Copyright needs to be protected, because it is costly for a publisher to produce a book. But, it might be a worthwhile thing to make an inexpensive version available to students who could ill afford to pay for the original. I learned later that McGraw-Hill does produce an International Student Edition (ISE) of textbooks they publish, as a paperback for sale at a low price in Europe and Asia. The hardcover version is available to the latter areas, too, but it is primarily aimed at the American and Canadian markets.

My Name as a Verb?

From the book-adoption list McGraw-Hill shared with me, I noted that my book was used in class at all sorts of colleges and universities, ranging from top-ranked Ivy-League schools to colleges I had never heard of. I was glad that my publisher showed enough interest in me to show me those data. But, unlike a textbook at the *Principles of Economics* level, my book had a relatively limited market at the junior–senior or beginning graduate level. Later, the news that the top universities all list my book as a prerequisite to entrance into their graduate programs in economics was the most gratifying aspect of this book.

One day, a group of four or five students from another college came to UConn for a visit, and they made it a point to come to my office to meet me. "We are here to tell you that we like your book very much for its clear and patient explanations," one of them spoke for the group, "but our professor is tricky; he assigns a different book that's hard to understand, then lectures straight out of your book." I could not believe that a professor would do such a thing, so I asked them how they happened to find out about this trickery. "Oh, we saw him reading your book in his office. So, we got your book, and follow the material there, as he does. We call this 'Chiang-ing it'!"

That was the first time, and only time, I heard my family name "Chiang" used as a verb. I felt honored, even though the honor was very local in scope.

My Worst Competitor

Only a couple of years after publication of the first edition, McGraw-Hill wanted me to write a second edition. A new "edition" is not the same thing as a new "printing." A printing of a book is a batch of so many copies printed at one time. After a particular printing has been sold out, a new printing can be ordered either with no changes in the text material, or with some minor changes such as corrections of typographical errors. But a new edition implies substantial rewriting with extra material added. Since I did not feel the need to rewrite something that basically remained satisfactory, I of course declined.

"Do you want a new edition because we need to fight against a serious competitor?" I asked the editor. "Well, your book is still the leading text in the field, but it does face a serious competitor." "What's my competitor's name?" I grew curious. "It's Alpha Chiang; it may sound strange, but you are your own worst competitor." Could that be true?

It turned out that the used copies of my book were competing with the new copies. Students sell their textbooks for a nominal sum to used-book dealers in May or June, and the used-book dealers will sell them in college book stores in the fall at a price somewhat lower than new books, but still for a huge profit. Publishers will therefore ask their authors to "revise" their books, not necessarily to an extensive extent, but with a little bit added here and there, so as to make the older edition obsolete. Killing the used-book market is thus the principal purpose of new editions.

Even after becoming aware of the need for revision, I did not publish the second edition until seven years later, in 1974. And the third edition had to wait another 10 years before its birth. Each new edition of mine did feature substantial changes rather than window dressings. Frequent revisions might mean greater financial gains, but they also entail a lot of work, aside from the consideration of professional ethics.

Cover Designs

The cover design varied from edition to edition. I especially like the cover of the third edition, by Carla Bauer, which elicited many favorable comments. It features an abstract drawing of an abacus with multiple columns of beads. Its light blue color on white background presents a simple, neat, picture of the Chinese calculating device dating from antiquity. I really loved the original sketch of it, except for a major inaccuracy in the drawing regarding the number of beads. In the real Chinese abacus, each column contains seven beads, two in the upper section and five in the lower. When the Japanese adapted it for their use, they economized and took away one bead from each section, leaving a one-to-four configuration instead of the two-to-five original. What the designer drew at first was an abacus with one bead in the upper section, and five in the lower, making it neither Chinese nor Japanese. At my insistence, she reluctantly redrew it in the correct Chinese version. But I neglected to tell her that traditionally there should be an odd number of columns. Her new drawing showed eight columns. Since this remaining error was due to my own negligence, I did not request her to redo it again. Charge it to "artistic license." Besides, only the very meticulous will count the columns and declare: "Hey, this is unauthentic!"

On the third edition cover, I also introduced an innovation. I asked the designer to include a seal (or chop) of mine showing my Chinese name. This will provide an official linkage between the author's name, Alpha C. Chiang, and my given Chinese name 蔣中一.

I show in Photo 30 in the front of this book the cover design of the third edition of *Fundamental Methods of Mathematical Economics*, with the abacus motif, and with my chop in red near the bottom. In the same photo is the cover of my later book, *Elements of Dynamic Optimization* (McGraw-Hill, 1992, later taken over by Waveland Press), also with an abacus-motif design by John Hite, and my name chop in red at the bottom.

Translations

The ISE is not the only means for readers outside of the United States and Canada to gain access to my work. There have been many translations into foreign languages. Even though the translations bear my name, I actually played no direct part in their preparation and production. For the authorized ones—yes, there are unauthorized ones as well—McGraw-Hill contracted the translators and designers. I was notified about each translation project and received a few copies upon its publication. Since I was not versed in most of the language involved, I could only treat them as souvenirs.

In later years, McGraw-Hill stopped notifying me about new translations, let alone sending me copies. The ones I do have on my bookshelf are Spanish, Italian, Japanese, Chinese (traditional font) and Chinese (simplified font), Korean, Indonesian, Portuguese, Polish, Turkish, and Croatian. I heard of others, but have not seen them.

Photo 31 in the front of this book shows a view of my books in various editions, with their foreign language editions (not complete).

Who's Who

Many of my friends had the misconception that the popularity of my textbook made me wealthy. I only wish. The market for this book is limited to upper classes. Hence, even "big" sales are in fact quite small. Besides, I have been my worst competitor. So, the book has not made me wealthy.

But *Fundamental Methods of Mathematical Economics* did give me name recognition. One form of this is the listing of my name in *Who's Who in Economics: A Biographical Dictionary of Major Economists 1700-1986*, second edition, edited by Mark Blaug, The MIT Press, 1986.

The words "Major Economists 1700-1986" in the subtitle made this listing quite prestigious. I appreciated this honor, but, no way could I qualify as a "major economist" on the basis of the journal articles and books I had written! I may have made some contribution to economics education, but not much to economics as such. However, that biographical dictionary had an established formula for inclusion, namely, the frequency an author's work has been cited in other economists' writings. Hence, even though my listing represented a gross overevaluation of my contribution, I was in no position to negate it. It made me feel easier when the next edition of this biographical dictionary came out under the more modest title *Who's Who in Economics*, third edition, edited by Mark Blaug, Edward Elgar, 1999.

Dicky from the Class of 1943

Dicky—Richard Cheng (鄭賢永)—a classmate at St. John's Middle School in Shanghai, was a soccer star in school, not too fond of books. On the other hand, as a bookworm, I was not at all into sports. But somehow, he used to visit my dorm room, and we even made home visits to each other back in Shanghai. There was no easy explanation for the bond between us. In fact, after I came to the United States to study, we lost contact with each other altogether.

For this reason, when he called me at Connecticut out of the blue, circa 1970, more than 20 years after we last met, it was a great pleasant surprise.

"Where are you, Dicky? And how did you find out where I am?" I asked him. "Oh, I came to San Francisco to set up a branch office for the Shanghai Commercial Bank," he said, "and I found out you are in Connecticut, because the professor teaching the evening class I am taking told me that I must read the book by Alpha Chiang. When I heard your name mentioned, I couldn't believe it. I told my professor that Alpha Chiang and I were classmates in high school!"

I was so pleased that my book had unexpectedly served as a bridge to reconnect two old friends. In fact, even more friends of the Class of 1943 became reconnected, because Dicky and his wife Deanna (舒甸娜) were instrumental in arranging a reunion of those of us residing in the United States. That reunion, held in San Francisco in July 1973, was attended by eight classmates and families. In view of its success, this first reunion was followed by subsequent ones in Los Angeles (1978 and 1983), Honolulu (1986), Vancouver (1988), Los Angeles (1993), Las Vegas (1998), followed by cruises in Alaska (2000), Mexico (2002), and Hawaii (2004)—arranged and hosted by various classmates and their respective spouses.

Dicky's family is shown in Photo 40.

Another Kind of "Replica"

The pirate edition is a literal replica—a photocopy. But is a plagiarized version a replica, or a pseudo-replica?

A few years after my book came off press, McGraw-Hill received a new manuscript submission in the math-econ field. An economics professor who reviewed that manuscript for McGraw-Hill reported that it was just a "paraphrasing of Chiang." The strange thing is that the author would send it to McGraw-Hill, my publisher, instead of some other competing company. McGraw-Hill's reply to that author was diplomatically worded: Write a book with your own personality.

When my UConn colleague Dennis Heffley reported to me in 1985 what he suspected to be a case of plagiarism of my book, it was not a manuscript, but a book in print that he brought back from Great Britain. At his urging, I checked the book out, and was distressed to find that in many places it read just like mine. The organization was same, the graphs were the same, and many paragraphs were word-for-word transplants from my book. Flabbergasted by such a "replica," I pondered what I should do about it, when I discovered to my dismay that this book was published by McGraw-Hill, UK, a sister company of my own publisher. With any other publisher, I could just refer the matter to McGraw-Hill, and let their legal department handle it. But McGraw-Hill, UK and McGraw-Hill in this country are siblings or cousins. They were unlikely to fight against each other.

Taking the advice of some fellow members of the Storrs Community Church, I asked Gerald Garfield, Esq., at the law firm Day, Berry, Howard in Hartford to advise me. He warned me that the case was not hopeful. First, plagiarism is difficult to prove; second, the situation is McGraw-Hill against itself; third, it is almost impossible to estimate the financial damage caused by the replica book on mine.

Nevertheless, I made a detailed cross-referencing exhibit of the "sameness" found in the two books, including the table of contents and the word-for-word paragraphs. But the professor of Columbia whom McGraw-Hill hired to referee the case would not come out with a definitive verdict of plagiarism. Even though Gerry and I made a special trip to New York in December, 1985, to negotiate with the McGraw-Hill lawyers, in the end we only got a nominal monetary settlement for damage, plus a promise that there would be no more printing of the UK book.

I thought of reporting this plagiarizer to the university where he was teaching, but I decided not to. I chose to "forgive those who trespass against us."

A Chance Encounter at the Hibachi

Except for big birthdays, like the 80th, I tended not to celebrate birthdays seriously, not any more than to have a dinner out. In 2011, yielding to the lure of a discount coupon that arrived in the mail, I took Emily to a birthday dinner at a newly opened Japanese restaurant, called Banzai, in Hartsdale, New York, not far from White Plains where I resided soon after retirement. It turned out that the restaurant was Chinese-owned, and the chef who cooked for us at the hibachi and entertained us with tossed knives and flying condiment containers while cooking, was also a Chinese.

Soon, a couple with a young daughter joined us at the same hibachi, and the gentleman and I had a peasant chat. His name is Yawah Shah, and he came to the United States as a student as I did. Though poor, he was able to complete a Harvard degree, plus a Harvard MBA, and his wife has a Harvard PhD. "I am a banker," he added. When I told him my name, he gazed at me and asked, "Have you written a book on mathematical economics?" I answered, "Yes." Then he smiled graciously, and said, "That's a book my professor highly recommended. I am very glad to meet you, the author." I smiled back, and told him that I was happy to have his family as my dining companions on my birthday.

At the end of the meal, I was surprised to see him take out a discount coupon just like mine. Oh, the alluring power of discounts! After he had settled his payment, I asked the waitress for my check, but she said, "No check for you. That gentleman already paid for your dinner." People do sometimes have "uninvited guests," but what I had was an "impromptu host" instead. What an amazing "side effect" from my writing.

I thanked him, of course. But we never met again. Out of curiosity, I googled my impromptu host, and discovered that he is no ordinary banker, but holds several high titles at Citi.

The Son of *Fundamental Methods*

I wanted to include the topic of dynamic optimization in the book, but it would make the book too bulky. Therefore, I chose the alternative of making it the subject of a separate book. It would be a sequel volume, written in the same style. Jokingly, I referred to it in private as "the son of *Fundamental Methods*."

Unlike the first book, which I wrote in earnest day and night in two years, the "son" volume was written over a long period of time.

Meantime, word processing on computer had made its way into our lives, and there was even special software to handle manuscripts with mathematical symbols and equations in them. I vaguely remember that the name of the software I bought was "TechWriter." It took me some time to learn it, and even longer for me to teach it to Emily, who again "volunteered" to type the final manuscript. Emily's antipathy toward the computer in general, and the technical software in particular, made the situation quite difficult. It even inspired me to draw a Christmas-card cartoon showing a computer "mouse" saying "hi" to Emily while she was trying to run away.

At any rate, the sequel volume came out with the title *Elements of Dynamic Optimization* in 1992, on the eve of my retirement. While *Fundamental Methods of Mathematical Economics* was dedicated to Emily (later to Emily, Darryl, and Tracey), I dedicated *Elements of Dynamic Optimization* to my dear parents.

McGraw-Hill was the publisher, and the cover designer, John Hite, again used the cover designer, John Hite, again used the abacus as the background at my request. And, again, a chop with my Chinese name adorned the front of the cover and on the spine (see Photo 30). But the small size of the market made McGraw-Hill decide to stop printing it. The manner in which they did it was rude: I did not know about it until The Waveland Press, Inc., in Illinois, notified me that they have taken over this book from McGraw-Hill in 1999.

17.1 The computer mouse and Emily! (A cartoon from my 1990 Christmas card).

The Fourth Edition

I was already about halfway on the revision work for the fourth edition, following my retirement and move from Connecticut to White Plains, New York, but had to proceed at a slow pace in view of my advancing age. Besides, I had become even more meticulous about my objective of lucid writing. But Lucille Sutton, my editor at McGraw-Hill, became extremely impatient with my progress and seemed to be interested only in tight deadlines. Unlike my previous editors Dick Fenton, Jack Crutchfield, Gail Gavert, and Scott Stratford, who all maintained cordial editor–author relationship with me, Lucille Sutton was all business. What finally happened was that McGraw-Hill proposed to arrange a coauthor to help me hasten the revision. Thinking that this would quickly wrap up my work and set me free, I agreed. But since the coauthor, Professor Kevin Wainwright of British Columbia Institute of Technology and Simon Fraser University in Canada writes in a very different style from mine, it was necessary for me to unify the writing by going over every word in the text. And, of course, I had to check his mathematics, too. Thus, my workload was not lightened to any extent.

But I indeed am grateful to Professor Wainwright for his cooperative spirit, and for his willingness to handle the onerous job of preparing the final manuscript, as well as all the supplementary stuff. He also excerpted the basics of dynamic optimization from my second book and made them part of the fourth edition of *Fundamental Methods*. More importantly, I appreciate the gentle amount of pressure he put on me to wrap up the whole business expeditiously.

For the fourth edition, I am the senior author and Professor Wainwright the junior author. If and when there is a fifth edition, our roles will be reversed. And by previous agreement, I will have no further revision work to do. The old material I wrote before will remain in the book, and my name will remain on its cover. But that'll be it. So, even at this moment, I can already wave a fond "farewell" to *Fundamental Methods of Mathematical Economics*, my baby born way back in 1967.

18

Class of 1943 Reunions

To facilitate my attendance at the first reunion of the Class of 1943 in San Francisco, organized by Dicky Cheng, I requested him to select a date in July 1973 to coincide with my return flight from Hong Kong on a visit to my parents. Thus, my pleasure of a parental visit was immediately followed by the excitement of a class reunion, 30 years after our high-school graduation.

The First Reunion

By Dicky's arrangement, this reunion took place at Beverly Plaza Hotel, just outside of San Francisco Chinatown, in close proximity to delicious food. Emily and our children Darryl (5) and Tracey (3) also attended, as did the family members of some other classmates. Eight classmates participated, including T. J. Mao, Y. C. Lee, and Otis Shao, whom I will introduce in detail below.

In our plenary session, the attending classmate took turns in reporting on our respective "lives after St. John's Middle School." To Emily's surprise, our meeting was conducted entirely in English instead of Chinese. She did not realize that English WAS the language at St. John's. Besides, using English at meetings served a practical purpose. If we used Chinese, it would have to be the Shanghai dialect, because St. John's operated in Shanghai, but some family members in attendance might not understand the Shanghai dialect.

After the life stories, we collected the current addresses of attendees plus the known addresses of other classmates residing in the United States, or even in other countries. A sumptuous banquet ended the evening. A picnic the next day in the Golden State Park brought the reunion to a close.

It was generally agreed that, after this successful reunion, we should hold regular reunions in five-year intervals. A few reunions later, however, as advancing age loomed as a factor in our lives, we shortened the interval from five to two years. We also switched from a pattern of two-day gathering to weeklong cruises.

Las Vegas

The subsequent reunions took place in various locations, organized by different classmates and their respective spouses. We held two successive ones in Los Angeles (1978 and 1983), one each in Honolulu (1986), Vancouver (1988), Los Angeles (1993), and Las Vegas (1998), followed by cruises in Alaska (2000), Mexico (2002), and Hawaii (2004).

I attended many of these, but for some reasons I harbor special fondness for the 1998 reunion in Las Vegas, organized by a committee headed by Dicky, and attended by more than a dozen classmates and family members. Three of the attendees were actually members of the Class of 1942, but we still had as many as a dozen participants from our own class. The venue was the casino Bally's.

Why did Las Vegas occupy a special place in my memory? First, it was so well-attended. Clinton Kung (孔慶貢), who was my fellow devotee of Chinese calligraphy in our high-school years and who used to send me long letters in excellent penmanship, attended our reunion for the very first time. And, as usual, Wellington Lo (羅明開) and his wife Iris (王蓉珍) came all the way from Singapore to join us, in a touching display of loyalty to our class. David Liu (柳和豐) had passed away, but his wife Irene (董雅玲) came in his place. And the general atmosphere at this reunion was the most cordial I had ever experienced.

Second, in preparation for a stay at a casino, I had purposely read up on blackjack skills, with the hope that I might be able to finance my trip to Las Vegas with my prospective winnings at Bally's. But, as I reported in Chapter 3, I met with unmitigated defeat at the blackjack tables. Though a defeat, it was fun.

18.1 Class reunion in Las Vegas, April, 1998. From left: Larry Ma, Wellington Lo, T. J. Mao, me, Y. C. Lee, Dicky Cheng, Frank Cheng; back row: Percy Yau, Kenneth Li, Stanley Chen, Clinton Kung, Martin Su, Lincoln Luke, and Harry Chang.

Third, I thoroughly enjoyed the fabulous "Jubilee" show at the casino, which we classmates saw as a joint activity. At this show, my poor eyes, like those of the others, suffered a severe fatigue attack when 200 or so beautiful showgirls, all in sparkling but scanty costumes, paraded on stage in long lines that traveled in diverse directions. Trying to take in as much of their beauty as I was physically capable of proved to be a most taxing job. In the end, too many attractive showgirls bunched together just resulted in a big, big blur. A lovely blur, but still just a blur!

There was also an interesting incident one day. Arriving at the general meeting of the reunion 10 minutes late, and before I could utter my apology, I heard the chairman announce that, "Alpha Chiang has been elected the Editor of the Reunion Report." I wrote reunion reports before and after the reunion in Las Vegas, but to be elected *in absentia* as an editor was something new. That ought to teach me to be late to meetings!

It took me more than a couple of weeks to collect, integrate, and edit the biographical sketches submitted by the classmates. The resulting comprehensive report with 13 single-spaced pages, plus 2 pages of addresses, served as a good souvenir of a wonderful class event.

Some Brief Sketches

While preparing for this chapter, I took time to reread the biographical sketches I had edited. The stories of my classmates are no less interesting and absorbing than when I first read them. And I still marvel at what we as a group had accomplished in our respective career paths. But a sad feeling inevitably accompanied the realization that many of the classmates have since gone to another world.

Dicky Cheng (鄭賢永) was among those who were no longer with us. But I was still in touch with his wife, Deanna (舒甸娜). Dicky used to come to Connecticut to see me whenever he took a business trips from San Francisco to New York. And I always visited him and Deanna either on our way to Hong Kong, or on our way back. His interest in soccer and my interest in books did not coincide, but we did have a few things in common. Their elder son, Patrick, is the same age as my son Darryl. They both won the national writing contest as high-school seniors. Moreover, both Patrick and Darryl went to Harvard Law School. Darryl, being unsure about the acceptance prospect, applied to as many as six law schools. When I asked Patrick how many law school applications he sent out, his short reply was, "Just one." He graduated from Yale summa cum laude, and saw no need to apply to any other law school besides Harvard. What a bright, confident young man. Patrick (see Photo 40) practiced law for a few years, but then decided to study theology and become a clergyman.

The name Otis Shao (邵鴻義) I have mentioned before. He was a participant in our extemporaneous English-speaking practice sessions in Shanghai. Following the footsteps of the Three Musketeers, Otis also attended the University of Colorado, where we were able to arrange a scholarship for him. He then went on to earn a doctorate at Brown University. He taught political science at several colleges, and later became a college administrator. His positions included Academic Vice President at Occidental College and Dean of the Graduate School at the University of the Pacific. He was married to Marie Sheng, but had no children.

The special thing about Otis was that he had the best American accent among us classmates. That was because he had lived with an American family for many years in Shanghai. In contrast, the other classmates tended to speak with a hint of the British, with a pinch of Shanghai or Cantonese accent mixed in. He had a rich vocabulary, plus a love for big words. Aware of my strong interest in English, he was fond of testing me on English words, hoping to hear me say, "I don't know," so that he could reveal the answer with a triumphant smile. One time, walking together after an afternoon class on the St. John's campus, he tried his favorite pastime again, and asked me, "What is the English word for 頭皮屑 (flakes of dead skin on the scalp)?" My quick answer, "Dandruff," took him aback, for he was quite sure that I would be stumped. He explained to me why he was surprised: "This is a word we were never taught in any classes or in any assigned books." He was curious where I learned this word. I took advantage of my turn to smile at him with a tinge of triumph, but did not answer him.

So, how did I know this word? It was actually quite simple. By a strange coincidence, that very morning, in the school library before classes, I happened to flip through an American magazine lying on the table, and saw a shampoo advertisement with the word "dandruff" in it. I looked it up in the dictionary then and there. *Voilà*! After Otis and I parted that afternoon, a question suddenly arose in my mind: Why did he ask me about this word at that moment that day? Could it be that he also had just learned that same word from the same magazine that same morning?

Ever since my "dandruff" feat, he made no further attempts to stump me.

T. J. Mao (毛子仁) and I were academic rivals, but we were good friends. The Three Musketeers visited him in Cincinnati, on our way from Colorado to New York way back in 1948. For reasons I do not recall, he acquired the nickname "Pope" at St. John's, and many us just called him Pope more often than T. J. Pope was a top student in our Class of 1943. Our long academic rivalry did not affect our close relationship. A good example of our good relationship involved a photograph of a girl. At St. John's University, Pope became an ardent admirer of a lovely young lady, Jane Fang (方全), who happened to be a good friend of my cousin Ellen Chiang (蔣懿然). A loyal friend that I was, I requested Ellen to obtain a picture of Jane, which I then presented to Pope as a gift. Pope did not request this favor; I did it all on my own initiative as a friend. For a long time, Pope and Jane could not be together as they wished, but they did eventually get married after Jane came to the United States years later.

After his MS degree at the University of Cincinnati in leather and tanning, Pope later earned his PhD in chemistry at the University of Florida. He joined the General Motors Research Laboratories in 1960 as a Senior Research Scientist in their Polymers Department, and rose to Head of the Polymers Department in 1981.

In view of his position at GM, it was quite natural that he drove a Cadillac when he came from Detroit to Storrs, Connecticut to visit me. My little son, already into cars though still small, was impressed by his automobile. Normally, my son would, in accordance with the Chinese tradition, address Pope as "Uncle Mao." But, because of his car, Darryl referred to him as "Uncle Cadillac Mao." This was for unmistakable identification against another of my visitors, "Uncle Toronado Chang."

Roommates

There were six beds in the dormitory room where I resided in my first year at St. John's Middle School. Amazingly, the biographical sketches I collected for reunion reports included as many as four former roommates.

One of them, Y. C. Lee (李榮就), had his bed adjacent to mine, and our desks faced each other, so we were close study mates for a whole year. But then we were assigned to different sections, and grew apart. In correspondence after coming to the United States, though, I gathered the impression that he did graduate work in accounting, but according to his biographical sketch, he actually worked primarily in computer-related engineering fields, variously at RCA, GE, and Xerox, from which he retired.

He was best known as a champion table tennis player. At one of our class reunions held at his home in Palos Verdes Estates, California, I noticed that one of their rooms was overflowing with shelves upon shelves of the trophies he had won in this sport. In the year 1999, he achieved the rare honor of being inducted into the California Hall of Fame in Table Tennis early in the year, and then into the USA Hall of Fame in Table Tennis later in the same year. He was even a certified "International Referee" for this sport.

Aside from his trophies, I also noticed his auto license plate: "2 at MIT." I asked him what that inscription meant. He answered proudly, "Both of my daughters are studying at the Massachusetts Institute of Technology." I felt I had to take my hat off to him and his wife, Fae (李鴻妃), although I wasn't wearing a hat at that time.

Then, there was Wellington Lo (羅明開), who specially flew in with his wife Iris (王蓉珍) from Singapore for the reunion. When Wellington and I shared a dormitory room at St. John's, he frequently tried to annoy me by bumping against my shoulder every time he passed by my desk where I was hard studying. I realized that he did it only out of mischief, not malice, but I truly resented it. Since I could not avoid him because my desk was next to the door, I could only grin and bear it. It was only when, after many years, we met again in Hong Kong, where he happened to be a neighbor to one of my uncles, that we began a friendly relationship.

An economics major in college, like me, Wellington built his career mainly in the textile field in Hong Kong. For years, he was assigned by his employer to Lagos, Nigeria, as the General Manager of HK Synthetic Fibre (Nigeria) Co., producing African prints. Iris told us that, while in Nigeria, Wellington had as many as 10 servants in his home, including two chauffeurs, one for daytime and one for nighttime. What a life he led! Back in Hong Kong, Wellington and Iris were very hospitable to

Emily and me whenever we visited our parents there. One time, they invited us to a special herbal medicine dinner, where each course of the dinner featured some Chinese herbs beneficial to certain organs of the human body. It was not only healthful, but tasty and memorable.

In an attempt to reciprocate their hospitality, when their son, Raymond, went to the prep school Hotchkiss in Connecticut, I invited Iris and Raymond to come to our home first, then I drove the young man to his new school. Raymond later graduated from Stanford University and became a principal of an American investment firm in Hong Kong.

David Liu (柳和豐), another former roommate, was at St. John's only for one semester, after which he moved with his family to India. But I remember him vividly as a fantastic mimicker of many Chinese dialects. And he was funny in other ways.

With absolutely no contact with him for decades, I was really shocked by his sudden appearance at my University of Connecticut (UConn) office one late afternoon in 1985. How did he find me after more than 40 years? It turned out that he, a chemical engineer, was teaching part-time at a branch campus of UConn, and came on that day to the main campus in Storrs to attend a departmental meeting. He had noticed my name in the university catalog, and decided to give me a surprise visit. Luckily, I habitually stayed late in my office. Otherwise, he would not be able to find me after his departmental meeting. It was hard to believe, but we still could recognize each other without difficulty after so many years.

David told me that he was living in Princeton, New Jersey. And, just before parting, he said something uncanny to me: "If your children ever come for an interview at Princeton University, please look me up." I considered this statement extremely incredible because I indeed was going to take my son Darryl to visit Princeton University in a few days. On that trip, I did indeed look up David and his wife Irene (董雅玲) there. And after Darryl enrolled at Princeton, "Uncle David" and "Aunt Irene" took very good care of him throughout the four years. They even allowed Darryl to store a lot of his belongings in their home during summer vacations.

Before David passed away, he was busy editing a handbook, and he called me often to discuss the various questions that came up during the publishing process. The finished product, *Environmental Engineers' Handbook*, a monumental tome the size of a thick New York City telephone directory, eventually came out posthumously, and Irene held a dedication ceremony in September, 1997, in Princeton. She invited several speakers to mark the occasion, each a friend during one particular phase of David's life. I was honored to be one of them, relating to his high-school year at St. John's.

Stanley Chen (陳宣享) was the other former roommate. His bed faced mine on opposite sides of the room, and we were closest to the door. Seeing that I was a serious, hard-working student, he looked up to me, and we always maintained a friendly attitude toward each other. On one occasion, he even said to me, "You know, Alpha, my younger sister is quite pretty, and I would like very much to introduce you to her." I felt very much honored by his offer, but he never took any action on it. To tell the truth, though, even if he did, it would not bear any fruit, for I was too shy at that stage of my life to socialize with a girl, especially a pretty one.

Stanley, a civil engineer, studied and worked in the construction business after coming to the United States in 1951, and eventually started his own business, Stanchen Construction Co., Inc., in Boston in 1972. Among other things, he built several high-rise apartment buildings for the elderly. Although geographic distance prevented us from meeting in person often, he and I were in frequent phone communications.

A few years ago, Stanley called one day, and stunned me by asking me for financial advice, "Alpha, I have just sold a building, and have on hand five million dollars in cash. What do you think I should do with it?" Wow, what a tough problem my former roommate had to struggle with! Since I was not known as a good investor, I don't understand why people—even colleagues in my economics department—wanted my opinion on what to do with their money. Since it was not in my place to suggest to him what to do with such a large sum of cash, I only offered him a general discussion of the pros and cons of different investment vehicles: stocks, bonds, real estate, and precious metals, things that he probably already knew. I never learned what he decided to do. Later, I learned that Stanley and his wife Josephine have become generous philanthropists, establishing scholarship funds, and joining many civic projects.

As I relate the stories of these classmates, I marvel at the diverse directions they had gone in their lives, and the varying ways they had made their marks in society. Hall of famer, builder, professor, academic administrator, editor, banker, . . . Class of 1943, you are not too shabby!

Most of these classmates I wrote about in this section and last are, to my regret, forever gone, though. May they rest in peace.

To conclude this chapter, I present here a picture of the attendees of our reunion cruise to Mexico, in October, 2002.

1 Fae Lee	2 Y. C. Lee
3 Irene Liu	4 Jane Mao
5 T. J. Mao	6 Margareth Cheng
7 Frank Cheng	8 Emily Chiang
9 Alpha Chiang	10 Wellington Lo
11 Stanley Chen	12 Josephine Chen
13 Iris Lo	14 Emily Su
15 Martin Su	

18.2 Mexican cruise, 2002, "formal night."

19

The Latecomers

Being an only son in a Chinese family, I have a moral obligation to produce a male heir. It would not be a punishable crime to fail this obligation, but to make the family happy, it would be preferable to have one heir, or more. I knew child-rearing is a life experience I do not want to miss, and Emily felt even more strongly about the joy of being a mother.

Road to Parenthood

Right after our marriage, at the start of my teaching career, I could not consider having children on account of the demand on my time it would entail. As time gradually ripens for adding children to the family, we seemed to be facing a closed door. Since hoping and waiting yielded no result, we had to resort to proactive quests.

Emily underwent gynecological tests, and I took fertility test as well. Verdict: Nothing is wrong with either of us. Advices: Relax; take vacations; spend time in warm-climate places. Warning: Children will come when it is most inconvenient for you!

We did try to relax, but obviously never reaching the required level. We spent my sabbatical leave in Hong Kong, hoping that its subtropical climate would do the trick. No such luck. Friends and relatives offered us various secret recipes and wonder diets. And my parents suggested adoption, which I firmly rejected for a good reason: I was fully confident that I will someday have my own children, and if I adopt now and later have my own, I cannot trust myself to be entirely impartial between the adopted and the natural children. Any partiality that may likely come up will gnaw at my conscience, and I must nip that eventuality in the bud.

People asked me: "How can you be so confident about having your own children?" My answer was: "My fortune, as foretold by my 'eight words (八字)' indicates that I shall have children, late." It might be laughable to some that I would believe in fortune-telling. But the "eight-word" fortune-telling is unbelievably accurate, as I will explain and explore in Chapter 45.

The Pivotal Advice

The pivotal advice regarding child-bearing finally came from our opera friend Julia Wu (伍杜天薌), who performed the opera "A Fisherman's Tale" with Emily at the China Pavilion at the World's Fair in Flushing Meadows, Queens, New York, in 1964. She had solved her own fertility problem with the help of a Dr. Liu (柳淑媛), a lady gynecologist/surgeon trained in Shanghai as well as at the University of Pennsylvania. Dr. Liu's husband and Julia's husband were schoolmates at Columbia, and that was how Julia got to know Dr. Liu's medical practice.

Upon Julia's strong recommendation, Emily decided to consult Dr. Liu at her office in Chinatown in Manhattan. Since we were living in Connecticut, some distance away, Emily was lax in setting a date. In March 1965, however, taking advantage of her stay in New York for the opening of the first solo art exhibition of her elder sister Chinyee, Emily called on this genteel Chinese lady doctor. Right away, Dr. Liu diagnosed Emily's problem as endometriosis, recommended surgery, and confidently told Emily, "You'll have a baby two years after an operation."

Her prediction turned out to be entirely correct. Two years following examinations and surgery by Dr. Liu, Emily became a mother to our first child, a son, born a week before Christmas in 1968 at the New York Infirmary. The due date Dr. Liu gave us was December 18. Our son beat the deadline by 11 minutes, arriving at 11:49 p.m. on the due date.

My parents, who came to the United States for the occasion, were overjoyed. Asked to select a Chinese name for the newborn, my father thought of the Chinese maxim "君子之交淡如水 (The friendship between true gentlemen should be bland like water.)" and suggested "淡如" for his name. I liked his suggestion, and immediately chose the similar-sounding English name Darryl to go with it. Later, following the suggestion of Emily's father, we altered "淡如" to "澹如."

Dr. Liu's reputation spread at lightning speed among our friends and relatives, and many families sought her medical help, with success in every case. When we were expecting our second child, we of course would have loved to seek out Dr. Liu again, but already with a child to take care, we found it more practical to stick to an obstetrician closer by. It was Dr. Philip Sumner who smoothly delivered our second child in the Manchester Memorial Hospital on July 15, 1970. This child is a daughter that we were hoping for. In honor of Julia Hsu (徐張粹文) whom Emily and I both consider to be *the* most beautiful lady we have ever met face to face, I named her 粹似, using one word from Julia's Chinese name, and at the same time chose the similar-sounding Tracey as her English name.

My mother was kind enough to stay with us in the United States for a whole year to care for Tracey, while my father took care of his Shanghai Christian Church in Hong Kong alone, without her by his side with her customary valuable assistance. Both of them sacrificed a lot for us.

Playpen and Beyond

Emily kept Darryl in the playpen longer than necessary because she got pregnant again, and could not easily lift Darryl up. As an inmate in the playpen, Darryl would climb up and fall, then climb up again and fall again, showing a lot of tenacity. He also tried to walk within the small square area inside. Finally, when we let him out of the playpen, he could excitedly walk from one end of our extra-long living room to the other without difficulty. Then he discovered that the uncarpeted floor surface in the adjoining dining room had a different surface.

After using his toe to test the floor and finding it solid, he then ventured out to the new territory. He even quickened his steps into a run.

Tracey, one and half years younger, also tried to climb up in the playpen. But after two unsuccessful tries, she would give up, and just stay in the sitting position. We thought she lacked perseverance. But, actually, she had a weak knee. That was one reason we sent her to ballet lessons later.

Photos 10–12 in the front of this book show Darryl and Tracey as youngsters. My parents had the Chinese dress and hat in Photo 10 custom-made for Darryl in Hong Kong.

It was fun to see them learn this and learn that, especially in speech. In their early years, we intentionally spoke to them in Chinese only, since we felt that was the best time to train their flexible tongues for the sounds and tones unique to the Chinese language. Emily and I spoke to them in Mandarin, but they also picked some Shanghai dialect from my mother.

Once they were in school, we expected they would learn English in no time. That was not entirely true. In nursery school, Darryl could not understand the teacher's instructions at all, and the teacher worriedly told Emily, "I think your son may have a serious hearing problem, you better have his ears checked out soon." Whenever the time came for singing nursery rhymes, Darryl had no clue what was going on. Fortunately, he had seen the Lawrence Welk Show on television. So, he just stood up and conducted! Gradually, he picked up English, and even spoke English to Tracey at home. With some vocabulary in English when she went to school, Tracey did not have the opportunity to alarm her teachers as having a hearing problem.

The Thespian

The fact that Darryl instinctively played Lawrence Welk at nursery rhyme time signified his predilection for acting. Around 2 years of age, he saw the moon landing on TV, and immediately did a life-like imitation of the slow-motion moon walk. Amazed by Darryl's imitation, my mother was moved to declare, with great conviction, that "Darryl's walk is more authentic than the astronaut's!"

Expectedly, Darryl participated regularly in school plays. Roles in elementary-school plays were, well, elementary. A more formal role came his way when his middle-school teacher recommended him to play one of the village children in the Shakespearean play "The Merry Wives of Windsor," produced by the Theater Department of the University of Connecticut in 1979. The producer of the show, Professor Nafe Katter, at first rejected Darryl on the ground that it would be an anomaly to have a Chinese boy in the Windsor village in Falstaff's era. But he relented because Darryl's teacher was persistent in recommending him. His participation in all 12 shows in the run of the play taught Darryl a lot about the stage, including the preshow vocal and physical exercises the performers routinely went through.

Darryl has a special gift for remembering show dialogues. One time, probably when he was in middle school, he and I watched a TV police drama together, and afterward, he recited the whole show dialogue for me, with him playing all the roles therein, smoothly with all the scenes in correct sequence. I was totally amazed. In 1981, at age 12, he played a Texas oilman in the musical "On Broadway," in which he even put on a believable Texas accent to the delight of the audience. One time, there were two shows of "The Wizard of Oz" on two successive days, and he played the Scarecrow in one, and the Wizard in the other. Memorizing scripts was easy for him; I suspect he knew the lines for the other roles, too.

A climactic episode in Darryl's show experience was his audition in 1986 for a role in the movie "The Last Emperor." His age was suitable for the role of the teenage Emperor, Pu-yi (溥儀), and Emily gladly took him to New York for the audition. The lady casting director rehearsed with him the scene in which the young emperor met his English tutor, Sir Reginald Johnston, for the first time. She was deeply impressed by Darryl, especially when he declared his decision to do the same scene a little later, without script, in front of the director Bernardo Bertolucci himself. Ultimately, though, as one of the two finalists, Darryl lost the role to a Chinese youngster who lived in Beijing.

Tracey was not into drama. But she was one of the dancers in "The Frogs of Windham," a musical based on "the great frog fight of 1754" in Windham, a town next to where we lived.

Closer to their parents' interest in Chinese opera, both Darryl and Tracey had been drafted to do small roles in our stage productions in New York. They appeared on stage with makeup and in costumes (see Photo 24 in the front of this book). Even though the remuneration was meager, I think they had some fun. Tracey even had a brief speaking part once—a good thing that I insisted on homeschooling of Chinese language for them.

Chinese Lessons—Yuck!

I had to teach them Chinese by myself, because no children's Chinese language classes were available near our home. Even if there were, usually on Saturdays, I might still add lessons of my own, because I am convinced that language learning should be done on the daily basis, with constant contact, not only once a week. Darryl and Tracey already understood spoken Chinese, but I wanted them to be able to read, or even to write.

I procured some introductory textbooks from Taiwan, but found them to be too far removed from the living environment in the United States to be suitable. Thus, I made up my own teaching material that is pertinent to their own life experiences. For example, after we flew back from Hong Kong on a visit to my parents, I would teach a term they already heard: "空中小姐 (airline stewardess)," and then use each of the four words in the term to construct other phrases, such as "空氣 (air)," "中國人 (Chinese person)," "大小 (size)," "兄弟姐妹 (elder and younger brothers, elder and young sisters)," and so on. The process I used involved a lot of work for me, but the approach proved effective.

Compulsory daily Chinese classes naturally produced psychological resistance. They usually came to the 20-minute lesson every night with long faces. But years of cultivation did yield some fruits. I was pleased when, before going to college, Darryl told me that he wanted to continue with the study of Chinese. And, since I thought highly of the Chinese language program at Princeton University after I met an American girl from Princeton who speaks Chinese as if she grew up in Beijing, I steered Darryl toward Princeton. True, Columbia is also good, and my good friend Roger Yeu was teaching Chinese there. Finally, however, we decided on Princeton. While on the campus interview there in 1985, as a courtesy call, I took Darryl to meet Bill Bowen, the president of Princeton at the time, who happened to be a former student of mine at Denison University. I guess Darryl developed a special respect for his dad during those 20 minutes in President Bowen's office.

Another time I sensed genuine filial respect from my son was when, after installing a chinning bar for him in the basement, I raised myself up on the bar to test it, which resulted in an unintended show of physical prowess. Awed by what he saw, he commemorated the occasion by drawing a picture of a man in academic cap and gown doing the chin-up, and gave it to me as a Christmas present. Unfortunately, after several residential moves, I could no longer find that miniature drawing. That chinning bar reminded me of my early days in primary school when I was into basic gymnastics. I could do tricks on a horizontal bar and, I could even descend on a slide in the standing position. But then for some reason I distanced myself from athletics as the years went by, and joined the rank of purist nonathletes.

At Princeton, Darryl took three years of Chinese. His first-year teacher, Ms. Ren (任長慧) was so good that Darryl used to look forward eagerly to the early-morning Chinese classes. When the semester came to an end, Darryl was moved to present her a red rose.

Tracey also tried to continue with the study of Chinese. But, at Brown University, she had an American lady teacher who could not even speak Chinese as well as Tracey. Understandably and forgivably, she decided not to continue.

Brown versus RISD

Tracey's decision to pursue fine arts made the Rhode Island School of Design (RISD) her college choice. In a summer program at RISD, in 1987, while still in high school, Tracey produced a remarkable portfolio in the enjoyable weeks she spent there. I was especially attracted by one multipanel drawing she did, titled "Metamorphosis." The first panel shows an insect, a beetle. The middle panels show stages of detailed gradual transformations. Then, in the last panel, *voilà*, a car: a Volkswagen Beetle! RISD is a great school, but it is a technical college, while Emily and I wanted her to have a more liberal arts education. The compromise we found was: attend Brown University, a close neighbor to RISD, with "cross registration" with RISD, too. What "cross registration" means is that the students from either institution are free to take courses in the other. As it turned out, the benefits of cross registration were illusory. Art courses at RISD mostly take three consecutive class periods; thus, taking one RISD course will preempt three class periods at Brown. Consequently, Tracey could not really take as many RISD courses as she desired, and as we thought she could. This is good proof that parents do not always know best.

Arts Rather than Sciences

Both of our children are capable of doing well in both arts and sciences. But they both lean toward the former. Part of the reason, perhaps, is that on our numerous auto trips from Connecticut for New York to visit relatives and friends, or to do Chinese opera, the four of us usually played word games in the car, and rarely or never math or science games.

Surprisingly, Darryl had picked up many big words since an early age, such as *ubiquitous* and *lackadaisical*. From where? I don't know. While he never gave me a precise definition of each of such words, I have always found his usage and context to be correct. He was editor of *Virtù*, the high-school literary magazine at Edwin O. Smith School. He won a nationwide writing contest as a high-school senior, with an original short story.

Tracey's vocabulary is good, too, though she is not into big words like her brother. She also served as editor of *Virtù*, for which she wrote many poems and the magazine featured her cover designs. She also got inducted into National Honor Society, as Darryl before her. When brother and sister were both at Edwin O. Smith School, Darryl tended to dominate the scene. But after Darryl left high school, Tracey came out of the shadow in a big way. She won 10 awards at graduation, as compared to Darryl's five. She even won the Female Scholar Athlete Award, a statewide honor. And, as the Treasurer of the Class, she made a great speech at the Commencement, and that speech was extensively highlighted in the local newspapers the next day.

College and Beyond

After his BA degree in history, magna cum laude, from Princeton in 1990, Darryl spent a year in Taiwan to teach English and learn Chinese—actually also working for a law firm, Huang & Partners. Then he went to Harvard Law School for a JD degree, which he earned, cum laude, in 1994.

His first law job was to clerk for Chief Judge Judith Keep of U.S. District Court, Southern District of California in San Diego. Guess what Judge Keep's opening statement to us was when Darryl first took us to see her? It was: "Darryl shouldn't be a lawyer!"

Emily and I were shocked. "I always thought he writes well," I said. "Oh yes, his writing is excellent," the judge replied, "and he should be a creative writer. He often uses big words that I have to look up in the dictionary. Just this morning, I read a brief he wrote, and had to look up the word 'soporific.' The legal profession means a waste for him."

Further into the conversation, Judge Keep mentioned that a lawyer must take a stand on an issue and make arguments from that standpoint. Darryl, on the other hand, tends to see good reasoning on both sides of the issue.

In his later jobs with a couple of law firms, Darryl did not find the work enjoyable, and decided to work for business corporations. I once posed a crucial question to him: "If there were absolutely no constraints of any kind, what would you prefer to do as a life pursuit?" He thought for a while, and said, "I would enjoy producing films."

That response immediately rang a bell, for I remember the happiest times he had when he was wholeheartedly engaged in the production of a 25-minute video "Kung Fu to You Too" with his friends Dylan Shaw and Jesse Lerner, all high-school juniors. It was a parody on Bruce Lee, which he co-wrote, co-starred, co-directed, and co-produced. Being the chief coordinator for the project, he spent hours every day planning, notifying all the volunteer actors and actresses where they should be at what time, and be prepared for which scene, and so on. Exhausted by all this work, he would come to dinner with a look of triumph and accomplishment. The final video production, which I have watched with interest and pride several times, was considered by the high-school faculty as an exemplary social science project.

For a long time, Emily and I thought he might quit law any day. But, after trying a few corporate jobs, and joining Google in July 2006, he seems to be quite cordial toward the legal profession now.

Tracey also went on to graduate studies after Brown. Worried that an art career may not be life-sustaining, Emily advised Tracey to get a degree in art education, to have teaching to fall back on. Tracey agreed and earned an MA in art education in 1994 at the School of the Museum of Fine Arts, Boston, which is affiliated with Tufts University. However, her teacher certification from kindergarten to 12th grade completely went to waste, because her practice-teaching assignment to an inner-city school immediately scared her off. Many of the students carried knives, and one of them even dared to ask her for a date. In the meantime, a professor of photographer who noticed much creativity in her work said to her, "Why do you want to teach art? You should let your own creativity flourish!" The result of this admonition was her enrollment at the School of Visual Art in New York, where she earned an MFA degree in photography in 1996, and received the Paula Rhodes Memorial Award in Photography upon graduation.

Soon after, she became a published artist. Her submission of a portfolio to a photographic book project was accepted, and the editor gave her an 8-page spread in *Twenty-Five and Under/Photographers*, edited by Alice Rose George, Double-Take Book published in association with W. W. Norton & Co., 1997. The work consisted of a series of Tracey's self-portraits, with lines and texts scratched across the negatives, that depict her inner struggle with the dual cultures that she was born into. For the haunting images, her work was singled out for mention by a reviewer of the book in an art magazine. The following year, a Swiss collector contacted her and bought four of these self-portraits. I will come back to this in Chapter 22.

Then, she published an essay with a photograph of herself in the book *Our Grandmothers*, edited by Linda Sunshine, Welcome Enterprise, Inc., 1998. This is a collection of the writings of 74 granddaughters, selected out of 152 submissions. Hers was one of few that won unanimous YES votes from the judges.

Since such creative activities did not produce steady income, she turned to graphic designing, and worked for some small firms. At Kiyoshi Kanai, Inc., she had an extraordinary experience. Mr. Kanai, who owns a house in Japan as well as a villa in Italy, likes to vacation there for long periods of time. One day, Mr. Kanai waved a nonchalant goodbye to Tracey and took off for a couple of weeks, leaving the entire job of producing a forthcoming issue of *American Craft* magazine to the only employee in his office, a novice. Maximally stressed out, Tracy somehow pulled it off. She admitted to me, "I learned a lot from that job."

Since September 2004, she has been working at Nickelodeon, and now carries the title of Associate Director, Production Illustration.

Second-Generation Latecomers?

Do latecomers breed latecomers, too?

On August 2, 2003, Tracey married Jonathan McGrath, a son of Giles and Yvonne McGrath. A skateboarder, part of the "McGrath Brothers" team, Jonathan injured himself during a show, and had to quit the sport, unlike his friends who became rich as sports stars. He is a street photographer. I print their wedding picture as Photo 66 in the front of this book.

Their two sons, Emmett and Kieran, came in 2004 and 2007, respectively. They are not so late. Interestingly, both of them happened to pick special days for their arrival into this world: Emmett on

Groundhog Day (February 2), and Kieran on April Fool's Day (April 1). They are also alike in their love for Chinese food. To them, the world's best dish is the aptly named "Heavenly Chicken" served at the Chinese restaurant Cheng Du 23 (川園) in Wayne, New Jersey. It's always fun to take them there, and watch them savor that chicken dish, as well as their scallion pancakes (葱油餅) and soup dumplings (小籠包).

The McGraths can be seen in Photo 76.

With Darryl, it is a different story. After a brief marriage after finishing law school, he remained a bachelor for 21 years until 2016. Then, on September 10, 2016, he married Dr. Andrea Jue, the daughter of Mr. Joseph Jue (居紹敏) and Mrs. Olympia Jue (居伍瑛芝). An ophthalmologist trained at Brown University, Andrea has her own medical practice in New York City.

Their wedding is depicted in Photos 78 and 79 in the front of the book. But I would also like to show below three pictures of speech-making at the wedding: Photos 19.1–19.3.

Darryl and Andrea were told to expect a son in early March, 2019. But the stork could not wait, and decided to make delivery about 10 days early. Like his cousins Emmett and Kieran, Julian chose to enter into the world on a special day, February 14, 2019, Valentine's Day. I was 41 years old when I welcomed my first child, Darryl. Darryl welcomed his first child at age 50, beating me in the "lateness contest" by almost a whole decade!

19.1 A speech by the bride's father, Joseph Jue, at the 2016 wedding.

19.2 A speech by Emily, the groom's mother.

19.3 A speech by Tracey, the groom's sister.

Julian Chiang is shown in Photo 84 (at 6 months) and Photo 85 with his parents (at 9 months) in the front section of this book.

And, on Thanksgiving Day, 2019, Emily and I had a picture taken with all three of our adorable grandchildren. This is printed as Photo 86 in the front of the book.

20

Kiddish Words and Deeds

The utterances of small kids and their early deeds often are funny, witty, thought-provoking, and revelatory. I believe that children in every household are likely to make cute sayings and do interesting things, but they do not always get recorded. When my kids grew up, I made sure to write down their words and deeds, so that I could relive those cute moments years or even decades later. There was also a more urgent reason: my parents living faraway in Hong Kong had an insatiable craving for reports on their grandchildren's sayings and doings.

I'll report some of these below, with my personal comments shown in brackets.

First Taste of Coke

One of the ancient written records I have on file relates to the Chinese word 辣 (*la,* meaning spicy or biting, or pungent). Darryl (3) and Tracey (1 and 1/2) had not learned any English yet at the time, and Tracey commented in Chinese on her first taste of Coca-Cola, "有一點 *la*. (It tastes a little *la.*)" Darryl right away told her, "Of course it tastes *la*. That's why it's called Coca-CoLA."

[Taking one syllable of an English word, he assigned a Chinese meaning to it on the basis of its pronunciation. It sounded logical. My parents, with understandable bias, thought it was ingenious.]

Food Alternative

Thinking that, as a father, my life's mission was to stay home and play with him, Darryl (3) attempted to block my exit whenever he saw me heading for the garage to go to the office. Emily would pull him away, explaining that, "Daddy must go to work to earn income. Otherwise, 我們沒有飯吃 (we'll have 'no rice to eat'—the Chinese way of saying 'no food on our table.'"

Darryl had a quick response, "沒有飯吃, 我們可以吃麵啊! (If we have no rice to eat, we can eat noodles instead!)"

[This response seems to have been borrowed directly from Marie Antoinette. But there is absolutely no plagiarism involved here because it can be proven beyond any doubt that Darryl had not even heard of Marie Antoinette at that age.]

An Unjustifiable Justification

One day, Tracey (4) farted, quite audibly. Somewhat embarrassed, she offered a justification: "我的屁股在說話. (My buttocks are speaking.)"

[She had not yet learned that speech involves sound, but the converse is not true.]

Fifty Percent

Our good friends Roger and Lilian Yeu (樂亦平陳霖伉儷) came to Connecticut to visit. As they entered into the house, I pointed to Roger and asked Tracey (4) in Chinese, "Do you remember who this is?"

"Roger," she replied in a low voice.

"No, you should say 'Uncle Roger,'" I tried to correct her.

"我只說 一 半 (I just say one half of it)."

[Her arithmetic was entirely correct. One word out of two was precisely one half.]

Narrowing the Field

Emily just made a long red skirt for Tracey, and Tracey just loved it. Wearing it proudly, she came straight to me and asked in Chinese, "Daddy, whose clothes are the prettiest?"

In a teasing mood, I didn't give the answer she desired, "Oh, I think my clothes look the best."

Frustrated at my response, she said, "No, I mean children's clothes."

Continuing in the teasing game, I pretended to ponder, and then said, "Darryl's clothes."

"No," she began to speak with agitation, "I mean GIRLS' clothes!"

"Okay, Tracey, I think your clothes are the prettiest, especially this red skirt."

She finally put on a smile.

[I probably should not have teased her, she was only 4. But it was fun to watch her narrow down the fields successively from all clothes, to children's clothes, then to girls' clothes, in a logical order.]

The Unthinkable Restaurateur

Gradually, our children became more and more bilingual.

Darryl (4) received a toy cash register at Christmas, and wanted to open a play restaurant. Guess who would be his customer? His sister, of course.

"Welcome to our restaurant. We serve great food. What would you like to order?" Darryl showed much courtesy to his very first customer.

"Mm, mm," the customer had to think hard since she had never ordered food in a restaurant by herself before.

"Oh, let me help you with ordering," Darryl said, "How about some chicken?"

Relieved of the problem of choice, Tracey replied with joy, "Yes, yes. I'll have chicken."

But the restaurant owner had a strange reaction: "So sorry, we are out of chicken. Please order something else."

"Mm, mm, . . ."

[A restaurant owner would normally push and recommend what he is overstocked with. To suggest something that's known to be out of stock is unthinkable, hence hilarious!]

Empirical Evidence

After seeing "The Wizard of Oz" on TV, Darryl (4) announced a general discovery he had made about the world. "There are three things in the world that can melt," he said, and then counted them out one by one on his fingers, "tissue paper, ice cream, and witches."

[A statistician in the making?]

Professor's Suit

Tracey (5) saw me take out my academic regalia from the closet on my way to a commencement exercise, and asked in English, "Is that your professor's suit?"

[I took this opportunity to teach her the names of the three individual pieces of the regalia: a cap with a square top with a tassel, a black gown with blue stripes on the sleeves, and a hood with colors that serve to identify the school conferring the degree.]

Clone?

At a critical suspenseful moment in a TV show, we called Darryl (5) to get ready to go out with us to a restaurant. Reluctant to leave his TV show, he yelled, "How I wish there were two of me, one to go to dinner with you, and one to stay here to finish watching the show!"

[If he had grown up to be a scientist instead of a lawyer, would he have devoted his life doing research on cloning?]

A Mistaken Identity

Some visitors to our home brought a delicate piece of ivory carving as a house gift. Emily showed it to Tracey (6), and said, "Look at this lovely piece of art, it's made of ivory." She had a natural follow-up inquiry: "Poison ivory?"

[The two words "ivory" and "ivy" do sound deceivingly alike.]

Tooth Fairy Tale

The legend of Tooth Fairy was prevalent in the children's world. I used to put a quarter under a child's pillow in exchange for a fallen tooth. But ever since our neighbor's daughter Debby made it known that her Tooth Fairy gave her a dollar per tooth, Tracey (6) felt cheated. One night, as I was tucking her in, she cast a sly glance at me, and then sighed, "Too bad we have a cheap Tooth Fairy in our house!"

[I just smiled, but did not bother to explain to her that: (1) Some Tooth Fairies are richer than others. (2) More importantly, when some Tooth Fairies ignore the going market rate, and recklessly overpay, they are violating a sacred law of the Fairyland.]

Introduction to Alcohol

At Pizza Hut, I ordered a glass of beer to go with my pepperoni pizza.

Darryl (7) was curious and asked, "What does beer taste like, Dad?" I pushed the mug toward him, and said, "Why don't you take a sip, and find out?" He savored the liquid, and then remarked that "It tastes just like Scotch."

In another restaurant on another occasion, I ordered a gin-and-tonic, and let Tracey have a taste of it from a chopstick that I had dipped into the drink. Her response was simpler, "Mm, not bad."

[These two responses indicated the different personalities of the two children. Darryl had never tasted Scotch before, and probably had barely heard it mentioned, yet he daringly chose to cite Scotch as a reference drink. Tracey's response was less pretentious; she chose not to pretend to be more worldly than she actually was.]

Net Worth

After he started to receive a weekly allowance, Darryl (7) bought a combination-lock toy safe for his savings. But he would often broadcast the amount of money he kept in the safe. I admonished him to keep his financial information to himself.

He asked me, "Why should I keep it secret?"

"It's not a question of secrecy. But financial information should be kept private and confidential. It is not good manner to tell people how rich or how poor you are."

"I shouldn't even tell that to Tracey?" He wondered.

"Not even to Tracey," I affirmed.

"But she's my sister."

"Even so."

Darryl thought for a second, and then said, "I think you are right, Dad. She might be a double agent."

[Double agent? At what point did we enter into an espionage drama?]

What Did He Say to God?

I saw Darryl (7) praying at night, and asked him, "What did you say to God?" He responded briefly, "I just said 謝謝儂 ('Thank you' in Shanghai dialect), and 多福多壽 ('Have lots of good fortune, and enjoy a long life' in Mandarin)."

[The well-wishing phrase "多福多壽" was what our whole family said to one another in unison with raised glasses at dinner, and what the children were taught to say to guests as a toast. It became funny when these wishes were offered to God. It would have been even funnier, had we taught them a more full-fledged version of this well-wishing phrase, and it had then been repeated to God: "多福多壽多子孫" ("Have lots of good fortune, enjoy a long life, and produce many children and grandchildren!").]

A Serious Health Worry

Darryl (7) appeared seriously worried one day, and told me in a hushed voice, "Dad, I think I am doomed; I may have VD."

"VD?" I said, "Do you know what VD means?"

"Yes, I know what it means: venereal disease," he said, confidently.

"I am sorry to hear that. But where and how did you get it?" I had to probe.

"Well, Stephanie kissed my hand five times yesterday, and this morning when I tried to tie my shoelaces, my fingers felt weak."

I almost laughed out aloud. To put him to ease, I gently patted his head and said, "Don't worry, son. You are absolutely fine. I can guarantee that your fingers will recover tomorrow."

[Where did a little 7-year-old boy hear of the term VD? From his classmates? Then, the question is: where did his classmates learn of the term?]

Wife's Consent

Darryl (7) tended to make promises far into the future. One day, he announced out of the blue to Emily and me that, "When I grow up, I'll buy you lots of things."

"Oh, that's very nice of you," I said, then added, "But, after you grow up, you will be married, I think you should first check with your wife before buying things for us. She may object to that, you know."

"Okay, I will check with her. But if she does not agree, then I'll divorce her!"

"Divorce? Isn't that too drastic?"

"No, I'll divorce her if she objects," he said, in a resolute voice, "but I'll keep the child."

[A 7-year child already heard about divorce, and the related question of child custody. Didn't that say something about our society?]

A Fraternal Pledge

Emily and I did not lecture the children formally too often. But sometimes, we emphasized to them that they should value their sibling relationship, and help each other whenever the need arises.

To show his willing acceptance of our advice, Darryl (8) instantly made a pledge: "If I become a millionaire, I will give Tracey one hundred dollars."

Emily of course did not think kindly of the $100 offer. "Darryl, if you have four hundred dollars, and offer one hundred to Tracey, it shows generosity. But if you have a million dollars, and only offer one hundred, that only shows stinginess."

Darryl then did some more mental calculation, and said, "All right, but 8,000 dollars is my highest bid!"

[Actually, he meant "the highest offer." But, hey, now we had graduated into the realm of high finances, talking about millionaire, bid and offer, etc.]

The Asking Price?

At the dinner table, we often talked randomly about how things were in China when Emily and I lived there as youngsters, before and during the Sino-Japanese War (later merged into WWII). We also introduced them to dynastic history of China. One time I told them that way back in time, when floods and droughts plagued our native country, some families near starvation had to sell their children in order to survive, and to give the children better lives in the families that could afford to buy them. Darryl and Tracey expressed due sympathy toward such tragic circumstances.

Then, in a moment of frivolity, I posed a hypothetical question to Darryl (8). "Darryl," I said, "it's illegal to sell children in this country. And I'll never sell you even if it were legal. But suppose we were living in China during a severe drought, and I had no alternative but to sell you, how much—what price—do you think I should charge for you?"

I thought he would either say, "I have no idea," or "Ask for a million dollars." But after some thought, he came up with an extremely modest amount: "$49.99."

Then, after two seconds, he shook a raised finger, and added with emphasis, "Plus tax!"

[I was admittedly crazy to have raised such a hypothetical question during a dinner conversation. But his answer about his own estimation of his market worth was interesting to me for two reasons: (1) At a young age, he had already noticed that price tags often do not show whole dollars, but a penny less, so as to end in the form $ __9.99. (2) He had also noticed that "tax" is an automatic concomitant to the price. Here, he was of course referring to the sales tax. He would learn about other kinds of taxes soon enough.]

Husband Choice

One weekend, Emily's brother Johnny invited us to see his new house on Long Island. It has a nice layout, attractive furniture, a spacious backyard with a wide deck, neat lawn with automatic sprinkler system. Tracey was impressed, and expressed her admiration by saying, "I think I will try to marry a millionaire."

Hearing her spoken-out plan, I said to her, "Tracey, you should not think of marrying someone rich; you should think of studying hard, working hard, and become financially well off by your own effort."

She thought for a while, and replied, "Okay, I'll study hard and work hard, but if I don't succeed, I'll marry a millionaire."

[Good thinking, daughter. You should always have a Plan B.]

Death of a Tadpole

Tracey (8) once caught a tadpole, and kept it as a pet in a glass bowl. Unsure about the tadpole's true gender, she arbitrarily named it Richard. And, ignorant about the need to feed Richard, she provided nothing for it. Poor Richard died in a couple of days.

Darryl (10) felt sorry for Tracey's loss, and offered to conduct a funeral service for Richard in our living room. With due solemnity, he asked Tracey to be seated, and then delivered a speech: "Dearly beloved, we are gathered here today to say our last farewell to Richard, the tadpole. We are sorry that Richard has passed away, but let's shed no tears, for death is part of life, and there is life beyond death. . ."

At this point, driven by curiosity, Emily was already standing near the living room. Seeing Mom, Darryl turned, and asked, "Isn't that right, Mom?" Emily said approvingly, "That's right."

Then Darryl turned to Tracey, and said, "Tracey, before we bury Richard, let's have some music." Obligingly, Tracey stood up and walked to the piano that we just bought a few days ago. Even though she had not started piano lessons yet, she knew she had to play something in Richard's honor. So, with two fingers, she tapped out eight notes: so do do do, so re si do. The wedding march wasn't quite appropriate for the occasion, but it was music nonetheless.

Emily could not believe that Darryl was capable of saying something as profound as "death is part of life, and there is life beyond death." She felt the urge to call me at the office, and excitedly describe to me the whole episode. "Your father is a Christian minister," she added, "and I won't be surprised if Darryl follows his grandfather's footsteps someday."

I, too, was astounded. Once home from the office, I asked Darryl to repeat to me what he said at Richard's funeral, and he repeated those same words. Proudly, I patted his head, and said, "Those thoughts are quite profound. I am proud of you. How did you think of them?"

"Actually, Dad, I didn't think of them myself. I got these words from 'The Odd Couple' show."

[So, Darryl was not a pastor in the making. But this episode again exemplified his special gift for remembering theatrical scripts. He asked me whether I was less proud of him because those words were not his own. I told him that, though the words were not original, I was still proud of him for remembering them and applying them correctly on the appropriate occasion.]

Embarrassment

At a dinner at Rosal's Restaurant one night, Emily ordered a steak, medium rare. When the steak they served her turned to be well done, she calmly asked the waiter to send it back to the kitchen. Darryl (10) considered Mom's request to be "rude" and confided to her, "Mom, I am so embarrassed by this." Emily tried to relieve him of his anxiety with the explanation that, "There is no need to feel embarrassed, Darryl. If the food served is not what is ordered, then the customer has the perfect right to ask for a substitution. I don't feel embarrassed at all."

Unable to accept this point of view, Darryl retorted, "Of course you are NOT embarrassed, because you are the embarrassOR, and I am the embarrassEE!"

[I have heard of "lessor vs. lessee." But "embarrassor vs. embarrassee" is all new. Somehow, this kind of wording sounded like an attorney in the making, no?]

Summer Day Schedule

For the summer months, I told Tracey (9) to set up a time schedule to organize her daily activities. She dutifully presented to me a neatly written schedule in a couple of hours:

Schedule for week days Summer 79 Tracey

9:00 tom and jerry

9:30 fred flintstone and friends

10:00 mike douglas

11:00 lavirne and Shirley

1:30 sew

2:00 paint or draw

3:00 free time

4:00 Piano

4:30 munsters giligans island my three sons

5:00 wait till your father gets home

7:00–8:00 any tv show

8:30–9:30 free time

[So funny. Very organized. No capitalization except for the word Piano. Laverne is misspelled as lavirne. Poor kid: she only had two hours of "free time" each day!]

Applied Math

Darryl (12) sometimes impolitely referred to one of his fellow students as a "wimp" or a "jerk." Just to make conversation, I asked him, "Which is worse, a wimp or a jerk?" He said, "Equally bad."

Then, as a joke, I said, "Could someone be a 'wimpy jerk'?"

"Of course, that's what Bret is."

I should have stopped right there, but I continued to ask, "And could someone be a 'jerky wimp'?"

"Oh, that's what Bret is, too—because of the Commutative Law of Wimpiness."

[I laughed hard. He had obviously learned about the Commutative Law of Addition, $a + b = b + a$, and the Commutative Law of Multiplication, $a \times b = b \times a$. And, laudably, he was able to apply what he learned in one context to an altogether different one.]

Dad's Income

I don't recall how old Darryl was when he suddenly asked me one day, "Dad, how much do you make as a professor?"

Surprised that he wanted to know my income, I said, "Financial information like this is private and confidential. You should never ask anybody a question like that."

"But you are not 'anybody,' you are my dad, and we are family. You can trust me, you son; I won't tell anybody."

"Even so, you should not ask, and I wouldn't tell you."

Dissatisfied by my noncooperation, he reluctantly dropped the subject. But two days later, he flashed a big smile to me and said, "Dad, I know how much you make in salary." I asked him how he found that out. His source of information was a simple one: UConn professors are Connecticut state employees, and their salaries are public information.

"Jesse and I looked it up in the UConn library this afternoon," he said, "And, by the way, Jesse wasn't happy; you are making $10,000 more than his father."

[Resourceful kids indeed. They knew how and where to look for essential information.]

Scientific Nomenclature

Somehow a sound of passing gas erupted during our dinner one night, and that phenomenon became the subject of our conversation. Darryl asked, "How do you express that in English?" My answer of "flatulence" did not satisfy him, because he wanted a scientific term.

"For scientific nomenclature, you probably have to go to Latin, but I have no knowledge of Latin to speak of, so I am sorry I can't give you an answer," I said.

Tracey (12), who usually did not participate in our conversation, uncharacteristically joined in at that moment, and burst out with a great answer, "*Magna farta!*"

Everybody laughed.

[This unexpected bit of fake Latin from a 12-year-old Tracey should provide a fitting end to this report on my kids' early words and deeds.]

21

Castles in My Life

The first house I have ever lived in was the spacious Chiang family home in Baoshan, with lots of rooms, courtyard, banquet hall, and a garden with fruit trees. I think it qualified as a mansion. But I did not live there long. And, of course, after so many decades, it no longer existed, as Baoshan underwent inevitable modernization.

After Mother and I (at age 5) moved to Shanghai in 1932 to join Father, we shared a modest house with another family in the original walled city area of Shanghai, called Nanshi (南市, the South District). Several moves within Shanghai took place, but we remained renters, never the sole occupants of an individual dwelling.

The Sino-Japanese War, which broke out in 1937, spawned a vast, urgent wave of migration of Shanghai residents into the special areas of Shanghai known as French Concession and International Settlement (or British settlement), which, under foreign governance by treaties signed during the Qing Dynasty, afforded protection from the Japanese invasion forces.

34 Mei Lan Fang

The battle to get housing in the French Concession was fierce, but Father was able to purchase a unit, No. 34, in the compound called Mei Lan Fang (梅蘭坊) on *Rue Amiral Bayle* (貝勒路). The 80 or 90 houses in the compound had the same floor plan, with the front door facing south and opening to a miniature courtyard and the reception room, with a stairwell and a kitchen in the back. The narrow stairs led to a small so-called pavilion room (亭子間) at a landing turn, before reaching the main room on the second floor. Going up from there, we met another pavilion room at the turn of the stairs before reaching the third floor main room, and an open terrace atop the pavilion rooms.

To me, at age 10, that house was eminently impressive. It was quite new, clean, and even equipped with modern plumbing. Besides, the name of the compound, Mei Lan Fang, sounded exactly like that of my Chinese opera idol Mei Lan Fang (梅蘭芳). And the two digits of the house number, 34, add up to 7, a lucky number. Above all, I was joyous over the prospect of living in our own individual house for the first time!

My joy soon proved to be premature. Since the demand for housing in the French Concession and International Settlement far exceeded the supply, Father was inundated by requests from friends and relatives to rent to them part of the house. Finally, a Chen family and a Hsu family occupied the ground floor and the third floor, respectively. And, moreover, several of Mother's relatives had no place to go but to move in with us. As a result, No. 34 became a very crowded house. We even had to construct new attic-like sleeping spaces to accommodate us all. Under the extraordinary circumstances of resistance against Japanese aggression, I could not have a big room to myself, or even a pavilion room. In fact, I had to sleep in my parents' room on the second floor for years during the war. Under the circumstances of war, I could only accept such reality without voicing any complaints. But no complaint did not mean I was pleased. I strongly wished for spacious living quarters, like those of some of my friends and classmates. Anyway, I secretly made a promise to myself: someday, I will live in a nice, spacious, well-decorated house—a "castle" of my own.

A tiny step forward occurred when my seventh *jiujiu* (mother's youngest brother) decided to leave Shanghai, and the pavilion room he had occupied became mine. It was not spacious, but it would be my own room, where I could look out the window and watch the goings-on in the lane down below. Soon, I noticed a four-word phrase written in pencil on the windowsill. To my consternation, it was a derogatory remark against my family. While its authorship was unknown, there had been only one previous occupant in this room. My heart was broken, because I had always held this *jiujiu* in high regard because he had taught me many things. He taught me an easy way to draw parallel lines with a pair of triangles: just hold one triangle fixed and slide the other along its edge. He also taught me to play the harmonica: Merry Widow, Skaters' Waltz, and so on. Since my parents were extra-generous with him, paying all his expenses including tuition, and providing him a monthly allowance, that penciled derogatory remark showed inexplicable ungratefulness. I hesitated about relating this incident. But it was an important moment in my life: it was at that moment that a dose of cynicism entered my innocent mind for the very first time.

I could not forgive him until, decades later, I saw him in person again in Xian, on one of my trips to China. He looked frail, but could still recall a small incident in my childhood. I was sure he no longer remembered the windowsill remark he wrote. "Chung-i (中一, my Chinese name), do you remember the night you sang 'Moonlight and Shadow' on a children's program on radio?" he asked. "Yes, I do," I replied, surprised that he could even name the song (from a Dorothy Lamour movie) that I sang, "I did it, all because I wanted a pair of free sun-glasses, which I never actually got." The radio program was a promotion sponsored by an optical company. They issued an open invitation to all children in Shanghai to join a singing marathon on radio, and promised a pair of free sunglasses for each participant. I had no way to get to the radio station till my third *jiujiu* agreed to take me there in the evening. By that time, they had already run out of sunglasses.

The reminiscence about this little incident somehow softened my feelings toward this *jiujiu*. Thus, I continued our conversation in Xian with 100% politeness, as a good nephew should.

After China won the Sino-Japanese War in 1945, the Hsu family left No. 34, and I finally moved from the pavilion room into the big room on the third floor, which I had expected to be mine to begin with. If nothing else, I now got the space I long craved, though in no way could I consider it as my castle.

Rentals Galore

Becoming a graduate student in the United States meant renting living quarters. In Boulder, Colorado, the Three Musketeers lived in a hotel for a while before I rented a room in the Vaniman house. After moving to New York, I first roomed with several friends, and then rented a room from Mrs. Fisher on West 124th Street, near Broadway. After a number of years there, I rented a room on Fleet Street, south of Queens Boulevard in Forest Hills, to concentrate on writing my doctoral dissertation. Then, before I got married and left New York, I shared a two-bedroom apartment at 640 Riverside Drive, with Chris Wu (吴肇勳), James Yu (尤紹新), and S. C. Siao (蕭孫祺).

Even in Ohio, after I started full-time teaching in 1954 at Denison University, we lived in a rental. The university-owned, one-bedroom apartment in the College Town House was within walking distance of the campus. The rent we paid was unbelievably low, and it even included utilities and furnishings. We resided there for six years, until we went to Hong Kong during my sabbatical leave. Then, upon returning from Hong Kong, we rented a bigger university-owned apartment in Stone Hall. This time, we had two bedrooms, one of which I used as my study, a luxury. Financially better off than before, we bought furniture of our own for every room.

The next rental, at Prince Albert Apartments on Whalley Avenue in New Haven, Connecticut, during my National Science Foundation Fellowship tenure at Yale University, remained in my memory for three things. First, in the back of the apartment building behind the parking lot, there was a rugged mountain precipice that looked like a classical Chinese landscape painting. I loved taking a long look at that mountain every morning as I started the car, reminiscing about the days in Shanghai when I was studying Chinese landscaping painting.

Second, for the first time in my life, I made an expensive purchase on impulse. On a particular stormy night, answering a knock on the door, I faced a young man who looked tired and was wet. He was selling Collier's Encyclopedia, which I did not need. But he appeared to be desperately wanting to make a sale, and I somehow envisaged his family waiting anxiously for him to return home with food money.

It pained me to see him go through his sales ritual amid the ominous thunder and lightning. I wrote a check to him right away. The many volumes of the encyclopedia graced my book shelf for years, although I did not use them much. My children probably found more use for those bulky volumes as they grew up. Then, during one of the moves later, it was necessary to discard the whole set. Nowadays, of course, when all kinds of information are available on the internet, the word "encyclopedia" has become of historic interest only.

The third thing associate with Prince Albert Apartments was the momentous news of President Kennedy's assassination that came over the radio. We were sadly shocked and badly shaken, along with the whole nation and, in fact, the entire world!

Emily and I did not think of buying a house until I joined the faculty of the University of Connecticut in 1964, where we decided to settle down. To allow ample time for house-hunting, though, we still rented a house for the first year. Norman Kogan, Professor of Political Science, and his wife Meryl planned to spend a sabbatical leave in Italy in 1964–1965, and we rented their house on Eastwood Road, within walking distance to the campus.

The Kogan house was significant for me, because that was where I wrote the first pages of *Fundamental Methods of Mathematical Economics*. I used my own portable typewriter at first, before the delivery of the IBM Selectric I requisitioned for the office.

For house-hunting fun, we ventured out far and wide every weekend. But every house we looked at seemed to contain one or two design flaws, if not more. In one case, as soon as we stepped into the building, we got turned off by the layout, and wanted to turn around and leave right away. In another house, closet space was woefully lacking. We had to keep looking week after week.

Southwood Road

Then, our real-estate agent Lynn Bobb showed us a ranch-style house that fulfilled most of the needs we had in mind. It had a spacious living room with a big picture window, two bedrooms, a dining room with a modern tri-globe chandelier, a kitchen with lower-than-normal counters (ideal for Emily), and a flight of stairs leading to a walkout basement and a huge backyard beneath the living room window. Attached to the house was an enclosed porch, plus a two-car carport. Our furniture fit in well, although we needed to buy something for the basement and the porch. Being on a short street with very few houses, this house did not even carry a house number. It was easy for Emily and me to make a positive decision.

Lynn Bobb and her husband had built this house for their own use, but later sold it. We bought it in 1965 through Lynn from a Mrs. Jeraldine Withycombe. Interestingly, when we later sold this house in 1971, it was again through Lynn as our agent. With so many successive transactions, this house certainly proved to be a vastly profitable property for her!

We did not need to make major changes to this house. But, to give it a more positive, hopeful, and uplifting look, we later changed the outside color of the house from steel gray to barn red. That became my first "castle."

21.1 The first house I owned: Southwood Road, Storrs, Connecticut, 1965–1971.

Memories from the First Castle

To us, the Southwood House was most memorable for the birth of our son Darryl in 1968 and our daughter Tracey in 1970. My parents came from Hong Kong for Darryl's birth, and we of course set them up in the master bedroom, and moved ourselves down to the basement. We had arranged for permanent residency in the United States for my parents and, as part of the legal requirement, they had to be physically present in the United States for a stipulated number of days each year. On this visit, we took them to see New York City, and showed them Columbia University where I studied, toured the United Nations, and enjoyed a spectacular show at the Radio City Music Hall.

Unlike many Chinese, my parents did not mind American food in restaurants. In fact, Father soon developed a taste for pizza with pepperoni topping, and Mom, salad bowl with sliced ham and boiled egg on top for lunch. But mostly we ate Chinese at home. Mom was an excellent cook, and Emily learned a great deal from her. Mom was also an extraordinarily skilled mahjong player. So, naturally, we played mahjong often, asking her to teach us. That was for fun, not for gambling. Whoever won was required to put the money in a tin can, and when there was sufficient fund, we went out to dinner. Guess who was the biggest contributor to the can?

Father showed an interest in driving. I gave him driving lessons in a deserted parking lot after hours. In turn, he spent a lot of his leisure time on washing the car, making my Dodge Lancer the cleanest automobile in town.

After Tracey's birth, dear Mother kindly agreed to stay on with us for a whole year to help out with the new baby, and poor Father had to take care of himself while tending to his church in Hong Kong. What sacrifices they were willing to make for us!

Relating to my career, the Southwood Road House was memorable because it was there that I did a tremendous amount of overtime work on the book. After coming home from the office, I would regularly follow the routine of taking a short nap after dinner, and then resuming writing till midnight every night. Seven days a week. Fifty-two weeks a year. This high-intensity effort was what made it possible to beat the deadline for manuscript submission to McGraw-Hill. Strangely, and luckily, I remained completely healthy throughout the solid two-year period of hard work without a single break.

Also memorable were a couple of joyful opportunities to witness the power of nonverbal communication with a child. When Darryl knew how to walk, I installed a collapsible gate at the top of the stairs to prevent him from falling downstairs. One time I needed to go down to get something, and he followed me to the stairs. I stepped down, turned around to close the gate, and raised my pointing finger, and said, "等一下 (Wait a moment)." He could not yet understand my words, but he also raised a pointing finger to mirror my gesture, and patiently waited at the same spot for my return. A few days later, he followed me again to the stairs. He raised his pointing finger before I raised mine to signal him to stop and wait. I marveled at the ease of nonverbal communication between father and son.

As Darryl's walking ability progressed, we allowed him to venture into the front yard. Emily held his hand and led him through the permissible walking space. But at the edge of the street, she drew a line with her hand, and shook her hand to signal that he was forbidden to go beyond that line into the street. To test whether Darryl understood the nonverbal instruction, she released her hand and let Darryl walk by himself over the grass. He did walk to the edge of the street, and each time he obeyed the restriction. The hand signal did work.

We didn't use a similar communication signal for Tracey, because we moved out of Southwood Road before she could walk.

35 Beech Mountain Road

The completion of my book, and the growth of my family, prompted us to look for new housing. Lynn Bobb took us through quite a few houses, all problematic. However, one house, on Beech MountainRoad in Mansfield Center, a few miles south of the University of Connecticut

(UConn) campus in Storrs, impressed both Emily and me as a lovely and lovable residence. Because of the terrain, half way up the mountain, the houses on one side of the street sat higher above the street, whereas those on the other side were situated below the street level. The house we liked, 35 Beech Mountain Road, a ranch-style building on a corner lot, rose above the street with a gravel U-shaped driveway in front, and a paved driveway leading from a side street to its garage on the side of the house. With the garage on the side, the front of the house only showed a stately double door in the middle, a wide picture window of the living room on one side of the double door, framed by bricks, and some bedroom windows on the other, dotting the aluminum siding.

Inside, a foyer with slate floor led to a sunken living room on the right with a fireplace, framed by bricks all the way up to the cathedral ceiling. A suite of four bedrooms was located to the left of the foyer. A wall facing the front door hid a dining room behind it. Toward the back of the sunken living room, we found an all-electric kitchen with a dining area, and a good-sized family room, a porch, a deck, and backyard with tree after tree.

Everything was to our liking except two features: (1) On the outside, the narrow stone path from the U-shaped driveway in front to the double door was not only narrow, but ended with a shabby-looking, step-stool-like connection to the wide landing in front of the house. It looked totally incongruous with the imposing double door. (2) Inside, the wallpaper on the wall facing the front door featured an ugly, objectionable Oriental motif. It looked fake. The plastic plants lying limply down below were even worse. The good thing is that those defects could be fixed with relatively little effort.

But one thing was hard to fix: the owner's asking price was so high that it probably was the highest ever heard in that region: Mrs. Martha Calise was asking $57,000—way beyond my professorial means! Emily and I could only look at each other with regretful expressions.

At the Election Queue

A few months later, while waiting in a long queue at the 1970 Presidential election site, a "hello" came from behind, and it was Lynn Bobb lining up right next to us. We greeted each other, and the subject inevitably turned to the housing market.

"Do you remember that Calise house?" Lynne said, "It hasn't been sold, and in fact she hasn't received any offer at all. So it's still on the market. If you still like it, why don't you make an offer on it?"

"I wish I could, but the figure we had in mind was only $45,000. That would already be a stretch for us, yet way below the asking price. To make an offer like that would be too insulting to the owner." I said.

"You never know, Alpha. I would encourage you to make an offer anyway, at $45,000. The worst is that she'll reject it. What have you got to lose?"

What happened was that we did make the offer. And the seller and the buyer agreed to "split the difference" between the asking and offering prices. Thanks to the capable Lynn Bonn, a deal was struck at the astronomical sum of $51,000. In May, 1971, we became its new owner. Our decision to assume Mrs. Calise's 15-year mortgage meant a substantial monthly payment for a very tight mortgage period, a financial stretch for me for quite a few years.

At that point, I discovered a mysterious set of similarities between the Southwood House and the Beech Mountain Road house. In both cases, the house was the fourth house on the left on the street. In both cases, we bought from a divorced lady. And in both cases Bobb was our agent. And, lastly, in both cases, the previous owner had to search for the house keys we asked for. Imagine: the doors were never locked in those days.

I now had my second "castle."

Our Botanist Neighbor

We were overjoyed to learn that our next-door neighbor, Professor Howard Pfeiffer, taught botany at UConn. He was not only knowledgeable about plants, but actually kept more than 200 species of plant life in his backyard. When we invited him over for a drink, he was kind enough to offer us several excellent suggestions on landscaping.

First, he suggested a dogwood tree and a variety of flowers to plant, including rhododendron, azalea, and *boule de neige* (snow ball), which tended to bloom at different times, so as to prolong the flowering season. Second, the planting should be done far enough away from the house so as to be viewable from inside the living room, as well as from outside. For that reason, most of the planting should adorn the living room side of the house. Third, the path from the U-shaped driveway to the front door landing should be drastically widened, and, with pressurized railroad ties and gravels, built into gently rising steps, very wide from the bottom, but gradually narrowing till the highest step matched the top landing in width. That added a stately entry walk extending a palpable sense of welcome.

I followed all of Howard's advices. In addition, I bought a truckload of big, odd-shaped rocks and placed them strategically on the two sides of the railroad-tie steps. I made sure that the bottoms of the rocks were duly buried in dirt, to avoid the look that those rocks were just floating on top of the soil. I love the external appearance of this house, and captured it in Photo 7 in the front of this book. Photo 33 also shows a partial frontal view of it.

Rick Repko

Turning to the inside, the first thing I did was to take down the Oriental-motif wallpaper in the foyer, and root out the plastic plants in the small rectangular planting area on the floor. But there was some question as to how to finish the foyer and what furniture to buy for the four-bedroom residence. Fortuitously, an advertisement in the newspaper caught my attention just then. Rick Repko, a young interior designer, was opening a furniture store in nearby Manchester, and offering free interior design service to furniture buyers. I immediately dialed his number.

He appeared very young and artsy. He wore platform shoes, but did not sport a weird hairdo, or outrageous clothing. Articulate, and mindful of our likes and dislikes, he impressed us with many interesting suggestions. For the foyer wall, (1) use a cork-based wallpaper, (2) look for a shapely dead branch in our backyard, paint it white, then anchor it in a heavy, black planter pot, with white stones in the pot as well in the empty planting area at the foot of the wall. All of these should go well with the black slate floor in the foyer and the cork-based wallpaper. "And be sure to let the main branch point to the right," he said, "that way, the entering guests will naturally follow the direction of the branch to walk towards the right, into the living room."

The branch I picked out from the backyard stood out distinctively against the cork wallpaper that revealed scattered glittering blue spots from behind. But, to add a more personal touch to it, I also designed and carved a seal on a one-square-foot block of wood, bearing the name I gave to this house: 別趣山居 (Bie Qu Shan Ju), with several possible meanings. From its sound, the name could simply mean "A Residence on Beech Mountain," but the words could also be interpreted as "A Residence with Extraneous Charms," or even "The Home of One with Varied Interests." Such was the admirable richness and flexibility of the Chinese language! My own preference was for the third meaning; to characterize myself, accurately, as a person with many hobbies—Chinese art, Chinese opera, dancing—which could serve as a good apologia for my less-than-full attention to my chosen field of work, and failure to attain my "potential" in it. Painted in red and white like the seal used on Chinese paintings, and hung on the wall near the pointing branch, this seal greeted our visitors for two decades. The white branch and the red seal are shown in Photo 8 in the front of this book. Another view of the foyer is captured in Photo 48, depicting our family in a frivolous moment of impromptu acting mood. The white branch is on the right, against the cork-based wallpaper; the hallway next to it leads to the bedrooms; on the left are the back sides of the double door.

For the lengthy living room, Repko selected for us two long sofas (partially visible in Photo 9) to be placed perpendicularly to each other, in blue-on-blue pattern (our preferred color), with a corner table connecting them. The coffee table he found for us was a unique round one topped with four marble petals sitting around a wooden cross on a chrome base. And, for seating with the back toward the foyer, he found us two modern chairs in royal blue, again in beautiful, modern chrome frames. He maintained that the chrome frames were important because the backs of those two chairs would be the first thing to enter into guests' eye view, so they must look attractive. I liked the fact that he thought of such a subtle yet important point. That was why I immediately said okay to his proposal to design the furniture for the children's rooms instead of purchasing ready-made ones.

For each child, Repko designed a desk, book shelf and chest of drawers, all in white, and all made to measure to fit the bedroom. In view of Darryl's fascination with automobiles, the face of the chest was graced with bold cutouts of two colorful cars instead of the usual pullouts. Tracey, who had not yet shown any special objects of love, got colorful cutouts of flowers instead. Blue walls were for Darryl and yellow ones for Tracey.

The bedroom for my parents was decorated more traditionally, with curtains rather than vertical blinds, a double bed, chest of drawers, and a custom-made desk with a piece of glass on top, the way my father wanted.

For the dining room, we asked Repko to design a round banquet table with oak finish, with a matching Lazy Susan. Surprisingly, he delayed its delivery again and again. Only after I pressed on him hard, did he confess that there was a problem with his design. The single post he had chosen for the table was too slim to support the heavy table top, causing the top to sway. I quickly solved his problem by suggesting the replacement of the single post by a bigger square column. Soon the finished table and Laze Susan were delivered, to everyone's satisfaction. He was also able to find 10 sleek but sturdy chairs, in blue, with short arms so they could be tucked under the table when not in use. I love this custom-made table, but had to give it to a friend when we moved, because it could not fit into our new house. In Photo 35, we had Emily's cousin Alice Ho Li (李何娟蓉) and her husband Shu-Tung Li (李樹東) over for dinner. Shu-Tung was a graduate student at UConn at the time (1975), but later founded a very successful company, Collagen Matrix, in 1997, that makes artificial body parts such as tissues, bones, and so on. See also Photo 36 for a fuller view of the dining room.

Repko came to our house several times, and we had lots of conversation. One time, he mentioned in passing that he owned a Rolls Royce that once belonged to the Shah of Iran. Thinking that he was just bragging, I simply said, "Oh, marvelous." Then a couple of months later, while driving in Manchester, I saw a Rolls Royce in the oncoming traffic, and lo and behold, it was indeed Repko steering that classic beauty! He then won my complete trust, and I became very proud to have had him design my Beech Mountain House, a house to my total liking, my second "castle"!

Memories from the Second Castle

Life in my second castle was by no means all happiness. In the basement, where a dungeon would have been located in a real castle, there was a movable partition in a big room aside from a sizable storage room. I kept a study on one side of the partition, and a ping-pong table on the other. I was pleased with this setup, but rain water obviously shared my fondness for the basement, and it always tried to enter through the hatchway door in the backyard every opportunity it had. We installed a curtain drain around the hatchway. It did not work. We re-graded the backyard, creating more of a slope away from the hatchway. But the backyard was not deep enough for this to work either. What finally gave us a dry basement was a big drain at a low point in the backyard, with a big underground pipe leading away from the house at a steep angle. It cost me a lot.

At one time, termites also discovered the charm of my castle, and moved in uninvited. When I saw a few of them on the foyer floor, I was disturbed, and then I saw more of them, and became really alarmed. Fortunately, a good exterminator answered my urgent call, and fed pesticides into holes he drilled inside and outside the house. I was happy to see that just a single extermination treatment was sufficient to fix this serious, thorny problem.

Mostly, though, life in this castle left good memories. I finished writing another book, *Elements of Dynamic Optimization*, while living on Beech Mountain. The subject matter of this book was in fact a continuation of the contents of *Fundamental Methods of Mathematical Economics*, thus I jokingly referred to it as "the son of *Fundamental Methods*." While working on this volume, I could not muster the same work intensity as when I was younger, but I still worked into the nights often, in my study down below in the dungeon area downstairs. Photo 30 in the front of this book shows the cover designs of both of these books.

The children grew through elementary school, middle school, high school, and college, and beyond in those years. I gave them daily lessons on the Chinese language, which they hated of course, at least at first. They sometimes helped me rake the leaves in the fall, and clear snow in the winter off the 100-foot long, paved side driveway, especially when there was a huge storm, like Storm Larry, which happened to occur on Chinese New Year's Day in 1978, causing Governor Grasso to declare that day a holiday. The whole family joined forces in shoveling snow; I didn't appear in Photo 37, only because I was taking the picture.

I started a new hobby, piano playing while residing on Beech Mountain. Also, Emily and I began our serious training in ballroom dancing during our residency there. These, I will elaborate on in Chapters 26 and 33, respectively.

Neighbors

Beech Mountain was a friendly neighborhood. There were home visits, and parties. One funny incident has especially remained alive in my memory. Our next-door neighbor, Howard Pfeiffer, habitually worked on his plants in his backyard bare-chested and sweat-covered. At one dinner party, one of the lady guests, seeing Howard fully dressed, with tie and all, said to him in a voice audible to all, "Hi, Howard, I can hardly recognize you with your clothes on!" Everybody roared with laughter. But other conversations were more conventional, and not as report-worthy.

Halloween was great fun for the neighborhood kids, of which there were many, mostly in two or three age groups. Since the houses on Beech Mountain were located far apart from one another, some parents arranged hayrides for the young kids going from one house to the next on Halloween. Some volunteer parents would lift these kids up to the hay truck and help them off at each stop. And some older kids would run ahead of the hay truck to warn the successive homes, "They are coming! They are coming!" Later, at the end of the evening, all the adults would gather at the estate of the orthopedic surgeon Dr. Sage Sikand and his wife Fran, for a party of our own. The Sikand family had the largest home in the area, and they regularly hosted our July 4 cookouts, as well as New Year's Eve parties.

Photos 18 and 19 carry memories of Halloween on Beech Mountain.

Visits of My Parents

My parents visited the United States from Hong Kong many times. The permanent resident status we had obtained for them required them to be physically in this country every year, and they did come every year. But the mandatory travel soon became a burden to them. Unwilling to give up his church in Hong Kong, Father decided to give up the permanent residency. After that, they still came, but on visitors' visas instead.

Mother was with us to help with the care of Tracey when we bought the Beech Mountain house. And Father came to bring her back to Hong Kong about the time we made the actual move. So, all three generations formally began our occupancy of the Beech Mountain "castle" in 1971 together, filling all the four bedrooms. But after one full year of Mother's stay with us, she went back to Hong Kong with Father.

Once again, they came to Beech Mountain in June, 1975. To celebrate Father's 71st birthday, we took a family trip to Niagara Falls, a famed sight Father had always wanted to see. Emily and I had been to Niagara before, but it was new for my parents and children. The sight of the ferocious running and cascading water, plus the Maiden of the Mist boat ride behind the Cataracts, made a treasured impression on my parents. It was a great birthday celebration. But, after celebrating Mother's 70th birthday with a banquet in New York, they again returned to Hong Kong.

A full nine years passed by before they visited Beech Mountain again. This time, we celebrated Father's 80th birthday, in August 1984, by taking them on a tour of Washington, DC. Father had always been an avid newspaper reader and follower of world events, and he was interested in seeing the seat of American government and politics. We obtained White House tour tickets from our Congressman, but the lines outside the White House were like those for a hot rock concert. Luckily, since I was pushing my mother in a rented wheelchair on account of her ill health, a security agent was kind enough to signal me to follow him to a side entrance. Avoiding stairs, he led us into a small old-fashioned elevator inside, up to a floor, through a small room to rejoin the tour group. I thanked him for his kindness, and asked him what that small room was for. He told me that it was President and Mrs. Reagan's private dining room. I told Mother that we had just gone through a part of the White House that no other tourists could see. Father was envious when I told him about this minor but special detour in the White House for Mother and me.

The Beech Mountain House became very dear to me, especially after we fixed up all the problems that vexed us. I would not have minded to live in it forever. But after I decided to retire from UConn by accepting an early retirement package, Emily expressed a strong desire to move to White Plains, New York, to be near her elder sister Chinyee. By then, the children had already flown out of the nest. Our longtime friendship circle and Chinese opera association in New York also counted as an argument for moving. In addition, I would welcome the relief from the daily raking of leaves in the fall, and the seasonal worries about snow. So, I resolved to abandon my second "castle" in May, 1994, after a 23-year ownership.

8 Cottonwood Lane

In one conversation I had with my father soon after that, he seemed to indicate his willingness (finally) to join us in America on a permanent basis, even specifically suggesting that we get two apartments in the same building, so that we could be close to each other, yet still maintain our mutual independence. Accordingly, we bought a second apartment in White Plains, where we already owned a rental property, on Nosband Avenue, a very short but lovely street. But when we discovered that Mother was displaying early Alzheimer's symptoms, we had to revise our thinking, and consider buying a single house for the whole family instead.

In May, 1995, our stay on Nosband Avenue in White Plains came to an end as soon as the construction of a town house at the Ridgeway in White Plains was completed to our specifications. We chose the particular house, at 8 Cottonwood Lane, for several reasons. First, the front door faced south, the preferred direction in the Chinese culture. Second, the house number is 8, a lucky number in Chinese superstition. Third, it had all the features we desired: four bedrooms upstairs, a living room on the ground floor with space for a baby grand piano I had just bought at Emily's instigation, a kitchen with an island, a dining area to the side of the long kitchen with a window to the backyard, a formal dining room, which we converted into a family room, plus two and half bathrooms, as well as a basement.

We did have to ask the builder to correct one seemingly minor, but really pivotal, defect outside of the house. The builder had planted a big tree straight in front of the front door, thus violating a major rule of *feng shui*. Literally meaning "wind-water," *feng shui* is an ancient Chinese pseudo-science relating to spatial relationships between men and the environment. It prescribes dos and don'ts about the positioning of a house in relation to the street, and the arrangement of doors, stairs, furniture, lighting, and other aspects of the house. One rule is that the back door should not be located such that you can see it from the front door. Another states that the stairs should not directly face the front door. There are many others that even a nonexpert like me knows by heart.

The problem posed by the big tree straight in front of the door was that it blocks the flow of *chi* (or *qui*, energy) into the house. I had to insist that the builder move the tree away from the direct path of the front door. To me, that was quite essential. An indirect proof of the correctness of my decision soon emerged from what happened to the house next to ours. That neighboring house not only had a sizable tree in front of the front door, but a huge rock next to the tree, giving it a double blockage. On first seeing that *feng shui* fault, I predicted to Emily that whoever occupies of this house would have problems. And, sure enough, there occurred in the next few years an abnormally high turnover of residents in that house. Several families successively moved in, but each one left within a few months for one reason or another. The only good thing was that it proved a boon to real-estate agents. Was the high turnover just a coincidence? I tend to think *feng shui* had a great deal to do with it.

One eye-catching feature in our house was a two-story-high foyer with a chandelier, facing a railed walkway upstairs that linked all the bedrooms. A finished basement provided a space for dance-step practices and Chinese opera rehearsals after we installed special mirrors on one complete side of the wall. I used one side of the basement for as extra study space, and Emily used the other side as her sewing quarters.

Photo 55 in the front of this book shows the external view of the Cottonwood Lane house. A wonderful feeling of liberation enveloped me after we moved to this house. No leaves to rake, and no snow to plow. The Homeowners' Association took care of those chores. A corner of our living room can be seen in Photo 21.2.

The house was attractive enough for me to consider it as my third "castle." I gave this residence the name of 餘廬 (Yü Lu), with three implied meanings. While the second word (Lu) in this name simply means an abode, the first word (Yü) could be alternatively interpreted to mean "leftover," or "avocational," or "surplus." All of these three

21.2 A corner of our living room on Cottonwood Lane.

interpretations seem to fit in with this new residence. First, when we left Connecticut, we had to discard a large percentage of our belongings; what we retained were literally the leftover stuff. Second, I made a promise to myself that in my remaining years, I will let my hobbies—avocational interests—rule my daily activities. Third, like everybody else, I cherish the hope that I would have a surplus at the end of every year. I carved another wood block and painted it in red and while as a Chinese seal. The seal is visible on the wall in Photos 56 and 68 in the front of this book.

Of these three implied meanings, the first was simply a statement of fact. The third was a wish, with an outcome beyond my control. The only control I had was over the second, regarding the pursuit of hobbies. My intention has largely been fulfilled. I certainly could not leave the baby grand piano to stand all alone at one end of the living room. So I often played on it with abandon at any hours of the day. My favorite time was at the end of the day, close to midnight. No neighbors could hear the sound anyway, and I would not be disturbing them even at that late hour. For my Chinese calligraphy hobby, I had rice paper and ink spread out in one of the bedrooms at all times, so that I could practice whenever my whim sent me there without having to set things up every time. Emily and I did a lot of Chinese opera singing, and took a lot of dancing lessons, both group and private.

Many friends and relatives visited us in White Plains. In particular, we had a gathering of some of my cousins in White Plains in 2004, on the occasion of a visit of my cousin Zhongquan Jiang (蔣中權) and his wife Shufen Li (李樹芬) from Dalian (大連), China. He and I share the same family name, but they now spell it differently under the new transliteration in Mainland China. One year my junior, he was one of the youngsters who went to the levee in Baoshan together, where I suffered a fall from the cliff. But that happened some 70 years ago! I was happy to host a dinner in his honor, and invited some other cousins residing in the United States to meet him and his wife. In Photo 68 in the front of this book, I gave the English names of the people; here I add their names in Chinese. The five in the front are, from left, Zhongquan Jiang, Clark and Julia Chiang (蔣中寬程靜梅夫婦), Diane and James Chow (周爾恭關明珠夫婦); the three ladies in the back are Shufen Li (half hidden), Eva Tien (蔣懿範), Emily; and the two men in the back are Rex Tien (田元) and me.

Cousin Clark and Julia lived on Long Island, and so did James and Diane. Because they had different circles of friends from me, I did not see them often. Eva and Rex joined us from Warwick, Rhode Island, near Brown University. I did not see them too often either, but we are grateful that they kindly took good care of Tracey during her college days at Brown.

But the post-retirement years were not all fun and play. I also worked on the fourth edition of *Fundamental Methods of Mathematical Economics*, although not at top intensity on account of my advancing age.

Parents' Quarters

The primary reason for us to give up the Nosband Avenue apartments (where we stayed from 1993 to 1995) in favor of a town house on Cottonwood Lane was to accommodate my parents, who could no longer live independently in separate apartments in view of Mother's

Alzheimer affliction. We reserved two of the four bedrooms for their use, one for sleeping and the other for sitting. Yet, Mother never set foot in this townhouse. She died in Hong Kong before the construction of the house was completed. Father did come for seven weeks between October and December 1995, mainly to participate in Darryl's wedding ceremony, saying a prayer in Chinese at the altar, but also to visit Mother's grave near our home and call on some friends and relatives. But he never came to live us on a permanent basis. Unfortunately, Darryl's first marriage was not permanent either; it lasted only for a year.

Memories from the Third Castle

Emily has always been very close to her elder sister Chinyee. During our years at Cottonwood Lane, the two sisters lived within five minutes of walk in the same compound. Close proximity was one of the reasons why we chose that house to purchase in the first place. Short, spur-of-the-moment visits were frequent, a treat for the two of them. Once in a while, Chinyee and her husband H. Y. Sung (宋錫元), Emily and I would play a low-stake mahjong game together after dinner, more for the conversation than for the game itself.

Emily's second elder brother Johnny Ho (何欽翔) and his wife Pearl (周淑婉), residing on Long Island, saw us less often. But we still tried to have dinner together as our respective time schedules permitted. An electric engineer by training, Johnny became a successful entrepreneur after he and some friends started a corporation, Frequency Electronics, years ago. He is extremely handy, and is very generous with his time and skills. His house-warming gift to us at Cottonwood Lane was a complete set of dimmers for all our light switches. But Emily only accepted two, one at the kitchen island and another at the dining table. But just a few months later, the dimmer for the light over the dining table stopped functioning. Since such a small repair job would not interest an electrician, Emily naturally thought of Johnny for help. She invited Johnny and Pearl to come for dinner, but added, "By the way, one of the dimmers is not working, please bring your tool box, plus a new dimmer." Johnny obliged as usual. As we greeted them on

21.3 Emily's elder brother John Ho and his wife Pearl.

our driveway on the appointed day, and as Johnny was taking out his tool box from the car trunk, Pearl made a casual remark: "Could the problem be just be a burnt-out light bulb?" That remark hit me like a rock. "Oh, no," I silently said to myself, "let it not be a bulb. We would look so foolish and stupid." Well, no such luck! When I changed the globe bulb, the light came on instantly! That was the most embarrassing situation we had experienced in a long, long time.

Our participation in the Chinese Opera Association of New York naturally became much more active now that we had moved to White Plains, New York. Aside from involvement in the performances the group put on, usually at the auditorium of the Fashion Institute of Technology in Manhattan, I also edited and published special booklets to commemorate special shows. In October, 2001, it was a 66-page booklet for our Golden (50-year) Anniversary show with several essays and lots of photographs. See Photo 64 for its cover. Then, 10 years later, I did another 30-page booklet for our Diamond (60-year) Anniversary show in October 2011, with stories and new photographs. They were meaningful souvenirs for my long involvement with the Chinese Opera Association of New York.

We were invited to many private dinner–dance parties, usually with 100 people attending. In turn, we hosted many such parties. Many of our friends were serious dancers, taking lessons regularly, and inviting their instructors as their dance partners. I will report on these in more details later in Chapter 33.

Waving Goodbye

Again, I felt that we could live in this third castle forever. But Emily grew worried about the future days when we would not be able to drive, and would be pitiably stuck in this compound far away from shops and restaurants. She then took the initiative to start a search for a retirement community with medical facilities and meal plans. That search eventually landed us in a retirement community in northern New Jersey, called Cedar Crest, in Pompton Plains.

With mixed feelings, I waved goodbye to our third "castle" in 2012, taking with us 17 years' worth of memories.

22

Art on the Walls

I studied Chinese classical landscape painting with a private tutor when I was young, and brought many of my works with me to the United States. But they were all unmounted, in a wrinkly state, unsuitable for display. More importantly, I grew tired of the style I studied, and intended to switch to a more impressionistic style. But schoolwork and social activities prevented me from pursuing that hobby to any fruitful extent. And I never adorned the walls of my "castles" with my own paintings.

A Chinyee Gallery

The principal artist that I do feature on my walls has been Chinyee Sung (宋何欽翼, 藝名青意), Emily's elder sister. A major in fine arts, she has produced many lovely watercolors, and acrylic and oil paintings in her life. For many years, she had worked as a simultaneous interpreter of Chinese language at the United Nations, but she never really stopped her art pursuit. And after her retirement from the United Nations, she has maintained an art studio near her home, and spent most of her time painting and drawing. She has held numerous exhibitions, in the New York area, as well as in Hong Kong, Tianjin, and Shanghai, China, and published several art catalogs.

The first piece of her work that I own is an abstract oil painting (36" × 51") I bought at her very first solo exhibition in New York in 1965. Its blue motif, with sky-blue background and dark blue mass on top and strokes of lines cascading down to a white mass and a brownish-yellow shape below, is suggestive of a rainstorm. But there is no feeling of tempest, only a sense of quiet cleansing. It fits in perfectly with our blue furniture in the living room on Beech Mountain. You can see a partial view of it in Photos 9 and 77 in the front of this book.

Chinyee also gave us some watercolors and a collage over the years. One of my favorites is a 17" × 17" work with blue, purple, and red masses strategically positioned against one another. It is visible in the upper right corner of Photo 32 in the front of this book.

The collage, a small square work of black, gray, with red blotches, had an interesting origin. When trying to thin out her accumulation of watercolors, the thought occurred to her that she could tear those watercolors to pieces and then reassemble them into collages. The resulting pieces were the most beautiful collages I have ever seen. The one I hang in my bedroom now is mostly black and gray, so I print here in black-and-white as Photo 22.1.

22.1 A collage by Chinyee, 1997.

Chinyee has a great sense of color, and her composition is always unerringly well-proportioned, regardless of the medium chosen. It is fun to observe how she would use a well-placed bold streak near the border of a painting to balance a sizable mass on the other side, or employ just a few dabs of color here and there to dress up a gaping void. As any good artwork should, her paintings have depth in the sense that they contain layers and layers of meaning to be explored, discovered, savored, and appreciated, viewing after viewing.

Since I cannot enjoy the luxury of showing more of her artwork here, I strongly recommend that the reader google "Chinyee," or "Chinyee artist" to have the enjoyment of her creations.

A Masterpiece at Three and Half

In his nursery school days, when Darryl could not yet speak a word of English, his teacher used to give him a piece of blank newsprint every day and let him play with some acrylic or paint. He would bring home a daily artwork. Some days, the paintings were a scene of chaotic strokes. But one day, he brought home what Emily considered a "masterpiece." It shows a big mass of black at the bottom, with the upper half of a round orange-colored object near the upper left, and a group of quick, forceful black strokes close to the upper border pointing to the right. It could be a sunset; it could also be an approaching storm. In either case, it is very powerful! Unfortunately, the teacher folded the painting in the middle harshly, leaving a sharp crease. See Photo 16 for this young artist's work.

When Emily showed me this painting on a 17" × 23" newsprint, I was quite amazed by the maturity of the strokes. It could pass for a work by a grown-up, but Darryl was not quite 4 years old. At that time, Darryl could not yet write his name. But, by his sixth sense, he left a space on the upper left corner of the painting, so that he could retro-sign it "DARRYL 1972" as soon as he learned to write.

I decided to frame this painting. Not only that. I also commissioned Repko to design a black buffet to go on a side wall of the dining room at the Beech Mountain house, to serve as an anchor for this painting.

Photo 36 shows this painting and part of the buffet below. I chose a white frame for this painting, so that the black mass in it would be left free, not bounded by a colored frame.

After Darryl grew older, he was puzzled at my sustained fondness for this painting. Once, he pointedly asked me, "Dad, what qualities about this painting make you like it so much?" I could not answer right away, for I had not formally thought about it in that manner. But I was able, later, to gather up five points for the answer. First, had the big black mass been solidly filled, it would have been a dull sheet of color, but Darryl did leave specks of white space within the black, allowing the big mass to "breathe." Second, Darryl let the orange paint for the "sun" drip down into the black, and, by creating a flow, provided a contrast in texture. Third, he used forceful dried black strokes above the "sun," and, by varying the degree of dryness in the multiple strokes, added several layers of further contrast in texture against the black mass, as well as against the dripping orange. Fourth, he put irregular-shaped dots on the dried black strokes, thus adding points to lines and mass. Fifth, he added some orange dots as well, to provide an echo effect to the orange figure over the black. These desirable effects might all have been unwittingly executed, but they nevertheless coalesced to make this an exceptionally worthy painting.

Equal Opportunity

Opposite to the wall where I hung Darryl's painting over the custom-made buffet, was a smaller wall space without any art work on it. The vacant space on that wall did not escape Tracey's awareness, and soon afterward, she started to show me a painting on newsprint from the nursery school every day, asking, "Dad, do you like this painting?" I wished I could accept her work to fill that vacant wall space quickly, but for one reason or another, nothing she produced seemed suitable there.

It took about two months or longer for her to come up with one with design and color congruous with the rest of the dining room at Beech Mountain. It was a piece of paper towel dip-dyed with two colors, blue and brown, in a simple but pleasing pattern, mostly symmetrical, but with some variations to make it interesting. The two colors also went well with the dining table and chairs. I praised her, framed it and hung it opposite Darryl's painting. Thence, she left me in peace.

I habitually view and review these young artists' work with joy and pride. The only regret was that they were done on impermanent media. The newsprint on which Darryl painted has yellowed quite a few shades over the years, and the paper may someday crumble. The dyes in Tracey's paper-towel art have suffered from fast fading through long exposure to light, although the story behind it will always remain fondly in my mind.

Art off the Wall

Darryl's interest in art continued, but it was drawings, especially the comic-book type, that absorbed his attention. Of course, no more memorable paintings came out of his hands. That caused our neighbor, Bill Ryan, to tease Darryl as "the painter who peaked at age three and half." Bill had a good reason to needle and make fun of Darryl. Being the President of the Williams College Alumni Association, Bill was eager to recruit Darryl to go to William College. When Darryl chose Princeton instead, Bill was palpably and understandably upset.

Darryl did produce some off-the-wall art. In elementary school, he produced a comic book as a project for the special education class. Since I don't have a copy of it anymore, I cannot describe the details. But I remember helping him assemble the various pages in special sequence, so that when the Xeroxed pages are folded and stapled together, the pages will appear in the correct order as a booklet. I helped with the duplicating job, and used a specially bought saddle stapler to gather the pages into the book form. He set a price of 25 cents, which did not even cover the cost of production.

Mrs. Betty Shibles, the special education class teacher, liked the booklet, and brought a few copies of this comic book to show other teachers at a conference out of state. She actually sold several copies of it. When she came to our house to give Darryl the sales proceeds, something like $1.75, Darryl gladly took the money, and gave a dime to Mrs. Shibles. When I later asked him about the dime, he said, "Oh, I was giving her a tip." A big tipper he was not! But, at least, he knew that if someone has done you a favor, you should show appreciation. I am glad to report that, growing into adulthood, he did develop into a generous tipper.

His interest in comic-book art was persistent. Later, in 1984, he produced a more full-fledged, 16-page comic book, labeled as DComics No. 1, "*The Uncanny X-Wing*," with five mythical characters. I don't know how many copies he sold. This time, he set the price at the formidable level of $1.50.

Later, at Princeton University, he turned to designing T-shirts for some friends who produced and sold them to fellow students. "How much do your charge for your artwork?" I asked him. When he told me that he was doing it for free, I advised him that, if the T-shirts were to be sold for charity, then he should contribute his services free, but if it were a business venture, then he should claim his due share. A few weeks later, he reported to me, "Dad, on my latest design job, I asked

22.2 Darryl's *the Uncanny X-Wing*, 1984.

for a percentage." From "no charge" to a "percentage share" was such a giant step that I found it hard to hide my pleasant surprise. But when I followed up with the question: "Percentage of the price, or percentage of profit?" he did not have an answer. He still had a bit more to learn about how "business" goes.

Identity-Inspired Artwork

The two pieces of art of Tracey that I have displayed with pride in my bedroom are both related to the theme of self-identity. One is an oil painting from her art class at Brown University. The other is from her photography class for her MFA program at the School of Visual Arts.

The oil painting from Brown, an odd-sized vertical work, measuring 57" × 14", has as its background a strip of Oriental rug, with tiny, white tassels at its left-hand edge. On the rug are four apples, two located on the rug proper toward the right, and the other two lying directly on the tassels on the left. Her professor at Brown, questioning Tracey about the meaning of the painting, was very much impressed when she explained that, "This painting depicts my family. My parents are immigrants with a Chinese heritage, an Oriental background; hence, I represent them as two apples sitting on the Oriental rug. But my brother and I, both born in this country, are neither strictly Chinese, nor regularly American. We have a dual, mixed, even confused identity; hence, the other two apples are sitting on the borderline." This explanation impressed me as much as it did the professor.

The elongated shape of this oil painting makes it difficult to find a suitable spot on the wall for it. I finally had the solution: In the Cottonwood Lane house, it was hung near the end of the wall, so that it was totally visible, but away from and unhindered by the bulk of my baby grand piano. At Cedar Crest, it was again hung near the end of a wall, unblocked by a bed and the night table. This painting of four apples is shown in Photo 17 in the front of this book.

Her photography piece on our wall, with more conventional dimensions, 27" × 22", is a self-portrait from her work at the School of Visual Arts, already published in a book. It is a work even more explicitly related to the theme of self-identity. When her professor told her to submit some artwork to a person named Alice Rose George, she had no idea that her work was an entry for competition for inclusion in a book project—a compilation of works by young photographers 25 years or under. In that book, which came out in 1997 under the title *Twenty-five and Under/Photographers*, Tracey was given an 8-page spread of her self-portraits, all in black and white.

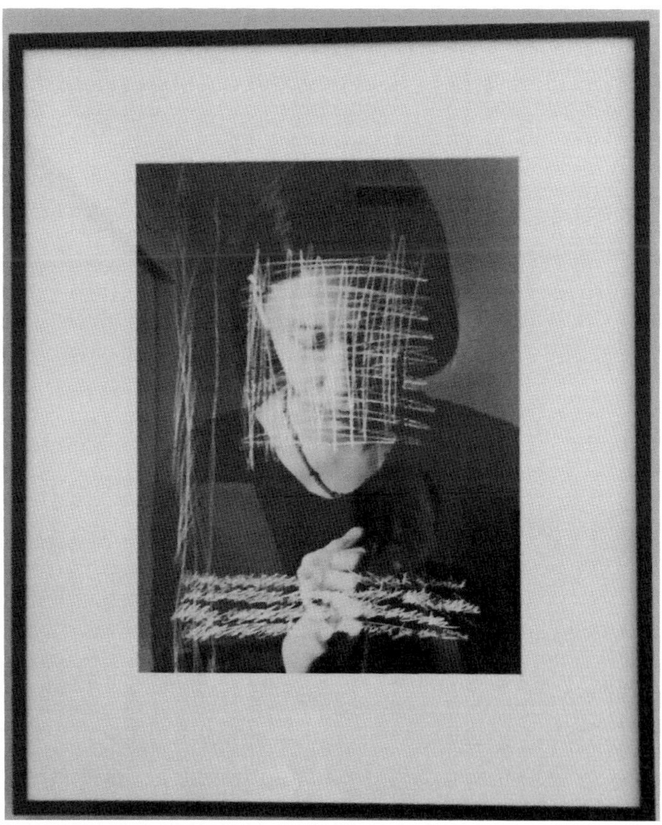

22.3 One of Tracey's self-portraits, published in a book in 1997.

No ordinary portraits, these photos have lines and words scratched across the negatives to portray her inner struggles. This is her own explanation of her work: "As a child growing up in a white community, I wish my Chinese-ness weren't so visible; as an adult living in a non-Chinese society, I am afraid of losing the intangible elements of being Chinese. In America, a woman is respected if she can stand up for herself in a situation that she believes to be intolerable; in Asia, a woman is respected if she has the inner strength to tolerate and survive. I am never enough of one thing—Chinese, American, passive, aggressive—to be seamlessly whole, but I am afraid to be too much of one thing and, as a consequence, lose the other entirely. My work is about wanting to be understood without having to speak out loud in English or in Chinese, simply through my own visual language."

The editor commented that "[Tracey Chiang] struggles to decipher her individual equations of rootedness and disconnection, and through her self-portraits and almost ritual markings, finds a voice to speak eloquently about race, gender, restriction, and generations."

And a book reviewer singled out Tracey for mention as a promising young photographer, and expressed the hope that she will continue to do creative work. But, alas, in real life, the considerations of livelihood often direct people to a path other than the one most desired. In Tracey's case, she eventually found it necessary to become a graphic designer instead of a photographer. She is working at Nickelodeon as Associate Director, Production Illustration.

From the Old Man's Camera

On the castle walls, I did not display any of my own artwork except the wood blocks carved with the names of the residences in ancient Chinese scripts. After moving to Cedar Crest, a retirement community in Northern New Jersey, however, I decided to claim a small wall space as my own gallery, to show three enlargements of landscape photos I took at Huang Shan (黄山, Yellow Mountain) in China. This, I guess, revealed a diminution of modesty at old age.

My visit to Yellow Mountain was inspired by Stanley Chen, my high-school roommate who had huge paintings of that famous scenic region in his living room. "Make sure you tour that mountain region while you are still mobile!" he urged Emily and me. He was serious, and I took him seriously. Thus, when we planned to fly to Shanghai in May, 2002, for the 100th birthday of my Aunt Lizhen (see Photo 81), we also booked a three-day tour after the birthday celebration to Yellow Mountain.

A mere one hour's flight from Shanghai landed us in a town nearby, and a private guide and a waiting car took us to a cable car and up the mountain. Stanley was perfectly right! The natural beauty of the Yellow Mountain region was awe-inspiring, confirming everything we had heard about the intricately shaped pine trees, the picturesque rocks, and the majestic rolling sea of clouds. The sea of clouds makes its appearance only when there was enough vapor in the air, and some tourists never had the opportunity to see it. Luckily, we did.

I took many scenic photos of the Yellow Mountain, and used five of them on the front and back covers of my home-made Christmas card for 2002. The panel of four scenes on the back cover of that card

22.4 The pines of the Yellow Mountain (2002 photo).

is reproduced as Photo 28 in the front of this book, and I am reprinting the front cover of that card here as Photo 22.4. (The original photo is a silhouette of pines, so printing it here as a black-and-white picture does not really detract from it.)

For the wall display, I enlarged a few of these and printed them on 11" × 18" boards. With three of these up on the wall, I have officially joined the estimable company of the other three artists: Chinyee, Darryl, and Tracey.

23

The "Christmas-Card Uncle"

I have been given a couple of nicknames over the years. One, "Albie," was a gift to me from Mrs. Fisher, my landlady in New York, who mistook Albert to be my name, and added the "ie" ending for affection. For many years I lived under that name, and, just to mock me, even some friends of mine called me Albie for a long time.

Another nickname, "the Christmas-card uncle," was how some of my friends' children referred to me—also with affection. In the Chinese culture, children automatically address their parents' friends as uncles and aunts. If they met me face-to-face, they would call me "Uncle Alpha." But those who had not met me would usually append a descriptive phrase in place of name. To some of them, what distinguished me from other "uncles" were the homemade Christmas cards I have been sending out since 1953, the year before I got married.

Besides the traditional wishes for a Merry Christmas and Happy New Year, I customarily report about the events that occurred during the year, sometimes with a little humor, and often with cartoon illustrations. They seemed well received by my friends, and even their young offspring gradually developed a liking for my cards. In some years, when my cards got printed late, friends would worry about the missing Christmas cards, and call to make sure that I was not sick in bed, or disabled, or deceased.

The McGuire Calendar

What started me on this personal-message tradition was the Christmas letter I received from Professor Carl McGuire, my MA thesis supervisor at the University of Colorado. In his "McGuire Calendar," he divided the regular letter-size paper into 12 compartments, one for each month, and filled these compartments with a minimalist but humorous explanations, in words and cartoons, of what happened to his family, and when. The drawings were crude, usually with matchstick figures, but humorous and expressive. The words were concise, but catchy. These were done with the ditto process, but later with offset printing.

One year, Professor McGuire gave a lecture to the American Society of Engineers at Michigan State University. What he drew was a speaker, with a couple of snoring listeners, all in matchstick figures. And another item for the same trip, accompanied by Mrs. McGuire, was the statement: "Esther realizes her life-long ambition—sleeps in men's dorm." Even funnier, reporting on his convalescence after a hernia operation, he drew a man in a hospital bed. Seeing a nurse approaching, the man shouted out: "Who goes there? Friend, or enema?"

Imitation as the Best Compliment

I was fascinated with the McGuire Calendar, so much so that I decided to create an imitative version of my own. But I did not have access to ditto papers and the duplicating machine. And I was not venturesome enough to explore more formal ways of printing. All changed when I found employment, while still writing my dissertation, at the Chinese Government Procurement and Services Mission, an amalgamated New York office of several state agencies in Taiwan. The availability of ditto gave me the impetus to do my first Christmas message, simply titled "Greetings!" The only copy I have kept of this 1953 work is now quite faded.

I did two more ditto Christmas greeting messages after going to Denison University with Emily, my bride, before I upgraded to offset printing for 1956. This duplicating service run by the Denison staff, charged reasonable fees, and gave much more legible and permanent cards. Yes, I did say "cards." Now, instead of a flat sheet, I began to fold the regular-sized paper twice to form a card with four quarter-sized pages. I named it "Inside the Chiangs," but for subsequent editions, changed the title to "Empha Card," where, obviously, the "Em" is from Emily and "pha" is from Alpha.

Cartoons

Words may be good for imparting information, but cartoons are better for heightening interest and inducing chuckles. That was true of the McGuire Calendar, and I must follow its example. I was no cartoonist, and I had to learn, borrow, adapt, or invent. Sometimes using thin line pens, and sometimes medium, my drawings do not exhibit a consistent style. But it was not the artistic quality of the cartoons, but the fun-enhancing effect, that mattered to me.

Often, when lacking reportable events for the cards, I needed to manufacture a news item by "making a mountain out of a molehill." Getting the first driver's license should not be a big deal. But, when Emily passed the test in Ohio, I drew a cartoon showing her fainting in the arms of the police officer upon hearing the news that she had passed (Photo 23.1).

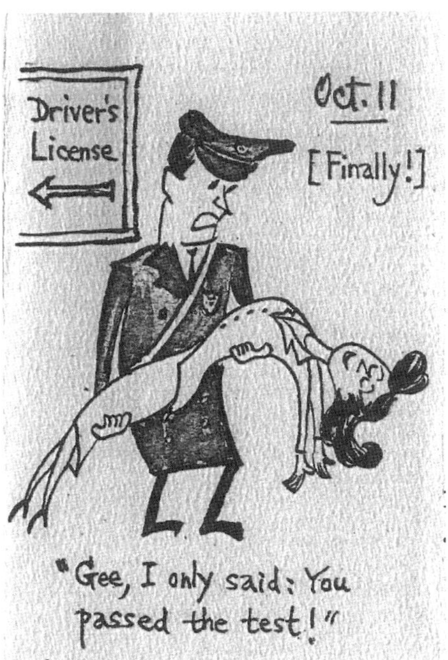

23.1 Emily passed the driving test, 1957.

As another example, I elevated my ingrown toenail operation in 1963 to the status of a major event. And, for ridiculous effect, I drew a cartoon of a podiatrist wielding a big saw (Photo 23.2).

The birth of my son Darryl in December, 1968 (after 14 years of marriage) was, on the other hand, a true "big event." But how could I announce it in a non-bland way? After some thinking, I decided to let my son emerge from an egg. Since he was born late in the year, after the 1968 Christmas card was already printed, I reported that the next year.

We took my visiting parents to tour Washington, DC, in 1984, despite my mother's apparent subpar health (later diagnosed to be

23.2 Alpha's ingrown toenail operation, 1963.

hypothyroidism). Pushing her in a rented wheelchair during the trip was my first experience as a caregiver. Her disability afforded her and me special treatment at certain places, even in the White House, where a security person took us upstairs in a private elevator. To add some zip to the cartoon of the wheelchair, I drew it as a speeding one. But that, of course, was just a cartoonist's exaggeration. I was a consistently careful pusher (Photo 23.3).

During the semester-long stay in the Netherlands in 1989, when I took a group of students from the University of Connecticut on a Study Abroad program at Limburg University, Emily and I traveled frequently to different places in Europe. We enjoyed the hospitality of Emily's elder brother James Ho (何欽羽) and his wife Belinda (李薇) in Vienna where James was working. Among other things, they treated us to the most tasty fish dinner we had ever had at a restaurant by the Danube River, which I memorialized in a cartoon of a chef catching a fish by his bare hand. And, in Paris to see I. M. Pei (貝聿銘)'s ingenious but

23.3 Mom in wheelchair, Washington, DC, 1984.

23.4 Best fish dinner ever, Vienna, 1989.

controversial Pyramid, which he built at the *Louvre*, I drew a cartoon with a strange, hypothetical question (Photos 23.4 and 23.5).

23.5 At the Louvre, Paris, 1989.

While the manuscript of my *Fundamental Methods of Mathematical Economics* was written on an IBM Selectric typewriter, the sequel book *Elements of Dynamic Optimization* was done, in a different era, on a computer. I decided to purchase a scientific word processing software designed to handle mathematical symbols and equations, and learned it with some effort. When I taught it to Emily who was to prepare the final manuscript, she had to overcome a deep-seated phobia about computer. (Her first big peeve about my computer: Why is the power button labeled "1/0" and not "On/Off"?) My cartoon depicting her running away from the "mouse" has already been shown in Photo 17.1.

Lastly, I include here a cartoon about a visit to the San Diego Zoo from the 1995 Christmas card. We visited Darryl when, after Harvard Law School, he was clerking for Chief Judge Judith N. Keep of the United States District Court, Southern District of California. The San Diego Zoo was one of the sights we saw. The humor lies in the fact that the photographer was aiming his camera too low, and the lady, obviously his wife, was trying to tell him to aim higher, the object of the photo being a tall giraffe (Photo 23.6).

23.6 The photographer and the giraffe, 1995.

Can't Judge the Card by the Cover

In the one-page flat format of a calendar, there was no cover. After I changed the format by folding the paper into the shape of a card, there was a new job to do: design the cover. For many years, I handled the cover design myself. But when I noticed the artistic bent in both of my children, a great idea occurred to me: let the children do the cover design, making the Christmas card a family project, even though its name remained as Empha Card, with no mention of Darryl and Tracey. And what role did Emily play? Well, she held executive "veto" power over the contents. If she said, "Take this part out," that part must be taken out, no questions asked.

The children's first cover appeared in 1974, when Darryl was 6 and Tracey, 4 and half. They each drew a snowman, dark blue ink on brown paper, with artists' signatures. For the next 18 years, they, as alternate cover artists, produced as many beautiful covers, all printed on colored paper, in colored ink. I have introduced some of my cartoons above; it's only fair that I now introduce some of their cover designs.

Three of Darryl's covers are shown in Photo 41, and three of Tracey's are shown in Photo 42 in the front of the book.

Darryl's 1975 cover shows two people having a sleigh ride. You can almost hear the jingling of bells. His 1979 scene of two deer in snow is notable for the simplicity of composition. By leaving a big empty space, he succeeded without drawing anything in suggesting the boundlessness of the snow-covered land around the two deer. And the two solid letters N and E provided interesting contrast to the two letters O and L left not inked in. The solid letters also echoed the trees in the background, as the letters O and L echoed the land of snow. And in the third one, with Santa conducting a choir of reindeer, the traditional role of the reindeer as transport workers was switched to that of music makers, a novel idea. Also, have you noticed that, showing only the backside of Santa obviated the job of drawing his face altogether?

Among the covers by Tracey, the one with the angel (1978) is interesting in a couple of ways. First, she broke the square frame around the angel at the top line, to allow room for the angel's halo.

Then the broken frame became semi-reconnected by the tiny halo. Second, the angel's nose was visible only as a suggestion. Third, no mouth is shown. In the next cover, for 1982, she reversed the roles of Santa and the reindeer, made Santa pull the animals, which provided the humor. And, talking about humor, look at her 1991 cover design. Examine carefully, and you'll see something unusual happening among that school of fish. The fish at the bottom was heading in the wrong direction! This is a point easily missed by the casual viewer, but I would rate it as the most intriguing part of this design.

To be fair to myself, I felt I should present here a cover design of my own. On second thought, since I will have occasion to show throughout this book many kinds of work I did, including cartoons, landscape painting, calligraphy, photography, and even seal carving, it's best to skip Christmas card designs.

Chinese Supplement and Color Xerox

Two things in the early years of the 21st century caused major changes in the format of my Christmas cards. First, in 2001, Emily and I suddenly realized that, even though I had trained Darryl and Tracey in Chinese language and culture, they, now in their early 30s, had never set foot in Mainland China. To rectify that omission, we decided on a grand tour of China in the spring of 2001, covering all the must-see points of interest. This trip not only opened the children's eyes, but also my own, because my previous travels in China had been severely limited.

Here is a quote from the 2001 Christmas card regarding the trip: "Two natural wonders stood out among the lovely sceneries we saw in China: the majestic Three Gorges (三峽) on the Yangtze River, and the picturesque limestone hills along the Li River in Guilin (桂林灕江). 'Breathtaking' may be a cliché, but it is a most appropriate adjective here. And the top man-made wonders? Our votes go to the Great Wall, completed during the reign of Qin Shi Huang (秦始皇 'The First Emperor'), 221-210 B.C., and also to the thousands of terra-cotta warriors (兵馬俑) excavated from his royal tomb near Xian (西安). It is striking that both of these wonders are legacies of a single despotic ruler. Perhaps only an extremist despot could have conceived such ambitious projects, and commandeered the immense manpower (no machines) required for their execution."

My Christmas cards up to 2000 had been in English. But reporting on our China visit in English somewhere did not quite satisfy me as a raconteur. I needed to add a Chinese-language supplement to feel fulfilled as a writer. From 2001 on, my Christmas card has been bilingual.

Another thing that altered the Christmas card format was the increasing popularity and lowering of the price of color Xerox. Printing cards with color photos was previously too expensive. But my printing shop suggested the possibility of using color Xeroxing for the Christmas cards, and it worked well. Thenceforth, I introduced color photos, and reduced the use of cartoons to make room.

Retirement Plan?

For decades, Thanksgiving Day had been the starting day for the planning of the Christmas card of the year. Going over my pocket diary to select the "events" to be reported on; writing the text, possibly with some humor (but keeping in mind that Emily might object); considering what cartoons (now photos) to use; cutting the text to fit into the available space on the card. These would be followed by visits to the printing shop, selecting the paper stock and the ink color; purchasing postage stamps; addressing, stuffing, and stamping the envelopes; and, finally, mailing them out.

It was a time-consuming process.

Emily has suggested several times that I put the annual Christmas card routine to an end. And I did consider her suggestion. But it seems a shame to cut short an enterprise that I started in 1953, more than six decades ago, and has been sustained without interruption. What I have decided to do is to keep alive the tradition, but simplify the process.

Instead of printing a card in a size to fit an A-6 envelope, now I just write a Christmas letter, one page of English text, with a couple of color photos, and a back page of Chinese text. Besides, I have adopted the easier, if less polite, way of communicating—by email.

In this simplified mode, I hope to be able to continue for a few more years. Who knows? I might even do cartoons again.

24

Viewing a Floral Show on a Trotting Horse

Among the travels we took, perhaps the most meaningful in purpose, as well as the most extensive in scope was a tri-generational tour of Europe in 1979, from August 16 to September 3, covering 9 countries in 18 days. Yes, it involved 3 generations, 6 people, 9 countries, and 18 days—coincidentally with all these numbers divisible by 3. In the numerical sense, there was another interesting thing: the trip was for celebrating (1) my father's 75th birthday, and (2) my own 25th wedding anniversary with Emily. We thus also had an interesting equation, 75 + 25 = 100, adding to a good round number. This number quite naturally contributed to inspiring us to undertake this family tour.

To tour 9 countries in 18 days was clearly an overly ambitious undertaking. At best, it would be little more than an impressionistic journey, as described by the Chinese saying "走馬看花 (Viewing a floral show on a trotting horse.)" The "floral show" consisted of England, France, Switzerland, Liechtenstein, Austria, Italy, Germany, the Netherlands, and Belgium. And our "trotting horse" took the form of a bus with 53 passengers plus a tour guide.

Connecting at Heathrow

Instead of going to Hong Kong to accompany my parents to Europe, we asked them to join a European tour organized by Jade Tours in Hong Kong, which would directly take them to London. Emily and I, and our two children would then join their group in London at the Heathrow Airport, where the tour guide, Tony Lau, found us with little problem, and we soon greeted my parents and the other fellow tourists from Hong Kong on the bus.

After a six-hour flight, we needed to go to our hotel to freshen up before lunch. And the group from Hong Kong, who had an even longer flight, must have felt the same way. But, sorry, we needed to take our lunch first, because our hotel rooms would not be available until in the afternoon. Knowing the food preference of Hong Kong people, Jade Tours considerately arranged for our lunch at a Chinese restaurant, Jade Garden (翠園). In fact, our group was to sample Chinese meals whenever and wherever available, in Paris, and also in Rome. Even in Lucerne, where there was no Chinese restaurant, they chose a Swiss restaurant with an ample supply of rice—a staple food for the Chinese—to satisfy the Chinese appetite.

With no sightseeing scheduled for the rest of the day, our family activity consisted of exchanging gifts in the London Metropole Hotel. My parents brought slippers, underwear, and other clothing items from Hong Kong for each of us. Darryl presented to Grandpa a bookmark he handmade, plus a drawing of pine tree (symbol of longevity), with Chinese calligraphy on rice paper, for his 75th birthday (see Photo 26 in the front of this book). Tracey gave him a handmade ceramic cup, with the inscription "Grandpa, I love you," and a wooden vase stand she had designed. To Grandma, she presented a pair of pot holders she made. My own gift to my parents was more mundane and unimaginative: a check for their travel expenses.

Going out to dinner on our own that night, I thought I would see a lot of English people. But the hotel lobby was filled with numerous people in flowing Arab garb, which explained the presence of the long row of Rolls Royce cars parked outside. There were also many Pakistanis and Indian, although they were mostly working as service people in the hotel. I did not envisage London that way at all.

Even though nothing really happened on August 17, this counted as the first day of our European tour.

A Glimpse of London

The second day of our journey started with a tour of London, or, more accurately, a glimpse of London. From Westminster Abbey, to the changing of guards at the Buckingham Palace, to the display of crown jewels in the Tower of London, we had to follow closely our guide, Tony Lau, in order not to get lost into some other similar tour groups surrounding us. Also, unless we stood within a foot of the guide, we could not hear him clearly. But since he was obligated only to make explanations in the Cantonese dialect for the tourists from Hong Kong, Emily and I and the children could not understand him anyway. In one instance, when he was introducing a brief history of the Westminster Abbey, referring to it by its translated Chinese name "西敏寺," I truly thought he was talking instead about "三明治 (sandwich)," which sounded similar to me. In kindness, a fellow tourist in our group, Amelia Ng, who spoke Mandarin, offered to translate the general idea of the guide's explanation to us, but we tried not to impose on her often. My father was better off, because he understood Cantonese 75%–80%, but my mother, not as much.

I had of course seen the Westminster Abbey on TV before, most vividly for the coronation of Queen Elizabeth II in 1953. But setting foot in the Abbey gave me a vastly different feeling. A sense of awe naturally arose at a place where more than 3,000 notable people were buried, including Charles Darwin, Sir Isaac Newton, Charles Dickens, Dr. Samuel Johnson, and Rudyard Kipling, not to mention the many other famous people who were commemorated, though not buried there, including William Shakespeare and Jane Austen.

The changing of the guards at the Buckingham was a colorful show. I loved the contrasting colors between the red coats and the black hats and trousers. But the palace is, in my opinion, located too close to the street. Proximity to people might be desirable to signify the royal family's affinity to the subjects, but some geographical remoteness would seem necessary for the mysterious and fable-like traits of a palace.

After lunch, again at Jade Garden, we continued our tour to the Tower of London. Even the mere mention of the name of the Tower itself instantly called to mind the name of Anne Boleyn, the second wife of Henry VIII. What a tragic and bloody story that was, a queen beloved, betrayed, and then beheaded. The display of the crown jewels in the Tower, beautiful as they were, could not fight off the cruel execution scene from my mind for the longest time.

France-Bound

The hovercraft crossing of the English Channel the next morning, on the third day of the tour, took 40 minutes to get us to Calais, France. It was a bumpy ride over the Channel waves. We then boarded the bus which would take us across the European continent for the next two weeks. The driver, a stout Dutch fellow named Krien Kleer, proved to be an excellent driver, courteous as well as accommodating. Emily and I were especially glad because we could easily communicate with him in English.

The route to Paris took almost five hours. Everyone was hungry at the end, and welcomed the Chinese dinner waiting for us at the restaurant *Aux Délices de Chine*, with the Chinese name 周家飯店 (Chow's Restaurant). And the hotel, PLM-St. Jacques, with the rooms modern if not spacious, was more comfortable than the Metropole in London. We were glad to be given three rooms, one for each generation.

That evening being free, I decided to spend it at the renowned nightclub *Moulin Rouge.* Darryl and Tracey were old enough to be left

24.1 Krien Kleer, our Dutch bus driver, with Darryl and Tracey.

by themselves at the hotel. And we four adults spent $45 per person for a not-so-spectacular show at the nightclub, even though the many showgirls were pretty and glamorous. The stage was much smaller than I expected, and no singer sang at the level of Edith Piaf. While sipping champagne that came with the admission price, and watching the cancan dancers, I was thinking all the time of the 1950s movie *Moulin Rouge*, starring José Ferrer as the painter Henri de Toulouse-Lautrec. The details of the movie story had already become vague to me, but the image of the painter with the stunted legs painting away at the boisterous nightclub remained clear in my mind. My parents probably did not have much appreciation for that evening's outing, but I assured them that this nightclub was one of the must-see spots in Paris.

Paris Kaleidoscope

The fourth day of the tour was jam-packed with sights to see: the Eiffel Tower, Napoleon's Tomb, and *Notre Dame* in the morning; *Place de la Concorde, Arc de Triomphe,* and *Champs-Élysées* in the afternoon; and a cruise on the *Seine* and an "illumination drive" through the town in the evening. This list included many stops, and at each stop the loading and unloading of people took a lot of time. Besides, the guide had to take time to count heads, to make sure that nobody had strayed off from the group.

There are two observation platforms on the Eiffel Tower. Probably for cost economy, our tour only went up to the lower one, which afforded an adequate but not comprehensive overview of Paris. We had a family picture taken at the foot of the Eiffel Tower (see Photo 44 in the front of this book). Napoleon's Tomb did not excite a lot of interest, especially because we had to pay for admission fees ourselves. Only the two children and I ventured in. The cathedral of *Notre Dame* was, on the other hand, a famous structure everyone longed to see. Unfortunately, the stately edifice with beautiful stained glass windows was filled with multitudes of tourists crowding against one another, which dissipated the atmosphere of serenity I expected. Just our own bus alone would pour into the cathedral as many as 50-odd visitors all at once. And there were several other buses parked outside.

Arriving at the *Place de la Concorde,* I found myself thinking of two tragic figures in history. Who? King Louis XVI and Marie Antoinette, of course. Mostly, I re-envisaged the scenes from the old movie *Marie Antoinette*, starring Norma Shearer, Robert Morley, and Tyrone Power. Emily must have the same reaction, since we saw that movie together. But we had to brief my parents about the story of the French Revolution. The six of us then took a long walk together on the famous Parisian boulevard, with a refreshment stop at a sidewalk café, before we took a ride in the Metro (a much cleaner subway system than its New York counterpart) back to our hotel.

The evening cruise and drive were nothing to write about. But, guess where we had lunch and dinner that day? Yes. Chinese food at the same place: Chow's Restaurant.

The Mona Lisa Moment

I had left out one significant item from the above itinerary, on purpose. Our tour did include a visit to the *Musée du Louvre.* But either by accident or by design, we arrived at the museum just shortly before closing time. So, we had to hurry in, almost running after Mr. Lau our guide, until he called a halt abruptly near a crowd surrounding a particular painting. "This is the famous Mona Lisa," Mr. Lau shouted out to us, "Please take a quick look, because the museum is closing soon." We had to limit our homage to this famous painting to—literally!—one moment. Then we hurried out at the same speed we hurried in. Nevertheless, if we were asked the question: "Have you ever seen the real Mona Lisa?" we could reply, in all honesty and without any trace of embarrassment, "Yes, at the *Louvre*!" There is no need to tell the whole truth by adding, "Only for a moment."

Lucerne

The most annoying aspect of land tours is the almost daily need to pack and unpack the suitcases. Even worse, passengers must leave their packed suitcases outside of their hotel rooms by 10 p.m. or so at night, to be loaded onto the coach for the trip the next morning. Emily had extra work to take care of my belongings and those of the kids. And the poor hotel staff had to take all of the luggage pieces down into the cavernous cargo space under the passenger seat on our bus.

On the fifth day of our tour, we entered into Switzerland at Basel. But it was a long drive to Lucerne, our destination. There was apparently no Chinese restaurant in Lucerne, but the young waiter serving us Western food in the local restaurant obligingly came out with a huge container midway through the meal, asking enthusiastically at each table, "Want more rice? Want more rice?" Some in the group took second and third helpings.

Our Fellow Travelers

It was during meal times and at some relatively lengthier sightseeing stops that we could take time to socialize with fellow passengers seated faraway on the bus. And we got to know many interesting people.

There was this youthful, petite couple on their honeymoon who never talked to anybody. An older, more sociable couple, Mr. and Mrs. Leung, joined this tour because they were sending their 14-year-old son, Andrew, to England to study. Andrew, their only son with five sisters, was a treasure to his rich parents. As a sign of his favored status, he touted an expensive Canon A1 camera, equipped with the most powerful zoom lens. But I wasn't sure whether he should be considered lucky, or unlucky, to be sent to boarding school in a foreign country at the tender age of 14. Andrew often kept company with Darryl, younger by four years.

One young couple had an eye-catching quality: Ying Fai Wong, an architect, and his wife Christine, a travel executive, both spoke good English and dressed fashionably. Somehow, they heard that Darryl had commented to someone that they, the Wongs, were the smartest looking couple among us. Mrs. Wong soon bought a big toy car for Darryl, after finding out that our boy was keen on automobiles. Another young man, Addy Chow, honeymooning with his beautiful bride, had a high position in the Hong Kong police department. In a reassuring tone, he said to my father one day, "Rev. Chiang, if you get into any kind of trouble, just look me up in the Police Department, I can fix it for you for sure." Jokingly, my father said, in his broken Cantonese, "Okay, now I won't be afraid to pick a fight with anybody!"

My parents were the oldest people in our group, but they never lagged behind when walking from place to place. The guide, annoyed with the slow people, often said to them, "Why can't you follow the example of our eldest couple, Rev. and Mrs. Chiang?"

During driving hours, the passenger seating was assigned for the day. To give equal opportunity of front-seat view for all, there was a seating rule on the coach: Everyone got promoted to the seat one row ahead by the next day; and the first-row people would go to the back of the bus. But under this rule, we still kept the same circle of people as our seat neighbors. The young lady, Amelia Ng, who was very friendly and often translated the guide's Cantonese commentaries into Mandarin for us, always sat right in front of Emily.

Luckily for us, a repulsive and generally disliked couple had their seats far away from us, and we never sat at the same dinner table with them. The male member of that couple liked to play with his false teeth, taking them off and putting them on again and again during dinner, thereby ruining every dining companion's appetite. Aptly, he was soon given the nickname "Dracula." His wife did not have removable teeth, but she had the habit of making senseless photo poses, such as holding a pen in each hand and raising both arms high in the shape of a V—signifying what? Some people in the group nicknamed her "雪山飛狐" ("The Flying Fox of the Snow Mountain"), the nickname of a peculiar, abhorrent antiheroine character in a Hong Kong martial arts movie.

10,000 Feet Above Sea Level

The "floral show" continued. The "trotting horse" dutifully kept on.

The schedule for the sixth day included a cruise on the Lake Lucerne, an ascent to Mt. Titlis, and a walk-through the Ice Palace. Mt. Titlis is 10,000 feet above the sea level, reachable by cable car (once) followed by aerial trams (twice). We soon became surrounded by mists or clouds. At lunch, the shifting clouds outside the windows created a dynamic scene, with constantly appearing and reappearing mountain tops all around.

And the Ice Palace, a walking path carved out of a huge ice block, convincingly proved how penetrating the cold temperature could be. I could not believe that I was capable of such a high walking speed to hurry away from the cold air in there!

Vaduz and Innsbruck

On the seventh day, we drove by Lake Zürich, had a photo stop, and arrived in Vaduz for lunch. Vaduz is the capital of Liechtenstein, a 64-square mile principality, defended by a team of no more than 15 policemen. Had it not been for this tour, I would never have set foot here. In view of its miniature size, it would have been easy to pass through it without realizing we had entered it and left it.

The overnight stay at Innsbruck, barely into the border of Austria, was probably included so that it could be claimed as an additional country covered by this tour. The stay was so short that the guide decided not to allow us to unload our big luggage pieces. The hotel, Innsbruck Holiday Inn, had a swimming pool, but with the kids' swimwear locked up in the inaccessible suitcases, we had to buy new swimwear so that they could show grandpa and grandma their swimming abilities. By the same token, with our clothes locked up in the bus, we could not take advantage of the washer and dryer facilities this hotel offered.

Discoveries in Venice

Crossing the border into Italy the next day was an extremely casual affair. There was not even the ceremonial, perfunctory stamping of our passports. Our first destination was Venice, but our hotel was in nearby Mestre. Hotel Plaza was the worst hotel on the whole trip, small, dark, and drab. The saving grace was that it was in this old hotel that I got to see a crude wooden blind, which might be an example of the original Venetian blind. When fully closed, it worked as a solid barrier inside the window, but, when opened, it let in varying amount of light through the slits. I would not have encountered it in a more modern hotel.

Another interesting discovery at this hotel was one that stumped me: a toilet-flushing mechanism I had never seen before. I had used pull chains, levers, push buttons before, but here I found a knob on top of the tank cover that could not be pushed down; nor could it be turned left or right. I never considered myself to be a dumb person, but it took me three or four minutes before I figured out how to flush this toilet. In a "zen" moment, it occurred to me to pull the knob UP instead of pushing it DOWN. Then the desired "whoosh!" came on cue. From that moment on, I have never forgotten that, whenever the effort in one direction fails to work, I should just try the opposite direction.

Visits in the morning of the ninth day to the famed St. Mark's Square, impressive for its spaciousness, and to the stately 14th-century Doge's Palace were made more interesting because we had an Italian local guide explaining things to us in English. But it was the afternoon visit to a glass factory that gave a really absorbing, novel experience for the whole family. To our astonishment, the blow glass worker could make a life-like small horse just with a few twists of his fingers. Other animals appeared out of his fingers just as easily. Tracey touched my

24.2 Pigeons at the St. Mark's Square, Venice.

heart deeply when she spent her entire allowance money to buy me a glass rabbit to add to my collection of rabbits, leaving no money to buy anything for herself. Being born in a year of the Rabbit, I had kept a collection of rabbits, large or small, made of wood, marble, stone, pewter, and jade. That rabbit from Venice made a treasured addition. But the piece in my collection that I value the most is a rabbit in a relaxed pose, made of clay that Tracey designed herself when she was around 8 or 9 years of age, which she gave me as a Christmas present.

That evening, we had a gondola ride with live musicians playing accordion music for us. The moonlight did a kind thing: it rendered unnoticeable the not-so-clean water in the canal, and the familiar Italian songs around us held all our attention as the gondolas for our group floated leisurely along. When I saw an old lady on the shore enthusiastically dance to the gondola music

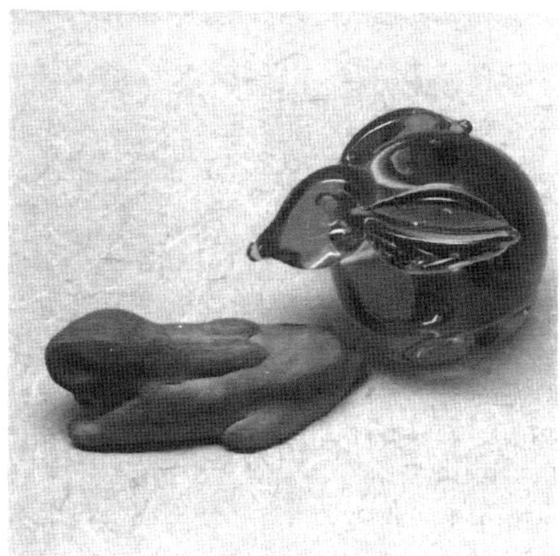

24.3 The two rabbits Tracey gave me.

24.4 My rabbit collection.

all by herself, I felt a strong sense of discovery: Italian people tended, in contrast to people of some other countries, to live joyfully, even though the environment might be lacking in some respects, even appearing dirty and disorderly.

Rome and the Vatican

Leaving Venice behind amid rain, we drove slowly on toward Rome on the 10th day. From the sixth-floor window of the *Hôtel de la Ville* where we stayed, we could look down and see the patio restaurant below, with thatched umbrellas over the tables. We had dinner late, and decided not to join the others to the Roman Fountains outside of Rome, but to walk down the Spanish Steps nearby. Darryl wanted caricatures of him drawn by two different artists working on the Steps, but neither one showed close likeness nor humorous exaggeration, the hallmark of good caricatures.

Our tour of Rome actually started the next morning, with a visit to the Trevi Fountain. Had it been an evening visit and had the fountain been deserted, there could have arisen an illusion of Anita Ekberg cooling off in the water, as in the movie *La Dolce Vita,* but with the big crowds around the fountain in broad daylight, there was no way the image of Anita could be conjured up. Instead, another movie set in Rome, *Three Coins in the Fountain,* did come up in my thoughts. For fun, I followed the custom of throwing a coin into the fountain which, according to legend, would bring the coin-thrower back some day. The legend seemed to work: Emily and I did come to Rome again some years later.

The Colosseum did not interest me much, but it was nevertheless a must-see tourist attraction. See Photo 45 in the front of this book. More movies came to mind, with hot fighting scenes. As a souvenir of the visit, I decided to have pictures taken with local youngsters dressed up in gladiator costumes—for a fee, of course.

The Vatican was next on the itinerary. The expansive St. Peter's Square was impressive for its immensity and majesty. And the cathedral was amazing in that, even when full of tourists, it appeared neither noisy nor suffocating. But one thing turned me off: the

Michelangelo-designed uniforms of the Swiss Guards for the Pope. The green-yellow color combination and the checkered design were not congruous with their paramilitary mission. Designer clothes? Of course. Successful? Not in my view!

Lunch at a Chinese restaurant named 黄河飯店 (literal translation: Yellow River Restaurant) gave pleasure to our group from Hong Kong. After lunch, Tracey needed a rest, and my mother volunteered to keep her company. The other four in our family spent time at the Vatican Museum and Sistine Chapel. There were too many items to look at and read about in the Gallery of Tapestries, the Gallery of Maps, and so on. We had to get quickly to the Sistine Chapel. Many tourists there were from Japan, all with fancy cameras. Unfortunately, no flash was allowed, and there were only a few small, high windows to let in natural light. I did not bring fast film, and could only try a few shots of the ceiling painting by Michelangelo at 1/8 second shutter speed, trying my very best to hold my hands steady. Even at that speed, with a relatively long exposure, the pictures still turned out underexposed.

24.5 At St. Peter's Square, with Mr. and Mrs. Ying Fai Wong (on the right).

We had often looked at the attractive patio restaurant below from our hotel room window. On the last night at the hotel, Emily and I could not resist its call to have a night cap there. Emily Yu, a single fellow tourist, seeing us going there, remarked with a sigh, "How romantic!"

A Bridge and a Statue in Florence

The next morning, on the 12th day of our "floral show," we spent most of the time on our "trotting horse" on the way to Florence—or *Firenze,* a name that sounds much prettier and more melodic than Florence. After lunch, we walked over the well-known bridge *Ponte Vecchio* ("Old Bridge"), with many shops along its sides. Believed to be constructed during Roman times, the shops used to sell meat and fish, until a decree around the 16th century prohibited butchers and fishmongers on the bridge for the stench they created. Now only goldsmiths and jewelers could do business there.

I was not aware at the time, but later I learned that this bridge got mentioned by name in the popular soprano aria "*O mio babbino caro*" from the opera *Gianni Schicchi* by Giacomo Puccini. In that story, the young girl Lauretta pleads with her father (*Schicchi*) to allow her to marry her young boyfriend, threatening that if the father denied her wish, she would jump from the *Pont Vecchio* to drown!

There are several versions of Michelangelo's Statue of David in Florence. The one we saw is located in a square that commands a panoramic view of the city. The colossal statue impressed us all, of course, and its sight tended to predominate in impact the other sightseeing spots, such as the Duomo and the Baptistery, the most acclaimed attractions in this city of the Renaissance.

A Shopping Stop Too Short

As part of the tour, we were also led to a leather factory for a shopping frenzy. Given a limited time, with around 50 people rushing in at the same time, everyone tried to select some souvenirs from the goods displayed on several huge tables. And then everyone had to vie for the attention of the cashier. The tour guide should certainly have allowed much more time for this shopping stop. As I understood, tour guides who bring customers to such shops are customarily rewarded with commissions. A longer period of shopping would mean more compensation for the tour guide. So, why did our guide impose a severe limit on the stay? I could not figure out the economics of this at all.

Geneva and Frankfurt

The drive toward Geneva, on the 13th day, led us away from a landscape of vineyards toward more rugged terrain. Passing by Mont Blanc, which is situated partly in Italy and partly in France, we enjoyed good scenery, but it was already late afternoon when we arrived in Geneva. All we saw was Lake Geneva, the *Jet d'Eau* (water jet), and the offices of the United Nations.

The next day, we were on the road most of the time. After lunch in Basel, we drove on to Germany, through the Black Forest area, arriving in Frankfurt at dusk. A drive around the city after dinner completed the day. Our "trotting horse" did a lot of trotting, but we did not see many "flowers" in Geneva and Frankfurt at all!

Loreley, on the Way to Amsterdam

On the way to Amsterdam the next morning, on the 15th day, our group left the bus at a small town, *St. Goar*, to board a ship for a one-hour cruise on the Rhine to view the *Loreley,* a huge rock in Germany. This rock is associated with the legend of a siren. A beautiful maiden who had jumped into the Rhine in despair, over an unfaithful lover, was transformed into a siren who used to sit on the rock to lure sailors to shipwrecks and death. There is supposedly an echo audible when a ship passed by the rock, but I did not hear anything.

We left the ship at Boppard, where our bus was waiting for us, to continue our land journey. After lunch in Cologne, this time non-Chinese, we finally arrived in Amsterdam for dinner—again at a Chinese restaurant. This restaurant had a unique name: 一定好 747 ("Indubitably Good 747"). It was a spacious venue well-deserving the 747 designation. Unfortunately, the other part of its name seemed to be guilty of exaggeration.

That evening was brightened by a surprise visit to the bus by three unfamiliar people, a lady and two young children, a boy and a girl, about the same age as my children. They turned out to be the family members of our driver, Mr. Kleer, whose home was near Amsterdam. Since all of us in the tour group had become very familiar and friendly with the driver, all of us were genuinely glad to meet his lovely family.

Red Lights

But the next event that evening was much more venturesome: a walk through the red-light district in Amsterdam!

It wasn't appropriate for my parents or my children to go, and Emily expressed no interest. Thus, I was the only one in our family to join the group. The narrow streets we walked through were lined with a multitude of narrowly spaced display windows, each showing a woman sitting on a high stool in an alluring dress, ready to receive clients. Actually, a few days earlier, when our bus first arrived at Paris from Calais, we also drove through a similar window-display district, but that was only a hurried drive-through. Here, in Amsterdam, we were instead taking a leisurely walk-through.

Some of the windows only showed a chair, either with a woman on it (waiting) or left empty (in business), and a curtain hid the bed behind, but some windows left the curtain half-open, revealing a bed and a wash basin in the rear. What amazed me was some of the prostitutes were very beautiful, and even elegant and intelligent-looking. What could have driven them to this line of business? Even more amazing was that some of them were not attractive at all, or even unsightly. Given men's preference for good looks, I wondered how much income these less attractive women could earn, with a lot of competitive windows within a few feet of them. The economics of the whole line of business left more questions than answers in my mind.

Even more venturesome than the walk that night, was the subsequent visit to an adult theater. The program consisted of three parts: (1) a movie, (2) a striptease show, and (3) live acts. Ten of us going together had the same desire to skip the film part of it. Being more daring than the rest, I volunteered to negotiate with the manager for a group discount. It turned out that even though we did not want to see the film, we still had to wait out the film time. But since I bargained with him, the manager offered to give us a 20% discount, from 50 to 40 *guilders* (about $25 to $20) per person. For that feat, I received not only the gratitude of the group, but also the (undeserved) honorary title of 領隊 ("Captain").

A Transaction Aborted

Amsterdam being a big center for the global diamond trade, our itinerary inevitably included a lengthy tour of the Coster Diamond Factory in the morning. With the intention of buying a diamond ring for Emily for our 25th anniversary, I spotted one with nine small diamonds arranged in a square. Priced at $775, it seemed to be a suitable choice. But just before I took action, a Mr. Leung from our bus (not Andrew's father) whispered to me not to buy. It happened that Mr. Leung was the manager of the jewelry department of Lane Crawford, the major department store in Hong Kong. With his full knowledge of the diamond trade, he told me that the diamond price in Amsterdam was way too high, about 40% higher than in Hong Kong. Besides, in his opinion, the nine diamonds in this ring were too small to serve as a store of value, making the purchase of this ring economically unwarranted. After some hesitation, I decided to accept his expert advice. Sorry, Amsterdam: no sale. Sorry, Emily: no Dutch ring.

Canals, Windmills, and Clogs

On the canal cruise in flat-bottomed boats in Amsterdam that followed, the commentaries by the Dutch young lady guide were neither informative nor clear. Still, the canals in Amsterdam are something that inspire wonderment. And a novel I studied at St. John's Middle School, *Hans Brinker, or the Silver Skates,* set in the Netherlands about a skating race on the canal, momentarily came to my mind. But, of course, during my visit, the canals were not frozen, and there were no skaters.

Windmills are a well-known Dutch icon. The first time I saw the inside of a windmill was eye-opening. There was more intricate machinery than I imagined. We all walked gingerly by, taking care not to touch anything.

Clogs are another Dutch icon. In a clog factory we toured, Emily bought a small pair, red on a yellow base, not suitable for wearing, but big enough for keeping loose change. Mr. Kleer, our driver, went deep inside the workshop, and came out with two unpainted clogs, as gifts for Darryl and Tracey. Since unfinished clogs were never for sale, these presents to our children became unique souvenirs.

From Brussels Back to London

It was the 16th day now. Entering into Belgium, we stopped by the site of the 1958 World's Fair. And in the evening, a drive-through Brussels ended at a major tourist spot, *Le Grand Place*, a huge square with palatial buildings surrounding it, colorfully lighted and full of tourists. The lighting effect was very dramatic, but nothing else was going on, and the scene came off as a bit monotonous.

It was hard to believe, but the next morning we were already on our return trip to London through France. Saying goodbyes to our friendly driver, we boarded a hovercraft in Calais. The ride over the English Channel was so choppy that it was a wonder that my mother did not throw up. And the Pepsi bottles in the children's hands almost flew away into the air!

Toasts at Jade Garden

On the bus trip to London, we planned to mark the end of our European tour at a good restaurant, for an official double celebration of Father's 75th birthday, and our own 25th wedding anniversary. We intended to first wash up in the hotel, then dress up and go out. But our plan did not materialize; instead of depositing us at the hotel as we expected, our bus took us directly to a restaurant. Where? Good old Jade Garden, of course! We now had to wash up after dinner, and seek out a good place just to have some desserts for our double celebration.

During the dinner at Jade Garden, however, there did occur a surprise. Without our pre-knowledge, Darryl stood up, called the group to attention, and proposed a toast to Grandpa for his 75th birthday, then another one to Emily and me for our 25th anniversary. Tracey then followed suit. These toasts brought forth rounds of applause, and prompted many friends in our group to come over to offer us their good wishes. That created a little commotion in the crowded restaurant, but it also added a festive atmosphere appropriate for our final group dinner.

Did we go out for our planned desserts? No. It was raining too hard. Following Plan B, we just had something in the lobby Lounge of the London Metropole Hotel.

Farewell at Heathrow

The tour had finally come to an end on this 18th day. In the beginning, "9 countries in 18 days" sounded good. But, in the end, "viewing a floral show on a trotting horse" (走馬看花), left us with only rough impressions with no depth. If we consider the fact that the 1st day (arrival in London) and the 18th day (goodbyes at Heathrow) did not really involve any sightseeing, the tour was actually even shorter than as advertised.

What did my parents think of the trip? It was a worthwhile novel experience, seeing so many foreign countries firsthand. It also provided a fountain of fond memories and conversation topics. But most importantly, they treasured it as a source of good family togetherness. I concur.

Since my parents' flight back to Hong Kong took off earlier than our flight back to New York, we could see Father and Mother off, along with the others in the group. Father and Mother were emotional, and Darryl cried while hugging Grandpa and Grandma farewell.

A Sequel

Only three years after the European tour, we made another attempt at "viewing a floral show on a trotting horse." The destination this time consisted of Malaysia, Singapore, and Thailand. Taken in August, 1982, it involved 3 generations, 6 people, 3 countries, and 11 days. However, if we deduct the 1st and the 11th day, which we learned from experience would not cover real sightseeing, we would get nine days, giving us a number pattern of 3-6-3-9, again with all the figures divisible by 3.

Skipping the details, I'll just make a few brief comments about this trip.

First of all, we found Singapore to be unbelievably clean. The severe penalty for littering in this city, plus strict enforcement of the law, made Singapore the cleanest city in the world. Why couldn't its example be followed by other countries (I wondered)? Arriving in Singapore from Malaysia made the contrast so sharp and clear. A couple of dubious gentlemen in our tour group made a special effort to search for cigarette butts, candy wrappers, or food crumbs in the lawn or on the street pavements in Singapore. Absolutely no success!

Singapore is not only impressive for its cleanliness. It's also more modern in appearance. The Coralarium (showing undersea life) and the Jurong Bird Park (a specialty zoo and sanctuary) were uniquely interesting.

When we arrived in Thailand, we again noticed a sharp contrast in cleanliness. One incident was especially amusing. Our tour guide bought bananas for us from the floating market in Bangkok,

24.6 An elephant ride for grandpa and grandson, Bangkok, 1982.

which we all enjoyed. Later, when we asked him, "What do we do with the banana peels?" he responded with a smile, "Do as the locals do, just throw them into the river." As we did that, some women were washing clothes in the river about 60 feet from our boat, and some young kids were bathing in the same water.

But, in Bangkok, the Cultural Show in the Rose Garden left us with indelible impressions. It featured delicate Thai dances, an unusual Thai boxing match, a fierce cock fight, and an elaborate, colorful Thai wedding ceremony. But the top prize for exotic experience undoubtedly should go to a short, rough, but unforgettable elephant ride we took. Not only was it different, it was probably not easily available elsewhere in the world.

25

Travel Tidbits

It would be too tedious to report on all the travels I had. But some unusual or unexpected tidbits about those travels, about either the places visited or some of the people I met, are worth telling.

A Slow Boat to Japan

During the academic year 1960–1961, I took a sabbatical leave from Denison University to reunite with my parents in Hong Kong. They had taken advantage of a rare opportunity to leave Shanghai for Hong Kong in 1957, and were eager to see me, and even more so to meet my bride Emily for the first time. We intended to travel by air. But our Chinese opera friend, William Cheng (程威廉), a manager at the China Merchants Steam Navigation Co. (招商局) in New York, suggested a more exotic alternative: take a freighter of his company from America to Taiwan, and then fly to Hong Kong. "I'll even give you a big discount," he said. He made the deal irresistible.

The freighter we took, Hai Ming (海明輪), sailed from Los Angeles on July 10, 1960, with only 11 passengers. There was a diplomat, a Minister to a country in South America, returning to Taiwan with his wife. There was also a returning medical doctor, Dr. Hsu (徐嗣興), after a year's study of virus in the United States, who turned out to be a distant uncle of Emily. The others included a couple of single nurses, who had to stay in the infirmary throughout the voyage because of seasickness. In view of the fewness of passengers, every dinner was at the Captain's Table. One day, we all volunteered to wrap Chinese dumplings (包餃子) for dinner together. The group was congenial; we played cards, chatted, and truly had much fun together.

The Captain (whose name I can no longer recall), an excellent raconteur, had many stories to tell us. At the end of WWII, he headed a mission to ship Japanese prisoners of war (POW) back to Japan from China. To avenge the brutalities and barbarities the invading Japanese military had inflicted upon the Chinese people, our Captain imposed rules and restrictions designed to make lives difficult for those POW's. For every such instance he mentioned (such as not allowing the POW's to leave the company to go to the washroom, resulting in their having to dirty themselves up right on the spot), those of us who had suffered various indignities under the Japanese invaders loudly cheered and applauded him.

But the Captain also had a sad story about a tragedy in his own family. His elder son had developed throat problems resulting from tonsillitis, and the father wanted the younger son to have tonsillectomy to avoid the problem that had troubled the elder son. The young son, a well-behaved child good in scholastics, with no tonsillitis and fearful of the procedure, begged the father to spare him. But the father's insistence, plus the promise of a movie as a reward, finally swayed the boy. Little did anyone suspect the massive hemorrhage that would occur, causing the boy to die in the operating room. Sensing that he had in effect "murdered" his own son, the Captain found it almost impossible to live on. To ease his own pain, he decided to carry a portrait of his son to a movie theater, in order to keep his promise. He watched the movie from beginning to end, with his son's portrait facing the silver screen, and with tears cascading down his own eyes!

One other memory from that freighter had to do with a whale. One day, while taking a stroll on the deck, Emily and I witnessed a collision of our ship with a small whale. It was a rare, unexpected sight to see—somewhat scary, but luckily with no serious consequence. Two other passengers witnessed the same accident, but when we reported this collision to the rest of the passengers inside, none of them would believe us. "Collision with a whale? No way," they must have thought. Truths, I learned, may not spread as facilely as rumors.

Our ship made a scheduled stop in Kobe, Japan for loading and unloading cargo. We decided to get off the ship in Kobe instead of going on to Taipei. We had plans to go to Taiwan, of course, but since that would be my first visit to Emily's home, I thought it best to wait for a time when we could stay with my in-laws for a longer period of time. Therefore, we abbreviated our stay on the freighter to 17 days, with fond memories.

A Thing of Two about Japan

Our one-week tour of Japan was enjoyable enough. But here I will only report on a couple of things we encountered there.

One day, at lunch in a fast-food restaurant, Emily asked the Japanese waitress for some ketchup. The waitress showed no understanding of the request. Emily then repeated, slowly, "K-e-t-c-h-u-p." Only after pondering for nearly 10 seconds, did the waitress suddenly put on a smile, and said, "Oh, kechopu!" This incident was interesting to me for two reasons. One, Japan had obviously adopted many foreign words as its own, including "ketchup." But, second, the Japanese language is such that, they cannot pronounce a consonant unless it is followed by a vowel. Thus, the last consonant "p" in the word "ketchup" must be augmented by a "u" to form the "pu" sound. This was indeed true, because I found out later that the word "ball" (think of baseball, popular in Japan) has also been adopted in the Japanese language, but it must be pronounced "ballu." Similarly, if you pronounce (or mispronounce) "milk" as "miloku"—with two vowels *o* and *u* added—you can count on being understood with ease.

Another interesting thing I discovered at the hot spring district of Hakone (箱根) was the high priority accorded to a bath in that region. When we arrived at a Japanese inn one late evening, the innkeeper courteously met our train. And, as soon as we stepped into the inn, he asked us, in broken English, to take a bath. Being famished at that latc hour, we asked for dinner first. But the innkeeper would not yield an inch to our request, and just repeated, "*Dozo* (please). *Dozo.* Take bath." After 10 minutes, on Emily's advice, we had a denouement: Bath before dinner. The lesson from this incident: If you go to a hot spring resort in Japan, remember that BATH must come before anything else.

Mile High Swinging Bridge

When Roger and Lilian Yeu invited us to join them on their weeklong "time share" vacation in May, 1997, we gladly said "Yes." They had been our good friends for 40-odd years then, during which Roger had been my musical partner on the Chinese opera stage in New York in many shows. We were happy to join them. The drive to our vacation destination, Beech Mountain, North Carolina, was quite long. But a nice two-bedroom apartment was waiting for us there at Cedar Village at the end of our journey.

The main attraction of the trip was supposedly George Vanderbilt's Biltmore Estate in Asheville, North Carolina, the largest private home in the United States. With 8,000 acres, and several gardens in different styles, the living space is located in a big mansion with 250 rooms, including 35 bedrooms, 43 bathrooms, and 3 kitchens. Among other things, there are also 65 fireplaces here and there, 16 chimneys punctuating the steeply pitched roof, and a staircase with a three-story, winding and highly decorated balustrade. I could not quite imagine living there.

What excited me more on this trip was a simpler man-made structure, a special bridge. Located in Linville, North Carolina, the Mile High Swinging Bridge is a 228-foot suspension bridge that spans an 80-foot chasm on Grandfather Mountain at an elevation more than one mile. Because of its suspension nature, even a person's gentle stepping would cause the bridge to swing and sway. And when there is any wind force, the swinging action could turn wild, even violent. Can you guess the wind speed that prevailed when I tried to walk over that bridge? It was around 60 mph! Since I was also a mile above the land down below, I felt I was walking in a "4-dimensional space," being thrown up and down, to the left and to the right, each second with an unpredictable direction. The thought entered my mind that the situation was not real; it was a Hollywood special effects team at work!

Emily did not walk on the bridge, but Lilian was more daring.

Strangely, the deepest impression I retain about North Carolina is not any tourist spot, but the excellent food we enjoyed at almost all the restaurants we ate at. We did not consciously look for restaurants with reputation. But, one meal after another, and whichever eatery we chose to sample at random, on a main street or on a side street, we were invariably surprised with delicious food, courteously served and reasonably priced. Never again have I experienced such a consistent record of excellence. Bravo, North Carolina!

A Question about Napoleon's Portrait

Our trip to Baton Rouge, Louisiana, in January 1999 was for the celebration of the 80th birthday of my Aunt Daisy (蔣陳允娟), where I also met her children, my close cousins. But our plane landed in New Orleans first, and we had a chance to join a swamp and plantation tour of New Orleans before going to the birthday festivities in Baton Rouge.

Many aspects of New Orleans appeared to be new and different. We had fun looking for little alligators during the swamp boat ride, and listening to the tour guide's tales about the smuggling operations of Jean Lafitte, the pirate in that very area. Lafitte and his comrades were captured by a U.S. naval force. And, in return for a legal pardon, Lafitte *et al.* helped General Andrew Jackson defend New Orleans from the British in the final battle of the War of 1812.

The most striking tale the guide told us, however, was not about Lafitte, but about Napoleon. The big plantation we visited was owned by a family who immigrated from France, and their ancestors knew the Bonaparte family. According to the guide, those ancestors laughed hard when they saw the widely circulated portrait of Napoleon, because that portrait is the likeness not of Napoleon, but of his brother. It was believed that Napoleon's father selected the "brother portrait" to be circulated because the brother looked more imposing than Napoleon himself.

Could that be true? Or was that just a made-up story? I have wondered often. As a matter of fact, I have also wondered about history in general. How much of the history we have learned in school or outside of classes is an accurate depiction of actual happenings?

How much of it represents fabrications, or facts distorted by value judgments, political whitewashing, or plain ignorance?

Taking Our Children to China

For years I made special efforts to teach Darryl and Tracey Chinese language and some aspects of Chinese culture when they were young. Understandably, they showed resistance to my lessons, since they felt little affinity to a foreign culture and an altogether different system of language. My efforts did bear some fruits, though. And Darryl actually thanked me later for forcing him to learn Chinese. One regret was that I did not have time to take them on a tour of Mainland China. Prior to 2001, they had only been to Taiwan and Hong Kong.

That omission was rectified in 2001, when we took Darryl and Tracey on a two-week China tour, covering Beijing, the Great Wall, Xian, Guilin, the Three Gorges on the Yangtze River, Wuhan, and Shanghai. In view that my previous travels in China were extremely limited, this trip was an eye-opener for me as well as for the children. Being retired, with more free time than the children, Emily and I went a few days earlier to visit some friends in Beijing first.

Special Friends in Beijing

Before the children joined us in Beijing, we looked up Dr. Qian Yijian (錢貽簡), a former roommate of mine at St. John's Middle School, later a famous physician who served as the attending physician during President Nixon's visit to China. Yijian kindly treated Emily and me to a sumptuous banquet with his family. At that restaurant, I witnessed for the first time a novel gadget—a motorized Lazy Susan. To call any dish to your front, just push a button, and the Lazy Susan will rotate to deliver it. How much more mechanized can a dining experience get?

Yijian also took us to the Great Hall of the People on a prearranged special tour. Because he had been instrumental in the establishment of a medical office at the Hall, and was Honorary President of the hospital for top government leaders, the administrators at the Great Hall of the

25.1 Lunch with State Dinner menu after our tour of the Great Hall of the People, May 25, 2001. From left: Mr. Yu Tao (于濤, Deputy Chief of the Protocol Office of the Great Hall, our host), Dr. Qian Yijian, Emily and me, and Dr. Chang Huiqin (常慧琴).

People treated him, and therefore us, with great courtesy. They assigned a private guide to show us the various reception halls, including those off-limits to the ordinary tourists. We were even invited to lunch as guests of the Deputy Chief of their Protocol Office, where we were served a meal with the State Dinner menu.

It was also during our stay in Beijing that Kang Yao accompanied us to see the Musketeer George. See Photo 63 in the front section of this book. Emily and I also paid a visit to Peter Hao, my fraternity brother who co-founded the Chinese opera group in New York with me. And, Mr. Chien Kiang (錢江), a well-known amateur Chinese opera singer of the young male role (小生), whom we had met not too long ago, invited us to several dinners, including a singing session in his private opera club attended by many famous professional singers.

After these visits to special friends, we, with the children, enjoyed touring the Forbidden City, the Temple of Heaven, the Summer Palace,

25.2 On our way to the Temple of Heaven (in background), Beijing, 2001.

and Tiananmen Square in Beijing. A picture of the family at the Great Wall is shown in Photo 47 in the front of this book. Here I print a picture, Photo 25.2, taken on our way to the Temple of Heaven. The Temple of Heaven is a gigantic structure, but being far away in the background in this photo, it appears disproportionately small.

Back to Shanghai

My return to Shanghai after an absence of 54 years was quite a strange, emotional experience. For Emily, who had lived briefly in Shanghai when she was a teenager, it was probably also a nostalgic event. But, for my children, Shanghai was some place all new.

The first thing Darryl requested to see in Shanghai was my last residence in Shanghai before I left home for the United States. I was touched by his interest in my past life. I called a taxi to take us to Mei Lan Fang, to take a look at No. 34. But my former residence looked rather dilapidated after half a century. It also appeared smaller than how I remembered it. I didn't know who were living there, and decided not to knock on the door to ask to see the inside. I let bygone be bygone, forever.

Darryl also requested to see St. John's University and Middle School in the western part of Shanghai, where I studied. While the taxi driver waited at the gate of the campus, we walked through the campus from the university area in the front to the middle school area in the back. The campus looked pretty much the same, but the old university actually no longer existed and its campus was now used by another school. I could not quite believe that I would have this opportunity to revisit, with my family at my side, the place where, at age 14, I used to bury my head in the pages of the dictionary every day and, with clenched teeth, engage in a desperate struggle with the English language, to cure my lexical anemia.

A Session on Family History

On this trip to Shanghai, an aunt of mine, Lizhen Jiang (蔣周麗珍), at age 98, held a long chat with me for no less than four hours, filling me in on the happenings in our extended family since the day in 1947 when I left Shanghai for the United States. The reason for that special session was that I didn't give her enough attention at a banquet I hosted for the relatives in the Chiang family. So she asked one of her daughters, Yilian Jiang (蔣懿蓮) to take her to our hotel for an exclusive chat. I was totally amazed by her razor-sharp mind and lucid recollection of events past. This indefatigable raconteur told her stories in clearly demarcated strands of family history, a feat rare even among professional storytellers.

This Aunt (see Photo 81), the wife of my father's younger brother, gave birth to many children. Her sons therefore share with me not only the same family name (now spelled as Jiang instead of Chiang), but also the generational indicator. But a funny thing with regard to names happened: whereas the names of two of her sons (蔣中權 and 蔣中銓) sound distinct in the Shanghai dialect, they happen to be homonyms in Mandarin, both transliterated as Jiang Zhongquan. The elder of the two, Zhongquan (中權), one year my junior, was not the academic type in his youth, but ended up as a professor of accounting at the Dalian Institute of Technology. He is shown as the first person from the left in Photo 68. The younger one, Zhongquan (中銓), became an architectural engineer in Beijing. And the latter's son, Fan Jiang (蔣凡), has had a successful career in the field of high finances in the United States. After earning a doctorate at Notre Dame University, and after some years at Goldman Sachs and JPMorgan Chase Bank, he is now a Managing Director at Citi.

Before my aunt parted from my hotel, she reminded me that, in accordance with Chinese tradition, she would be celebrating her 100th birthday in her 99th year, in May, 2002. Could I and Emily be there? Having never attended a 100th birthday before, I was happy to promise her that Emily and I would definitely be there at her centennial party.

25.3 The younger of the two Zhongquans, at the Great Wall, 1990.

25.4 Fan Jiang (middle) talking to Emily. Andy Sung (left) and David Kwo (right) are Chinyee's sons (2000 photo).

Sea of Clouds

After the well-attended, festive 100th birthday party of my aunt in Shanghai, with many speeches, we undertook a three-day visit to Huang Shan (Yellow Mountain) in Anhui Province (安徽), a famous scenic area my friend Stanley Chen had long recommended as a "must-see" sight in China. This was a rare opportunity to follow up on Stanley's advice since, conveniently, Huang Shan was only a one-hour flight away from Shanghai. We booked a private guide who would meet us with a car at the airport in a town at the foot of the mountain.

Huang Shan is renowned for its grandiose rocks, its picturesque pines trees, and its spectacular sea of clouds. The rocks and the pines are always there, but the sea of clouds appears only under opportune weather conditions, and it depends entirely on the luck of the tourists whether they can get to view the spectacle or not. Our first day of arrival was literally a washout. It rained so hard that we got thoroughly drenched during the 40-minute walk to our hotel from the mountain-top station of the cable car, even though we bought plastic ponchos and umbrellas right then and there. Through our hotel window, we could see no rocks, no pines, . . . only rainfall. We were obviously out of luck, and had to lower our expectation to the bottom level.

The next morning, however, we were awakened by glorious sunshine. And, as a big surprise, the water vapor from the rain the day before produced a dramatic sea of clouds, one that our guide considered the best he had ever seen in his career as a guide. The fast-rolling clouds set off the rugged, unusual rock formations and the twisty pine clusters at their most photogenic. I didn't realize that what seemed like a total disaster one day could end up as something perfectly wonderful! A good lesson on optimism that was.

I took many pictures at Huang Shan. A panel of four scenes, in color, is shown in Photo 28 in the front of this book. A fifth one, showing shapely pine trees in black and gray, was shown in Photo 22.4.

A Big Scare

But a big scary thing happened that afternoon on Huang Shan, when, on a photo walk by myself after a nap, I became attracted by the sight of thousands of padlocks attached to the wires on the guardrails along a wide precipice. As I was wondering about those padlocks, large and small, even in different colors, a voice came from behind me: "Are you Mr. *Chiang Chung-i* (my Chinese name)?" The question took me aback. If I could claim any measure of name recognition, it would be in two circles, academic economists and Chinese opera fans. How could someone here on remote Huang Shan know my name! In my mind arose frightening questions: Have I been under surveillance since I arrived here? Have I violated any regulations to cause questioning and possible investigation? Am I about to be arrested?

I had to turn around and answer that person, "Yes, I am *Chiang Chung-i.*" But what I saw was a young man not in police uniform. I immediately asked, "How do you know my name?" To my relief, he smiled, and said, "Your wife was here in the morning, and bought a padlock from me. She gave me your name, her own name and the names of your two children to be engraved on it. I remembered your name because it is unique. Somehow, when I saw you come, I guessed the name fits you."

In response to my queries about those padlocks, he explained to me that many honeymooners, or lovers, who come to Huang Shan, like to have their names engraved on the padlock, then have it secured onto the guardrail and throw the key into the ravine down below, vowing that the two of them will never be separated from each other. Emily had our names engraved, along with the words "永保平安 (Tranquility and security for our family forever.)" The key? Deep in the ravine.

To Earn Our Lunch

In May of 2003, Emily and I took a Canyonlands tour with Tauk Tours.

Normally, when a tour bus arrives at a lunch stop, meals can be ordered as soon as the tourists are seated at the tables. But on this tour, the stop for lunch at the restaurant Chuck Wagon Cookouts in Kanab, Utah, was anything but normal. The manager of the restaurant, in Western garb, announced on the loudspeaker that, sorry, lunch would not be served until we had "earned" it by participating in a mock Western drama on the spot. He outlined a story, and did the casting right away—cowboys, Indians, homesteaders, soldiers, saloonkeepers, waitresses, and songstresses. We were then sent to an adjacent room to put on our costumes, and escorted to our assigned locales for the drama about to unfold according to his roughly sketched script.

Why was there a condition imposed before the meal? Maybe it was just a gimmick to make us hungrier by the delay, so that the food served would seem tastier. But the official reason given was that Kanab, Utah, known as "Little Hollywood," often served as the locale for Western movies and TV shows; it was therefore only proper that we did the "local thing" and played a Western drama while visiting there. Emily and I were cast as a pioneer couple who had to guard their home against trespassers. We didn't have much to do, but Emily kept busy washing clothes, and I used my rifle a lot. An hour's theatrical work, plus the excitement of it, did make the lunch taste good.

25.5 To "earn" lunch, we had to play a "pioneer couple" (2003 photo).

The Canyons: A Fantasy of Food Comparison

This Canyonlands tour mainly covered three places: the Grand Canyon in Arizona, the Bryce Canyon, and Zion National Park, both in Utah.

The word "Grand" in Grand Canyon is a most apt adjective, because words like "big," "widespread," "extensive" cannot adequately convey its grandeur. The problem for the tourist is that, because of its scale, if you move a thousand yards away, your view remains pretty much the same. Also, in view of its more or less flattened top of the canyon, I found it photographically challenging to find angles that show interesting lines in the pictures.

At the rim of the Bryce Canyon, I for the first time saw something called "hoodoos," irregularly shaped rock columns seemingly grown from the bottom of the valley. The irregular shapes of the columns resulted from the freezing and unfreezing of water over thousands of years, which displaced the less solid components of the rocks, and kept only the hard ones.

The Zion National Park is located at a low spot surrounded by high mountains. Instead of the down-looking viewpoints at the Grand

Canyon and the Bryce Canyon, here we had to look up from below, an altogether different experience.

After returning from the trip, a fantastic thought occurred to me. I considered a situation of some ants placed around some food, and formed in my mind a comparative picture of the Canyonland tour spots as follows: (1) Put one half of a watermelon on the table, use a spoon to dig out random pieces of the melon, some deep, some shallow, to create an irregular-shaped ravine. Now place an ant on the edge of the half melon. What the ant sees is something like the Grand Canyon. (2) Dig out the middle of a birthday cake, and place in that space birthday candles of varying heights and varying widths. Now invite a small ant to take a walk along the edge of the birthday cake. It would resemble the Bryce Canyon. (3) Cut a group of bamboo shoots into mountain shapes, some big and fat, some short and stubby, and arrange them in a circular pattern. Now place an ant inside the circle. What it sees would be like the Zion National Park.

Why did this thought occur to me? I don't know. But those who have visited these resorts might agree that my fantastic ant food comparison is apropos.

25.6 Doesn't this scene at the Bryce Canyon look like a Chinese painting?

Disappointments on the Baltic

In August 2005, a group of friends joined force to take a cruise to Northern Europe. The large group meant interaction and fun, but the trip itself also brought me disappointments—as many as three, in fact.

The first had to do with the iconic statue of Copenhagen, The Little Mermaid. Justly famous, the statue is based on a fairy tale of Hans Christian Andersen about the love affair between a mermaid princess Ariel and a human prince Eric. The bronze statue, depicting a mermaid becoming human, sits on a rock in the water. Even though it is situated not far away from shore, however, its 4-foot size looked unimposing. I fully understood that the word "little" means "small." But the impression the statue gave me was "miniature" rather than "small," totally failing to fulfill my expectation. Despite my disappointment with it, I deplored the incidents of vandalism that had occurred in various years, including pouring paint over the statue, and even, unimaginably, decapitation!

The itinerary of our Northern Europe cruise included a stop at Gdansk, Poland. But a big storm made it dangerous to approach the port, and the Captain of our ship decided to omit Gdansk from our schedule. That was my second disappointment, since it deprived me of my one rare chance of visiting Poland.

The third disappointment was of an altogether different nature. In the splendid Catherine Palace in Pushkin, built for Catherine I (not Catherine the Great), the guide told the rather fantastic story of the rise of a servant woman who first became the mistress of Peter the Great, and later his wife and the Empress of Russia. Born in one of the small Baltic states, and orphaned at age 3 after losing both parents to the plague, this woman, originally named Marta Skowronska, was raised by a local pastor. She worked as a laundress, and later married a Swedish cavalryman. In a war between Sweden and Russia, she was taken as a prisoner, and was passed around several times as servant/mistress, ending in the household of Prince Alexander Menshikov, the best friend of Peter the Great. Then Peter the Great met her, and took her as a mistress, initiating an incredible change in her life.

After hearing such a story, what could I imagine her to be like? She must be a woman of exquisite beauty, plus infinite charm and irresistible feminine qualities. A few minutes later, the guide led us to a huge portrait, and pointed her out to us as Catherine I. My immediate response was: MY GOODNESS! What I saw in the portrait was so far apart from my imagination that I could not believe my eyes. Thick eyebrows amply suggested masculinity. That was fortified by a visible mustache. I was shocked by Peter the Great's taste! Catherine must have many good qualities not ascertainable from such a portrait. I can't imagine what.

A Whirlwind Win at Blackjack

The standard design of cruise ships places the casino in the middle of the ship on the main activities deck. The Star Princess, the cruise ship we were on in August, 2005, was no exception. You want to go to the dining room? You have to pass the casino. You want to go to the theater? You have to pass the casino. Normally, I just walked past the casino quickly. But that evening, I saw Sissi Lu (盧柯嘉惠) at the blackjack table by herself. An old friend, she is a sharp cardplayer who had once won the blackjack championship in a tournament in Atlantic City. I went to her, and jokingly asked her, "Sissy, can I join you as a partner?" She graciously said, "Of course. My capital is $100. Give me $100, and we'll be equal partners."

I reached for my wallet, but before I could hand her my $100, Sissi said, "I have reached the target of a $200 winning. We should quit now. You and I will split $200." She did not accept my $100 capital. On the contrary, after cashing in the chips, she handed ME a $100 bill.

She is a phenomenal cardplayer; not only does she play well, she knows when to quit. She is also a most gracious partner.

No Smorgasbord in Stockholm

On this same 2005 cruise, our stop in Stockholm was a short one, but we had time for lunch on our own. My desire was to have a smorgasbord, which should be easily available on the pedestrian street we were on. But before I found one, a particular sign attracted Emily's attention—a sign in Chinese. It was a Chinese restaurant.

She said, "Let's have a Chinese lunch." My reply was not characterized with politeness, "Are you crazy? Eat Chinese for our only meal in Stockholm?"

"Why not? We had Chinese meals in London, Paris, and Rome," she retorted.

"But that happened on a tour group from Hong Kong. We are now on our own!"

Her response was silence.

You guessed it. We ended up with a Chinese lunch as our only meal in Stockholm. It was a totally forgettable one. No, on second thought, it was a totally "unforgettable" one.

The Bonnie Banks o' Loch Lomond

Having been a Princess Cruises passenger in 2005, we were offered a discount for another Princess cruise in 2006. Finding it difficult to refuse a 50%-off deal, we booked a trip in August that would take us to Dublin in Ireland, Loch Lomond in Scotland, Bergen in Norway, Rotterdam and Delft in the Netherlands, Bruges in Belgium, and Le Havre and Honfleur in France.

But the main attraction for me was Loch Lomond. Loch just means "lake." What made this particular lake special to me? It was a song, "The Bonnie Banks o' Loch Lomond ('Loch Lomond' for short)," which I learned way back at St. John's Middle School in Shanghai. As the song lyrics intimated, two lovers who used to frequent the banks of Loch Lomond now faced permanent separation. The reason for this fate was never fully explained, and, in those high-school days, I lacked the time and resourcefulness to dig out the details. Still, the song stuck with me for all these years:

By yon bonnie banks and by yon bonnie braes
Where the sun shines brightly on Loch Lomond

Where me and my true love were ever wont to gae
On the bonnie, bonnie banks of Loch Lomond

O ye'll take the high road and I'll take the low road
And I'll be in Scotland afore ye
But me and my true love will never meet again
On the bonnie, bonnie banks of Loch Lomond

Evidently, both the lovers were returning to Scotland from some place. Why were they away? On their returning trips to Scotland, why did they not travel together and take different roads? And, once back in Scotland, why could they never meet again?

The tour guide in Loch Lomond supplied the missing part of the story. During an ancient war, many Scottish soldiers were captured by the enemy. The enemy commander, an eccentric, declared an outlandish policy: Each and every day, he would set one captive free, and put another to death—at random. The lover of one captive took an arduous journey for days from Scotland to look for her beloved. The good news was that she succeeded in locating him in the prison camp. The bad news was that her lover had been selected to be executed the next day. That doomed soldier then wrote the song. What did he mean by the "high road?" It was the road traveled by living human beings. And by the term "low road," he meant the road traveled by the soul of the deceased.

Was that a true story? Or just a legend? No matter, here I was, physically standing on the bonnie banks of Loch Lomond—a lake seemingly like many others, yet very special in its own way to my mind. I lingered there for quite a few minutes, thinking about that tragic couple, and also thinking about my young days, singing "Loch Lomond" with my teenage schoolmates in the huge Assembly Hall of St. John's Middle School in Shanghai.

A Humorous Local Guide in Santorini

In 2008, some of my Chinese opera friends were eager to try out a new ship of the Cunard Lines, Queen Victoria, and invited Emily and me to join them. I was a bit wary, because new ships might not have had time to work out all the "bugs," and might well be subpar in their services. Still, it was a congenial group, and the 12-day itinerary was interesting, covering quite a few places that we had not been to. Starting from Rome and ending in Venice, the trip would include stops at Pompeii and Sorrento in Italy, Santorini and Athens in Greece, Ephesus and Istanbul in Turkey, and Dubrovnik in Croatia.

One of the deepest impressions about this 2008 trip was our conversation with a humorous local tour guide in Santorini. Instead of a straight narration about the island, he asked us for answer to his questions. "You see two houses in Santorini; one has marble floors all over, and the other, wooden floors instead," he asked, "what can you conclude from this observation?" Normally, marble floors would signify a family richer than the one with wooden floors. But the way he posed the question led me to choose the opposite conclusion. If so, marble would be the cheaper material, and from simple economic demand-and-supply analysis, Santorini must be a marble-producing place. On this thinking, and seeing that nobody else had answered his question, I volunteered the answer: "The house with the marble floors belongs to a poorer family, because marble is cheap here." And that indeed was the correct inference.

The next question he posed related to the large number of churches our car passed by on one street after another. "Can you conclude that Greek people are abnormally religious?" he asked. From the way he posed the question, I again chose a contrary answer: "No." "Why then," he continued to ask, "do you find churches one after another?" I did not have a ready explanation. It turned out, however, the reason again related to economics. The Greek law at the time stipulated that a religious organization can engage in business, with its profits tax free! As a result, every astute businessman would first form a church, and then conduct business under the church's name, in open abuse of the tax law. What I could not understand was why the government did not see through this gaping tax loophole, and tried to close it.

Hairy Tales

Many cruises we had been on had postage-stamp-sized dance floors, hardly big enough to do any reasonable steps for one couple, let alone two or three. And the bands usually played for limited time each session. On the other hand, Queen Victoria, the ship of our 2008 cruise, features a full-size ballroom, with a ceiling two stories high, and an orchestra that played music for two full hours. Besides, the ship provides as many as four "dance hosts" who would dance with ladies with no partners of their own. With such a good dance floor and a nice orchestra, Emily and I took advantage of it almost every night.

One night, as we sat down after a dance, one of the dance hosts, in navy blue blazer uniform, walked briskly toward our table all the way from the other end of the dance floor. We both noticed him, and had the common thought that he was coming over to compliment us on our dancing. But no such luck! He addressed himself exclusively to Emily, and said, "Lady, you have a great haircut!" A compliment on haircut? From a dance host? Well, yes. This gentleman happened to be a hairstylist from Boston. A dance enthusiast, he always took a few months off from his hair work every year to serve as a dance host on cruise ships, enjoying visits to different parts of the world into the bargain.

Strangely, there was also a hairy tale off the dance floor on this cruise. In Pompeii, while walking back to our bus after seeing the ruins, Emily struck up a conversation with a beautiful lady, for an unusual reason: They admired each other's hairdo! I naturally also started to introduce myself to her husband. This couple, David and Margaret Vowles from England, were easy to talk with. Since David is a banker, he and I talked about the current financial condition in the world. And later, we had several cocktail dates. (Actually, a few days later, the news of a global stock market crash reached the ship, causing a great deal of consternation to all.)

Returning to the subject of hair, I must admit that both Margaret and Emily wore attractive hairdos. Look at Margaret in the Vowles

25.7 Captain's Reception on the Queen Victoria, 2008.

picture in Photo 88, and Emily in the foreground of Photo 25.7 here, and many of you may easily agree with me.

Provoked Bows in the Theater

Aside from dancing on the Queen Victoria, we also tried to catch the shipboard shows in the huge theater, usually after dinner. One night, we arrived a few minutes late to the theater, and knowing that it would be difficult to find seats in the rear but that there always tended to be a few empty seats in the front rows, we entered through the side door in the front. The featured performer, comedian John Evans, seemingly annoyed by the commotion caused by the late arrivals, started to mock us to shame, telling us that we had missed a lot of his good material already, and so on, and so forth, . . . , without end. It irritated me enough after a few minutes to feel compelled to do something about it. But I had no access to a weapon (microphone), which left me only with the possibility of doing some passive parry. I unhesitatingly stood up, turned around to face the audience, and after waving my right hand, I took a bow. To the surprise of the comedian on stage and myself, the audience laughed and applauded! In reprisal, the comedian intensified his mocking effort. And, not to show weakness, I stood up to face the audience again and took another bow. This time the audience really roared. And soon, to my relief, the comedian decided to end our "fight." Frankly, I couldn't believe that I was capable of such an impromptu antic!

At the end of the show, I went up to the comedian and apologized to him for my disruption of the proceedings. And he apologized back to me, too. Then, on my way out of the theater, several people sought me out and excitedly said, "We enjoyed your show!" I had to emphasize to them that I wasn't a part of the show.

We had a post-show date with David and Margaret Vowles to have drinks together in the Commodore Club. The Vowles was at the show, sitting just a few rows behind Emily and me. So, among other things, we talked about my provoked bows in the theater. Regarding my behavior, I mentioned to David that I was actually a "shy" person by nature, not at all bent on making a scene. He wryly replied, "Yes, Alpha, you proved it tonight."

Ruins: Antiquity and Present Day

For our tour of the Acropolis in Athens, we had the worst possible local guide. Her commentaries were inexcusably brief and uninformative, and she couldn't wait to let us roam on our own, so that she could step away to reunite with her cigarettes. It was a good thing that Emily and I had just finished studying a DVD course on Greek Mythology, so we knew that Athena, Goddess of Wisdom and patron deity of Athens, was the daughter of the mighty Zeus, and that she had no mother, but came out of Zeus' head already grown-up. The Parthenon, the major attraction at the Acropolis, was built for her. From the high spot of the Acropolis, we could see the temple for Zeus down below near the center of Athens. But, to see the temple of Poseidon, the God of Sea, and brother of Zeus, we had to drive some distance from Athens.

What we saw in Athens were ruins left from antiquity. The time of our visits to these ruins—October, 2008—unfortunately coincided with the time of financial ruins to many brought on by a severe stock market crash! Ironically, most of our fellow tourists were having a bad time while trying to have a good time.

Professor's Professor

The quality of local guides had a 180-degree turn in Istanbul, where we were served by a very intelligent lady with an excellent command of English. She briefed us clearly about the celebrated tourist spots like the Blue Mosque, which has 21,000 azure tiles inside, the Topkapi Palace, which was built by Sultan Mehmet II, with its Harem, and the Hagia Sophia, a mosque converted from a Christian church and now a museum. She also guided us through an intercontinental round trip between Europe and Asia on our bus, which took just a few minutes over a simple bridge.

Since I was seated in front on the tour bus, I could easily talk to this guide when she was not busy with her official duties. After complimenting her of her great service, I asked her, "Are you familiar with the name Tansu Ciller?" "Of course," she said with a smile, "she was the Prime Minister of Turkey a while ago, and before she became Prime Minister, she was my professor of economics in college." I told her that Tansu Ciller received her PhD degree in economics from the University of Connecticut where I taught in the Department of Economics. The guide, excited to meet a professor of her professor, became extra attentive to me. Actually, I never had Tansu in class, although I was once her academic advisor. I was happy to meet this student of a student. And I felt obliged to tip her double at the end of the tour.

Several factoids about Istanbul long remained in my memory:

The "Blue" of the Blue Mosque had nothing to do with the outside color of the mosque. The epithet originated from the ceramic tiles inside the awe-inspiring structure. Unlike other mosques, which normally had two or four minarets, the Blue Mosque has six. Why? Because of a misunderstanding. When it was built in the 17th century, Sultan Ahmed I ordered that this mosque should have "*altin minareler* (gold minarets)," but the architect thought the Sultan wanted "*alti minare* (six minarets)." Hence, it featured six minarets. But this created a problem: only the Prophet's Mosque in Mecca was authorized to have six minarets. To resolve this conflict, it was decided that one more minaret be added to the Prophet's Mosque.

At the Hagia Sophia, I noticed a big double door, with a vertical arrow ↑ in gold on each panel. I asked the guide, "What's the significance of this arrow symbol?" The answer struck me as funny, and ingenious. Now a museum, the Hagia Sophia was originally built in the 6th century as a Greek Orthodox Christian Cathedral in the then-named Constantinople in the Byzantine Empire. It was converted to an imperial mosque, with four minarets, in the 15th century when the Turks conquered Constantinople. The symbol on this double door used to be two golden crosses, which now had to be dismantled. But taking the crosses off would ruin the doors. As a simpler way out, they just took down the horizontal component of each cross, and repositioned it near the top of the vertical component as two diagonal lines of an arrowhead. The upward-pointing arrows have no symbolic significance; they are just the reincarnations of crosses that had become out of place in the reign of the Ottoman Empire.

The Topkapi Palace was the residence the Ottoman sultans for 400 years between the 15th and the 19th centuries. Amid its many splendors, its Harem might be expected to be the most curiosity-arousing feature, at least to male tourists. But it also could be the most disappointing. Once the Harem was inhabited by many lovely women, and lots of exciting things happened on the premises. But, now, all the curious tourists could see is an empty building, with lots of ceramic tiles and stained glass windows, but no enchanting ladies, no intoxicating music, and no alluring dancing. The quarters for the concubines are small and cramped. The windows are very high, beyond human reach. Was that meant to prevent escape?

Istanbul at Dusk

The Queen Victoria left Istanbul at dusk. From the balcony of my cabin, I was enthralled by a perfectly beautiful view the setting sun made: a stunning silhouette of the Blue Mosque with its six minarets, and the Hagia Sophia with its four minarets. Hurriedly, I took out my camera for a parting shot of this lovely city.

I used this picture on the back cover of my Christmas card for 2008. When our friend Alice Fei, who was on the same cruise with us, saw it, she called to tell me specifically how much she liked that picture, "This photo completely captured the very essence of Istanbul, with the two icons Blue Mosque on the left and the Hagia Sophia on the right."

I wanted to share it with you here but, unfortunately, I could not find the original print. All I can do is to have the image on the Christmas card back cover reproduced here. My apologies to you the reader, and also to Istanbul the city.

25.8 Istanbul at dusk.

26

An Oddball Student

At a UConn colleague's dinner party back in 1986, the conversation turned to the subject of piano. After one of the guests, an avid jazz pianist, voiced high praise of his piano teacher, Sue DeWolf, I was glad to tell him that Sue was also doing a great job teaching my son Darryl and daughter Tracey.

"Oh, so you know Sue. Did you hear that she has just accepted a new adult student, a complete oddball;" he said, "this guy does not read music, refuses to practice scales, and insists on avoiding beginners' songs and plunging into Chopin right away?"

I should have remained quiet and let him continue with his story. But, to avoid possible embarrassment, I decided to cut him short. Calmly, I said: "That student is me."

A Substitute Pupil

To start piano lessons at age 59 was by no means a premeditated decision of mine. But when my son, then in high school, announced one day that he was absolutely too ill-prepared to face his piano teacher, something drastic was called for. One should never cancel a lesson at the last moment. So, if he could not go, someone must go in his place.

Question: Who?

Answer: Who else?

Surprisingly, Sue showed little hesitation in accepting me as a new adult student, in spite of my oddities cited above. My inability to read music—more accurately, to *sight-read* music—meant that she could not teach me out of a music sheet. As to me, I would have to face the laborious process of determining what each successive note is, and what kind of musical phrase a bunch of notes collectively make. As I don't read music, I must memorize all the music I learn.

To ease my job, I chose as my initial piece Chopin's "Raindrop Prelude" (Opus 28, No. 15, in D-flat Major). My son had played that piece before, and I already knew the tune by heart, needing only to figure out the finger work. Still, it took me quite a few weeks before I conquered that piece, and played it for Sue. Of course, there were many mistakes to correct, but I made sure that they were all duly rectified one by one.

Then a series of other Chopin pieces followed. Also, to expand the horizon, I detoured into Beethoven ("Moonlight," 1st movement) and Debussy ("Clare de Lune"). None of the pieces came easy to me. But I persevered through the task of determining the finger combinations for every beat: right hand, left hand, and the coordination between the two.

Adult Recitals

Piano teachers in the local region regularly held recitals to showcase their respective adult students. Unlike the young students, however, adult pupils were not required to memorize their music. Thus, almost all of them brought their music to the piano during recitals. Every time, differently from the others, I walked to the piano empty-handed, the other performers and the audience would utter hushed sounds of astonishment. They must have wondered what kind of an idiot or masochist I must be, to take the (non-required) trouble to memorize the music?

Another significant difference between me and the others was the eye position when playing. They all looked straight at the music sheets, whereas I habitually looked downward at the keyboard. This fact precipitated a big disaster for me during one recital held at the home of a piano teacher in another town in 1989. As I sat down at the piano, I discovered to my horror that several keys on her piano had broken ivory pieces, exposing the rough wood beneath that made the surface uneven. To make things worse, a tree lamp, ill-placed to the left of the piano, was casting three different shafts of light onto the piano, producing layered shadows from the black keys. As a result, the keyboard was transformed into the equivalent of a diabolic face staring straight at me!

While the other performers were not perturbed by this disfigured keyboard, because their eyes were focused upon the music sheet, my mind was instantly thrown into distraction as I had to look at the disfigured keyboard. My fingers froze up, and I could not even start the first bar. The audience, trying to help me, shouted: "Bring out your music! Bring out your music!" They did not know that the problem was not my memory, but the scar-faced piano itself.

After a long, strenuous mental struggle, I finally managed to play the piece through. The resulting pitiful rendition of "Raindrop" dunked me in a deep pool of shame. The worst part is that I strongly felt the guilt of letting my teacher down!

Fortunately, the pain of that disaster was offset by an auspicious recital in 1991 held at the Steinway dealership, Clinton's of Hartford. The owner kindly let us use a full-sized Steinway concert grand, with a beautiful look and gorgeous sound. My "Moonlight" smoothly sailed through without mishap.

Hiatus

After six years of lessons with Sue, I moved from Connecticut to White Plains, New York, upon retirement. My interest in learning new pieces never waned, but I realized that I could not keep on expanding my repertoire. Without sight-reading ability, I needed to commit every new piece to memory and to practice it constantly to keep alive the hard-won muscle memory. An oversized repertoire would crowd out everything else in my daily schedule. As it happened, I have indeed lost a nocturne and a waltz over the years simply because of inadequate practice. For this reason, I have remained a "minimalist" as far as the number of pieces is concerned.

It was only after a long hiatus, that God graciously introduced a second teacher into my life. She would not only oversee my playing, but also, uncannily, lead me into a totally unexpected realm of musical adventure.

The Generational Inequality

When our children were taking lessons, my dear wife would habitually shower them with encouraging words, and urge them to practice "ten minutes more." For me, however, her treatment was altogether different. Often, even before I reached the piano bench, she would shout out: "You are going to play again?"

Actually, Emily's reaction to my practice sessions was easily justifiable: Whenever I hit wrong notes here and there, and tried diligently to repeat the phrase over and over again to get it right, what was intended to be music would unforgivingly turn into noise. Who could tolerate a long barrage of that?

To show my apologetic heart to her, I drew a cartoon for our 1986 Christmas card, showing me banging away on the upright piano we owned then, while Emily was being "driven up the wall."

Gradually, as in everything else, time provides a cure. As my playing improved, though at a snail's pace, the waves of wifely complaints ebbed. One time, I could swear, she even said: "Not bad." But the brightest moment occurred when, after hearing about a going-out-of-business sale at A. Michael's Piano, Inc. in Waterford, Connecticut, Emily insisted that I buy a grand piano as a retirement gift to myself. A very expensive gift!

After trying out all the Steinways and other grands at Michael's, I fell in love with a particular Mason & Hamlin for its superior sound quality. And when Sue, my piano teacher, independently selected the same piano as the best, I boldly plunged and splurged. That choice was also applauded by my piano tuner, who told me that after CBS acquired the Steinway company, they adopted unwise business policies (such as production quotas) that angered the skilled craftsmen, because they were forced to use wood materials before they were fully cured or

26.1 "Driving Emily up the wall" (1986 cartoon).

otherwise prepared, in order to fulfill the production quotas. Many of these skilled workers defected to Mason & Hamlin instead, raising the quality there and lowering that of Steinway. Thus, after retirement, I enjoyed playing on a baby grand piano, much to the envy (and complaints) of my children who had only a Kawai upright to practice on in their piano years.

To commemorate the new, improved atmosphere surrounding piano playing, I was inspired to draw another cartoon for our 2006 Christmas card, exactly 20 years after the earlier "driving her up the wall" one. This drawing shows me frolicking at my new baby grand, and Emily murmuring, "Play it again, Sam."

This quoted line is supposedly taken from the movie *Casablanca*, but of course Ingrid Bergman never uttered it in the movie. And neither did Emily in our living room. I used that line because, if I used the caption "Not bad," the drawing would just be a drawing, but the caption "Play it again, Sam," would unquestionably change its nature into a cartoon.

26.2 "Play it again, Sam" (2006 cartoon).

27

Commencement Exercises

The word "commencement" means "beginning." But a commencement exercise at an educational institution is a ceremony marking the "end" of an academic journey, and celebrating the successful completion of a study program, and the conferral of an academic degree. Happiness naturally abounds at the event, most directly for the degree recipients, but perhaps even more for their parents who, presumably, have given them financial and moral support.

It is only fitting that special academic regalia adorn the ceremony for solemnity, as well as festive effect. Every participant, student or faculty member, wears an academic cap, usually square, topped with a tassel fastened to the middle of the top of the cap. The academic gown, usually a black robe, has different sleeves for the different degrees: pointed sleeves for bachelor's degree; oblong sleeves, open at the wrist, for the master's degree; and bell-bottomed sleeves for the doctoral degree, with black or blue velvet stripes on the sides. But the hood, worn at the neck with the larger part of it hanging down at the back, is where the colorfulness comes in, based on the school colors, and the fields of study. The faculty, with degrees from many universities, can provide a rainbow-like display of hoods for the eyes of the graduating students and their guests.

A Lesson from My First Commencement

My first commencement exercise was the one at St. John's University in Shanghai, in the summer of 1946. It was the year after the end of WWII, with China victorious over the atrocious, barbarous invaders from Japan. Even though a civil war was already on, the Chinese people were optimistic about the arduous task of national reconstruction still ahead of us.

That day, the glorious sunshine provided a balmy atmosphere for the outdoor commencement event by the iconic, big camphor tree on the St. John's campus. The proceedings lasted quite long, mainly because the first of two speakers, the President of another university (滬江大學) took his time to read to the congregation not only his lengthy speech in English, but also its Chinese translation. Most of the students gradually became visibly bored. Besides, sitting in the sun under black, heat-absorbing gowns rented for the occasion, soon made us feel hot. It was thus a great relief when the bilingual speech finally ended, with a perfunctory applause. In sharp contrast, the next speech, delivered in English by Dr. K. C. Wu (吳國禎), Mayor of Shanghai, was direct and to the point, and he finished in no more than 10 minutes. Understandably, that speech was greeted by a thunderous applause.

If I got nothing else out of this commencement, I definitely learned one important lesson: an effective speech is one that's concise and to the point. Make the point(s), then conclude it.

A DIY Conferral at Colorado

For my MA degree, I not only donned cap and gown, but also an academic hood with school colors on it. For the University of Colorado, the colors are gold and black. The 1948 commencement at the University of Colorado was lengthy, because there were as many as four different categories of degree recipients: for bachelor's degrees, for master's degrees, for doctor's degrees, and for honorary degrees.

It was my expectation that, to receive the MA degree, I would be called up to the platform, and a university official would place the hood over my head to signal the conferral of the degree. That was not to be. In view of the large number of degree candidates, only the doctoral candidates were called up to the platform one by one to be individually hooded. These candidates also received their diplomas on stage. Honorary degree awardees even got to sit on the stage.

In contrast, the MA and MS candidates for each field of study, already wearing their respective hoods, were simply asked to stand up *en masse*, and flip the tassels on their caps from right-front to left-front, and then sit down. That tassel-flipping action signified the conferral of degrees by the university, but it was done with our own hands, DIY (Do It Yourself) fashion. Somehow, that was not as satisfying to me as a ritual performed by a university official.

At that time, I already knew that I would go on to pursue a doctoral degree. "Wait till the time I finish the next degree," I said to myself, "I will then be officially hooded up there on the stage."

I did not pay that much attention to the commencement address. The other Musketeers, Stephen Li and George Hsu, who were sitting beside me, and who flipped the tassels on their caps at the same moment, did not listen that carefully either. Our minds were filled with too many other thoughts, like winding up our stay in Boulder, preparing to go to New York, planning the return trips to China (for Stephen and George), and the enrollment at Columbia (for me).

A picture of the three of us in caps and gowns has been shown in Photo 5.6.

Not Again!

Starting the doctoral program at Columbia in 1948, I did not finish until 1954. It should not have taken six years, even though the writing of the dissertation did involve a lot of work. But the need for income after the breakdown of the remittance channel from my father necessarily diverted my energy from my studies. Indeed, for quite a long period of time, I held a full-time daytime job in New York; I also had a part-time teaching post in the evening in Connecticut for three semesters.

With due excitement, I was finally to receive my PhD degree on June 1, 1954. Following instructions, I joined the other degree candidates at the West Corridor of the Low Library on the Columbia campus. Then we were led to our designated areas for the open-air commencement. There was a sea of black gowns, seemingly thousands of us. My seat was right on 116th Street, far from the platform by the Low Library, where the university officials and the candidates for honorary degrees sat. At that distance, I could not see them well, and could not hear the announcements, loudspeakers notwithstanding. Emily, my bride to be, was at the commencement, but there was no way she could locate me, a mere droplet in that sea of black gowns.

There were speeches, hardly audible. Then came conferral of degrees. In view of the large number of candidates for degrees, only those for honorary degrees were properly hooded on stage. Regular doctoral candidates, let along master's degree candidates, received their degrees as follows: All stand up, flip your tassels, sit down.

Long story short, I did not get hooded, again! As a consolation, at least there was no rain on that day to spoil things further.

27.1 Columbia's ALMA MATER statue on W. 116th Street, New York City, 1954.

27.2 With Emily after I received the PhD degree, June 1, 1954.

The Hooding of Emily

A few days later, on June 5, Emily received her BS degree from Georgian Court College, a girls' college (now a coed University) in Lakewood, New Jersey. I of course attended her commencement, with her brothers James and Johnny, and her sister Catherine (Chinyee). My friend Steve Ying, his wife Mildred (吳建華), and their son Chris also attended the happy event.

The sunny day showcased the gorgeous campus of Georgian Court at its best, so named because of the Georgian style of its buildings. Formerly the winter residence of Jay Gould, the American leading railroad developer in the 19th century, this campus has a lot of land, with a Japanese garden, as well as an Italian garden, and a beautiful fountain. But the student body at the college at that time only numbered around 200. And Emily's graduating class had only about 50 young ladies.

To my envy, during this commencement ceremony, every single graduate went up to the stage all by herself to get hooded and receive her diploma. Not only that, each one of them even got to choose her favorite music to be played while she walked up to the stage. (But they didn't go as far as allowing a "lady-in-waiting" for each candidate.)

27.3 After Emily's commencement, June 5, 1954. On the right: Mildred and Steve Ying (holding Chris).

An Annual Show

After I started full-time teaching, I purchased my own academic regalia, because I would need to dress up at the end of every academic year to participate in the commencement show for the graduating class and their families. Cost considerations made me choose velveteen rather than velvet for the facing and the side stripes on the gown, and yellow-silk tassel rather than gold. But the hood is the standard one with Columbia colors, light blue and white.

Denison University had an enrollment of around 1,200 students, with a faculty of about 100. So the display of hood colors was quite impressive to make each commencement exercise a memorable event for the students and their families. I looked forward to this event each year, because I felt good about my students for their arrival at a milestone in their lives. I especially appreciated the opportunities to talk to the parents of my students, and discuss their future plans. As I mentioned elsewhere, one time, embarrassment befell me when I discovered that I was the one who spoiled the straight-A record of a student, William Berger, by giving him a lone B+ grade.

A commencement meant a lot to me in another way, because it also marked the initiation of a whole summer's worth of time for my own studies and research.

Reduced Participation

Once I joined the faculty of the University of Connecticut (UConn), my participation in commencement exercises was cut to half. The commencement exercises at UConn were held simultaneously at several locations, and because of the sizable faculty, each professor only had to attend the commencement in alternate years. There was less chance of my witnessing my own students receive their degrees in a queue marching up to the stage. But since I was now involved more in graduate courses with few students, I did not in actuality miss seeing that many students.

By that time, I have heard Edward Elgar's march "Pomp and Circumstance" so many times I could hum it backward. I still enjoyed hearing it. But I normally held no hope for truly inspiring commencement addresses.

What I always looked forward to at my biennial attendance was to see the awardees of honorary degrees, some of whom I heard of, and some not. Sometimes they were the commencement speakers, with interesting personal experiences to tell the audience. Victor Borge, the pianist–comedian, a resident of Connecticut, was given an honorary doctorate in 1983. Three years later, Ray Bolger, the dancer who played the Scarecrow in the movie "The Wizard of Oz," was an honoree, but he could not come to the 1986 commencement because of illness. I regretted very much for losing this rare opportunity to see the Scarecrow in person.

Miss China as an Alumna

In September, 1966, right after sending the completed manuscript of *Fundamental Methods of Mathematical Economics* to McGraw-Hill, we went to Ithaca, New York, to start my visiting professorship at Cornell

University. Even away from UConn, we received the news that a former Miss China, Anne Lien (連方瑀), had come to Storrs as a faculty wife. Indeed, Dr. Chan Lien (連 戰), her husband, had accepted the post of Assistant Professor of Political Science at UConn. Being away, we did not have a chance to make their acquaintance. But after our return from Ithaca, we became good friends with the Liens during the following academic year.

Chan Lien's office and mine were both in the Social Sciences building, one floor apart. Eloquent as well as elegant, he had built up a reputation by the time I first met him. As to Mrs. Lien, Emily saw this attractive young Chinese lady one day in the one-and-only local supermarket, and correctly assumed that she was Anne Lien. They instantly developed a cordial friendship.

As I mentioned in Chapter 5, Anne worked for a master's degree in biochemistry during her stay at Storrs. She received her degree at the 1968 commencement. Since Chan Lien and I both attended the same ceremony, we three took a photo together as a souvenir (see Photo 43). Chan's academic regalia look different, with a round-shaped cap and an extra colorful gown. The reason is that his PhD degree is from the University of Chicago, which has its own design of cap and gown.

The Liens decided to return to Taiwan at the end of that academic year, but our one-year friendship continued on, and we have kept on seeing one another in New York and in Taipei in later years.

Dr. Lien went into politics in the Republic of China in Taiwan after teaching at the National Taiwan University. His positions included Mayor of Taipei, Governor of Taiwan Province, Premier, and Vice President of the Republic of China. During his Vice Presidency days, he was sent to the Dominican Republic to attend their Presidential Inaugural in 1996. Stopping in New York *en route*, he and Anne invited Emily and me to dinner at Tang Pavilion (山王飯店) with a group of dignitaries on May 6. Since they insisted on seating us by their sides, a close-up photo of the four of us appeared in the Chinese newspaper *World Journal* (世界日報) the next day. It caused a stir among our friends, many of whom, not knowing that Dr. Lien and I were once colleagues at UConn, could not understand why Emily and me would be sitting together with the Vice President and his wife at the banquet table. That picture at Tang Pavilion is shown as Photo 59 in the front of this book.

Attending Children's Commencements

I participated in countless commencements as a faculty member, for the benefit of students and their parents. Eventually, my turn to attend commencements as a parent came when Darryl graduated from Princeton (BA, History, high honor) in 1990, and Harvard Law School (JD, honor) in 1994; and when Tracey graduated from Brown University (BA, Visual Arts) in 1992, then from Tufts University/ School of the Museum of Fine Arts, Boston (MAT, Art Education) in 1994, and the School of Visual Arts (MFA, Photography, Paula Rhodes Memorial Award) in 1996.

I experienced on these occasions what the typical commencement-attending parents would go through: (1) It's difficult to get overnight lodging, when hundreds of families swarmed, like a cloud of locusts, to the same destination. The hotels in Cambridge, Massachusetts, blatantly jacked up their room rates three-fold, and also required a three-night minimum for reservation. (2) Parking on the campus is next to impossible. We found it necessary to park the car far, far away, and take a taxi or subway ride to the campus. (3) If the school is one of substantial enrollment, one cannot expect to see their particular candidate in the sea of academic gowns with everybody's head covered by a cap. We had to take it on faith that our son or daughter was in that crowd.

Princeton and Harvard Law

Even though I could not locate Darryl at the commencement, I did catch a shot of him marching toward the ceremony with his friend Jeff Oberstein (Photo 49). And we had a family portrait taken at the Graduation Ball (Photo 50).

At Harvard, the ceremony was divided into two parts, the first being the University-wide one, and the second, the Law School ceremony where the diplomas were distributed.

I was able to get close for a picture at the second ceremony at the Law School. See Photo 51.

Marching at Brown

Tracey's commencement at Brown University, though, gave me an extraordinary experience: I marched in its procession even though I was not on the Brown faculty. The reason was an invitation from Dr. Vartan Gregorian, President of Brown University, for all graduates' parents who are educators to join in the commencement procession. This was a unique opportunity, and I accepted it with pleasure.

Two things fondly remained in my memory. First, in academic regalia, Tracey was among the degree candidates lined up on the side

27.4 A picture with President and Mrs. Gregorian of Brown University.

of the procession path, and as soon as she saw me approach, she ran toward me, gave me a hug, and presented me with a bouquet of flowers. Instead of parents giving the candidate flowers, here, the candidate was giving flowers to a parent. It was deeply touching. That scene was captured in Photo 53.

Second, that day, near the end of May, was abnormally cold and windy. Almost every year, my academic gown normally tended to make me sweaty at commencements. That particular day, however, I could not have been more grateful for the protection from the penetrating cold and the cutting wind that my good old academic gown afforded.

Photo 54 shows Tracey holding her diploma from Brown University. We also took a picture on that day with President and Mrs. Gregorian of Brown.

Tracey's MAT degree (Tufts University/School of the Museum of Fine Arts, Boston) and MFA degree (School of Visual Arts) were awarded without the usual formal commencement ceremonies. Students attended the ceremonies in regular attire. Hence there is no cap-and-gown photos.

She is certified for teaching art from kindergarten through 12th grade. But she was scared away from the teaching profession by her unfortunate practice-teaching experience. She was assigned to an inner city school where quite a few students looked like fighters, and carried knives. And one of the older students even tried to date her.

28

The Itinerant Professor

My first full-time teaching post at Denison University in Granville, Ohio was a 10-year affiliation, although I was away at Yale in the 10th academic year. That was followed by a 28-year association with the University of Connecticut (UConn). I was thus a reasonably "stable" educator, with no interest in jumping from post to post for economic or noneconomic gains. My claim to being an "itinerant" professor, if at all valid, was because I did accept a few visiting professorships along the way, at New Asia College (新亞書院, now part of the Chinese University of Hong Kong (CUHK 香港中文大學); Cornell University in Ithaca, New York; Lingnan College (嶺南學院, now University) in Hong Kong; and Helsinki School of Economics and Business Administration in Finland.

A Job I Could Not Decline

When I took a sabbatical leave from Denison in 1960–1961 to go to Hong Kong for a reunion with my parents, my plan was to get away from teaching, to concentrate on studying mathematics on my own. But an uncle of mine, Charles Chiang (my father's cousin, 蔣繼惠), informed me right after I arrived in Hong Kong, that there was a teaching job waiting for me. What happened was that Uncle Charles' former professor, Dr. J. M. Yang (楊汝梅), Head of the Department of Business at New Asia College, heard of my coming, and wanted me to join New Asia. Since I had already made study plans, I immediately paid a visit to Dr. Yang to thank him for his confidence in me, but to decline his offer. But he was politely persistent, and my uncle also tried to urge me to accept the post. Finally realizing that my "No" answer would cause my uncle to "lose face" in a big way, I decided to accept this offer. Since I planned to stay with my parents for a whole year with Emily, whom my parents were meeting for the very first time, I ended up teaching at New Asia College for two semesters.

At that time, a proposal was afoot to form a new CUHK, by combining three existing colleges, including New Asia, with government funding. Dr. Yang invited me to stay on permanently. But I had to insist on a "No" answer at this point, because I was legally obligated to return to Denison upon completing the sabbatical leave.

I didn't realize it at the time, but Dr. Yang was famed as one of the four foremost accountants in China. His PhD dissertation, "Good Will

28.1 Dr. J. M. Yang (left), Hong Kong, 1960.

and Other Intangibles," at the University of Michigan, was considered a classic in accounting theory. Naturally, he had held many high positions as Chief Accountant, including at the major banks in China.

What I taught at New Asia were some basic junior- or senior-level economics courses. But I suffered from some daunting difficulties in class. I had learned the economics terminology entirely in English, but in Hong Kong I had to teach in Chinese. The need to learn some Chinese translations of economics terms took extra time. As to the Chinese language, I can only use Mandarin and Shanghai dialect with ease, but many students in Hong Kong use Cantonese. With heartfelt apology, I somehow got by with a combination of English and Mandarin, but my teaching was unsmooth at best, and perhaps unintelligible to some at worst.

One great pleasure of teaching is to have bright and diligent students in class. There were a few of them at New Asia, but only two of them have kept in touch with me ever since. Dr. Yak Yeow (Y. Y.) Kueh (郭益耀) and Dr. Joseph C. H. Chai (蔡俊華), good friends yet academic rivals of each other, both received their PhD degrees in Germany. Y. Y. (aka Yiyao) taught in Australia as well as Hong Kong, and Joseph settled in Australia. Both of them had kept in touch, and even come to Connecticut to see me during their respective stays at Harvard-Yenching Institute at Harvard University in Cambridge, Massachusetts. Y. Y. brought his bride, Hsiao-hu Li (黎曉瑚), and Joseph brought his German wife, Karin, and we became good family friends. On my many trips to Hong Kong to visit my parents, I always tried to get together with the Kuehs and the Chais. In one interesting turn of events, Y. Y., once my student, later became my "boss," a story I shall recount below.

However little the students benefited from me, I personally benefited from New Asia. I attended many public lectures regularly scheduled at the college. The most educational were the lectures by Ch'ien Mu (錢穆), a founder, and President of New Asia College, with a great reputation as a master historian of China. He always lectured without script, but what he uttered invariably came out as an elegant, well-organized essay. The only regret was that, being born in Wuxi

(無錫), China, he spoke with a heavy local accent, which I (luckily) could understand, but many in the audience probably found difficult.

There were other benefits at New Asia College: I visited classes in Chinese classical painting and calligraphy, which were my reluctantly estranged hobbies. I participated in the Chinese opera club, which gave high-standard stage performances. Occasional organized student trips took me to parts of Hong Kong I would not have otherwise seen.

Meeting a Historic Figure

Emily, like me, did not find the Hong Kong climate agreeable. But we did reap some important unique experiences during our year in Hong Kong, 1960–1961. One was our meeting a famous personage in the modern history of China, a lady named Yu-Yi Chang (張幼儀), the mother of our good friend C. K. Hsu (徐積鍇), who was living in Hong Kong at the time. It was through the kind introduction of C. K. that we had the opportunity of calling on his mother. We naturally called her Aunt Hsu at first, because she was once the wife of the poet Chih-mo Hsu (徐志摩), C. K.'s father. But the poet initiated a historic divorce case that made big news and rocked Chinese society in the 1920s, and she was now, after so many years, married to a Dr. C. C. Soo (蘇記之). Thus, we called her Aunt Soo instead.

From the vehemence with which Chih-mo Hsu pursued his demand for divorce, one would assume that his wife, Yu-Yi Chang, must be an unattractive, awkward, and unintelligent woman. Nothing could be more untrue. I found Aunt Soo to be a most gracious and elegant lady, and also good-looking. We could communicate easily in the same dialect, and in fact I learned to my surprise that she was born in Baoshan, my own native place. We had a grand time at a lunch she and Dr. Soo hosted at Repulse Bay (淺水灣), an upscale area in the southern part of Hong Kong.

Aunt Soo was familiar with many things and people in Hong Kong. She wanted to know whether Emily had any special interest or hobby to pursue, so that she could recommend an appropriate resource person to contact. As soon as Emily mentioned her fondness for sewing, Aunt Soo recommended a Shanghai-style master tailor who was giving lessons to a group of ladies. Emily was thus able to join that group, and learned many professional tips she has successfully applied for decades to come. Most of these tips are ingeniously simple, and all of them simply ingenious.

We saw Aunt Soo often that year in Hong Kong. Many years later, after Dr. Soo passed away in the early 1970s, Aunt Soo moved to New York to be near her son, C. K. And we were happy to reunite with her in Manhattan, together with C. K. and Julia, our old friends. Much later, we even got to know socially two of her granddaughters (C. K. and Julia's daughters) Angela Hsu King (金徐琪) and Fern Hsu Tse (支徐放), extending it to a three-generation friendship.

After C. K. and Julia Hsu passed away, the family needed someone to render their Chinese names for their burial chamber. I was honored to be asked to undertake this task. With cordial respect, I chose to write their names in the *li shu* (隸書) style of calligraphy.

Hong Kong High Society

Meeting Aunt Soo was one of the highlights of my year in Hong Kong. Another was to rub shoulder with the high society in Hong Kong, though only briefly.

This unexpected event started when Lionel Crocker, Professor of Speech at Denison, hearing that I was going to Hong Kong for my sabbatical leave, said to me in earnest, "In Hong Kong, you must look up an alumnus of Denison, Kai-yin Chau, whose father is the Mayor of Hong Kong. Kai-yin will take care of you and show you around." I thanked Lionel for the suggestion, but privately laughed at his information (or misinformation). A British colony at that time, the government in Hong Kong was headed by a Governor appointed by the British. There was no such thing as a "Mayor of Hong Kong."

Nevertheless, after a few months in Hong Kong, I did try to call up Kai-yin Chau (周啟賢). Surprisingly, sight unseen, he was palpably excited to hear from a professor from Denison, which he attended many years ago. We had no common Chinese dialect, so we talked in English, merrily chatting about "good old Denison," "good old Granville, Ohio," and so on. He still remembered Dr. Crocker. I told him about Dr. Crocker's misinformation about the "Mayor of Hong Kong." Kai-yin just laughed, and said, "Well, at least he got my name right, and I am glad that he asked you to call on me. I am very fond of Denison, and would like very much to know you."

A few days later, a formal, printed invitation came from Kai-yin, inviting Emily and me to a luncheon at the Royal Jockey Club in Happy Valley on a Saturday in late January, 1961. It was a party hosted by "Sir Sik-nin and Lady Chau," (周錫年爵士暨夫人), Kai-yin's parents. Though not a mayor, Kai-yin's father was an important personage in Hong Kong. A British-trained ophthalmologist, he had over the years branched into business and politics, and was the chairman or director of many business concerns and social welfare organizations. He was also a senior unofficial member of the Executive as well as Legislative Councils of the Hong Kong government.

In the British tradition, horse racing sets the stage for big social gatherings. What we witnessed was a lavish luncheon, held in Box One at the Royal Jockey Club, a room big enough to entertain 80 or 90 people. (Later, I found out that Box Two belonged to the Governor of Hong Kong.) That day, there were only about 40-odd people present. Kai-yin received us, introduced us to his lovely wife, and presented us to his parents. The whole family was gracious. Some of the other guests we met gave me their business cards; they all held high positions. I did not carry business cards, but was nevertheless greeted with courtesy, probably because of the traditional respect for professors in the Chinese culture.

Food was plentiful. And all kinds of drinks were served, including champagne. When each race was announced, the guests dispatched the waiting staff to go to the betting windows to make bets for them. Like them, I placed some bets. Unlike them, I went down to the windows to buy tickets on my own. Partly, it was because I wanted the experience. More importantly, I didn't want the waiting staff to handle my embarrassingly meager bets. Then when each race came on, we all went out to the balcony to watch the horses run. There were quite a few

28.2 With Mr. and Mrs. Kai-yin Chau, and Lady Chau, at the Royal Jockey Club, Hong Kong, January 1961.

races, and since I did have some stake in the results of each race, it was exciting to watch the horse I picked to either lead ahead or lag behind.

At the end of the races, I was preparing to leave. But Kai-yin said, "No hurry. Let the crowd down below leave first. Then we can go more comfortably. Come, have some more champagne."

Kai-yin was obviously very fond of Denison. He genuinely kept me in mind, and followed up with more invitations to other functions. But I soon awoke to the fact that it would be hard for me to reciprocate his hospitality in this high-society setting. Therefore, with reluctance, I gradually began to decline his kind invitations. But I have always cherished Kai-yin's offers of hospitality toward a professor from his alma mater who had never had him in class.

Frequent Banquets versus Long Famine

Since many relatives of mine had moved from Shanghai to Hong Kong by that time, we often had dinners together, with each family taking turn as host. Usually, those dinners were banquets in restaurants of various types of cuisine, which abounded in that colony. It was a bit on the extravagant side to me. That feeling grew stronger when one thought of what the people in Mainland China were going through in their economic lives.

In the years 1959–1961, China was still being plagued by the three-year Great Famine, caused by a combination of drought and flood, and economic policies inimical to farm production, under the ironic name of the "Great Leap Forward." As a result, people in Hong Kong were busily engaged in a care-package campaign. Strangely, there was a strict two-pound weight limit on these packages. Nobody in China was allowed to receive from Hong Kong more than two pounds per month. With so many relatives still in Shanghai, my parents spent a lot of time shopping for sugar, lard, and other necessities, and packaging them into two-pound packages, making sure not to exceed that weight limit. Often, we wrapped the packages with towels instead of paper, so the recipient could get a towel as a bonus, which was also in shortage there.

Emily and I naturally helped with those packages, packing as well as mailing them at the Post Office. The lines of senders at the Chinese-speaking windows in the Post Office were always long. We could take advantage of the English-speaking window, where the line was much shorter, and the service, much more courteous.

Two extraordinary packages caught my eyes. One was a package containing mushrooms, not a basic necessity. I learned that this was sent in response to a request from a gourmet aunt, who was also a gourmet cook. This aunt, named Lizhen (蔣周麗珍) was the wife of my father's younger brother (see Photo 81). And she was the aunt whose 100th birthday party Emily and I attended in Shanghai about four decades later, in 2002. She lived to age 108, two months short of 109.

Another package that was different contained powdered milk for a newborn boy, a grandson of the abovementioned aunt. There was a six-month limit on powdered milk, and my parents sent six such packages. This boy, Fan Jiang, grew up to be a good student and, with a little support from me, came to the United States to study, got a PhD degree, became a successful investment banker and a man of wealth (see Photo 25.4).

The Chinese University of Hong Kong

The proposed consolidation of three colleges in Hong Kong into a CUHK, initiated while I was at the New Asia College, came to fruition in 1963, two years after I left. Besides New Asia, Chung Chi College (崇基書院) and United College (聯合書院) also became components of the new CUHK. They moved to a beautiful, scenic campus in Shatin (沙田), in the northern part of Hong Kong.

I could not stay on at New Asia, as Dr. Yang wished, because I was obligated to return to Denison University at the end of my sabbatical leave. Years later, Dr. Choh-Ming Li (李卓敏), President of CUHK, contacted me for the position of Professor (Chair) in the Economics

28.3 With President Charles Kao (right) of the Chinese University of Hong Kong, 1989. He won a Nobel Prize in 2009.

Department at CUHK. But my roots in the United States had become too deep for a long-term move to Hong Kong. And a short-term appointment would involve too much disruption to my family. Thus, nothing came out of this. Nevertheless, I did maintain a cordial relationship with the Chinese University for many years, serving as an External Examiner for its Degree Examination in Economics. As such, I had to go to Hong Kong several times. On one such an occasion in 1989, I had an opportunity to have dinner with President Charles Kuen Kao (高錕) of CUHK, who, known as "the Father of Fiber Optics," was awarded the Nobel Prize in Physics in 2009.

An Invitation from Cornell

Just two years after I joined UConn in 1964, I accepted an invitation to a Visiting Professorship at Cornell University in Ithaca, New York in the year 1966–1967. I made sure to finish the manuscript of my *Fundamental Methods of Mathematical Economics*, and dispatch it to McGraw-Hill before we headed for Ithaca. We had arranged to rent the house of my old Chinese opera friend, Professor Ta-chung Liu (劉大中), who would be on leave from Cornell to spend a year at the Massachusetts Institute of Technology. Located on Cayuga Heights Road, not too far from the Cornell campus, the Liu house perfectly suited our needs, and even commanded a lovely view of Cayuga Lake down below.

A Sojourn in Bermuda

As soon as we finished depositing our belongings at the rented house, we hurriedly flew to Bermuda for a week of vacation, much deserved after the long, two-year toil on the book. What we actually needed was a monthlong vacation. Besides, we were due to celebrate our 12th wedding anniversary on September 4. But the Cornell commitment could only allow a weeklong sojourn in Bermuda.

In Bermuda, we stayed at the Carleton Beach Hotel, which owned a private beach and a private bay. Good dinners at the hotel, floor shows, and excursions to Hamilton and boat rides with music, or simply sunning on the beach—they all provided great relaxation. But the most memorable experience was a rare "walk on the bottom of the sea."

That excursion was officially labeled "Underwater Wonderland." Since Emily and I do not swim, I at first thought that such an adventure would not suit us at all. But the young lady at the concierge desk emphasized that, from her own experience, it involved no swimming. Thus, I felt a strong interest to try it, although it took me a long time to persuade Emily.

The tour guide, a muscular yet eloquent gentleman, took us, a small group of seven or eight people by boat, to a remote spot on the water. In shorts or swimwear, we descended into the water using a metal ladder on the side of the boat. Each of us was given a helmet with glass front, and even though it had an open bottom, the air pressure prevented water from entering into the helmet. Comfortably entering into the sea water, we did indeed land on the bottom of the sea. We could see things quite clearly through the glass front of the helmet, and we could walk on the ground beneath our feet, because the guide had set up underwater lights.

28.4 "Underwater Wonderland," Bermuda, September 1966.

The tour guide, now unable to communicate to us vocally in the water, signaled us to watch the tropical fish around us. He let us hold some mussels in our hands, so that the fish could eat out of our extended palms. He also waved the fish through a wired hoop he set up down there, as a dance show. He even took pictures of us with an underwater camera.

Emily, at first reluctant to join me, later ranked this underwater excursion as the top attraction of our Bermuda trip.

Big Hall and Co-teaching at Cornell

I had always taught small classes, no more than 25 students for undergraduate courses, and even less for graduate courses. But one of the classes I was assigned to teach at Cornell was a Principles of Economics course in a big lecture hall for more than 100 students. That proved difficult. I knew how to hold the attention of 25 people in an intimate room. But, in a big hall, inevitably with some students whispering to each other, some others with their thoughts patently wandering elsewhere, and yet some others trying to catch up on their sleep, my power of concentration got seriously challenged. I was not satisfied with my performance in that class. Big lecture was an unwelcome new experience.

Another new experience was a co-taught graduate micro theory course, suggested by Professor John Fei (費景漢), another Chinese opera friend. I first met John in Ohio, when he was teaching at Antioch College, and I at Denison. He then went on to Yale, and I joined UConn. Living only an hour from each other in Connecticut, he visited me regularly, and we wrote research papers together, aside from going together to New York for Chinese opera rehearsals and performances. For a few years, he was on the Cornell faculty, but eventually he returned to Yale. Co-teaching a course was not something I was used to, but since John and I knew each other well, I enjoyed the joint teaching. One thing that might have impressed, and perhaps also tickled the students, was that both John and I habitually used colored chalks to draw diagrams. Technicolor, the class was, though not necessarily CinemaScope.

A Protest in Class

Another new experience I had at Cornell was a jarring one. For the Graduate Price Theory course I taught alone, I assigned as required readings only current articles from professional economics journals. One article from the *Review of Economic Studies* dealt with a relatively subtle technical matter of analysis. During class discussion of this article, a woman student suddenly voiced a strong protest. With her hand raised, she proclaimed in an angry voice, "This article is totally irrelevant, and you should delete it from the reading assignments." This shocking utterance from a student, made not in private but openly during a class, unsettled me to the extreme.

For a couple of seconds, I could not decide how to respond. But quickly I collected myself, and tried my best to speak in a controlled tone. "I'd be happy to respond," I said calmly, "As the professor of this course, I have the responsibility and right to plan its contents. My purpose is to lead you through some current articles in the field that, in my judgment, will help in your training as professional economists. Every economics journal I consulted is a refereed publication. Each article submitted to the editor of a journal goes through a double-blind review. This means that the author's name is not shown to the invited reviewer, so that the latter will not be swayed by the reputation, or lack thereof, of the author. Similarly, the reviewer's name is not shown to the author when his comments are transmitted to the author, so that there should be no fear of retribution. The editor then decides whether or not to publish the article, after reading the reports of two or three reviewers. In view of this process, I daresay that each published article is bound to have something worthwhile to teach us. As to your opinion, I think you do have the right to disagree with me on the merit of the article in question. But you certainly do NOT have the right to tell me to delete it from the assignment list. Just to SUGGEST deletion would have been overstepping your boundary. To DEMAND deletion is outrageously out of line. Your only choice is either to stay in the class and abide by my assignment sheet, or to withdraw from this class."

That woman student was going to give a retort, but she was drowned out by a big applause from the class. When I started my long speech,

I had no idea how the class would react. The applause was incomparably comforting.

When I left the classroom, the professor teaching in the next classroom stopped me, and said, "We professors get applauded at the end of the semester. How come you get applauded so early in the semester. You must be an extraordinary professor!" I shook my head, and said, "No, that applause was not because I am an extraordinary professor, but because we had an extraordinary incident in the class."

By the way, that protester student decided to stay in my class. I somehow had the suspicion that she was a transfer student to Cornell from one of those universities where radicalism and protestations were rampant at that time. I was so glad that Cornell was not infected.

Speaking of applauding professors, I think only Ivy League schools follow that tradition. I applauded my professors at Columbia, and I was applauded by Cornell students, at the end of each semester course. Of course, some applauses could be spirited, and others could be perfunctory. But at other schools, even perfunctory applauses are not given. Ironically, therefore, a guest lecturer who speaks for an hour gets applauded at the end of the talk. But a professor, after 45 classes, receives no such recognition. One time, at UConn, I mentioned this difference between Ivy and non-Ivy schools to a graduate class. To my surprise, I got applauded in that class at the end of the semester. But that experience was never repeated; UConn is non-Ivy after all.

Outstanding Students

There were many good students at Cornell. But because of the short contacts with them, now—after half a century—only two names I can cite without checking my grade records. One is Alan Deardorff and the other is Robert Engle. According to the internet information, Alan Deardorff is John W. Sweetland Professor of International Economics at the University of Michigan, with International Trade as his specialty. Robert Engle taught at the Massachusetts Institute of Technology, the University of California, San Diego and, after retirement in 2003, teaches at New York University. He was honored with the Nobel

Memorial Prize in Economic Sciences, 2003. I should also mention that Robert Engle wrote his doctoral dissertation at Cornell with Professor Ta-chung Liu as his supervisor.

Emily: Icy Roads and Math Classes

The winter months in Ithaca are extremely inhospitable. Every evening we had a few hours of snow. To my complaints about the Ithaca weather, the Cornell colleagues would say, "You surely have snow in Connecticut, too!" To that, I would retort, "In Connecticut, snowing is occasional; it's like a dating situation. Here, in Ithaca, snow is with you daily; it's a marriage." The snow that visited every evening meant icy road the next morning. I found it difficult to negotiate the slippery roads, let alone finding a parking space on campus under such weather conditions. To catch my early classes, I had Emily drive me to Goldwin Smith Hall where my office was. Chauffeuring me on ice and snow every day, she quickly turned into an expert winter road driver. Whenever I complimented her for that, she would always say, "There is really nothing to it. Just go slowly, and never step on the brake hard and fast." Still, it's easier said than done.

We did not yet have children in 1960, and Emily was contemplating a career as a mathematics teacher. Teaching, as compared with other work, is attractive at least for the free summer months it affords, which will coincide with my free summer. To that aim, she took mathematics classes at Cornell, working toward an MA degree. On the days without classes of her own, she would go home after depositing me at my office. When she had classes of her own, she would hunt for a parking space.

One day, something extraordinary happened as she was walking out of her classroom. A handsome young man, perhaps a sophomore, approached her, and asked, "Hello, my name is X X. Can I carry your books for you to your dorm?" Wow! It was true that Emily looked very young for her age, but, for a lady in her mid-30s to get an offer to "carry her books"?! Understandably, she felt exhilarated for days, if not weeks.

Ta-chung Liu and John Fei

The gloomy climate condition was said to cause a suicide problem at Cornell. I have no actual information on this matter, but a graffito in a restroom stall that I saw was more shocking than funny: "The suicide rate at Cornell is declining. **Do your part!**"

Ta-chung Liu, Goldwin Smith Professor of Economics at Cornell, ended his life in 1975 by suicide. He was 60. The reason for the suicide was not the Ithaca weather, but the unbearable pain of worsening cancer. Just a few days before his death, John Fei and I called him on the phone from my Connecticut home, and he sounded optimistic that a new experimental drug could produce some substantial result to cure him. But soon the news of his suicide came.

Even more tragic than Ta-chung's suicide was the fact that his wife, Ya-chao Chi (戢亞昭), took her life at the same time, leaving their two sons, Ernest and Frank, simultaneously without father and mother. It was rumored that Ta-chung and Ya-chao had a long-standing pact to die together. But we don't know whether that was true. But Emily and I, both great admirers of Ya-chao, a most elegant and gracious lady, had always noted that, in Ya-chao's life, everything was centered around Ta-chung. The loss of the husband would therefore render her own life utterly meaningless. That might explain why she decided to die along with him in a room at the Holiday Inn near their home. She would even disregard the fact that she had two adult sons and two granddaughters.

Ernest Liu, their elder son, turned out to be a very successful investment banker, the first Chinese to attain Partner status at Goldman Sachs. It is such a pity that his parents left the world too early to witness and bask in their son's glory.

Like Ta-chung, John Fei was a close friend of mine with a double link of relationship: a fellow economist as well as a fellow Chinese opera fan. Unlike Ta-chung, who was almost a whole generation older than I, John was only four years my senior.

I first met John in Ohio, when he was teaching at Antioch College, and I at Denison, but did not become close until we both moved to Connecticut. Living only an hour from each other, he visited me regularly. For a few years he was on the Cornell faculty, but eventually he returned to Yale. My visit to Cornell coincided with his years at the same university.

In Ithaca as in Connecticut, he visited my house regularly, and we must have had hundreds of chats, long in time and wide in scope. They ran across Western history, Western music, Chinese history, Chinese opera, Chinese classical poetry, arts, politics, philosophy and, of course, economics. Emily usually joined us, too, in our enjoyable discussions and arguments. He and I used to play a game revolving around historic figures. For a specific personage selected, each of us was supposed to think of a one-word epithet to summarize his/her life. Controversy often arose as to whose epithet was more to the point.

I lost a most intimate friend when John died, at age 73, of cardiopulmonary failure in 1996 in Taiwan. His wife Alice (費張立和) asked me to speak at his funeral in Virginia. I took this honor seriously, and did my best to prepare a fitting eulogy. I mentioned our "epithet game," and revealed the life epithet I chose for him: Dedication. For he was always fully dedicated, to his research, to his friends, to his students, and even to his leisure activities, including Chinese opera. With his death, I lost a close professional as well as personal friend.

Lingnan College: A Semester of Hotel Living

The next visiting professorship did not occur until about quarter of a century later. I purposely tried to stay put in Connecticut, so as not to disrupt the children's schooling.

In response to an "early retirement package" from the State of Connecticut, I retired from UConn in 1992, after 28 years of teaching there. As soon as my retirement became known, Dr. Y. Y. Kueh (郭益耀), Dean of Faculty of Social Sciences at Lingnan College, Hong Kong, invited me to teach there for a year. I was of course glad to do that, but my parents were about ready to immigrate to the United States around that time. To accommodate them, I could only teach the fall semester of 1993 at Lingnan.

Such a short-term stay in Hong Kong, it would be difficult to arrange an apartment lease. As a result, Emily and I decided to live in a hotel, City Garden Hotel, North Point, near where my parents lived. Guess what? For those months, we slept on fresh sheets every day. A maid made up the bed every morning, too. And Emily accumulated so many plastic shower caps from the housekeeping routine at the hotel that it became a ridiculously large collection.

Y. Y. was my student when I taught at New Asia College in 1960–1961. But after earning a doctorate at Marburg University in Germany, he had a distinguished academic career, teaching in many colleges and universities (at one time the chaired professor at Macquaire University in Sydney, Australia), and publishing many books and articles on the Chinese economy. By hiring me to teach at Lingnan, he turned from a former student to my current boss. That was most interesting and satisfying for me!

Again, I could not be sure about the effectiveness of my teaching because most of the students at Lingnan spoke Cantonese only, whereas my teaching was in a mixture of English and Mandarin. For myself, it was a cherished experience, especially since Y. Y., the Dean, and his staff all showed me unusual courtesy.

28.5 With Dean Kueh (left), Lingnan College, Hong Kong, 1993.

Y.Y. is tightly bound with Chinese tradition. Even as my "boss," he called me "lao-shi" (老師, master), despite my request to him to call me by my first name. Today, he is a little more relaxed. But in his emails to me, instead of using the salutation "Dear Alpha," he still uses "Dear Alpha lao-shi." Very Chinese; very proper.

28.6 Colleagues at Lingnan College, 1993.

Incidentally, my parents were supposed to move to America with us after my stint at Lingnan. But my father changed his mind again. If I had known that earlier, I could have accepted Y. Y.'s invitation to teach for the whole year, and, instead of hotel living, rented an apartment.

Helsinki: A Semester in Three Weeks

On our way home from Hong Kong, we made a stopover in Taipei to see friends and relatives. But as soon as were home, there came an opportunity for a visiting professorship at the Helsinki School of Economics and Business Administration (HSEBA). Someone who accepted a teaching assignment had to withdraw, and HSEBA was looking for a last-minute replacement. This was reminiscent of the situation that led me to Denison University. We had never been to Finland, and a chance to visit there sounded exciting. I accepted the offer without hesitation.

The assignment was only to teach a single semester course in macroeconomics in their International MBA Program. The extraordinary thing was the "semester" would last only for three weeks. How could a semester be this short? It became clear only after I familiarized with the special setup at the HSEBA.

First of all, a semester course normally involves 45 class hours. What Helsinki does is to have each course meet five days a week (Monday through Friday), three hours per day (either morning or afternoon), making a total of 15 class hours per week. Thus, a whole semester of 45 class hours can be telescoped into three weeks. The course is extremely concentrated, like squeezing several days' meals into a single day. Even though I was already aware of the condensed nature of the schedule, I still felt flabbergasted when, after a single week, I had to start preparing a mid-term examination.

The International MBA Program at Helsinki has no permanent faculty, with all teaching positions filled by visiting professors. Having no permanent faculty means no tough promotion and tenure decisions to make. Each visiting professor is paid a set stipend, and provided with a free, furnished apartment. My semester at Helsinki was from April 11 to 29, 1994. A graduate student met us at the airport, and drove us to the designated apartment, and showed us around the campus.

My class, held in the morning, had about 20 students, most of them Finnish, but some of them were from Spain, China, and Russia. They had no problem with English. But, somewhat to my surprise, Finnish students tend to be much more reserved than American ones. In America, whenever I asked a question, many hands would go up, even from students who did not have the answer. In Finland, they tend not to volunteer to speak up, and prefer not to be called upon to respond. But we got along with one another famously.

Professor Charles Madden of Baylor University, who taught the afternoon course in the same semester, told me that he liked to

28.7 The International MBA class, Helsinki, April 1994.

invite students to have lunch with him at nearby restaurants, at their own expenses. I thought it was a good idea to foster teacher–student cordiality, and adopted his practice, to good effect.

At the end of the short semester, the class kindly presented me with a CD of the music of the Finnish composer Jean Sibelius as a souvenir for my brief stay in Helsinki.

Tour Plans Aborted

We had grand plans for weekend trips to Tallinn, Estonia; Stockholm, Sweden; Bergen, Norway; and St. Petersburg, Russia. That would make the trip to Finland even more fruitful.

The first weekend after classes started, we carried out our plan to visit Tallinn by ferry. It was already in the middle of April, but the sea water was still covered with big blocks and sheets of ice. An ice-breaking boat was therefore needed to open up a path for our ferry boat to proceed. In my Christmas card for 1994, I referred to this trip as a "cruise on the rocks," visually depicted with a cartoon of a boat floating over ice cubes in a stemmed cocktail glass.

The rest of the plans, however, had to be aborted, because, only 11 days into our stay in Helsinki, a long-distance call from Hong Kong informed us that both of my parents were in hospital for food poisoning. Emily immediately arranged to fly to Hong Kong. Finn Air agreed to refund our paid airfare to St. Petersburg, but we got a fat "*nyet*!" from the Russian hotel to refund our prepayment. Our visit to St. Petersburg was delayed to the next year, when we took a Baltic cruise.

I had to wait after the final examination before leaving Helsinki. Since Emily flew to Hong Kong without proper clothing for the hot weather in Hong Kong, I had to go back to United States first, to pick up summer clothing for her (and myself). It was a lot of little things to do in a hurry. Fortunately, my parents were in no serious danger. They got sick from a bunch of vegetables from China, which they didn't realize were more heavily applied with pesticide than the locally produced ones they usually bought, and thus failed to give them the extra cleansing needed. We made sure that they were out of danger before we returned to the States.

29

The Holland Semester

I have always liked trying out new experiences. When an opportunity opened up to take a group of University of Connecticut (UConn) students on a Study Abroad Program to the Netherlands (commonly referred to as Holland), I accepted it without even consulting Emily. Colleagues who had undertaken this mission to Holland before me all raved about their experiences, and one of them, the totally enamored Professor Imanuel Wexler, used to talk about "Holland this, Holland that," so frequently that I, with the support of the other colleagues, felt the need to proclaim, in jest, what became known as the "Chiang rule," which stated that "From this day forward, no member of the Economics Department at UConn shall use the word *Holland* ever again while on the campus."

In view of the rave reviews we had heard, Emily and I embarked on our journey to Holland in the fall semester of 1989 with full expectation of an enjoyable time. But not until we had lived through the four months at Limburg University, in the picturesque Roman city of Maastricht, did we fully realize how special and memorable that experience turned out to be.

A Modern Apartment in an Ancient Setting

Limburg University provided us with a charming duplex apartment in town, on the street named *Lakenweversplein,* within walking distance of my office. Although the outside wall of the apartment complex was kept as an ancient building, the apartments inside were all modern. Our duplex apartment occupied the top floors (third and fourth) of the building. The lower floor of our apartment consists of a living room, kitchen, and a dining area, with the front door opening to a narrow lane on a paved rooftop, with easy access to an elevator. But the opposite end of the apartment opens to a balcony facing a spacious courtyard down below. One weekend, a band in red uniform came to the yard and played a concert directly below our balcony. Seated there for the concert, we felt like royalty enjoying a command performance.

29.1 Our duplex apartment in Maastricht.

Of the three bedrooms upstairs, we used one as my study and another as a guest room. The first person to use the guest room was our daughter Tracey, whom we took to Holland for a two-week vacation before she started her sophomore year at Brown University. Later, Emily's elder sister from Taiwan, Chin-ling (陳何欽翎), and elder brother James (何欽羽), who was working in Vienna at the time, and his wife Belinda (何李薇), also came to Maastricht to visit. Photo 34 shows not only these visitors, but also the building in which we lived.

Dr. Leepo Yu (于鄭麗波), a longtime Chinese opera friend, for whose operatic performances I provided musical accompaniment numerous times on stage, spent a weekend with us, when she took a short break from her research mission in Hamburg, Germany for the National Institute of Health. We were pleasantly surprised that so many visitors could come during our short, four-month stay in Maastricht.

The apartment suited us perfectly for its convenient location. Just a hundred paces from our abode, we found a small Chinese restaurant (鏞記) that, despite its uninviting storefront, served excellent Chinese food, expertly prepared by a chef from Singapore. A block away, the town's Market Square was the locale of a weekly market, with stalls selling all kinds of wares, including fresh produce, even Chinese vegetables. A little further away was the main square of the town, *Vrijthof*, lined on one side with several restaurants offering a variety of cuisine. Years later, we noted with excitement that the famous Dutch orchestra leader, André Rieu, a native of Maastricht, once chose that square as the site of a big concert. We were delightedly nostalgic while watching this concert on TV.

Dutch People and Business Ethic

We originally harbored some worries about language and communication. Those worries proved totally unwarranted. All Dutch people seemed to speak good English—so much so that my attempts to use my recently learned rudimentary Dutch were invariably thwarted by their replies in English. The only time I did use Dutch successfully was to order a taxi for our guest Leepo, and that was because I spoke in one breath, not allowing any interruption. After so many years, though, my memory of the Dutch language has been reduced to two phrases, "*danke well*" ("thank you") and "*tot ziens*" ("see you later").

Two business transactions I had in Holland impressed me tremendously about the Dutch business ethic. First, since the shoes I brought with me to Holland could not handle the beautifully patterned but uneven cobblestones on the streets, I had to buy new walking shoes. The manager of the shoe store courteously recommended a good, reasonably priced brand, but, to my astonishment, graciously offered to shine my shoes whenever needed during my stay, for free!

I also needed a piano to practice my hard-learned music, even during my short stay in Holland, because I only played from memory, and needed constant practice to prevent forgetting. Unfortunately, renting a piano was not an option. Since we could hear the verbal fights of our next-door neighbors through the thin walls of the apartment, the sound of my piano practices would undoubtedly prove disturbing to them. For a solution, I consulted the owner of a piano store, Leyser & Hermans, located right on the *Vrijthof*, and he came up with an easy solution. "We have many grand pianos in the warehouse around the corner, and they need to be played on," he said, "so just come, get the key to the warehouse, and go in and play." When I asked him how much he would charge, his answer was simply "No charge".

29.2 Sampling all kinds of grand pianos in the Leyser & Hermans warehouse.

So, twice or thrice every week, I just practiced in their piano warehouse. As requested, I played on a different piano each time, and it soon became an uneventful routine. One time, however, after I finished practicing the few pieces in my repertoire, mostly Chopin, there was a big applause in back of me. I turned around, and found an audience of about a dozen people standing outside of the store window. With some embarrassment, I took a bow, and waved to them. And they applauded some more. How could I have ever imagined that I would one day give an impromptu piano recital in Holland ("Mostly Chopin")? Strangely, and luckily, I did not make too many mistakes in my playing on that particular day, perhaps because I did not think there were people listening. Then this funny thought came to me that induced a secret smile on my mouth: in the absence of seats on the sidewalk, what my audience gave me was, by default, a "*standing* ovation." Furthermore, the unintended recital was literally a "*standing* room only" event, with the entire audience standing on the street outside of the recital venue.

The Mystery Blond

Early every morning, we could see through the kitchen window the lady next door leaving home for work. But we had not seen the husband leave. Presumably, he worked at home. Then we noticed that, quite regularly, a young blond woman would come, and let herself into the next-door apartment with her own key. Because of the verbal fights we heard through the walls, the appearance of the blond aroused some neighborly concern. Who was she? Why did she always come after the lady of the house had already left home? Why would she have her own key? Could it be . . .? Oh, well, it was none of our business.

Soon, Emily found it necessary to talk to the next-door lady—not about the mystery blond, but about how to operate the washer–dryer machines in the apartment with the instructions all written in Dutch. The neighbor lady graciously came over to translate. That done, she asked Emily, "By the way, do you need a cleaning woman? I have a good one. She is Dutch, but just came back from Indonesia where she grew up. Somehow she did not get too much education, so she can only do domestic work. She is trustworthy; I even gave her a key."

Voilà, the mystery of the blond with a key was instantly resolved, in a satisfying way.

Thus, Emily got a cleaning woman. But we did not give her our key. And we never met the neighbor lady's husband.

A Surprise Photo

Since, in my role of the Resident Director of the UConn program, I only had to teach one course, International Financial Management, for our own students, I had time to audit all the courses (in English) our students were taking from the Dutch professors. That gave me the most enjoyable educational experience possible: learning, but without the pressure of examinations. I especially enjoyed the course Intercultural Communication taught by Professor Doctor G. Hofstede, a sociologist. But there did exist a downside to merely auditing those courses: no pressure to review the material for examinations meant a far less solid retention of the knowledge gained.

In my official duty as the Resident Director of our program, I saw Marc Daenen almost every day, because, as the Deputy Director of the Center for European Studies at Limburg, he was also the designated liaison for our program. In contrast, I had little to do with the Economics Department at Limburg, other than presenting a research paper at the Department at their request. However, a chance meeting with a young Economics faculty member, Tom van Veen, at the school cafeteria, yielded an amusing surprise. One day, Tom and I happened to share a lunch table. After our self-introductions, he immediately said, "Oh, I know of your famous book, and I must show you a photo I took some years ago in a small village in Indonesia." I knew many Dutch people took vacations in Indonesia which, until 1945, was a Dutch colony. But why would he want to show me a photo taken there? Maybe he thought I was Indonesian? No, he knew I am Chinese-American. But he declined to reveal anything more about the photo.

A couple of days later, he sent me a 12" × 18" enlargement of a photo showing pages from a book of mine, with my name clearly visible on the inside title page, serving as the liner of a plate on which packets of Indonesian food were displayed. Tom felt sad that pages torn out of a "famous book" could appear in an Indonesian village "in the middle of nowhere," being used for an alternate use far from the academic—wrapping food! So he snapped a picture. And it indeed was an amazing picture. What a coincidence it was for Tom to be at that specific place, at that specific moment of time, to see the food stall, and to have sufficiently sharp eyes to catch my name on that title page, to take that picture!

He told me with some excitement that he never thought he would ever meet me in person one day, to give me a copy of that photo. But I had to tell him that those pages in his photo were not from my *Fundamental Methods of Mathematical Economics*, the book he was thinking of, but from an earlier publication of mine, a workbook titled *Exercises in Aggregate Economics* (macroeconomics) that did not become famous.

The Hague

Limburg University provided tours for us to see Holland. An early one of these took the UConn group to The Hague, the capital city. We paid a visit to the Dutch Parliament, and had a group picture taken..

A more fascinating sight was *Madurodam,* a miniature city showing the typical Dutch buildings and landmarks on a 1:25 scale. Walking through that unusual amusement park of diminutive buildings, everyone would suddenly feel like a blown-up giant.

A Marred Field Trip

A one-week field trip was scheduled for October, to visit such places as the NATO Headquarters in Brussels, the Council of Europe and the European Parliament in Strasbourg. Emily and I joined the students, and learned along with them. But one incident during the bus journey marred the otherwise enjoyable field trip. In our hotel in Oberkirch,

29.3 The UConn group on a visit to the Dutch Parliament, The Hague.

29.4 At the Madurodam, The Hague, August 1989.

Germany, four of the students, while drunk, sneaked into the disco of the hotel after hours, and trashed the musical equipment and reduced the place to shambles. I was deeply ashamed for the irresponsible behavior of our American youth in a foreign country, and was of the opinion that those vandals should be duly punished. But, in the end, for fear of possible lawsuits from parents, UConn ignored my recommendation, and let the students off with very little punishment. That resolution devastatingly offended my sense of justice.

Aside from the field trip, the study-abroad students traveled on their own all over Europe on weekends: to the Oktoberfest in Munich, to see the Berlin Wall that just came down, among other places. In fact, most of them brought their suitcases to my class on Friday mornings, ready to dart out toward the train station the minute the class came to an end at noon.

Charlemagne's Throne

Emily and I took train trips on weekends, too. Since Maastricht is at the southern tip of the Netherlands, stepping a few feet to the east would place you into Germany, and walking a few feet to the west would land you in Belgium. In other words, these three countries almost meet at a single point, Maastricht. The geographical feature explains why, in those pre-Euro days, all the restaurants' checks showed the total charges in three different currencies, the Dutch guilder, the Belgian franc, and Deutsche mark. You could pay in any of the three.

The closest German town we visited, Achen, was full of relics of Charlemagne, the Emperor of the Holy Roman Empire in the 9th century. What really attracted my attention was a huge white marble throne, duly roped off from tourists. For some reason, this throne seemed to emit a warm invitation for me to sit on it. All my life, I have been a strict adherent to laws and regulations, which earned me the reputation of "the best-behaved boy" even in my early youth, thereby causing much envy and ill will toward me among my cousins of similar age. But, for some reason, the invitation from the throne was irresistible, and I quickly sneaked to the throne and sat on it when the tour guide temporarily turned away. During those few seconds on the throne, my mind raced back to the European History class at St. John's Middle School, where I, at age 14–15, first learned about Charlemagne

29.5 Charlemagne's throne, Achen, Germany, 1989.

(Charles the Great). Who could imagine that, about half a century later, I would actually be sitting on his throne here in Achen? The next moment, my mind came back to reality, and I strongly sensed the hardness and coldness of the marble. It was greatly puzzling why such a powerful ruler would settle for such an uncomfortable seat. Could it be that, in his great wisdom, he feared that comforts in daily life might corrupt and compromise his ambition and will?

Venice of the North

Brugge, Belgium, known as the Venice of the North, was renowned for its scenic beauty. We took Emily's sister Chin-ling and sister-in-law Belinda there during their visit to Maastricht.

A leisurely walk, followed by a carriage ride around town, and a boat ride in the canal, gave us a comprehensive view of that lovely city. Then, in a small church, we enjoyed a close-up view of a statue of Virgin and Child by Michelangelo, which added man-made beauty to the natural beauty of the town.

Finally, we experienced a leisurely, tasty dinner *al fresco* at the market square of Brugge, where colorful banners kept fluttering in the cool evening breeze, as if waving a cordial "Welcome," yet also bidding a sweet "Farewell." We felt reluctant to leave.

Viennese Wonders

Since Emily's brother James and his wife Belinda were residing in Vienna, we naturally wanted to visit them while in Europe, and they showed us the best sights in that fabulous city.

Among the sights, the *Schönbrunn,* Maria Theresa's summer palace, stood out in my memory, because of its yellow exterior wall. I was immediately struck by its color, since yellow was also the color designated for the royal families' exclusive use in the dynastic age of China. What a coincidence in color preference! What was so special about the color yellow that tied it to royalty? I wondered. As splendid as its palatial luxury, though, we must confess to having a much more exciting time at the imaginative *Hundertwasserhaus,* a unique, colorful house in Vienna with no straight lines to be found anywhere inside and outside of the structure.

Since our visit to Vienna coincided with the Double Ten Celebration (October 10 is the "July Fourth" of the Republic of China), we also had the unexpected pleasure of attending a concert with a full orchestra of Chinese music students from Taiwan, Singapore, and Hong Kong, studying in Vienna and nearby Salzburg. It was heartwarming to see so many music students of Chinese descent performing together with astounding virtuosity in the music capital of the world, Vienna.

We had many great dinners. But none beat the fish dinner James and Belinda took us to in a restaurant in Wachau, right along the Danube River. So impressed was I with that meal that I decided to commemorate it by drawing a cartoon, showing a man in a chef's hat catching a fish from the Danube, for my homemade Christmas card of 1989. See Photo 23.4.

At a couple of the restaurants in Vienna, we also had a chance to dance the Viennese Waltz. The music provided was the Viennese Waltz and nothing but the Viennese Waltz! "The Blue Danube?" Inevitably! It was among the music I learned to hum way back in Shanghai. As avid ballroom dancers, Emily and I were drunk with excitement doing the Viennese Waltz in Vienna. Whirling around to the beats of Strauss melodies felt so special that I easily forgave a rough, untrained fellow dancer who kicked my right leg several times on the floor, without even a single word of apology from his mouth!

Mozart's Salzburg

On the way back to Maastricht from Vienna, we spent two days in Salzburg, where we paid tribute to Mozart at his birth house. Music, music, music! The entire town fairly breathed music. You could hear music coming out of every other house as you walked by, on any street.

Uppermost in our memory, though, was a romantic evening stroll through a high-up fortress in a light drizzle. I memorialized this scene in my 1989 Christmas card thus: "For sheer poetry, . . ., we favor the twilight stroll through the mountain-top Hohensalzburg fortress in Salzburg, completely deserted because of light rain. With sonorous [church] bells in our ears, and a misty panoramic view of the city at our feet, the sensation was indescribable."

The Final Week

Even though the whole semester in Maastricht felt like a "vacation," we decided to take a genuine weeklong vacation before returning to Connecticut.

There were so many destinations to choose from, places we had not been, and places we desired to revisit. The question is: Which destination would yield the maximum enjoyment? We decided on Paris.

30

Chopin, Marie Antoinette, Oriental Painting, and Frogs' Legs

The fall semester of 1989 at Limburg University in Maastricht, the Netherlands, was of course academic in nature. But because of the opportunities to visit many places in Europe while we were strategically located in Holland, the whole semester felt like a "vacation." Now, at the semester end, Emily and I decided to remain in Europe for another week for a true vacation.

We happened to reach the same choice of destination: Paris. But why?

A Return Visit

The main reason was the incompleteness of our first visit a decade ago, in 1979. That year, I invited my parents to take a guided European tour from Hong Kong to celebrate my father's 75th birthday, and Emily and I, with our children Darryl (10) and Tracey (8), joined them in London for our 25th wedding anniversary. Our whole family, with six people spanning three generations, had a grand time touring nine countries in 18 days. The overly tight itinerary of the tour, however, left out many interesting things, especially in Paris, where we only had time to go to the lower level of the Eiffel Tower. More ridiculously, we targeted on just one single painting at the Louvre—the Mona Lisa! This time, with a more open schedule, we should have a better go at it.

Besides, this time we could also see something not available before—the famous Pyramids at the Louvre by the celebrated Chinese-American architect, I. M. Pei (貝聿銘), not yet planned during our first visit.

We also hoped to have a chance to look up Patrick Chen (陳禾嘉), an old friend from my Columbia days, who later settled in Paris in the early 1950s. (This was the "Patrick" my former landlady in New York once misnamed "Murphy.") But much to our regret, diligent inquiries about Patrick among the Chinese people we encountered in Paris, using both the Chinese and English versions of his name, yielded no leads. Neither did a search in the phone directory. It seemed that nobody had ever heard of him. We suspected that he must have left Paris years ago, or even passed away.

Aside from the search for Patrick, the other things to do and sights to see in our travel plan all went well. I will briefly review the highlights, but cite their French names without italics for simplicity. First of all, entering the Louvre via the main Pyramid, we had to marvel at how well the modern glass structure fits in with the original classical architecture of that famous museum. Once inside, we had a more leisurely walk among the art treasures, including but also much beyond the Mona Lisa. And the show at the Musée d'Orsay on expressionism and pointillism also gave us a day's pleasure, as did our return visits to the Versailles and Tuileries, the Eiffel Tower (to the upper level this time), Notre Dame (lighting a candle and saying a leisurely prayer), plus a fashion show at Galleries Lafayette.

To fulfill a personal wish, I even made a special effort to pay homage to my favorite composer, Chopin, at his grave at the Père Lachaise Cemetery, near the Bastille, even though I was running a low fever at the time. How could I possibly neglect Chopin after having visited Mozart's birth house in Salzburg only two months earlier during our Vienna trip?

All the things we intended to see and do, we accomplished in time. There was still a whole day left in our Paris sojourn. It would be a free day with nothing planned. Where should we go? What could be awaiting us on that final day? How we wished we could enjoy the guidance of Patrick Chen, my only friend in Paris, who had, unfortunately, defied all our efforts to locate him on this trip.

Chopin and Marie Antoinette

I checked the bulletin board of our hotel, and noticed an exhibition at a small museum, Musée Carnavalet, about the social life of Frédérick Chopin. My deep adoration of Chopin made this museum a logical primary destination. So, imagine my disappointment when we learned at the museum ticket office, that the Chopin exhibition had been moved to another museum far away, an impossible distance for us to travel at this late hour. Fortunately, the replacement show was one about Marie Antoinette, which sounded interesting enough. We decided to give up the romantic composer for the tragic queen. Unfortunately, this exhibition entailed a lengthy walk, without adding much new to our knowledge. And we could only go forward, not backtrack, in this museum. By the time we made it to the exit, we were extremely tired, not to say disappointed.

It was dusk now, and the mid-December air was penetratingly cold, made worse by the whistling wind. Emily found it necessary to stop for some coffee at the first café we saw, and it took fully 20 minutes indoors for us to become moderately revitalized. But as soon as we stepped outside, we felt the threat of the chilly air again, and had to duck hurriedly into the next available shop for relief from the cold.

An Oriental Painting

It was an antique shop, and two people were examining an Oriental painting. A French mademoiselle was holding the upper end of the scroll, and an Asian gentleman with long hair held onto its lower end while offering comments about the painting.

Warmth, not painting, was what lured us into the shop, but the painting piqued my interest, for I had learned classical Chinese landscape painting as a teenager in Shanghai. When we got close enough to the scroll, Emily asked me in Mandarin Chinese, "Is this a Chinese or Japanese painting?" I looked at the inscription on the painting, and replied, also in Mandarin, "It's Chinese."

At that point, the long-haired Asian gentleman turned toward us and said in Chinese, "Oh, you folks can speak Chinese." I said, "Yes, we can." Then, in an emphatic voice, he shouted, "Aren't you Alpha

Chiang?!" And, after an intense look at him, I exclaimed, "Aren't you Patrick Chen?!"

I could not recognize him at first because of his long hair. And we actually called each other by our Chinese names, to the consternation of the French mademoiselle. Patrick quickly let go the scroll, and we hugged each other for a long time in an unbelievable state of disbelief.

Inquiry after inquiry could not unearth this friend. But now, almost effortlessly, I walked right into him, propelled by nothing but the cold Paris air!

30.1 The end of the search for Patrick Chen in Paris, December 12, 1989 (compare Photo 1.2).

Why Was He in the Antique Shop?

I told Patrick that I had tried every possible means to find him, but nobody seemed to know his whereabouts. He explained that he had moved to the suburb after retirement some years ago, and now had hardly any contact with people in Paris itself. That day, he happened to come into town only to collect the accumulated fees for his translation work for this antique shop, *La Boutique du Marais,* at its main store in another part of the town. And he would not have come to this branch store, had the lady owner not recalled that there was this additional painting here for him to look at. He added that he was planning to head home in another 15 minutes or so, after completing his examination of this painting. We had caught him just before his leaving time.

The whole encounter was uncanny. On that day, Patrick traveled from his suburban home to the main store of the antique shop in Paris, and thence to the branch store. And Emily and I went from our little hotel to the small museum, stayed for the alternate exhibition, stopped at a coffee shop, and finally sought refuge from the cold wind in this antique shop. Then, bang! We ran into each other. What, besides divine guidance, could have directed us to move with such incredible timing, following two totally independent paths, to converge at a single spot in the big city of Paris, within a narrow time window of only 20 or 30 minutes? That was truly surreal!

Frogs' Legs

Naturally, we invited Patrick to have dinner with us. He agreed, but insisted on treating Emily and me. "Paris is my territory," he said, "and I just got paid for my translation work and have money to spend." He called home to ask his French wife, Josiane, to join us, but she declined simply because her trip would take too long, unduly delaying our dinner.

I had to ask him a personal question that I was withholding for the sake of politeness. Why did he keep his hair so long, necessitating the use of hairpins, totally unlike his old self? He said Josiane wanted it that way.

At the Chinese restaurant, called Great Chinatown, each of us ordered a dish, to be shared family style. The item in the menu that jumped out at me was "frogs' legs with ginger and scallion," and that turned out to be an excellent dish that lingered in my memory for the longest time. My mother used to cook frogs' legs back in Shanghai, one of my favorite dishes. In America, though, we do not see frogs' legs much on restaurant menus. Here in Paris, how could I pass up the opportunity to taste frogs' legs cooked in the Chinese style with a French flair, while reminiscing with Patrick about our bygone days in Manhattan?

"Do you remember your famous trademark at Columbia?" I asked him, "You used to carry a briefcase all the time, even if we were only going to a neighborhood restaurant for a quick dinner?" He burst out laughing, saying, "Yes, I was paranoid about fire breaking out in my rented room, so I had to bring my MA thesis draft with me. If it were burned up, I would never be able to rewrite it."

Patrick filled us with some details about his life in France since New York. After finishing his MA, he planned a roundabout journey from New York to China via Paris, because he wanted to visit his father's French friends on his way. But upon being warned by his father in China not to return to the homeland already under a new regime, Patrick just settled in Paris, working for intercultural organizations. Unfortunately, his decision to live in France made it necessary for him to divorce his first wife in China and marry Josiane as his second wife.

His first wife gave him two sons. The elder one, already married, stayed on in China. But the younger one joined him in Paris some years ago, and also married a French woman.

Then, . . .

We found Patrick too late in our Paris week for him to show us the Paris he knew, but Patrick and I henceforth exchanged correspondences and Christmas messages for many years. Then, one year, I received a short Christmas note, written by Josiane in French on Patrick's behalf. I realized then that he probably could no longer handle a pen, and maybe his memory was fading, too. I never received any more communications from him.

Among my friends, Patrick did not rank as one of the closest, nor of the longest standing. But, because of our uncanny meeting in Paris, he could eminently qualify as the most unforgettable.

31

Nobel Prize Winners

The Nobel Memorial Prize in Economic Sciences, not one of the original Nobel Prizes, was established in 1968 by a donation of Sweden's central bank, the Riksbank, to the Alfred Foundation to commemorate the bank's 300th anniversary. Even though it is not a Nobel Prize in the strict sense of the term, it is administered in the same way as the Nobel Prizes, and all the laureates, including those in economics, receive their honors at the same ceremony on December 10, the anniversary of Alfred Novel's death. The Nobel Prize in Economics is without question the most prestigious honor for any economist.

Over the years, there have been many winners of this prize. But I have had direct interactions with only eight of them. In chronological order of the years in which they were honored, the list includes

Professor Wassily Leontief (1973), for his input–output analysis

Professor Tjalling Koopmans (1975), for his study of optimum resource allocation

Professor James Tobin (1981), for his study of financial markets

Professor George Stigler (1982), for his study of industrial structure, and functioning of markets and effects of regulations

Professor Robert Solow (1987), for his study of theory of economic growth

Professor William Vickrey (1996), for his study of incentives under asymmetrical information

Professor Robert Engle (2003), for his contribution to econometric analysis of time series with time-varying volatility

Professor Edmund Phelps (2006), for his study of intertemporal tradeoffs in macroeconomic theory

In telling my stories about them, however, I will follow a different order, the order in which I met them.

George Stigler

In my first course of Microeconomic Theory at Columbia, I had Professor Stigler as my instructor. He had written a textbook on the subject, but he did not assign it in class. Still, students in the class all read it. In class, his lectures were always smooth going, and delivered at a high speed, yet not too fast for the class to follow. But no mathematics beyond geometry was used, although some journal articles assigned did involve more advanced mathematical techniques. It was around that time that economic papers began to get more and more mathematical, but there was no effort to offer courses to train graduate economics students to tackle those mathematically written professional articles. It was precisely the frustration I felt in this regard that sowed the seed for my plan to write *Fundamental Methods of Mathematical Economics* later, after an arduous journey of self-study of mathematics after I left Columbia.

The professors at a big school in a big city tended to be indifferent toward the students. I doubted that the instructors even bothered to know, let alone remember, the names of the students in their classes. Partly it was because professors' reputation was based not on how well they teach, but how much research they publish. Partly, many professors also held consulting jobs on the side. As a result, they kept very few office hours, and were generally hard to find on the campus. As I recall, I talked to Professor Stigler only once outside of the classroom in my first year, 1948, and then only for a brief time.

I stayed on at Columbia for a few more years, but Professor Stigler soon left Columbia for the University of Chicago, where he received his doctoral degree. He was a conservative thinker, and I suppose the University of Chicago was where he belonged. Even though he made great achievements in the field of economics, he acknowledged in a post-Nobel interview that his first ambition was to be a professional golfer rather than an economist.

William Vickrey

Professor Vickrey earned his PhD degree from Columbia, and stayed on to teach there. His field was Public Finance, and I got under his wings because my doctoral dissertation was in that field.

Actually, the choice of a dissertation topic was not easy for me, because I did not have a "favorite" field in economics. Although I did my MA thesis in International Trade, I felt no passion about it. Then, in a seminar in Public Finance, I developed some interest in the problem of jurisdictional conflict in income taxation in a federal state, where two levels of government have taxing authorities. That seminar was taught by Professor Robert Haig, and he agreed to be my dissertation supervisor. However, my work with him lasted only a short time. Professor Haig retired, and he died soon afterward (not on account of my dissertation, I am sure). I was then given Professor Carl Shoup as the mentor for my public finance dissertation, but shortly after, I was passed on to the younger professor, William Vickrey.

I had not taken any courses with Professor Vickrey, but I had heard a funny story—about his mode of transportation. He lived in Hastings-on-Hudson, a village along the Hudson River to the north of Manhattan. He could take a train from his home to the city, but instead of getting off at the Grand Central station on 42nd Street, far from the Columbia campus on West 116th Street, it would make more sense to get off on the penultimate stop on 125th Street at Park Avenue. But that left the problem of how to get from 125th Street at Park to 116th street at Broadway. The story I heard was that he used roller skates. I never asked him about this, and I never actually saw him roller-skating. But I did see him, an imposing figure, at the campus iron gate on Broadway one day, carrying a briefcase in one hand and a pair of roller skates in the other.

The economics department held frequent seminars with speakers from other universities. Not all faculty members would attend those seminars, and not all of them would engage in discussions, but Professor Vickrey was always a participant, an active one, regardless of the topic of the seminar. I was truly impressed by the range of his interest and knowledge. At each seminar, one could count on hearing some penetrating questions and relevant comments from the back of the room, where he used to sit.

Photo 5 in the front of the book is a picture of Professor Vickrey given to me by a fellow Columbian, Richard Yin.

In working with him on my dissertation, I found him to be a careful reader. He often offered good ideas of how to make my points more succinctly and forcefully, where to expand, and where to shorten. Our relationship was always cordial. One time, after he finished with his session with me, he said, "Come have lunch with me at the Faculty Club." He asked me, "Do you intend to have your dissertation published?" I said, "No." He looked at me and said, "Why not?" And I told him, "I am not sufficiently proud of it to think of publication. To me, it only qualified as an exercise in research and writing." I was telling the truth. My dissertation dealt with four countries with the "federal" form of government: The Commonwealth of Australia, the Dominion of Canada, the Confederation of Switzerland, and the United States. I had taken a bite bigger than what I could chew.

I had other good professors at Columbia, including Arthur F. Burns who later became the Chairman of the Board of Governors of the Federal Reserve System (1970–1978) among other things, but Professor Vickrey was the only one I kept up with. We exchanged Christmas messages (he also wrote and printed his own, though not as elaborate as mine). Once, while serving as department chairman at Columbia, he called me on the phone—to my great surprise. "Alpha," he asked, "did you ever teach the Economy of China? We need someone in that field here." Regrettably, I had to tell him that, despite my Chinese ancestry, Chinese Economy has not been my research interest.

The Nobel Prize came to him late, announced on October 8, 1996, when he was 82. But fate played a cruel trick on him. Professor William Vickrey, the newly announced Nobel laureate, died three days later. He was found slumped behind the steering wheel of his car on the Hutchinson River Parkway in Harrison, New York, near where I was living. He was on his way to a conference in Cambridge, Massachusetts, and apparently suffered a cardiac arrest on the road. He was lucky in that he died *after* the Nobel Prize announcement, for that prize is only awarded to living people. But he was unlucky in that he barely enjoyed the "bully pulpit" that the prize bestowed upon him to preach his economic beliefs.

I wrote him a letter of congratulations. But like many such letters, it never reached his hands before he left us for another world.

Edmund Phelps

In the September 1961 issue of the *American Economic Review* (the official journal of the American Economic Association), I read a fascinating article by Edmund Phelps, titled "The Golden Rule of Capital Accumulation: A Fable for Growthmen." Its fascination arose from the fact that, for the first time, I found an economics article written as a fairy tale. In this article, a mythical economist explained to the ruler of a mythical kingdom what the optimal savings rate should be, if every generation could agree to abide by the "golden rule" ("Do unto others as you would have others do unto you.") and adopt a uniform savings ratio to be adhered to by all generations.

Because of this article, one of the must-do things I did when I spent a year at Yale University, 1963–1964, was to look up Professor Phelps at the Cowles Foundation. I expressed my admiration for his writings, especially that article, and we had lunch together a couple of times. I expected to find in him a lively, humorous person. But the impression he gave me was entirely different, being deliberate and matter-of-fact.

Interestingly, there is a geographical link between Vickrey and Phelps. Professor Vickrey resided in Hastings-on-Hudson, and Phelps grew up there. (Coincidentally, this is also where my daughter Tracey and her family live.)

Somehow, I had never conceived the image of a young economics professor as a beer drinker and cigar smoker. But Professor Phelps fitted that unconceived image. There was foam from his glass during the meal and smoke afterward (smoking was not forbidden in restaurants then).

He was quite easy to talk to. But at that moment, he was vexed by the problem of whether he should accept an offer from the University of California, Santa Barbara at a higher rank, or just stay on at Yale. Even though he did not know me well, he sought my opinion. But, believing that a new acquaintance like me should not really state a position on a career question of such import, I merely analyzed the pros and cons of both choices, which I was sure he himself was already aware of and thought about.

I did not follow his career closely. But he did leave Yale a few years later, not to California, but to the University of Pennsylvania, and thence to Columbia.

Tjalling Koopmans

My relationship with Professor Tjalling Koopmans was very superficial, one based on common courtesy only. When I arrived at Yale in 1963 as a visiting scholar at the Cowles Foundation, I naturally paid a visit to his office as he was the Director of that institution. I thanked him for allowing me to spend a year there, and he graciously invited me to make use of all facilities at the Foundation. I could sit in classes or see the faculty for discussions. Since I had a project to work on, however, I regularly attended only one class, on econometrics taught by Professor John Hooper, and sat in seminars with topics that interested me.

Before I left New Haven, I invited Professor and Mrs. Koopmans to dinner at Far East, a Chinese restaurant in New Haven. Professor Phelps joined us too, but for some reason not Professor Hooper. That was in July, 1964. Neither I, nor Emily, had any idea that we had two future Nobel laureates as our guests at the same dinner. In fact, the Nobel in economics was not yet in existence during that time.

James Tobin

With Professor Koopmans, my contact was based on *courtesy*; he was my "host" at the Cowles Foundation. With Professor Tobin, however, the personal contact I had with him involved a measure of *discourtesy*.

During my year at Yale, I had no direct relationship with Professor Tobin, although I had on many occasions heard him commenting on the topics at seminars. But at the annual meeting of the Eastern Economic Association in March 1987 at Crystal City, Virginia, I was chairing a session at which Professor Tobin was a discussant. In my role as the Chairman, I was obliged to say something to him that bordered on being impolite.

At those professional conventions, it is a common fault that, in each session, too many papers are scheduled for presentation within a limited time. Each paper will involve two speakers, the presenter and the discussant. The first scheduled presenter usually takes too much time, and the later ones are thus unfairly deprived of equal time. Why doesn't the arrangement committee do the more sensible thing and schedule fewer papers for each session? The simple reason is that they want the convention to be well attended, and a sure way to have a member economist attend is to let him present a paper. Besides, the hotel where the convention is held always imposes a minimum order of rooms. For that alone, the organizing committee has a motive to squeeze more papers into each session.

Given my sense of justice about "equal opportunity" for all presenters and discussants, I started my session by announcing a strict time limitation: "According to my calculation, for equal access to time, each paper will be allotted 16 minutes, and each discussant, 5 minutes." Then, seeing that Tobin was sitting there, I added, "Nobel Prize winners get 5 minutes extra." I recall that there was some applause from the group for my unusual, yet sensible ruling.

Since I made a ruling, I perforce had to enforce it. The first presenter tried conscientiously to be concise, and he took half a minute beyond the 16-minute limit. I let him go without saying anything. The discussant was also cooperative. The second and third presenters, however, were verbose, and I had to cut them short before they finished. When Professor Tobin's turn came as a discussant, I announced that "Professor Tobin can have 10 minutes." But, unfortunately, not a fast talker, he went beyond his limit. I felt I must be true to my ruling. So, I said, "Professor Tobin, your time is up. Please sit down." He still went on, and I had to repeat my request. I knew it was impolite, and I had no intention of insulting him. But, I did have an unpleasant duty to perform.

When I told this incident to my colleagues later, none of them could believe it. "You mean you actually told Tobin to 'Sit down.'?" I had to acknowledge, "Yes, I did." I am likely the only economist who ever told a Nobel laureate to "sit down."

Robert Solow

Professor Solow of the Massachusetts Institute of Technology had been an economist I have admired for a long time before I met him at Cornell University where I was visiting in 1966–1967. He came to Ithaca to give a lecture, and I raised a question in the Q&A period. The exact question is no longer clear in my memory, but it was regarding something that his lecture did not deal with. His analytical model dealt with a steady state that the economy would approach as a result of a particular policy, "as time approaches infinity." My question was, aside from that conclusion of what would prevail in the far, far future—maybe after we are all dead—what could it tell us about the immediate effects while we are still alive? That was not meant to be a criticism, and I didn't think he took it that way. That, he probably said, would be the subject of a different paper.

As I was walking toward a cocktail reception for him in another building, Professor Solow who was a few steps behind me caught up with me, and asked, "Are you Alpha Chiang?" Quite surprised at the question, I said, "Yes, I am. But how did you know my name?" At that time, the book that would later give me some name recognition was still in press, and I was genuinely curious as to how he had heard of my name. He said, "That obscure you ain't!" I let it go at that, and did not pursue the question of how my name became known to him. At that point, I told him that I had a textbook in press, in which I cited his well-known growth model as an illustration of the use of differential equation in economic analysis.

The next time I saw him was in April 1986 when he came to University of Connecticut (UConn) to give a lecture. That was nearly 20 years after Ithaca. A small group of our faculty had dinner with him at the Altnaveigh, a relatively upscale restaurant near the campus. I told him that I was annoyed by the tardiness of the Swedish Academy to award him a Nobel Prize. And I went a step ahead to make a forecast: "Professor Solow, I predict that you will receive a Nobel Prize within 3 years." He was modest, and simply said, "Nobel Prize? No."

But my prediction was unerring, even a bit too conservative. He received the honor the very next year, 1987.

Wassily Leontief

Professor Leontief of Harvard was another professor whose work on input–output analysis was cited as an economic illustration of mathematics in my book.

He came to UConn to give a lecture in March 1971. Shortly after the lecture, Ann and Warren Fisher, two advanced graduate students came to me, and asked, "Professor Chiang, I hope you don't mind a spur-of-the-moment invitation. But could you and Mrs. Chiang come to have dinner with us tonight at our home? We have invited Professor and Mrs. Leontief to dinner, and they have accepted." Two big surprises! First, our graduate student couple had the initiative to invite a Harvard professor to dinner. Second, the Harvard professor, accompanied with his wife, gladly accepted. Emily and I gladly accepted, too. And my colleague Imanuel Wexler, a Harvard PhD, and his wife Betty were the other guests.

Ann prepared a good dinner, and the conversation was as lively as the food was tasty. I tried what little Russian I still remembered on Professor Leontief, and he just laughed, as my Russian was very rudimentary. Then I made a serious point, in English. "Professor Leontief, I predict that you will receive the Nobel Prize within three years." His response, like that of Professor Solow, was very modest: "Nobel Prize? No, no."

My prediction did come true. He received the honor in 1973. Too bad I didn't make a bet with him. Of course, knowing the odds in his heart, he probably would not have accepted my bet anyway.

A secret thought: I made two Nobel predictions, first for Leontief in 1971 and for Solow in 1986. Why can't I predict the stock market as accurately as I did Nobel winners?

Robert Engle

One day, late in 2003, Emily asked me at the breakfast table, "Didn't you mention the name Robert Engle to me before? A student you had at Cornell?"

"Yes, I recall that I did mention this name. But that was a long time ago, about 35 years ago. Why do you ask?"

"He has just been awarded the Nobel Prize!"

"It's not surprising. He was an outstanding student. He wrote his dissertation with Ta-chung Liu as his mentor."

Truth be told, even though I did have Robert Engle in class, I co-taught that course with John Fei, and I never had any personal contact with him outside of class. He never came to my office to see me, and I never had occasion to contact him after class on my own initiative. But I was happy for him for the Nobel, with an understandable smidgeon of pride that he was once in a class I taught.

32

Retiring So Early?

I have always enjoyed teaching. And, since there is no mandatory retirement age in college teaching, I could very well have continued with my enjoyable classroom interaction with students as long as my health holds. But I officially took retirement in 1992, when I was only 65 years of age. When I called Hong Kong to tell my father about my impending retirement, he bluntly asked me in a puzzled tone, "Why do you want to retire so early?" His negative attitude toward my plan did not surprise me. In his own case, he only started his second career as a Christian minister at age 61, and remained at his religious post for 31 years, until he died in 1997 at age 92.

So, why did I decide to retire? Here is the short answer: the temptation of an "early retirement package" from the State of Connecticut.

A Difference of a Few Dollars

From a budgetary point of view, it is easy to understand why an employer wants to encourage higher salaried senior staff to retire to make room for lower salaried junior replacements. The first "early retirement package" offered to University of Connecticut (UConn) professors by the State government did not contain attractive terms. Since I had no intention to retire, I paid zero attention to it. The next offer, to encourage people to retire in 1992, had much better terms, including payment of all health insurance premiums for me and my spouse, still did not attract my attention, until a friend from another department wisely suggested, "Alpha, you should do some calculations; compare what you would earn in continued teaching, with what you would receive as a retiree. That can provide the basis for a better decision."

The calculation, involving a plus column and a minus column, did not take long. As a retiree, I would pay no social security tax (a plus); I would receive social security benefit since I was 65 (a plus); I would save health insurance premiums (a plus); I would give up my regular salary (a minus); but I would receive my pension, calculated by multiplying my "basic salary" (the average amount of my last three years' salaries) by 2% for every year of my service at UConn. I had 28 years of affiliation with UConn, but, luckily for me, a recent legislation in the state permitted me to "buy in" the 10 years I taught at Denison, raising my total years of service to 38, and substantially increasing the amount of my pension.

The bottom line was unexpected: My total revenue as a retiree or as a continuing faculty member would differ only by a few dollars. In fact, it was higher as a retiree! There was one hidden drawback, though. The "basic salary" being fixed, there would not be annual increase of revenue from then on. To offset that disadvantage, the "package" included a cost-of-living adjustment (COLA) phrase.

When, in addition to that calculation, I put an arbitrary value on the free time I would enjoy, I was won over by the idea of retirement. I officially retired as of September 1992.

The Clock/Watch Retirement Gift

By tradition, I was supposed to receive upon retirement a clock from the State of Connecticut with my name inscribed on it. But there was a serious problem about giving me a clock as a gift. In the Chinese culture, the expression "giving a clock" (送鐘) sounds like "going to your funeral" (送終). So, giving a clock as a present is taboo. I could not ask the State to give me a different retirement present. All I could do was to warn the Head of the Department, Stephen Miller, my friend and research collaborator, about this problem.

At the departmental meeting convened for this presentation. Professor Miller made a short speech about my retirement, and then presented me the golden Hamilton clock with my name on it, while saying, "And here, according to tradition, we are presenting Professor Chiang with a big **WATCH.**"

In my thank-you speech, I had to explain to the puzzled colleagues why the cube-shaped, out-sized, unwearable "watch" I received could not be referred to by its legitimate name of "clock."

A Party of Hilarity

My colleagues planned a farewell party in my honor on May 3, 1992, at the Hillside Place, a catering venue on the UConn campus. My colleague in charge of venue and dinner arrangement, Steve Sacks, printed out an attendance list of about 50 people for me, with not only their names, but also their dinner selection of roast sirloin or chicken Kiev. Such parties could be rather polite and proper, or even drab, but mine turned out to be full of laughs, causing one of the guests to say after the party, "Hey, we should have fun parties like this every month!"

The success of the party should be attributed to the Master of Ceremony, William (Will) McEachern, the funniest MC one could hope for. He came in a tuxedo, as did I. But he wore a top hat as well, giving a grand, formal air to the party. He began with a hilarious monologue, to be followed by speeches of four colleagues, the old-timer Imanuel Wexler, plus the three recent department chairmen—Peter Barth, Arthur Wright, and Stephen Miller—in a joint effort to "roast" me.

Carnac the Mystic

It happened that my retirement was just a week apart from that of Johnny Carson, the celebrated host of the Tonight Show on TV. Our MC, Will, could not resist making a comparison of these two retiring persons: "Both Carson and Chiang started their last job at age 37. Both Carson and Chiang tended to keep people up at night. But both Carson and Chiang sometimes also put people to sleep." (Laughter.)

McEachern the MC then recreated a recurring act of Johnny Carson's, "Carnac the Magnificent," a mystic from the East with the ability to divine unseen questions in sealed envelopes. As Carnac, Will would first place a sealed envelope near his temple, think for a couple of seconds, announce his answer, and then open the sealed envelope to reveal the question relevant to that answer.

His first announced answer was: "Yellow pages." The question from the envelope was: "How do you know it's time to revise your lecture notes." (Laughter.)

Next answer: "Mission Impossible." Question: "Lisa, how would you describe the job of typing Professor XX's final exam?" (Big laughter, though not from Professor XX.)

Answer: "Alphabet." Question: "What did Professor Chiang do with this $5 chip from the Foxwood Casino?" (Gentle laughter.)

Another answer: "The good, the bad, and the ugly." The question: "How would you describe our three recent department chairmen?" (Loud laughter from everybody, including the three recent chairmen.)

The Toast and the "Roast"

Imanuel Wexler, the first speaker, was gentlemanly toward me. He mentioned how, through Paul Weiner, I became a job candidate at UConn; how my interview favorably struck him and the other colleagues; how the IBM Selectric typewriter I requisitioned after I joined the faculty became a conversation piece in the department, and so on. He also listed the things he and I had in common: both an only child; both an immigrant Asian minority; both writing a textbook around the same time; both with an MA from a state university, and a PhD from an Ivy university. Imanuel just "toasted" me, without "roasting."

Peter Barth, the next speaker, was in a widely different mood. When he started, he feigned bewilderment, and said, "Sorry, Imanuel, I could not listen to your speech, because for the last few minutes, I had a gnawing problem on my mind. I couldn't decide, of the other two chairmen to speak tonight, which is the *bad* one, and which is the *ugly* one?" (Laughter! The gall of anointing himself the *good* one!)

Peter roasted me about my hobby of analyzing stock-market charts. "Alpha knows a host of chart patterns to guide his investment decisions, such as 'head and shoulders' (not a shampoo), 'pennant,' 'ascending triangle,' 'descending triangle,' 'double bottom,' and so on. But all these intricate formations can be combined into one simple principle of investment: BUY DEAR, AND SELL CHEAP!" (Everyone laughed hard. Ouch! I could feel a direct hit.)

Peter then said, "One time, Alpha told me that I could be successful in whatever I do. I asked him why, and he said, '*You are tall.*'" (Laughter— largely because he had a direct hit again: I am short.) But he got this cheap laughter by truncating what I said. What I actually said was, "You can be successful in whatever you do, because you are tall, you are eloquent, and you have the ability to fool most people most of the time." He only quoted a part of it.

Being not as close to me as the other speakers, Art Wright did not have much material to roast me with. But he borrowed the pointer I used to use in class and made a joke out of it. He said, "Alpha is a strict teacher with high standards, yet he receives high ratings. What's the secret? I found out that he is a disciple of Teddy Roosevelt, who advised 'Talk softly, but carry a big stick!' He never goes to class without this stick [showing the pointer he borrowed from me]. I did send this stick to the lab. They found traces of blood on it." He then complained that whenever he interviewed job candidates at the economics association meetings, many of them would ask about Chiang, and he really got tired of having to answer such questions.

Stephen Miller started his speech with a reference to Carnac's chairmen-description question, and Peter Barth's reaction to it: "I guess I am the *ugly* one." (Laughter.)

Stephen and I had done joint research, and we had a good sense of each other's thoughts. Frequently, in the middle of a statement he made during our discussion, I could anticipate how he was to finish it. And vice versa. He usually wrote the first draft of the paper, and I, the last version. To mock at my habit of grading students' exam papers by marking with red ink "-1," "-2," or "-3," Stephen said, "When Alpha returned the first draft to me, it would be full of '-4,' and '-5' on the right margin!" (Laughter. He was cleverly self-deprecating. The former students of mine present at the dinner easily appreciated this joke.) He also added with some regret that the papers he coauthored with other colleagues usually got accepted by journals quickly, but the papers we two coauthored with me had to wait for four or five years before finding a publisher.

MY Little Bit

Then came the time for my own speech, or "rebuttal," so to speak. First, I offered an explanation of why I was retiring. "It's not because of the lure of the early retirement package the State offered," I said, "but because I want to save UConn from destruction. How? I have come to the realization that I have a high marginal propensity to jinx: things I touch would get into bad shape. Besides my marginal propensity to jinx is larger than my average propensity to jinx, which, in plain English, means, the tendency is getting worse. Thus, I must retire, in order to prevent UConn from deterioration, or even destruction.

"You want evidence? Well, Steve Miller just gave you a good example. His papers with other people easily get published, but when I am a coauthor, I jinx it. Also, as my first teaching position, I taught three semesters of evening class at the University of Bridgeport. Recently, Reverend Moon, the Korean evangelist has bought the University. As another example, Emily and I used to patronize Clark Restaurant in Willimantic. What happened to it? It's closed."

Before I could go on, somebody in the audience shouted, "Do you know that this place [our party venue] is closing tomorrow?" True, we held the party at the Hillside Place on its last day of business. Another piece of evidence of my propensity to jinx!

I originally intended to bust Peter Barth's truncated quote ("You are tall.") by giving out the complete quote ("You are tall; you are eloquent; and you have the ability to fool most of the people most of the time."), but felt that it would not be kind to mention about "fooling most of the people most of the time." I decided to skip it. But on the "Buy dear and sell cheap" principle of investing, I had to fight back. "Peter is also a devoted investor," I told the guests, "He does not use stock charts, but employs the so-called fundamentalist approach to investing. One time, he told me to buy Kidde, Inc. warrants. And I did follow his advice (maybe because he's tall), but the price of those warrants kept dropping to nearly zero. Somehow, on the expiration day of the warrants, Kidde announced some wonderful news, and the price shot up, and we made a profit. But his next recommendation, which he considered 'cheap,' got 300% cheaper in no time. The chart pattern I saw was actually bearish. But I took this tip from a tall guy seriously and bought, but had to sell it in a hurry. He did, too. The transaction was not pleasant to live with. But there was some comfort from this: At least I am not the only one that subscribes to the 'buy dear, and sell cheap' modus operandi."

Since Stephen Miller didn't really "roast" me, I didn't "attack back." On the contrary, I thanked him for being a great research collaborator, with apologies for my jinxing our coauthored papers. I also thanked him for advising me to take up the job of taking UConn Students to "Study Abroad" in the Netherlands, providing Emily and me a most enjoyable experience. I also thanked Imanuel for giving me the same advice about the "Study Abroad" assignment. And while on that subject, I could not resist telling the story to all the guests about the so-called "Chiang rule," which was promulgated by me, of course.

I told the gathering that Imanuel had such fun taking students to the Netherlands that, upon his return, he could hardly stop talking about Holland. "Holland this, Holland that" is intentional, for effect. So much so that every colleague got tired of hearing about Holland. Not being as polite as the other colleagues in the economics department, I took action, and promulgated the "Chiang rule," prohibiting the use of the word "Holland" on the premises of the economics department. Imanuel, a good sport, then carefully and conscientiously substituted the term "that country" for "Holland."

Yet, the "Chiang rule" notwithstanding, Imanuel's enthusiasm for "that country" did not abate. Instead, it rose to new heights. When the "Study Abroad" in Holland reached its fifth year, Imanuel was pushing for the idea of a celebration. At a cocktail party at his home, he said to me, "Alpha, don't you think that all of us who had served as Resident Directors for the Study Abroad Program should go to 'that country' for this 5th anniversary? Sort of a Jubilee celebration." Before I could answer him, Betty, Imanuel's wife and a great wit, responded to him first. She said, "Five-year Jubilee?! Why don't you wait another five years, and you can have a Ten-year Centennial!" (Big laughter, which was just what I expected, because I consider Betty's retort to Imanuel to be the funniest impromptu remark I have ever heard.)

Regarding Art Wright, I had this story to tell. When Art was hired as a new department chairman, I was on the Dean' Advisory Council, which had to approve the departmental recommendation. At the meeting giving the final approval, an associate dean made the remark, "I sincerely hope that this Arthur Wright will work out." I responded by saying, "Me, too. If he did not, we would suffer from ArthurWrightis." Everybody at that meeting laughed, and I was pleased that I uttered a "clever" saying. A couple of months after Art arrived in Connecticut, I related this story to him, thinking that he would be impressed by my originality. His response thoroughly punctured my ego balloon. He said, "Oh, yeah, my father's name was also Arthur Wright, and my mother used to claim that she was suffering from *double* ArthurWrightis." I got no credit for originality. In fact, Art's mother was one up on me.

I wish I could show some photographs of that festive party. But few pictures were taken that night, and none of them good. I did hire a professional videographer to record the proceedings. But a novice was sent over to do it, and all I got was a fuzzy videotape. That was fate. Maybe I jinxed it, too.

Gifts

I had told the organizers of the retirement party that I did not want any gifts for me. But I did bring some small gifts for some selected guests.

My colleague Steve Sacks had to endure the task of asking everyone signing up for the party the question "beef, or chicken?" I turned to him with a present, and said, "Thanks, Steve, for your great job. In case you have to do the same job about food selection again in the future, here are two file baskets, one for beef, and one for chicken."

Will McEachern did such a good job as MC. He had just come out with a new edition of his best-selling *Principles of Economics* book. The new brochure featured a beautiful Jaguar automobile, with the license plate 1991, and the name McEachern in big letters on the cover. I said, "Will, you have a popular book, and your publisher should give you a Jaguar. But they are cheap, and just put a picture of a Jaguar on the brochure. Tonight, I am giving you a car. Unfortunately, the Match Box selection at the local store is limited. Instead of a Jaguar, here is a BMW."

To Stephen Miller, I bequeathed my box of colored chalks. "By the way, these chalks were a gift to me from a former student, Barbara Beliveau, who got them from the Cowles Foundation when she was studying for her PhD at Yale. She's a great student, and I appreciate her effort to redistribute some Yale chalks to UConn."

My colleague Polly Allen and I were good friends, but we never had any business relationship. One time, however, she sought my investment advice, even though I wasn't known as a great investor. Her question was: "Alpha, what do you think I should do with $100,000 that just came to me?" Without much thought, I said, "Polly, knowing how you and your husband like New York City, my advice would be to buy an apartment in Manhattan. Then you'll have a weekend home in the city." She took my impromptu advice, and bought a co-op, but never told me its location. Only years later did I discover accidentally that the apartment we obtained for our daughter Tracey was also in the same building on West 13th Street in Manhattan. That co-op later rose in value by 500%.

To her, my parting gift was not as valuable as my investment advice. It was just a poster of a martial artist in a dynamic, crushing martial move, with a fierce facial expression. Upon looking at the figure, she laughed out aloud, because the martial arts shown in this advertising poster were a former graduate student that she had specifically told me she disliked. I got this poster because that student did get along with me, and he kindly gave me this poster as a souvenir. This poster was an excellent gift to tease Polly with.

Regarding this martial artist, there was an interesting incident of misconception about me. I was at one time invited to visit the evening class he was teaching in Willimantic, a neighboring town. Since I arrived before he did, the waiting students, all in martial arts garb, asked me who I was. Without thinking, I told them, "I am his teacher." What I meant was I was their teacher's professor of economics, but the students misinterpreted my words to mean I was his martial arts teacher, the master's master. I never received such looks of intense, almost religious awe and respect!

Letters of Remembrance

William (Bill) Lott, another colleague, was in charge of collecting a book of testimonial letters from economics PhD alumni on the occasion of my retirement. It was a time-consuming job, because these alumni were scattered all around the country and abroad, and many of them had not kept in touch with our department. Thanks to him, I did get a good number of them. And, I wrote each letter-writer a personal reply to thank him/her for the trouble of composing a heart-warming letter to me. Some of these letters brought a smile to my face. Some of them I read with moist eyes.

At the risk of appearing vain, sort of "pasting gold leaves onto my own face (臉上貼金)," I will quote from a sample of the letters I received, in random order, with the author's name and professional affiliation at the time of writing:

Roberta (Robin) Carey (The College of Staten Island, New York): It makes me very sad to think of future students who will not have the experience of a course with you.

John Darrow (Professor of Economics, Westfield State College, Massachusetts): To have been taught by you is to have had the fabled (but seldom found) "learning experience" because your classroom work always showed the hallmarks of the master teacher: punctuality, structure, enthusiasm, focus, pace, completeness, and the ability to anticipate what it is that students will have difficulty conceiving...

John Marthinsen (Professor of Economics, and Chairman, Babson College, Massachusetts): In the classroom, you were "Mr. Meticulous." Your considered, deliberate approach to mathematical economics was greatly appreciated; so was your first-day joke about all Americans looking alike.

(John also wrote about a call I made to him when he was a senior, offering him a full scholarship to attend UConn. I said to him something like "This is a very important decision, and you should take your time to think about it, and let me know tomorrow." But I do not recall using the word **"tomorrow."**)

Carlisle E. Moody (Professor of Economics, The College of William and Mary, Virginia) [This letter was addressed to Bill Lott]: In class, I remember Alpha being so patient, so methodical, so incredibly clear. I remember specifically when he would stop to explain why he had chosen a particular Greek letter to represent a variable, and the origins of the various mathematical symbols. . . . I don't remember a single incidence where Alpha became confused at the blackboard.

Jeffrey J. Wright (Assistant Professor, Lenoir-Rhyne College, North Carolina): One of my most vivid memories of my time at UConn is Economics 328 [Graduate Macroeconomics II]. One morning, I overslept and went into a panic when I realized that class for that day had already started. . . . I hopped into my car and drove the 50 miles to Storrs at a speed of 75 mph. It was only because the course was so worthwhile and because you were such an excellent teacher that I broke all speed limits on my trip from Rhode Island.

Nels E. Nelson (Associate Professor, Cleveland State University, Ohio): In the fall of 1968, I had enrolled in the PhD program in Industrial Relations at Cornell but just prior to the start of classes decided to return to UConn to complete my PhD in economics. When I suddenly arrived back in Storrs, you spent a considerable amount of time to arrange an assistantship for me. Without your help it would have been difficult for me to continue my studies.

Shyamala Raman (Assistant Professor, Saint Joseph College, Connecticut): To this day, I quote many of your remarks in my classes and model many aspects of my pedagogy after you. I still remember your comment about the applause to the professor at the end of a class.

Orawin Tailanga Velz (National Association of Realtors): I never cease to be amazed what a big celebrity you are. I remember one time about a girl from the Philippines who attended UConn. She begged Peter and me to arrange so that she could take a picture with you and get your autograph. She was a graduate student in math and used your book in the Philippines. I heard of rock star groupies, but this is a little bit much! [The intended meeting was never arranged.] Even here in Washington, DC, when people from all over the world hear that I went to UConn, all they can say was, "So, you took math with Chiang?" . . . Now that you are retiring, I'd like to tell you how much I appreciate your helping me during my long years at UConn. I could never forget your patience when you advised me on my dissertation. [I served as an associate advisor on her dissertation.]

Ming-Jer Wu (Budget Specialist, Office of Policy Management, State of Connecticut): Confucius defined a teacher as one who embarks on three missions for students: delivering principles, imparting knowledge, and helping solve problems. You went beyond these and extended your care to our family. Frustrated at times for being teased over short stature, we sought your advice. You comforted us by using the "dime versus nickel" analogy to illustrate that intrinsic value cannot be judged by appearance. This boosted our confidence.

Ann Fisher (The Pennsylvania State University, Pennsylvania): You also provided a role model for my teaching. The careful exposition in your lectures and in your book taught me the importance of choosing words carefully to convey exactly what is intended . . . Your use of colored chalks helped me recognize that students often need to see how a graph is constructed in order to understand and remember the concepts behind it.

Warren L. Fisher (Susquehanna University, Pennsylvania): When I was in residence, a popular song's lyrics included the phrase "What's it all about, Alfie?" Of course, we would walk around singing "What's it all about, Alpha?" In truth, there were no mysteries about your courses. . . . I was fortunate to have a few very good mentors, . . ., but you

32.1 Ming-Jer Wu and his wife ManLi Wang.

32.2 Ann and Warren Fisher, 2013.

stand alone as the one whose example makes me try to incorporate the principles of the scientific method into all facets of my personal and professional thought.

I can quote some more, but I should stop before you really label me as a vain person.

By the way, aside from UConn alumni, there were also well wishes sent digitally to me via Bill Lott from, variously, a person in the Department of Politics of Princeton University; a person at the University of Tennessee at Chattanooga; a group signed "UCLA economists"; and "A group of students at the University of Rome." I was deeply touched by all of these.

33

On the Dance Floor

As an untrained dancer in my youth, I had no fear of going onto the dance floor to do my thing, with whomever as partner. Though doing the steps wrong, my own perception was otherwise, and I could accept undeserved compliments without any compunction. At Emily's Senior Prom held at the Hotel Plaza in Manhattan, we were repeatedly told that "we stole the show." And we never felt the need to take dance lessons.

Things started to change when, almost close to my retirement, I took Emily to the Ballroom Dance Club at University of Connecticut (UConn), where a professional dance teacher was giving lessons. It was astounding that as many as 100 undergraduates were in attendance in the class. In such a huge class, not much personal attention could be expected from the teacher. Somehow, we caught the eyes of an older gentleman in the class, Roy Sergent, who, although neither faculty nor student, came to the UConn class anyway. He said to us, "You seem to have a genuine interest in dancing, but you can't learn much here. Let me take you to a dance studio where I am taking lessons."

Steps in Time

Steps in Time, the studio he took us to in August 1991, was located in Avon, Connecticut, more than an hour's drive from home. Run by Eddie Salgado and a partner named Kim, the studio had quite a few teachers, and we decided to sign up for private lessons.

Dancing suddenly became different; we had to observe lots of rules. But we were able to adapt. A couple of weeks into the lessons, Kim, our first teacher shocked us by saying, "We'll enter you into a competition." Competition? So early? We hadn't learned enough professional basics yet. Naturally, we said, "No," which ostensibly disappointed her.

Then we learned that competition is an important part of the dance instruction world. The dance studios enter students into competitions; then the students must take extra lessons in preparation; the teachers take the competing students to competition, with the students sharing the teachers' travel expenses; in each "heat" (about one to one and a half minutes long) of the competition, anywhere from four to eight students from the same level of learning compete with one another with their respective teachers as partners (the teachers are paid for each heat they dance); awards for "first place," "second place," and "third place" are given for every heat.

We heard that many students would regularly participate in several competitions in a year. At each competition, they tend to enter 20 or more dances, in as many heats. Thus, the expenses of entry fees, lessons, travel cost, teacher's partnering fee, can add up quickly to a handsome sum, not to mention the cost of dance costumes. But that is the economics of the dancing world. The students get a lot of pleasure and exercise; they also support the livelihood of the dance studios and dance teachers. Oh, yes, amateur couples can complete without incurring teacher expenses, except for the lessons. And professional dancers compete among themselves in professional competitions, for fame, status, and hence higher tuition rates.

The first thing I noticed from our beginning lessons was that the word "step" has two different meanings. A "step" could mean a single movement of one foot; it could also mean an amalgamation of individual steps. When a teacher teaches a "new step," it invariably means a new amalgamation. For example, the "crossover" in American-style rumba (also known as the "New Yorker" in international-style dancing parlance), involves (a) leading an "opening to the *right*" (turning from the face-to-face position of the partners to a side-by-side position with the lady on the left and the man on the right), followed by forward and backward steps and a return to the facing position; (b) doing an "opening to the *left* (the opposite direction)," followed by forward and backward steps and a return to the facing position;

(c) leading another "opening to the right" with the subsequent return to the facing position; and finally (d) leading the lady to do "an underarm turn." This basic variation in rumba, adaptable to cha-cha as well, spans a total of six bars of music, and consists of many individual steps of the feet. When several amalgamations are linked together into a long sequence, it constitutes a dance "routine." And it is the choreographer's job to fit a number of amalgamations into the framework of a piece of music to produce dramatic and artistic mix of music and movements.

Soon, Kim left the studio, and we were assigned another teacher, Brian. This young man loved dancing so much, and taught with a special fervor. He was the first one to point out to us how to put more energy into the cha-cha stepping, and make the crossovers look sharper. We liked him very much, but then suddenly he disappeared from the studio. It was a tragedy. By accident, a lady student stepped on his foot, and a heel of her shoes pierced through. Brian could never dance again, and his career was totally ruined! Dancing is meant for fun and enjoyment, but it can produce cruel and tragic results, too.

Guys and Dolls

Moving to White Plains, New York, after my retirement forced us to switch to other studios. Eddie of Steps in Time recommended that we continue with Nyemchek's Dance Centre in Pearl River, New York. But the distance of that studio from White Plains caused us some hesitation.

For a while, we studied with Brian Nash, whom we met at a Dance Weekend at the Concord Resort Hotel in the Catskills, in June 1994. He was teaching at Whippany, New Jersey, also far away from White Plains, but since some of our friends—Robert and Helen Rao (饒達德臧玉蘭) ... Tony and Susan Shen (沈繩同康書琴)—joined us for group lessons, we had fun dining and dancing together. We also took private lessons, and participated in student showcases in 1994 and 1995.

But eventually, to save time, we joined a new, local studio, Guys and Dolls, in the city of White Plains itself. Don Fischer and Betty Diamond taught us many steps in many different dances. Aside from cha-cha, rumba, tango, waltz, and foxtrot, we were introduced to mambo, quickstep, bolero, Argentine tango, Viennese waltz, merengue, samba, and paso doble, each with a host of new steps to learn. To deal with this constantly expanding body of information, I decided, with a serious academic attitude, to take detailed written notes after every class session. If you have ever tried to express with *static* words the *dynamic* movement of a dance, you will appreciate how difficult the task is! It's necessary not only to juxtapose the foot movement with the concomitant arm and body movements, but also link all of these to the rhythm of the music. There are simply too many things to describe all at once! Using colored pens to distinguish between distinct aspects of dancing helped a little, but the fundamental complexity of the task remained. I was able to develop my own system of notation, but it was far from perfect.

While we derived much pleasure from dance lessons, conflicts often cropped up between Emily and me. We understood the teacher's instructions differently, and had conflicting notions of what they meant. "The teacher meant this!" "No, he/she meant that!" I would naturally cite my notes as the authority. But Emily would argue, "What if your notes are wrong?" That response would not resolve the dispute, but it would terminate the argument. We must wait for the next lesson, when we could ask the teacher for clarification.

We stayed with Guys and Dolls for a long time, from 1995 to 1998. Toward the end of that period, Don Fischer left, and Betty Diamond was teaching alone. When she hired a new male teacher who, in our opinion, lacked even the basic qualification, we decided to quit, and tried Nyemchek's Dance Centre, as was recommended to us long ago.

By that time, we have already learned quite a lot of the dance lingo, enough to communicate with dancers and instructors intelligently. We could distinguish between (1) "international style" and "American style;" (2) "heel lead" (stepping forward with heel on the floor and toe up) versus "toe lead" (stepping forward with toe on the floor and the heel up); (3) "standard or smooth dances" such as waltz, foxtrot, tango, and quickstep (for which, one has to go around the dance floor counterclockwise, on the "line of dance") versus "Latin or rhythm dances" such as cha-cha, rumba, and swing or jive, which are danced within a limited area on the floor; "diagonal center" versus "diagonal wall" directions; and so on. But there are always more things to learn.

The Nyemcheks

John and Cathi Nyemchek were a junior championship team before they became a married couple. They evolved into undefeated Ten-Dance Champions, and then taught in their own studio in Pearl River, New York, coached professional dancers, and also served as judges at competitions.

When we first visited their studio in February 1998, John asked us to show him a few steps, so he could evaluate the level we were at. By that time, we had already had more than six years of experience, but John's first reaction to our short demonstration was not positive: "We'll clean it up!"

The Cleaning-Up Operation

To start with, John asked us whether we intended to compete. I said, "I do not want to compete, but I hope you'll teach me as strictly as if I am a competitor." That was perhaps not a good thing to say, because it caused John to treat me as a noncompetitor, to be more leniently trained. Emily's answer was even worse; she said, "Alpha is the one with the more intense interest; I am simply tagging along." This led John to treat her gingerly and less critically than normal, for fear that she would quit at the sign of any harsh remark from him.

Unlike the franchised studios (such as Arthur Murray and Fred Astaire), Nyemchek's Dance Centre never tries to ask students to sign long-term contracts. And students who sign up for private lessons can attend group lessons free, with Cathi teaching the international style, and John teaching the mixed American-international style. To take advantage what's available, we were willing to drive to Pearl River twice a week.

Most students desire to learn new steps rather than good techniques, and teachers have to satisfy such demand. Having had a few years of lessons, we had become more aware of the importance, not of new steps, but of how to do the old, basic steps better. Rushing a particular step to display more momentum, or delaying a step for half a second for effect, could make a big difference in the final result. Some minor embellishments to the movement may determine the artistic outcome of a dance. Sometimes, repositioning the man's body a bit may enable the lady to execute her part much more smoothly. That was the higher level of learning we aimed at.

Leading and Following

What is the most important—and most difficult—job for the male dancer? My own unequivocal answer is: LEADING. How to give the signal to the lady, and at which moment to give it, will determine whether the lady can respond comfortably and elegantly to do what she is supposed to do. Usually, though, teachers do not teach leading. Why? Because, in class, the men and ladies are instructed to do their respective parts of the dance, and when the two parts are put together, the ladies would do their part fine without requiring the men to lead the steps. Yet, when the men dance with ladies not enrolled in the same class, the ladies would not know what to do unless they are proactively and properly led.

I thought of a good way to learn leading. John has a reputation of being an excellent leader. To learn it from him, I asked him to dance with me, with me doing the lady's steps, so that I could feel how he actually managed to direct the lady. That process was effective in giving me the skill not often explicitly taught. As an early example, I became clear for the first time about the difference between leading a clockwise "underarm turn" (also called an "outside turn") and leading a counterclockwise "inside turn" (also call a "loop turn"). Although both are initiated by the man raising his left arm, his left hand is positioned differently for the two turns. The timing of the two turns is different also, because the former should be initiated when the lady's left foot is free to go forward, and the latter, her right foot. It was satisfying to know such a basic technique that nobody taught me before.

I did lady's steps quite often, to learn leading. While Emily learned to "follow" by dancing with John with no set routine. With no inkling of what steps John was going to use next, she had to remain alert to decipher each of the successive signals John gave.

A 14-Year Association

The "cleaning-up" operation, a cumulative process, took a long time. In fact, it could never end. Even the top professional dancers need coaches to fine-tune their skills. Our "cleaning-up" lasted for 14 years, from 1998 to 2012. It would have lasted longer, but for the fact that we were moving away to Cedar Crest, a continuing care retirement community (CCRC) in New Jersey.

The long association with the Nyemchek Dance Centre was enjoyable, not only because John and Cathi are good teachers and, more importantly, nice persons, but also on account of the many fellow students we studied in group lessons together, especially Damon and Pamela Tang (曾民興宋秀梅), who have kept in touch with us all these years. They are good dancers, especially in Jive. Another fellow student, Diane Discepolo, impressed us because we saw her join the studio as a total novice with zero background, and watched her grow with incredible speed into a superb dancer, similar to the case of Christina Zhang, whom we met early at Guys and Dolls and who built up quickly from a zero-experience dancer to a graceful one.

We did not compete. But, like many other fellow students, we did participate in showcases. I did a tango with Cathi once, while Emily did a foxtrot with John. Another time, Emily and I did a quickstep together. It was well choreographed by John, and adequately rehearsed, but I somehow messed up in the last few bars of the music, and found it necessary to improvise. By luck, with disorderly leading from me, Emily and I managed to end the dance with a matching ending pose on the last beat of the music, as if it were choreographed that way. That was a narrow escape from embarrassment.

I could not think of a reason why I messed up. It could not be the lack of confidence. Even before we joined the Nyemchek studio, we danced with enough confidence, especially at a birthday celebration for Emily at the Rainbow Room in Manhattan in December 1996. Not to brag, but we received more than 10 unsolicited compliments from other patrons of the Rainbow Room that night, for our display of energy and variety of steps on the revolving dance floor. But this Rainbow Room experience was unique. The enjoyment and excitement we experienced that night was a one-time affair of glory that never occurred ever again.

Dance Parties

Around the late 1990s, there arose a wave of dance parties among the Chinese dance enthusiasts in the Greater New York area. The first party Emily and I gave in June 1998 was a simple affair for about 30 people, with dinner at Sally Ling's restaurant in Westwood, New Jersey, followed by a dance at the Stardust Dance Studio nearby. The studio owner, Charlie Paragian, served as DJ. Our guests brought fruits, cakes, and other goodies. Richard and Maria Hsieh made chocolate-dipped strawberries, a big hit.

For entertainment, Robert and Helen Rao kindly agreed to dance a rumba. Emily and I did a paso doble. The rumba by the Raos was excellent; our paso doble wasn't. Based on the theme of bull-fighting, the paso doble requires a lot of machismo, which I miserably lacked. By all logic, we should not have chosen this dance, but we were temporarily blind to our limitations. I of course made sure to warn our guests beforehand that, even with John Nyemchek fine choreography, we could only present a "Medicare version" of the dance. What actually turned out was something much worse—a "Nursing-home version!" This truth came to light because two of our guests, Hung Yao Kuan and Nancy Kuo, were kind enough to videotape the proceedings of the party. Our forgiving guests did not boo us. But the videotapes surely did.

By the time we gave another party in the fall of 2002, a lot of things have changed on the dance party scene. Many Chinese dance lovers now took turns to host dinner dances. Parties had become larger, sometimes jointly hosted. Miranda and Hamburg Tang initiated a move to invite professional dance teachers as dancing partners, so that when you invite a couple, you had to save four seats for them, with the extra two for the teachers. This created a small problem about seating. At a round table for 10 people, two couples with teachers would take eight seats already. That would leave two seats, either for a single dancer with a teacher or for a couple coming without teachers. A couple not bringing teachers, like Emily and me, then became very convenient—and welcome—fillers for the two leftover seats. I hope that this was not the only reason for our popularity at these parties. Another couple that usually attended the parties without teachers are Steve and Nancy Kuo (郭子偉賈麗妮).

Some of our dancing friends are pictured in Photo 82. Arthur and Jenny Yu (Photo 39) and Cheng Sing and Della Lien (Photo 67) also came to my parties, although they are dancers that did not belong to our dancing-party circle.

Speaking of seating, I found that seating arrangement was one of the most vexing aspects of giving a party. First of all, not all of your guests are friendly with one another. You must know "who's unfriendly with whom," and seat them far from each other. Also, some guests are touchy about where you seat them. Some spots in the room are considered premium real estate by some arbitrary standards. And some people get upset if you don't place them at a table there. The most arrogant of them would even openly complain about it.

The entertainment at the parties had also undergone changes. Many hosts went to huge expenses to have famous professional dancers perform. The more extravagant ones would have one team doing a Latin show, and another doing a standard or smooth show.

Our Party in 2002

At our party in September 2002 at the Battista Dance Studio in Hackensack, New Jersey (later Rogers Dance Center, Hackensack, now closed), we had more than 100 people. The admirable Sally Ling catered a great dinner, and the physicist/dancer Peter Collins served nice dance music as the DJ. I wanted the entertainment program to be different, and added things other than dance showcases.

To start, I had vocal solo by Roger Yeu (樂亦平), my operatic musical partner who also has a beautiful baritone voice. He sang two songs: "Ol' Man River" and a Chinese song "紅豆詞." Then, as a cultural innovation, I thrust Chinese opera into dance parties. My large group of Chinese opera friends and my large ballroom-dancing friends belong to two separate categories like oil and water. I tried to mix oil and water together by including four arias from Chinese operas, sung by Emily (青衣), Herbert Chu (朱源興, 花臉), Mimi Pu Chang (張浦湘翎, 老生), and Chia-dann Chi (齊家旦, 小生), with George Yan (嚴仁安), Roger Yeu (樂亦平), and me as accompanists. To facilitate the appreciation of the mainly dancing group, I provided the Chinese lyrics in a printed program.

Lastly, there was a dance exclusive: John and Cathi Nyemchek danced together publicly for the first time in 13 years with a tango, and a novelty number. But Emily and I opened the show for them, with me dancing with Cathi in a waltz, and Emily dancing with John in a foxtrot. John also did a hustle with his 12-year-old daughter Jamie and a paso doble with Judy Liao, John's student of just three years. The dance by John and Cathi was great, and a rarity since they had not danced together in public for so long.

Several friends wrote or called to acclaim our party as a big success with regard to food, music, and the entertainment program. The letters of appreciation from Arthur Yu (俞潤身) and Cheng-Sing Lien (連健行) were written in such a high literary quality that I tried reading them multiple times in order to learn from them. We became close to Arthur and his wife Jenny Chen (陳澤容) because Jenny and Emily went to Georgian Court College about the same time. Arthur is trained as a chemist, but he writes like an English major. One time, they joined forces with us to look for suitable retirement communities. Arthur and Jenny appear in Photo 39.

Cheng-Sing Lien, a Professor of Linguistics at the Central Connecticut University, writes elegant Chinese with disciplined penmanship. His wife, Della Lee Lien (連李雲英), an avid dancer, and Dean of International Education and Professor of Computer Science at Quinnipiac College, is also a good friend. See Photo 67 for these two professor friends of mine. The Liens have an extra-special daughter, Mimi Lien, who received the prestigious MacArthur Award in 2015, for her outstanding contributions as a set designer for theater, dance, and opera. The MacArthur Award is commonly referred to as the "Genius Award." It is not something you can apply for; you have to be nominated, like a Nobel Prize. What a rare honor!

Michelle Officer

At this party, I noticed a beautiful, graceful figure on the dance floor, dancing with our guest Millard Chiang (姜義明), a brother of my old friend Allan Chiang (姜儀隆). Somebody told me that her name is Michelle Officer, several times United States American Ballroom Champion with her professional partner Edward Simon. No wonder her dancing was so impressively elegant.

When the party drew to a close, Emily and I stood near the door as all the guests came over to say goodbye. Usually, the professional dance partners would not bother to come to say thanks, but Michell Officer did. Not only that, she said to me, "At the next party, would you dance with me?" A little stunned by this unexpected, flattering request, I mumbled something like, "Of course, . . ., I would be honored."

Soon after that, I found on the internet a video of Michelle Officer and Edward Simon doing a waltz show in a palatial setting in Vienna. The choreography and its execution were flawless and truly mesmerizing. I viewed it three or four times, each time absorbing a little more of the details. Michelle became my dance idol. Unfortunately, that video was no longer available on the internet.

Was I courageous enough to ask her to dance with me? Yes, I did, at a later party in 2005. Millard, her partner did not dance much, and Michelle was available much of the time. The first time I asked her, we did a rumba. But Millard insisted that I continued with the next number, a cha-cha. I said at the end of the two dances, "I am afraid that's all the steps I know." Michelle, kindly encouraging, said, "That's a lot of steps you did."

I did ask her again at other parties. And, to my astonishment, she would often come over to my table to ask *me* to dance, to the wonderment of the other people at my table. After a few instances of this, I privately asked her, "Michelle, I appreciate your dancing with me. But why me over the others?" Her answer was very short, "I watched you dance; you dance from the heart." Her remark made a deep impression on me. From that moment on, I made conscious efforts to feel the music and dance "from my heart."

Michelle became a special friend, but little did I know at that time that, for my 80th birthday party in 2007, unusual circumstances would lead Michelle and me to partner up to do a show together. That story, a bit intricate, will be told in chapter 36.

I print here Michelle's business card showing her in an elegant pose.

33.1 Michelle Officer, dance champion.

Partnering with Professional Dancers

Cathi Nyemchek and Michelle Officer aside, I had occasions to dance with several professional dancers over the years. Even though Emily and I as a rule attended dance parties without our teachers as partners, I had opportunities to dance with teachers of friends seated at the same table.

Eric Kwan (關志良) often invited me to dance with his teacher Jennifer Morgan. Jennifer, an expressive, skilled dancer with big, bright eyes, was always fun to dance with. In Latin dances, the two partners are supposed to look at each other, something amateur dancers are often too shy or embarrassed to do, but not the professional dancers. Jennifer would of course never fail to do that. She would not only look at me, but would do so with high intensity. One time, her bright eyes became so overpowering that I was compelled to break the rule myself and look away from her. For standard dances, the two partners are not supposed to look at each other, and her bright eyes did not put the same pressure on me. In fact, while doing a waltz with her one time, we somehow synchronized our motions so well that she was moved to whisper to me, "I am elated." In honesty, I felt exactly the same way at that moment. She was so happy with that waltz that she added a dramatic ending to it all by herself. But this degree of "togetherness" was hard to come by, and it never happened again.

But, sadly, soon afterward, Jennifer could not dance any more. During one lesson, her student carelessly dropped her to the floor, and she suffered injuries that took dancing out of her life forever. It was a heart-rending tragedy. Moreover, she no longer keeps in touch with her dancing past, and I have no idea of her present whereabouts.

Hsing-ta Tao (陶行達) also asked me to dance with his teacher–partner, Aliaksandra Davydava from Belarus. She had won San Francisco Dancesport Championship, Ester U.S. Championship, and other awards. I usually did the cha-cha with her. And she always had kind words for me.

Whenever Ming-nan Sheng (盛明南), my fraternity brother, felt too tired to dance, he would habitually ask me to substitute for him. He had had several partners, and I danced with them all. Boriana Deltcheva, who and her husband Deyan Terzier were Bulgarian Latin champions and World Cup Latin champions, often danced an international rumba with me. J. T. Thomas, who and her partner Tomas Mielnicki were U.S. and World American Smooth Champions, also danced a couple of times with me. And the young, energetic Faina Savich, who was on the TV program "So You think You Can Dance," even became my frequent partner. She was so fond of dancing that she would try to force me off my chair every time she found me sitting, even if we were seated at different tables. Since Emily was having some back pain around that time, she didn't mind my dancing with Faina. Pretty soon, she became familiar with all my routines, and a smooth partnership resulted. In view of the many dances I did with her, I shared her with Ming as our joint partner at the later dance parties. Though enamored of dancing, Faina has a clear head and wise ambition. Instead of pursuing dancing, she decided to study law. After a few years of hard studies at Fordham University Law School, she is now a practicing attorney in New York.

I rarely had an exclusive professional partner. When Emily was at one time prohibited from dancing by doctor's order, I attempted to invite Michelle Officer to a party, but she had other commitment. And Boriana Deltcheva also could not make it, because she happened to be in Europe. Only many years later, I engaged Zoya Altmark as my partner, twice. She started her dancing when learning to skate. A skating champion at age 9, she was National Ten-Dance Champion in Israel at age 12. She has special talents in Latin dances and Argentine tango.

Group Pictures and Action Pictures

Many groups pictures of dancing friends were taken at our dance parties, but most of them were not clear, having too many people in them. I am showing one as Photo 82 in the front of the book. Here, I print here another one taken at a 2006 party hosted by Ann Hsu (許曼君) who was a swimming champion in Hong Kong in her youth.

33.2 At a 2006 dance party. From left: Sitting: Tida Chang, Angel Sheng, Emily, Ann Hsu, Ilse Chiang. Standing: Ming-nan Sheng, me, and Elliot Chiang (unrelated).

As to action pictures, it is not easy to take good pictures of dancers in action, mainly because dancing is a three-dimensional art, whereas photography is limited to two dimensions. A relatively good image of a waltz Emily and I did at our golden anniversary dance party is shown in Photo 73 in the front of this book. That picture, taken by Roger Yeu, appears a bit fuzzy because I had to crop it and blow it up from a small area of the original photo. But it serves as a great souvenir of that party.

The only other action photo I will show is one of Emily dancing a foxtrot with our teacher John Nyemchek in a showcase, also a good souvenir. There is none of my own.

33.3 Emily dancing a foxtrot with John Nyemchek.

34

Golden Anniversary

On September 4, 2004, Emily and I reached the golden anniversary (50 years) of our marriage. That was not an easy milestone, because we must fulfill the dual conditions of (1) still being together as a married couple, and (2) still being alive at the same time. It was obviously something worth celebrating. In fact, even a silver anniversary (25 years) could count as a worthwhile milestone. We held no party for our silver anniversary, but took a picture to commemorate it (see Photo 70).

For the golden anniversary, however, we planned two separate parties, one for our Chinese opera circle and another for our dancing crowd.

A Dinner–Dance Celebration

For convenience of venue arrangement, the dinner–dance was scheduled almost a month before the actual anniversary date, on August 8, 2004, at the Battista Dance Studio in Hackensack, New Jersey. We again depended on Sally Ling for designing the dinner menu, but she offered to do the table decoration as well. Peter Collins supplied eminently danceable music for the 130 people in attendance. These included our children, some relatives of mine, and Emily's siblings and their families, some coming as far as England.

The formal celebration program began with my speech titled "Reminiscence and Tribute," giving brief accounts of how Emily and I met, and how we lived through the struggling years as I embarked on my teaching career, and ending with a tribute to Emily for her contributions to my private life as well as professional career. A unique feature of my speech was my semi-scientific estimate for the number of meals Emily had served me over the past half century. The figure was staggering: 35,000! Most of the guests unconsciously uttered sounds of disbelief when they heard such a high figure. But even that figure could be an understatement.

Our son Darryl and daughter Tracey contributed to our celebration with a great speech "duet." I don't know how long they rehearsed it, but they sounded very much together, to the joy and gratification of their loving parents. They presented to us several gifts, including a golden, lacquered tray with a set of dishes. But the big surprise was a bottle of 1954 vintage Spanish wine, *Viña Tondonia*, which was the same age as our marriage! What a sweet and thoughtful gift idea!

Even though this was a dance party, we again included Chinese opera in the program. But the tight time schedule only allowed three arias, sung by Emily in the lady's role (穆桂英掛帥), Celine Foung (金茜琳) in the male role (搜孤救孤), and Herbert Chu (朱源興) in the hero's role (魏絳打嬰). Accompaniment was provided by our coach Mr. George Yan, me, and our old friends Roger Yeu and Peter Lu (嚴仁安, 蔣中一, 樂亦平, 盧德先).

Switching to Western music, we had a young lady, Patricia Lee, playing two famous violin solo pieces, "Meditation" by Jules Massenet and "Souvenir" by Franz Drdla. She was accompanied by her friend Alice Lu on the keyboard. When I was in high school in Shanghai, I used to hear a fellow student practicing these two particular pieces on his violin in the dormitory every afternoon, so that I quickly learned to hum the lovely tunes. It was by my specific request that Patricia played these, and she brought back a lot of fond memories to me.

Then, when our old friend Roger Yeu sang with aplomb his two Rodgers & Hammerstein favorites "Some Enchanted Evening" and "Younger than Springtime," they brought back fond memories of a yet different era.

Finally, for the dance portion of the program, I invited two teenage students from the Nyemchek studio, D. J. Collins and Olga Grant, to give a Latin show. I had previously seen them rehearse for a competition under Cathi's supervision, and were impressed with their skills at their young ages.

But, since it was our 50th anniversary, Emily and I felt that we should do a dance, too. After consulting with our teacher John Nyemchek, we decided on a waltz, and chose Nat King Cole's "Fascination" as the music. We rehearsed John's choreography over and over, for so many times that we eventually became "sick" of it. Still, with so much preparation, I did not do as well as I had hoped for. The saving grace was that I wore a tail coat (swallowtail) custom-made for me in London for this show, so at least I looked proper and respectable for the part. Emily was more energetic, and did a much better overall job than I.

As mentioned in Chapter 33, a photo of our dance show is included in the colored photo gallery in the front of the book as Photo 73. We are indebted to our good friend Roger Yeu for this shot. It is a good action shot, because it not only clearly captures the momentum of the dance movement, but also simultaneously displays the front view of both of us (instead of the front view of one and the back view of the other). The need of magnification from a smaller image, however, may have affected the quality of the print.

A more formal portrait of Emily and me on our golden anniversary is shown in Photo 71.

Eric and Lola Kwan (關志良張樂儀) kindly brought to the party an anniversary cake that, as beautifully decorated as it was tasty, added much to the enjoyment of our guests. A picture of Emily and me cutting the cake is shown as Photo 72 in the front of this book.

Richard and Maria Hsieh brought their specialty of homemade chocolate-dipped strawberries for our guests. Many other guests favored us with various presents, despite our earnest plea for "No Gifts." We received roses, assorted flowers, poems, Scotch (even Blue Label), picture frame, album, and so on. The most unique gift, from Celine Foung, involved "triple gold." Celine's maiden name is Jin, meaning "gold"; her gift was one share of the common stock of a gold mining company; it was meant to wish us Happy Golden Anniversary. Gold, gold, gold!

The Youngest Guest

Guess who won the honor of being the youngest guest at our dance party? It was Emmett McGrath, the 6-month-old son of Tracey and Jonathan, and our first grandchild. The amazing thing was that, amid all the goings-on, speeches, performances, Peter Collins' dance music and all, Emmett did not utter a single sound during the whole evening to cause any disturbance. A most cooperative kid he was.

When one of our guests, Ann Hsu (許曼君), a vivacious lady, happened to pass by our table, she took a look at Emmett, and liked him so much that she lifted him up from his carriage, and carried him to her own table to show him to the other guests. Tracey, a bit taken aback, said to Emily, "Mom, that lady in the pink dress took my baby away!" We went over to Ann's table after a few minutes and told her the story. Ann suddenly realized that she had taken away the baby without having said anything to anyone. "Oh, I'm so sorry, I guess I was a baby-snatcher," she said. We all had a big laugh.

The Chinese Opera Party

The other party, a Chinese opera singing gala, was held on September 5, 2004 (a day after our anniversary date) at Jimmy Sung's Restaurant (王朝飯店) on East 44th Street in Manhattan, with 60 guests attending. The party commenced at 2:30 and lasted till after dinner.

At such parties, everybody sings an aria, in the order the guests arrive. But I also arranged a short entertainment program. Tzen Chen (陳參) performed "drum singing (大鼓)," and Kenneth Huang (黃庚) did a comedy monologue (相聲), both well done in authentic North-China styles. Everybody genuinely loved these special treats.

Then, Chia-dann Chi (齊家旦) and Roger Yeu (樂亦平) gave speeches that "roasted" Emily and me, the hosts. Those called forth much laughter from the guests.

Individual singing that followed, with professional accompanists, had a wide range of roles (male, female, young male, hero–rogue) as well as singing styles. Lots of Chinese opera music, and all with high standard!

Ballroom dancing and Chinese opera singing had been the two main group activities for Emily and me in recent years. By giving these two parties, we were able to share our golden anniversary celebration with most of our friends in the Greater New York area. The only regret is that we could not share these festivities with many other friends who lived far away.

35

Opus 1

I do not remember exactly when I first met Tammy Lum (林嘉禧). But I can still visualize Tammy and her husband Leo Li (李耀強) walking into our "Advanced Latin" dance class one evening at Nyemchek's Dance Centre in Pearl River, New York. That dance class was not what they intended to take, but their inadvertent entry into the wrong class produced a significant effect on me: it brought me back to piano.

As soon as Tammy introduced herself as a Professor of Music, teaching piano and music theory at Nyack College, I had a revelatory feeling that, after my decade-long hiatus without a piano teacher since I moved to White Plains, New York, after retirement, God was sending me a new musical mentor. But, after I told her that I do not read music, she was hesitant to accept me as a student. In fact, she did not say "yes" to me until quite a few months later, in the fall of 2006.

Music Reading versus Music Writing

When I first started piano with Sue DeWolf, at the ripe age of 59, my intention was to learn enough pieces to form a "repertoire," to be committed to memory—since I do not read music. Now, with Tammy Lum, I had a more modest aim. At my more advanced age, just shy of 80, it would seem sensible to focus more on refining and improving the old pieces than on learning new ones. Tammy, on the other hand, had grander plans in mind. Among other things, she was determined to train me to read music. Sensing that flash cards and other elementary tools would meet resistance from me, she chose a novel approach—to teach me "music *reading*" through "music *writing*." To that end, she asked me to write out some music as an assignment.

"Choose some music you can hum, and write it out in the key of F," she said.

That assignment presented an interesting challenge, and I dutifully wrote out the Bridal Chorus from Wagner's opera, *Lohengrin*. The basics of the Western musical notation that I learned in junior high school in China were adequate for my piano playing, but I never applied it to writing. Still, Tammy was quite pleased with the Bridal Chorus. "You have demonstrated that you know how to write down somebody else's music. Now if you have your own music to write, the process will be no different, except you will then become a composer," she said encouragingly.

From Nowhere

What happened a few weeks later was surreal. One night, in a clear dream, a couple of musical phrases suddenly floated down from nowhere, and tenaciously hovered around my head, repeating themselves over and over again, so that there was no way I could ignore them. In the morning, I told Emily about this strange event, and she suggested that I jot down those phrases. I did it in a simplified musical notation that we use in Chinese opera, using 1 2 3 for do re mi. Then, a few days later, perhaps because Tammy's remark about "composer" had planted a seed in my head, I somehow felt inspired to do something with those musical phrases. Meanwhile, other phrases came to me or arose from my mind during the waking hours, though only in spurts at irregular intervals. One afternoon, on a street corner in New York City, I found myself humming out two bars of nice melody, without any serious effort. That happened during my short walk from my parked car to the hospital where my daughter Tracey was about to give birth to her first child. Little did I expect to be coincidentally giving "birth" too, outside the hospital, to new music. She had to suffer from labor pain; I only had to deal with a melody chain.

Soon, after I had accumulated enough material, I duly translated it from my original simplified notation into the standard Western notation, set out in four sections, in the common A-A-B-A pattern, plus a coda. *Voilà*, a newborn waltz! I did not learn to *read* music as Tammy planned, but I *wrote* a piece, in just about two weeks' time.

I chose the key of F Sharp for the waltz. That might be puzzling, because the key of F Sharp, with so many sharps, was not an easy key to play. But, for me, that particular key happened to be easy for the composing process. I always sang music using "do, re, mi, fa, sol, la, si" in mind, and adopting the key of F Sharp meant that I only had to concentrate on the black keys on the piano for the five main notes in the song: do, re, mi, sol, la.

Excited by this new baby, I was eager to show it to Tammy. I must hasten to add here that I only wrote the melody—the "bones" of the music, so to speak. But when Tammy played the simple handwritten music sheets I presented to her, she automatically added chords—the left-hand harmony that provided the "flesh" to wrap around the bones, making the music full-bodied. The difference between her version and my original bare-bone version was so huge that I could hardly recognize it.

Tammy expressed great delight in my waltz, and said she would play it in her next recital. "Be sure to label this piece as Opus 1," she added, "because I hope very much that you will continue to produce Opus 2, Opus 3, and many beyond that."

A World Premiere

For Tammy's recital program, I dutifully named my piece "Waltz in F Sharp Major, Op. 1." Since Tammy supplied the accompaniment, I considered Tammy to be a co-composer, but she insisted that she should be listed as an "arranger." Then, in a moment of silliness, I asked Tammy whether we should add the words "World Premiere" to my piece in the program. She laughed, and said, "Why not? It indeed *is* a world premiere."

The recital took place on May 12, 2007, about two months before my 80th birthday, at Pardington Hall, Nyack College, in Nyack, New York. After she played my piece, I presented her with a bouquet of roses, and took a bow with her on the stage. When I returned to my seat, I noticed Emily wiping the corners of her eyes with a tissue.

Opus 1.8

Two years later, Tammy played my second composition at a recital. Theoretically, this composition should be labeled "Opus 2." But since I felt that it was not in a really finished form, I jokingly called it "Opus 1.8," an unconventional but apt title. Naturally, it was another "world premiere."

Opus 1.8 is a more sophisticated composition. The A-B-A pattern suggested by Tammy involves a change of key from D Flat to A, then back to D Flat. Thus there are two transitions. By luck, a natural-sounding transition, from D Flat to A, came to my mind in a wink (it even won Tammy's praise), but the second one, from A back to D Flat, failed to satisfy the perfectionist in me. I became even more dissatisfied after hearing it played at the recital. Yet, revision after revision failed to please me. And it just happened that, meanwhile, Tammy was launching a major CD project. In order not to disturb her during her big undertaking, I began to put off my revision work on Opus 1.8. That was of course a bad decision, because procrastination bred laziness, and there resulted a multiyear disruption in my compositional endeavor.

The CD Cometh

Tammy had told me earlier that my Opus 1 will be included in her projected CD, "Ballades & Ballads," featuring Chopin's Ballades, and works by Gershwin and others. But when, in August 2015, she presented to me a real-life copy of her just-released CD, the thrill was still greater than expected. Not surprisingly, her arrangement of Opus 1, now renamed "Romanze in F Sharp Major, Op. 1," is even more virtuosic than the version at the recital. By the way, the word "Romanze" is not a misspelling; Tammy prefers to end the word with "ze" rather than "ce." Her performance throughout the CD is flawless and exquisite. It's Tammy at her very best. *Brava,* Tammy! (My friend Mary Chu (朱高曼琍), who spent many years as a youth in Rome, taught me that "*brava*," the feminine form of "*bravo*," should be used when complimenting a female.)

Photo 77 in the front of the book shows Tammy presenting a copy of her CD to me.

In the Chinese culture, to characterize someone as truly outstanding, we say he/she is like "a crane towering over a crowd of chickens (鶴立雞群)." When I saw my name appearing alongside those of Gershwin and Chopin, quite the opposite comparison came to mind; I felt like "a chicken crashing a party of cranes (雞闖鶴群)."

Later . . .

I did eventually finish revising the melody part of Opus 1.8 into a skeletal "Opus 2." But Tammy's concert schedule has not allowed her to work on the accompaniment end of it. Or, maybe she found that my new revision is not up to standard, providing little incentive for her to work on it. I did try to work some more on that troublesome transition. But the many other things I do in my life also demanded my time. Because of all of these, Opus 2 has so far remained an unborn child, waiting patiently for its delivery, someday. And the long delay made it easy for me to be further sidetracked into other endeavors than composing, including the writing of the present volume.

36

Suddenly 80!

Only three years after our golden anniversary, I arrived at another milestone: 80 years of age! It came rather suddenly and stealthily so as to cause me quite an alarm. Following the precedent of the golden anniversary celebration, we gave two parties, a dinner dance plus a Chinese opera singing gathering.

The Dance Party

For the dance party, scheduled for July 22, 2007, I booked the Fort Lee Hilton Hotel in Fort Lee, New Jersey.

On the party program I designed, I used the title "Suddenly, 80!" with a pine tree as the background. Pine tree is one of the traditional symbols for longevity, and I was glad that I could still draw it, even though I had not practiced Chinese painting for a long while. On the inside, I printed two ancient photos on the left-side page, one when I was 1-year old, and the other, taken with my mother when I was 5 years old—also reprinted in this book as Photo 2.1 in Chapter 2. On the right page inside, I listed the celebration program, consisting of (1) Emily's welcoming remarks, (2) my speech titled "On Becoming an Octogenarian," (3) Tammy Lum's speech titled "My Oddball Student," and (4) "Birthday Wishes: A Fairy Tale." Hardly noticeable was a very faint image of a crane in the background that I drew; cranes are another symbol of longevity in the Chinese culture.

36.1 Cover of the party program for my 80th birthday, 2007.

The Speeches

Emily's remarks were brief. And my speech only emphasized the point that my "psychological age" is much lower than my "chronological age" of 80. In addition, by virtue of my having spent time learning to tell jokes to overcome my shyness, I could not resist telling three or four age-related jokes.

Tammy, my second piano teacher, explained in her speech why she hesitated to accept me as a student, but was glad that I turned out to be a conscientious student. Pleasantly surprised by my Opus 1, she played it in her recital. Fortunately, that recital was recorded, so she could easily ask the DJ, Peter Collins, to play Opus 1 for the guests at my birthday party.

A Homespun Fairy Tale

A dance party usually has a dance show as an integral part of it. For my 80th birthday dance party, I originally wanted as the main attraction a professional showcase by my friend (and idol) Michelle Officer, who, after the retirement of her renowned co-champion Edward Simon, just found a new partner. She graciously agreed to do it. But, to provide an opening act for them, I envisioned a dance number I'll do with Emily. To add a twist, though, I wanted to perform it not just as a plain dance number, but as a dance within the framework of some story. It took me a few days before a concrete idea crystallized in my mind: I would write a fairy tale, with two characters, one male and one female; the female would be a fairy with magic power; the male would be someone with a few physical problems; and the storyline would lead to a dance sequence at the end.

After some rounds of deliberation, my fairy tale took its final shape. Titled "Birthday Wishes: A Fairy Tale," the story centers on a Prince Beta, twin to Prince Alpha in an ancient kingdom. Prince Beta, born crippled, did not please his father the King, and was forthright banished to the distant Land of Deformia, never to return. Thus, Prince Beta never really met his twin brother Prince Alpha.

The idea of Alpha having a brother Beta may very well have been inspired by my mother's tubal pregnancy, which resulted in a stillborn child when I was 19 years of age. But, in the fairy tale, Beta is deformed rather than stillborn, and the two brothers are twins instead of being 19 years apart in age. My stillborn brother was fact; Prince Beta is fiction.

To continue with the fairy tale, Prince Beta had heard that his brother Alpha, now King, was planning a grand ball for his 80th birthday. And Beta, having the same birthday, somehow developed a sudden urge to be reunited with his twin brother for the first time.

Feeling awkward about his hunchback, his limp, and his total lack of dancing skills, though, Beta hesitated to venture into such a reunion. He prayed hard for a miracle to occur. Then, lo and behold, there suddenly arrived out of nowhere a Birthday Fairy who agreed to grant him three wishes. In no time, the Fairy got rid of his hunchback; cured his limp; and, more importantly, downloaded into Beta's mind all the dance steps that had ever been invented. To test whether the downloading was successful, the Fairy and Beta tried a few dances, before the Fairy transported Beta to Alpha's ball in her "magic bubble."

Casting Complications

I was quite excited about this fairy-tale idea, and thought Emily would welcome the opportunity to play the juicy role of the Fairy. To my dismay, she poured ice-cold water on my red-hot project. "I think the concept of the fairy tale is fine," she said, "and if you don't mind making a fool of yourself, go right ahead and do it. But I am certainly not going to be part of it!"

Gee, I was suddenly short of a "costar."

Disappointed, but not yet discouraged, I turned to my dance teacher Cathi Nyemchek to play the Fairy. Her response was also negative! She said, "Alpha, I would love to dance with you in a show, but just last night I paid a nonrefundable deposit on a vacation rental, and would not even be in town on the day of your party. I'm so sorry."

It now appeared that my fairy tale was to be stillborn, like my brother! When I related my dilemma to Michelle Officer, she sighed and relayed an equally bad news of her own: her new partner could not make it to my party, either. So, both shows seemed to have gone kaput!

It took dear Michelle's incisive mind to come up with a solution. "Since both of us are short of a partner, why don't we combine forces?" she said. To my great delight and even greater awe, Michelle offered to play the Birthday Fairy, to my Prince Beta.

Some Highlights of the Show

The fairy tale was only about 20 minutes long. But Michelle and I spent more than 20 hours together to work out the details of the dialog, action, and the dances we would perform. To ensure proper timing, continuity, and flow, Michelle decided to have all the narration, dialog, and dance music for the show prerecorded on a CD. This way, the DJ only had to start the disk once, and let it play on without the need to splice separate pieces together. Michelle and I would just mime through the smoothly narrated story.

For some of the features in the show, Michelle and I planned with considerable care. She was to select the opening music, and her judicious choice was the Disney classic "When You Wish upon a Star." It filled the hall with such a fitting initial mood for the fairy tale. This musical overture then segued into the introductory narration, during which the limping, hunchbacked Prince Beta in royal regalia came on stage, with a coronet on the head, and a red sash hanging diagonally across his black jacket. I considered wearing a cape as well, but Michelle advised against it, because it might hamper the dance movements that would come later.

As the Birthday Fairy, Michelle wore a white tutu and carried a jeweled magic wand she made by her own hands. Originally a long wand, she had to cut it short for fear that its length would complicate the dance steps featured later in the story.

For the granting of Prince Beta's first two wishes (curing his hunchback and limp), the script called for a simple waving of the

Fairy's magic wand. But for the third (downloading all the dance steps into Beta's mind), the Fairy must stick the magic wand into Beta's ear for a minute or two. Since we should not have silence during that interval, we had to fill it with music. Michelle cleverly chose the "Final Jeopardy" theme from the game show "Jeopardy" to accompany her motion with the magic wand. I also added some hand motion seemingly to ward off the tickling sensation the downloading produced to my brains.

When, as a test of the downloading, Prince Beta and the Birthday Fairy danced together, I introduced another twist: Beta got stuck in a dance step, and froze in an awkward pose for a moment, obviously because of a glitch in the downloading. Only after another wave of the magic wand, could they resume dancing without further mishap.

We planned three dances: (1) a soft-shoe, which is not a ballroom dance at all, but suitable for the show as a novelty dance, (2) a bolero, one of my favorite dances with Michelle, with slow, expressive movements, and (3) a standard slow waltz.

Since Michelle is taller than I, I saw an opportunity to introduce some self-deprecating humor into the script. Before testing the dance steps, Beta suddenly came up with a fourth birthday wish, requesting the Birthday Fairy to make him a bit taller. Her scripted reply was: "Sorry, in fairy tales, we are only allowed to grant three wishes, no more." And when, toward the end of the story, the ever-persistent Beta pleaded once more with the Birthday Fairy to grant him the fourth wish, Michelle replied: "I'll grant this wish to you on your 90th birthday!" This turned out to be the line that elicited the loudest applause from the audience.

Having had all the sound and music prerecorded on a CD, Michelle and I just did pantomime. Luckily, there were no hitches during the performance. But, with insufficient rehearsal time for proper practice, my dancing was regrettably far below standard, and I had to rely on the gracious Michelle to carry me through. Nevertheless, the custom-written fairy tale made the party a unique, memorable 80th birthday celebration. The audience reception was graciously warm and cordial.

In my 2007 Christmas card, the back cover displayed a series of dance photos of the fairy tale, extracted from a video Leo Li, Tammy Lum's husband, kindly made for me. Another photo showed me, as Prince Beta, cutting a birthday cake. This back cover is reprinted as Photo 74 in the colored photo gallery in the front of this book.

The general dancing also went well, and the party lasted merrily till 11:00 p.m.

The Reaction

Many compliments came to me after the party, especially for the novelty of the show. A couple of professional dancers at the party told me that no professional dance show could ever compare with the fairy tale Michelle and I did. I would of course give the larger share of the credit to Michelle for her careful planning of the disk and for her skilled direction of my acting.

Proud of the creation of the fairy tale, I have kept to this day the coronet and sash I purchased as part of Prince Beta's costume. I have also kept the jeweled magic wand that Michelle made by her own hand for the show, and later kindly gave to me as a memento.

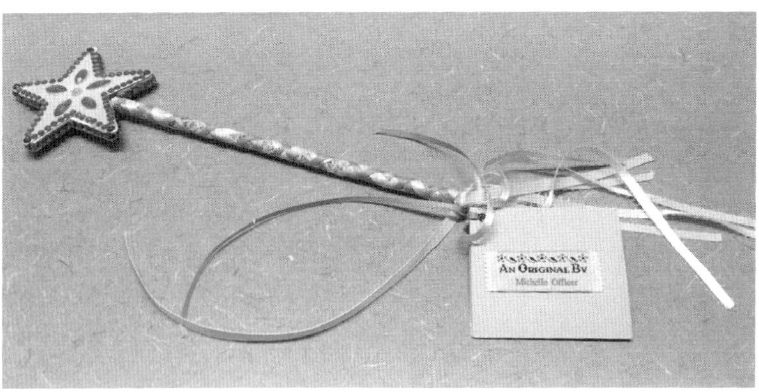

36.2 The magic wand Michelle Officer made for our show.

The Chinese Opera Party

The program I designed for the Chinese opera gathering was similar, with the same pine tree on the cover, but with changed wording. The ancient photos of me remained the same as well, but the celebration program now consisted of (1) Emily's "Welcome to the Party," (2) Darryl and Tracey's speech titled "Happy Birthday, Dad!" followed by (3) my "On Becoming an Octogenarian." To my deep regret, there was no way for me to share with my Chinese opera friends at this party the fairy tale about Prince Beta.

The venue, Evergreen Shanghai Restaurant (綠楊村) on East 38th Street in Manhattan, has a room on the second floor that can be closed off for singing. Somewhat crowded for the size of our group, we nevertheless had good vocal fun upstairs from 3:00 to 6:00 p.m., before going down to the main floor for the banquet, and the celebration program.

The Banquet

Among the 70-odd guests, I counted many guests who traveled from long distances to attend, two of my cousins among them. A picture with my cousins taken on that day, previously printed on the back cover of my 2007 Christmas card, is now shown in the bottom-left panel of Photo 74 in the front of this book. My cousin Jiang Zhongquan (蔣中權) came all the way from Dalian, China; he was at the extreme left in the said picture, sitting beside me (with bow tie). My economist cousin Kuo-tao Yui and his wife (余國燾劉公娟) who flew in from Victoria, Canada were the couple on the left in the back row in the same picture. Two other cousins in the picture, however, were residing in New York at the time: Kuo-tung Yui and his wife (余國棟向越華), front right, and Frank Wang and his wife (王曾冲施織芳), back right.

There were at least two other long-distance guests. Our singing and instrumental coach Mr. George Yan made the trip from Oakland, California. H was the one in white shirt, raising wine glasses with Emily and me in the center of Photo 74. Jerome Min (閔家榮), an experienced singer of the hero–rogue role as well as regular male role, came with his son from Shanghai to my party, although he was not captured in that group of photos.

The top-right picture in Photo 74 depicts Catarina Chi (齊陳寬泠) singing a Chinese opera aria. On account of my birthday, she made an exception to her long-standing policy of never singing in public. The picture directly below Catarina captures Darryl and Tracey laughing with me. And the picture directly below that shows Emily with Mr. Yan's daughter, Karen. The second picture from left in the bottom is interesting in that, Celine Foung (金茜琳, front) is a female singer of male roles, whereas Shu Ho (何恕, back) is a male singer of female roles.

Emily's welcoming remarks during the banquet were brief. Darryl and Tracey, who decided to attend the opera banquet rather than the dance party, both spoke. I had asked Darryl whether he would give a speech in Mandarin Chinese. He said, "Sorry, I can't." But when the microphone went to him, he delivered a smooth speech entirely in Chinese, which gave me a big, pleasant surprise. Tracy spoke in English, but she taught her husband Jonathan to say, in Chinese, the phrase "爸爸, 祝你生日快樂!" She even taught her 3-year-old son Emmett to say a well-wishing Chinese phrase, which did not quite come out clearly. I asked her, "Tracey, what did you teach Emmett to say?" She said, "*Shou bi nan san* (壽比南山)!" which means: Have a life as lasting as the South Mountain! My goodness, that phrase was definitely too difficult for a 3-year old with no Chinese-language background.

The program concluded with a last-minute impromptu contribution from Nancy Kuo (郭賈麗妮), singing the operatic aria "麻姑獻壽 (Celestial Longevity Blessing)."

The Mystery of the Longevity Peach

Emphatically, I pleaded in my party invitations for "No Gifts." Still, many guests preferred to go against my plea. Good wishes came in the form of leather album, carry-on luggage, chocolates, orchids, tie, a crystal ball with longevity symbols pine trees and cranes inlay, wallet and keychain, Tiffany cufflinks, Christofle picture frame and chopsticks set, recorder, and even gift card and cash gifts.

One present, a light-pink crystal peach with a single green leaf attached, caused a vexing problem. The gift was detached from its card when the many presents were piled together, so that I could not identify the person to whom to write a thank-you note. To add to the difficulty, I could not go over my guest lists and ask about the peach. All that time, the sender would be wondering why Alpha was negligent in acknowledging the gift.

Finally, after a long period, Angela King (金徐琪) casually raised the subject of longevity peach with me, and the mystery came to an end. She, a daughter of my old friends C. K. and Julia Hsu, was the one who sent me the lovely crystal peach. I finally could thank her with my deep apologies.

A Follow-Up to the Fairy Tale

Years have passed now. But a recent event—my annual medical checkup—made me think back to the fairy tale. Before I got to see the doctor, the nurse assistant routinely took my weight and height. Her announcement of the result was disheartening: "You have gained two more pounds since the last examination, and you have lost another half inch in height." I must have uttered an inaudible sigh, as my mind flashbacked to Prince Beta, and his fourth birthday wish about his height. Birthday Fairy, Birthday Fairy, where are you when I badly needed you?!

37

Count Alphonso

Another party we gave, in November 2009, at the Starlight Dance Center in Nutley, New Jersey, was co-hosted with Teresa Sun (孫魏珠). The theme of the party was quite ordinary—to celebrate the pleasing and comfortable fall weather. But, again, I want to have a different kind of entertainment. What I proposed to our co-host Teresa was a magic show, since no other dance parties had ever offered a magic performance. "Who will do the magic?" she naturally asked. My response took her by surprise: "I will do the magic, with you and Emily as the magician's assistants." Teresa was game, and said without hesitation, "Okay." Emily did not object either.

The World Premiere of "Comedy in Magic"

I have had an interest in magic tricks for some years, and I had taken lessons, and read books on magic. My initial motivation for this hobby was a desire to perform magic someday at grandchildren's birthday parties. But my original intention remained as intention only. Why? Birthday parties for kids have become fancy affairs. The tendency is to hire professional magicians, instead of allowing grandpas to do their half-baked or even fully baked tricks. Without occasions to perform these tricks, I easily got rusty. For this party, I had to select a series of tricks and weave them into a sequence. Then, practice, practice, and practice.

I decided to bill myself as "Award-winning Count Alphonso," and created the names of Emilia and Teresita for my "assistants." Audaciously, the show was labeled as the "World Premiere" of "Comedy in Magic." You'll notice the inconsistency between the adjective "award-winning" and the label "world premiere." If this were the very first show Count Alphonso had ever done, how could he have won any awards before? I hoped that some of the guests caught this joke and started to laugh even before the show started. I also hoped that the novelty of a magic show might please the guests.

The Show

At this party, there was no Chinese opera, or any other performance. Thus, I, with Emily and Theresa, were "on" from the very beginning. I made my entrance majestically in a tail coat (swallowtail), with a red sash across my body, and a medal of some kind hanging down my neck. The two "assistants," carrying an attaché case and a sketch book for me, looked their best beside me.

I began with a clarification of the name "Count Alphonso." "I am not a nobleman," I said, "and the title of *Count* is not a title at all." I made up this silly story: "I was a child prodigy with the ability to count from 1 to 10 in several languages when I was one year old. Being proud of me, my father would show me off when guests came to visit, telling me, 'Count, Alphonso. Count, Alphonso.' Gradually, I became known as Count Alphonso."

Then I explained why I chose the title "Comedy in Magic" for the show. It was because I want the audience to think according to the following rule: If a trick works, it should be considered as "magic," but if it doesn't, then it should be taken as "comedy." Either way, they should applaud.

Sooner or later, however, I must perform some magic tricks. What did I do? First, I looked for my magic red handkerchief in the attaché case, and failed it to find it. "Emilia, how come my magic handkerchief is not here?"

"I don't know," Emilia replied unapologetically, "Why don't you use your magic and create a new one?"

On that cue, I gave her a dirty look, and drew one in the sketch book, and painted it red with marker. Closing the sketch book, tapping with a magic wand three times, a real red silk handkerchief was coaxed out of the sketch book. (Applause.) This trick, by the way, was inspired by what I once saw on a TV magic show, except that on the TV show, what the magician produced from a sketch book was a heavy bowling ball, not a soft and light handkerchief.

That naturally segued into a coin trick. I wrapped a coin in the silk handkerchief, and squeezed the coin through the fabric without tearing it. This one, as some other tricks described below, I learned in an adult class magic course with a professional who calls himself "David, the Magic Man."

The "ball in the cup" trick consisted of several steps. I first dropped a ball into a cup, turned the cup over, and rested it on the table. After tapping the cup with the magic wand three times, I lifted up the cup, to show that the ball had vanished. No, it really had not vanished. It had gone into my pocket. After retrieving that traveling ball from my pocket, I put it back into the cup, turned the cup over as before. After the wand-tapping, I lifted up the cup again. This time, the single ball had now split into two balls. Wow! How could one ball produce its own clone?!

Out of the rope tricks I knew, I only played two. For the first one, I placed three ropes of unequal lengths one by one in position in my left hand, and, with a simple swiping motion of the magic handkerchief over the ropes, I transformed them instantly into three ropes of equal length. Yet, as I pulled out the three ropes one by one from the left hand, they were each restored to their original unequal lengths. And for the next rope trick, I asked for a guest from the audience to cut a piece of rope into two. Angel Sheng (盛李安琪) volunteered for the job. I then asked Teresita to cover my hands with the magic handkerchief as I mended the cut rope instantly into a whole piece again.

Of course, card tricks are necessary, too. But, by their nature, card tricks are close-up magic tricks, more suitable for an audience standing around a table. With our guests spread apart from one end of the wide ballroom to the other, card tricks would lose much of their attraction. So, I only played one. A volunteer picked a random card from the deck. After showing the card to the audience, I buried the card into the deck, and placed the deck on the table. Then, by moving my magic hands upward around the deck a few times, in an elevator-like motion, I made that specific buried card rise to the top of the deck. Wow! How did that card come up from the middle of the deck?!

The Sabotage

Another trick was the "answer in the sealed envelope" type. I asked for a volunteer to come up and do some arithmetic calculations on a sketch pad held up by my assistant Emilia away from me. Supposedly, the volunteer could choose any five-digit number, and after several prescribed steps of calculation, arrive at an answer. I would then open a sealed envelope, and ask the other assistant Teresita to help me unfold a big piece of paper with the correct answer on it. For comedic effect, I planned to hold the answer upside down on purpose. Only after the audience said, "Wrong!" would I pretend to be shocked at the mistake, and then, take a quick look at the paper and respond, "Oh, I'm so sorry. I had it upside down." Flipping the paper to the right position to show the correct answer would then call forth the expected applause.

That was the plan, but it was not what happened!

The volunteer who came up, who happened to be a highly educated scientist, had in mind evil fun. Intentionally, he fouled up the arithmetic calculations, so that his answer would not match what was in the sealed envelope! Actually, the moment Emilia had noticed the mistaken calculations on the sketch pad she was holding, she should have warned me about it. But, for some reason, she remained silent. As a result, this magic trick was totally ruined! This guest was not a close friend, but even so, it was shocking that any guest would play such a dirty trick on the host of the party. What a debased case of *schadenfreude*!

The Finale

I was deeply upset, but I had to stay calm and finish the show.

The ending I designed was meant to produce a last laugh. When I announced the end of the show, Nina (Katharina Marks), the owner of Starlight Dance Center, would come forward to present me with a very tiny, two-inch silver trophy cup. I would thank her, of course, but also ask her curiously, "Nina, it's so kind of you to give me this award. But, where in the world did you find such a tiny silver cup?"

Nina's prearranged answer was, "This is the cup you gave me before the show." A big laugh was expected at this point, and we indeed got it.

And, then I said, "If that's a cup I gave you earlier, then it must be a magic cup with something in it." I asked Nina to inspect the inside of the tiny cup, and assure the audience that the cup was empty. Then, I shook the empty cup, and pulled out from the cup yards and yards of colorful streamer! (The final applause.)

This finale is shown in Photo 75, with (from left) Emilia, Count Alphonso, Teresita, and Nina.

An Audit

In spite of the sabotage, the show was completed without any further mishap. Rita Ting (丁朱倫漪), a good friend, came to me with this remark: "After you have found out that that guy did the calculations wrong, you should have asked for an audit!" An audit? Didn't that sound like a comment from a Certified Public Account (CPA)? Well, it happens that Rita Ting indeed is a CPA. If she had made that suggestion during the show, I would definitely have followed it, and sought another volunteer (maybe Rita herself) to verify the math. But now the show was already over, so I must live with whatever had transpired.

38

Spices of Life

Somebody had said that "Variety is the spice of life." I prefer to alter the statement to: "Hobbies, or avocations, are the spices of life." I have seen friends dreading retirement, because they do not know what to do once they stop working, and no longer have the daily office routine to follow. On the other hand, people with multiple side interests may face the problem of how to apportion their limited time resource to the various interests in their lives. Obviously, the optimal thing to do is to develop some hobbies, but not too many.

Unfortunately, I belong to the category that has too many hobbies. "No time!" is usually my dilemma. But does that stop me from pursuing new interests? No! I still cannot help branching into new ventures or adventures when something novel comes onto the scene.

In Case You Haven't Noticed

Just in case you have not noticed from the preceding chapters the nonprofessional things I have fallen into, accidentally or on purpose, during my first 90 years, here is a short listing:

Chinese opera has been a lifelong avocation; I sang when I was young, up to 23–24 years of age, and focused on the instrumental side after that. I even co-founded a Chinese opera association while a graduate student at Columbia, which is still in existence, though no longer presenting stage performances.

Ballroom dancing is another, although formal training only began near my retirement age. The hundreds of private and group lessons that Emily and I have taken filled our lives with fun and supplied us with a motive to move our limbs and exercise our bodies. Showcases were fun, too, but there were more in the nature of challenges. And there were dance parties where friends with the same interest gathered to bask in the camaraderie.

I have also mentioned my ventures into piano playing, piano music composition, and magic. I had done piano recitals, written a piano piece "Opus 1" in 2007. And I even performed a magic show, with selected coin tricks, rope tricks, card tricks at a dance party that I co-hosted in 2009.

But there are other hobbies I have only lightly touched upon, or not yet at all.

Chinese Brushwork

Chinese brushwork is the basic skill at the foundation of the dual Chinese classical arts of calligraphy and painting. When I was in primary school, calligraphy was a required part of daily school work, not as training to become professional calligraphic artists, but as a necessary way to develop a presentable penmanship, the most outwardly observable attribute of an educated person. Dabbling into painting would be even more desirable. And the brushwork skills learned in connection with calligraphy could be easily applied to painting.

My father cultivated in me a strong liking for brushwork. Among my fondest memories of him were his efforts to take me to many calligraphy and painting exhibitions back in Shanghai. He would discuss with me the merits of the various exhibited pieces as he saw them. But I especially appreciated his willingness to get up early in the morning to help me prepare the ink by pouring water into the inkstone, and grinding the inkstick for me, something I should do for myself. For a long time, he also hired a private tutor to teach me landscape painting (山水) on Sundays. My fondness for these arts made me continue my study with C. C. Wang (王季遷, later renamed 王己千), the Chinese art collector and painter who came to New York shortly after I did, while I was working on my PhD at Columbia. Unfortunately, I had to quit it when my incipient teacher career took me to Ohio in 1954.

However, with the fountain pen and ballpoint pen replacing the brush as the primary writing instrument over the years, there was a noticeable general drifting away from brushwork as school work. And the long hours of practice required of a good brushwork artist inevitably altered the status of calligraphy to that of an esoteric art form. Youngsters in China no longer care as much about good penmanship as a desirable personal attribute. And, in the computer age, that probably does not matter, because most communications—emails, text messages—are nowadays typed out rather than hand-written.

After retirement, I did revive my practice of calligraphy for some years, but not painting. An occasion for a practical application of my calligraphy occurred, though not a happy one. My mother died in 1995 and my father in 1997, and I had their remains shipped over to be buried in the Kensico Cemetery in Valhalla, New York, near where we were living in White Plains. It was my sad duty to do the inscription on their gravestone (see Photo 6.3). Of course, my father could not grind the inkstone for me this time. I also wrote the names of C. K. and Julia Hsu (徐積鍇張粹文) for their burial chamber.

More recently, for a change, there was a happy occasion for putting my calligraphy to use. My daughter-in-law, Dr. Andrea Jue (居德琳), opened her own ophthalmology practice in New York City in September 2018, and she requested an art piece for the reception room of her office. I was of course tickled to be able to do it after a lot of last-minute practices. The inscription I composed reads: "慎施神妙保睛手術; 恒抱恭誠濟世胸懷." Translation: "Meticulous application of amazing surgical skills for eyesight preservation; consistent attitude of courteous and sincere service to the populace." (See Photo 38.1.)

I had also had occasions to apply my calligraphy to the Chinese opera performance programs I designed over the years. The cover of the commemorative booklet I produced for the 50th anniversary performance of the Chinese Opera Association of New York, shown in Photo 64, carries my writing in 行書 (running style). For some examples of my long-neglected painting skills, see Photo 27 (a birthday gift to my father) and Photo 36.1 (the pine tree background for the cover of a birthday party program).

38.1 My calligraphy piece for Andrea's office reception room, 2018.

Seal Carving

Seals, or chops (圖章), are used to add imprints, in red, on calligraphy and painting art pieces below or on the side of the inscriptions or signatures of the artist. They can show the name or nickname of the artist, or the artist's birth year, or even some poetic phrase describing the mood of the artist when the piece was done. Sometimes, the seals can be used as an additional tool for authentication of an artwork. Thus, seal carving is a closely related art to calligraphy and painting, and many calligraphers are also into seal carving.

In contrast to calligraphy and painting, done with a soft brush, seal carving entails the use of a knife to carve into hard stone, with the carving surface normally just a square inch, or less. Another difference is that what is carved on the stone must be the mirror image of the intended imprint, similarly to a date stamp. Usually done in an ancient script, a good carving artist will arrange the characters or words to be carved into an elegant and artistic design.

While in Shanghai, I studied the art of carving, and produced several pieces of work. As interesting as this art form is, I had to quit after I came to the United States to study. The lack of time made it difficult to put to use the stone sticks and carving knives my father packed in my luggage.

Poetry (詩) and Lyrical Poetry (詞)

Thinking back, I was struck by the fact that, in my Chinese literature training over the years, I never encountered a course in poetry or lyrical poetry. Then what factors gave rise to my interest in poetry? What caused me to self-teach the rules of poetry writing, including the format rules, the use of "couplets (對聯)" (two verses that contrast against each other), and the recognition of the tones (平仄) of the words used?

The simple fact was that I wrote my first poem, with eight verses of five words each, on the joyous occasion of China's victory, in 1945, over the Japanese invaders. A series of love poems followed, but everything poetic was put aside once I arrived at the University of Colorado. The academic work was heavy enough to keep me away from poetry for a number of years.

It wasn't until the second or third year of my teaching that I found the time to indulge in poetry again. By that time my interest was more in lyrical poetry (詞) which, being set to music in ancient times, has especially strict rules regarding the tones of the words chosen. There are hundreds of music patterns developed during the Song Dynasty (宋朝), 960–1279. The distinguishing feature of lyrical poetry is the varying lengths of the verses, as against the same number of words in each verse in the style of poetry of the Tang Dynasty (唐朝).

I have written quite a few of lyrical poems. Unfortunately, I have no training in English poetry, and find it impossible for me to translate them into English.

Photography

One of the early expensive purchases I made in the United States was a camera, a Kodak 35, which was mainly motivated by my parents' request to send pictorial report of my life in America. But the fun of photography soon won me over, and I became an eager learner, not content with plain snapshots. I read photography books and magazine articles. Kodak films, both black-and-white and color, costs of developing, printing, and enlargements all became regular items in the monthly budgets.

The basic sense of composition I already acquired from painting helped. But I also learned much from books and magazine articles. One of the basic principles is to avoid clutter. Each picture has a main subject to show, and all extraneous, distracting objects are best excluded from the scene. Have you ever seen a great photo with a disarray of stray of cups and glasses on the table, or a pile of toys on the floor?

A well-composed photo should have balance, unless you want to create an intentional imbalance for effect. It makes a difference, for instance, when a couple of smaller trees are included to counterbalance a big tree trunk on the other side of the picture.

An early compositional trick I learned is to "frame" a picture. Don't shoot a plain person, or a building or whatever, but try to include a little branch with a few flowing leaves in the top part of the scene, or something, to serve as a "frame." Sometimes, a nearby archway can frame a farther away landscape. The frame not only improves the composition, making it less monotonous, but also adds to perception of distance to the picture, the frame being nearby, and the main subject being farther away. An example of "framing" can be seen in Photo 7 in the front of this book.

A more sophisticated technique I learned is "selective focus." Once I saw a photo of a sharply focused rose against a fuzzy background with faint color. It struck me as 100 times better than a monotonous photo of a rose with a plain white background. It is also superior to a photo of a rose against a background of a wall with a painting hanging on it, or with a distracting wallpaper pattern. By including a fuzzy background of faint color, the rose is made to stand out, though not in a barren setting. This effect is achieved by using a wide lens opening, which reduces the depth of field, allowing the objects within a specific range of distances to stay in focus, but throwing objects beyond that range out of focus. I have used this technique for Emily's portraits, in Photos 13 and 14 in the front of this book.

Photo 14 also illustrates the use of "backlighting," with the main source of illumination coming from behind the subject, Emily. The backlit subject would then have some highlight on her hair, and the light on her back and shoulder will set her apart from the background, enhancing the feeling of depth. Of course, as a disadvantage, backlighting tends to make the subject's face appear darker. To remedy that, I used a while cardboard as a reflector of the sunlight, to give some modeling to Emily's face. I also made sure that the reflector produced some catchlight in her eyes.

Three Canons and a Lone Leica

Those two portraits of Emily were not taken by my Kodak 35. By that time, I had already graduated to more advanced cameras. I have owned a Canon FTb, a 35 mm single-lens reflex (SLR) camera, and later a Canon AE-1 Program, also an SLR. The so-called SLR has one feature I consider extremely useful: what you see in the viewfinder of the camera is exactly what will appear in that frame of film. This assures precision in pre-shot composition.

Later on, I bought two interchangeable lenses with different focal lengths. With the wide-angle lens, I am able to include more objects on my left and on my right into a picture. With the telephoto lens, on the other hand, I can make a faraway object appear closer, and look bigger in the picture. But since it takes time to dismantle one lens from the camera body, before installing another, it is inconvenient to use them when the subjects are a bunch of impatient people. For this reason, I also bought a zoom lens that allows me to change instantly from 35 to 105 mm focal lengths, by a simple twisting of the barrel of the zoom lens.

Once I acquired the zoom lens, I tended to rely exclusively on it for travel photos. I could easily select the wide-angle setting to shoot a group photo of many people, or switch to a telephoto setting to capture a snow-capped mountain located far, far away. The only drawback is that the zoom lens juts out in the front of the camera, like Cyrano's nose, and my Canon AE-1 looks extremely bulky, somewhat funny looking, and heavy to carry.

My Canon AE-1 with the zoom lens actually also served me well for photography of events. When John Fei (費景漢), a fellow economist and Chinese opera enthusiast, married Alice Chang (張立和), I took several rolls of pictures at the ceremony, as a wedding present. At such events, held indoors, flashlight was a must, and the photos necessarily came out looking more flat than without flash. But they were a well-composed record of the happy event. When the newlyweds took those photos to our opera association gathering, they duly impressed one of the ladies, whose understanding of photography involves nothing but "point and shoot." After looking at the wedding pictures, she exclaimed with excitement, "Alpha took those pictures? Wow, he has a such a wonderful camera!" To her, the camera is the key, not the photographer.

So many things have undergone drastic changes through the decades in a lifetime that it almost defies belief. The manual typewriter has evolved into electric typewriter, word processor, and computer. Eyeglasses have given way to hard contact lenses, and then soft contact lenses. Flying has gone from propellers to jet engines, to rockets. In photography, black-and-white film yielded to color films, and now photography has gone digital.

My interest in photography has waned enough for me not to step into the digital realm. But an opportunity to get a digital camera with "frequent-flyer miles," I decided to make the exchange. The digital camera is a Canon Power Shot 5X50 HS, with a built-in zoom lens with focal lengths from 4.3 to 215 mm. It took me a long time to learn to operate the new camera, but I did use it on a European trip, a cruise on the Danube. Soon, however, I discovered that the camera feature on the iPhone my son Darryl gave me is in fact an excellent instrument.

It's so light to carry (pocket-size), and so easy to operate (no special learning needed), and it even allows editing (such as cropping) right on the iPhone. These advantages are sufficient for me to retire all the fancy cameras I own. Of course, many of the creative photography functions are not there in the iPhone camera, but the picture quality produced is commendable to excellent.

A convenience feature that I have learned of late makes me treasure the iPhone camera even more. It's a shortcut access to the camera on the iPhone: After you turn on the phone, there is no need to enter the password, and click on the camera icon. When the phone is on, just swipe the screen to the left, and your camera comes on immediately, ready for picture-taking!

What about the Leica? Well, bless Emily, my Leica is an expensive surprise gift she kindly gave me. Its special feature is that, by inserting a filter in the film chamber, it can produce pictures in the panoramic format, not a very essential advantage. But its viewfinder, marked with white instead of black border lines, makes it difficult to determine the edges of the picture field. I did use it a few times, but despite its high price, it never became my favorite camera.

Caricatures

I experimented with cartooning ever since I started my homemade Christmas cards in 1953. Even though I admired people who can draw caricatures, likenesses of subjects with exaggerated and distorted facial or bodily features for satirical effects, I knew that I could never do them. For years, I eagerly looked forward to the works of Al Hirschfeld in the *New York Times*, all incredibly clever caricatures of theatrical celebrities, such as Frank Sinatra, Jack Benny, Katherine Hepburn, the Beatles, Marlene Dietrich, Luciano Pavarotti, and so on. He showed such simplicity, embodying in a few simple lines the essence of a face or a body that would unmistakably identify a particular personality. It's an almost impossible job.

Imagine my excitement when I learned that Tony Parisi, an artist and caricaturist, was offering an eight-week evening course on

Caricatures in the spring of 2003 at a venue close to my home. I was living in White Plains, New York, after retirement, and Mr. Parisi's class took place on the campus of the Scarsdale High School, only about 15 minutes away. Even with knowledge that I lacked the specific kind of talent, I nevertheless yielded to the temptation of another venture, and enrolled right away.

Mr. Parisi, a good teacher, started by teaching the basics about the human body and the human face. Regarding body proportion, he asked the students to draw a vertical string of eight ovals. The top oval should be where the head is. A horizontal line through the second oval indicates where the shoulder is to be located. The hip is within the fourth oval. A horizontal line through the bottom of the fourth oval pinpoints the location of the crotch. And, the last four ovals determine the position of the legs. This regular body proportion is, of course, subject to modification as demanded by the needs of exaggeration and intended distortion—such as for a person with an oversized head, or a stubby person with short legs.

A face can be shown in the front view, or side view, or something in between. It can be drawn as looking down, or looking up. Using an egg-shaped oval to depict the front view of the head, the eye level should normally be halfway from the top of the head. But, again, the level is adjustable up or down depending on the needs of distortion. What Mr. Parisi did in his demonstration was to start with a photograph of an actor from a movie advertisement, or of a politician from a news story. On regular sketch paper, he would first draw a normal likeness. Then, on a piece of translucent tracing paper placed on top of the portrait, he would alter the original by introducing some exaggerations into the (1) eyes (making them closer together or wider apart, and/or larger or smaller); (2) nose (longer or shorter, and/or wider or narrower); (3) mouth (widened or narrowed down, and/or showing more teeth or less). Other parts of the face, including eyebrows, ears, or the chin, would then be modified next. Then, with a second piece of tracing paper on top of the first piece, further distortions are added. This process went on until a final version is arrived at that portrays the subject's personality with sufficient emphasis on the prominent parts of the face and body (such as Jay Leno's protruding chin, Phyllis Diller's

38.2 Three caricatures I drew, 2003.

up-shooting hair, Jackie Gleason's bulging eyes, or Marlene Dietrich's sleepy eyelids) to enable the viewer to identify unmistakably to whom the distorted face belongs.

Those eight weeks of caricature lessons involved a lot of hard work and thinking, but the pleasure they gave me was commensurate. I show here three of the works I did for the class. I am sure you can easily tell that the two male characters are Woody Allen and Sammy Davis, Jr. The third one, a female, is more difficult to identify, partly because ladies' facial features, being generally softer than men's, are more difficult to draw. If you do succeed in recognizing her, more power to you! If you can't, sorry, the fault is entirely mine. If you must know, that face is supposed to depict the celebrated actress Meryl Streep.

Rabbit Collection

I have no recollection of when I started to collect rabbits—not live rabbits, but those miniature rabbits made of wood, silver, brass, jade, glass, crystal, pewter, ivory, marble, stone, and clay. There is a simple reason why I focused on rabbits rather than other animals: I was born in a Year of the Rabbit in the tradition of Chinese astrology involving a cycle of 12 real or mythical animals.

The latest count in my collection is 38 pieces. The first rabbit I ever had is a tiny one sitting on top of a column-shaped, uncarved seal stone. The idea was that I would one day carve it as a personal seal to be used on my painting or calligraphy pieces. But I never found the time and mood to do the carving.

Among the other rabbits in my possession, the smallest is a pewter one, a gift from my mother. Only ¾ of an inch long, it is easy to overlook it when it is placed alongside the others. In contrast, the largest one, which I bought in Mexico, is fully eight inches long and over five inches high. It is heavy enough to serve as a sturdy doorstop. In between these two of extreme sizes, I have rabbits made in various poses, standing, crouching, lying on one side of the body, or running.

Aside from the pewter one from my mother, which has obvious sentimental value, I especially treasure two rabbits, both being gifts from my daughter Tracey. I already referred to them briefly in Chapter 24, but some more details are in order here. One of these two rabbits, made of clay, was a Christmas present she made with her own hands when she was only 7 or 8 years old. It was well crafted, and she won a compliment from an artist who was at the party when Tracey presented it to me, especially for her treatment of the rabbit ears. She cleverly made the two ears lie flat on the rabbit's body, thereby obviating the difficulty of modeling upstanding ears. The other gift from Tracey is a glass one she bought when we were touring a glass factory in Venice in 1979. What made this rabbit extra special was that, for this purchase, she spent her entire allowance, leaving no money to buy anything for herself. I tried, for reciprocation, to find out whether she liked anything among the wares on display, but she said nothing there struck her fancy.

The two rabbits from Tracey are shown in Photo 24.3. Photo 24.4 shows my rabbit collection except for the huge doorstop one, which is too bulky for inclusion in the picture. The smallest rabbit, in the foreground middle, is my mother's gift to me.

City Pins

Another collectible item that has had my sustained interest over the years is city pins, mostly from European cities I visited on different trips. I display them on one side of a dark blue beret I bought in Maastricht, the Netherlands. Later, as the number of pins grew, I bought another beret, a black one this time, to accommodate the overflow. Finally, pins spilled over onto a baseball hat.

Some of these pins came to me easily. They were available at the small souvenir shops we saw on a trip. But, for some of them I had to hunt from store to store. Some cities either had no pins or somehow managed to hide them from me completely. (I don't have one from Maastricht, my favorite city, because none was available.) My collection does include pins from Brussels, Strasbourg, Salzburg, Vienna, Florence, London, Paris, Rome, Venice, Munich, Barcelona, Lisbon, Rotterdam, Prague, Budapest, Bratislava, Pushkin, Bermuda, Victoria, and Costa Rica. For each of these, some fond memories always exist. They are interesting in their own ways.

38.3 Two berets with my city pins.

The pin from Salzburg brings to mind the awesome visit to Mozart's birth-house, where I saw the handwritten score of a composition of his. I could not believe how neat it looked, almost completely devoid of corrections—in sharp contrast to Beethoven's manuscript, usually very messy with lots of changes. This pin also reminds me of the underground salt mine we visited there, using a slide to go down to the cave below. (*Salz* is German for salt.)

The Barcelona pin of course is dominantly associated with its landmark, Antoni Gaudi's renowned Church of the Holy Family, whose tall, slender spires bear a close resemblance to the rocks surrounding the Montserrat Monastery outside of Barcelona. Could those rocks have been Gaudi's inspiration? I wondered.

For me, the more memorable event in Barcelona was a dinner at a tapas restaurant, *Ciudad Condal*, recommended by the hotel where we stayed. Our friends, Herbert and Mary Chu, and Dann and Catarina Chi, went together with Emily and me, and we had a really delicious yet inexpensive dinner. Especially good were the baby squids, which we re-ordered as many as three times. The manager, a young lady, was very friendly, and I asked her the meaning of the restaurant's name. In spite of a language problem, she made it clear that *ciudad* means "city," but the word *condal* she did not know the English equivalent of. But, cleverly, she resorted to a roundabout way of explaining. She first signaled a crown on the head. I said, "king?" After saying "No," she lowered her hands. I said, "Duke?" She shook her head and lowered her hands another notch. Then I said, "Count?" and got an affirmative answer from her. That semi-conversation occurred in 1999. As I write this, though, I suddenly think of checking out this information on Google Translate. The translations for *ciudad* and *condal* are indeed "city" and "count," but when I punched in the two words *ciudad condal* together, the translation comes out as "Barcelona." Maybe those two words constitute a nickname for that city—like Big Apple for New York City?

What does the pin for Munich remind me of? One thing was the roasted chestnuts Emily and I bought from a street vender there. In my Shanghai days, I often used to buy roasted chestnuts from street stalls and stores in the fall season for snack. Many years later, I now encountered the same snack on the streets of Munich. Somehow, the Munich version was not nearly as flavorful as the Shanghai version. But the nostalgia factor made up for it.

A more costly purchase I made in Munich was from a department store in a Munich mall. During the evening stroll after dinner, we passed by this shop window with a good-looking vest on display. We went in and was waited on by a young saleslady of Asian ancestry. It turned out that she was from Hong Kong, although she did not show any special friendliness to us, perhaps because we could not speak Cantonese. But her facial features and general demeanor indicated beauty, elegance, and high culture. She patiently let me try on several pieces of that vest of different colors and patterns. Unfortunately, none of these would go well with the clothing I normally wear. After the sixth or seventh one I tried on, I felt obliged to buy one, and Emily helped me pick one with the color closest to what could go with my wardrobe. It was a well-made vest. I bought it in 1989 and, after so many years, I can no longer button it up. But I can still wear it with the front open, sometimes getting compliments.

The Vienna pin brought back the story of a late train in 1989. Emily and I were in Maastricht, the Netherlands, for a "Study Abroad" semester, and we planned to visit James and Belinda Ho, Emily's brother and sister-in-law, then residing in Vienna. Celebrated for punctuality, the German train we took for an overnight ride was nevertheless late for a whole hour. Emily became very much worried about her brother having to wait so long for our late train the next morning. But the first thing James said to us was, "I am so glad you are late! I got lost and I just arrived at the train station, too." The reason for his lateness was that he was only familiar with the geography of another train station, but we were arriving at a different one, new to him. When we got to their home, Belinda already prepared a delicious Chinese breakfast for us. She also related to us a call she received from James half an hour earlier:

"Hello, Belinda," James said with frustration, "I am lost."

"Oh, sorry. Where are you now?"

"I don't know where I am. If I knew where I am, I wouldn't be LOST!"

"Ok, then why don't you come home first and I'll go with you."

"But I don't know how to come home."

"Then why are you calling me?!"

Eventually, a kind Austrian gentleman who happened to be going to our train station asked James to follow him, and we met at the station without further problem. We all had a big laugh afterward, but the situation was not at all funny before it was resolved.

We had a wonderful visit with James and Belinda. We also enjoyed a concert given by an all-Chinese orchestra composed of the music students currently studying in Austria. So many of them with so much talent!

The pins from Prague and Budapest came into my possession in 2014 during a trip through Europe that Darryl invited us to for our diamond (60th) anniversary. Since he could not come to our anniversary party, he wanted to make it up by inviting us to a cruise. Prague was our first stop, and Budapest, our last. Darryl made reservations at Michelin-starred restaurants. At *Onyx*, a restaurant in Budapest, we had a big dinner, 6-course with wine pairing. At *La Dégustation Bohême Bourgeoise*, a restaurant in Prague, we had an even more elaborate dinner, 11-course with wine pairing. But I will report on that trip in more details in Chapter 41, in relation to our diamond anniversary.

Mini Crossword Puzzles

Having tried crossword puzzles several times in newspapers, I decided generally to avoid them, simply because they are too time-consuming. But once Emily alerted me that the *New York Times* has started a "mini" crossword puzzle feature, usually in the 5 × 5 dimension, I became interested in exploring it. Five-letter words are easy to find if the clues are clearly given. The fact that such mini puzzles do involve a measure of mild, but never overwhelming, challenges, and are solvable within three to five minutes, makes it a suitable pastime during breakfasts. I have made it a routine game at the beginning of a day. And Emily's interest in the same game has made the morning game a joint venture. The puzzles on Saturdays are larger, 7 × 7, but even those are manageable.

After many weeks of mini puzzles, I found an uncanny result in the solution for the puzzle of January 21, 2019. Emily was amazed, too. The excitement was strong enough for me to email the puzzle to Darryl and Tracey. After solving it, Darryl emailed back in a few minutes his reaction. "Supernatural!" he wrote. Tracey's reaction was, "What are the chances of that happening?"

What caused these reactions? It was two things: (1) The clue for 5-across is "Dominant personality," with the answer "Alpha." (2) The clue for 7-across is "Blunt who starts in the Mary Poppins remake," with the answer "Emily." Thus, both of our names happen to appear, horizontally, in the solution of the very same puzzle! And this awakened me to something I had not paid attention to before: Both of our names have five letters in them.

I also emailed the puzzle to my former colleague Peter Barth who is into this sort of puzzles. His reply was: "Amazing and fun. When do you and Emily leave for Paris and will you stop in Chile on the way home?" At first, I did not quite understand why he would mention Paris and Chile in his reply about that puzzle. But, after taking another look at the puzzle, I realized that, having placed my focus on the two names Alpha and Emily, I had neglected the other answers in the solution. "Paris" is the answer to the clue "Home of the Louvre Museum." "Chile" is the answer to the clue "Country that's around 2,650 miles tall but only averages 110 miles in width." In addition, I noticed the words "April" (Fourth month), "Lace" (Wedding dress material), and "Sale" (Black Friday event) in the solution. Putting these words together, I wrote back to Peter Barth, "Emily and I will go to Paris in April to take advantage of a sale of lace, and then return via Chile."

39

Donald Trump's Brother

Ever since I started learning English as a child, I have felt a strange attraction to long words. The multiple syllables make the pronunciation of such words a challenge to overcome. An equally weighty challenge is to master the spelling of these long beasts. One of the first of these is the word *manufacture,* with four syllables and as many as 11 letters in it. It was a moment of triumph when it dawned on me that both the pronunciation and the spelling would become easier if I compartmentalized the word into smaller units: ma, nu, fac, ture.

Sometimes, rarely used words also attracted my attention. But the fact that they are rarely used means that they can be easily forgotten. That would not be a big loss. But two rare words that I learned from a newspaper article years ago—actually decades ago—have for some unknown reason stuck in my memory, without any conscious effort on my part to remember them.

Two Minor Body Parts

Those two words are names for two minor body parts that, unlike hands, feet, nose, or ears, are not referred to very often. One is the vertical indentation extending from the bottom of the nose to the top of the upper lip. In the Chinese culture, this indentation, called *renzhong* (人中), is endowed with a great significance, because a long *renzhong* portends a long life in the pseudo-science of Chinese physiognomy. But, as far as I know, this indentation is not important for anything in the Western culture. Nevertheless, it has a name: *philtrum.*

The other minor body part I read about is part of a hand, the space between one's forefinger and thumb when they are extended away from each other—like the Nike logo. In Chinese, this is called *hukou* (虎口, literally tiger's mouth). I recall that, when I was a child, we used the *hukou* as a built-in measuring device in the absence of a ruler. By extending the thumb away from the forefinger, we use the linear distance from the tip of the thumb to the tip of the forefinger as a unit measure. Naturally, that distance would be called "one *hukou.*" This is never an accurate measure, it being directly dependent on the size of the person's hand. I am not sure whether Western children also use such a crude measuring device. But there is an English word for the tiger's mouth: *purlicue.*

Enters Trump

Those two words cannot be worked into conversations with ease. The only occasions on which I could call on them were when I said to my friends, "Do you know the name of that . . .?" Surprisingly, many of my friends showed interest in learning these words, but found them difficult to remember. To help them, I spent some effort in finding a mnemonic device for the word *philtrum.* Success came when I invented a fictitious brother for Donald Trump.

This fictitious brother, Philip Trump, has a fictitious rare allergy. He is allergic to the sound of the letter P when it appears at the end of a word, as in cop or tap. Unfortunately for him, both his first name and the last name end with the letter p. So, he has to do something drastic: drop the last letter to shorten his last name to "Trum." Similarly, he has to chop off the last two letters in his first name, shortening it to Phil. The letter P still appears in the first name, but since the two letters ph together are pronounced as the letter f, it does not bother him. Now, his official name becomes Phil Trum, which, by easy extension, leads to the word *philtrum*!

I don't know whether that story truly helped my friends to remember this word. But I myself have found it helpful.

I made a lot of additional effort to find a comparable fiction for the word *purlicue.* But no inspiration came to me. The only clue I can suggest is that it rhymes with curlicue, a word for the curly flourish at the end of a word in a person's handwriting. In fact, the word *purlicue* also substitutes as a synonym for the word *curlicue.*

I am still in search for a story as a mnemonic device for the word *purlicue*. If you, the reader, can construct such a story, please be sure to let me know. If it qualifies as an effective mnemonic device, I will gladly take you (plus a guest of your choice) to dinner at a fine restaurant of my choice. That's a promise.

40

An Omniscient Herbal Doctor

In my first 20 years, while a resident of Shanghai, we had access to medical services from two distinct types of doctors. Western-trained doctors took care of certain diseases, but Chinese traditional doctors would be preferred for other ailments. The former group prescribed pills and tablets manufactured by Western pharmaceutical companies; the latter group used herbs and plants for medication, although they also used mineral substances, available in Chinese-style pharmacies. In China, we refer to the two groups, respectively, as "Western doctors" and "Chinese doctors." But, here in America, since the term "Chinese doctors" could also mean "Western-style doctors who happen to be Chinese," I'll simply refer to the traditional Chinese-style doctors as "herbal doctors," even though they use mineral substances and even animal parts as well.

Herbal medicine has been practiced in China for thousands of years, and I have always had a strong respect for it. One of its nice features is that instead of targeting a specific point of ailment, herbal doctors tend to pay attention to the harmonious functioning of all organs in the human body together. But one aspect of herbal medicine turns me off: the herbs prescribed need to go through a long cooking process that produces a pungent odor around the house, before yielding a bitter-tasting potion most unpleasant to swallow.

Since coming to the United States, I did not see any herbal doctor even though a few of them are available in Chinatown. Then, in 2002, our good friend Catarina Chi recommended an herbal doctor to check Emily out after she developed a chronic shortness-of-breath problem.

Herbal Doctor Chang

Around the turn of the century, we were very active dancers. But Emily gradually found herself out of breath in the middle of a dance number. Then some pain on her shoulder started to bother her even more than the shortness of breath. Our family doctor, Dr. Preston Winters, reached an easy conclusion: the culprit is either her lung or her heart. “Let’s first consult a pulmonary specialist,” he advised, “and then, if necessary, a cardiologist.”

It took the lung doctor almost three months’ testing to determine, in April 2001, that Emily had no problem in her lungs. We planned to consult a cardiologist next. Before we did that, however, our friend Catarina Chi suggested that we should see a very good herbal doctor, Dr. Wen-chi Chang (張文旗醫師), who practiced in Vancouver, Canada, but also regularly came to New Jersey to see patients in this area.

We made an appointment with Dr. Chang for September 12, 2001. But the day before our appointed time, there occurred an earth-shaking event that drastically changed things. Early in the morning on September 11, I was awakened by a phone call from a cousin in Taiwan, urgently asking me, “Do you live near the World Trade Center?” Being rudely disrupted in my sleep, I was sufficiently annoyed to retort in a scolding voice, “It’s still early morning here! Why would you wake me up just to ask me where I live?!” She replied, “Well, I don’t have time to explain. Just turn on your TV, quick!” When I saw the airplane attack on the World Trade Center in Manhattan on the TV screen, I immediately apologized to her for my impolite tone, and expressed my appreciation for her concern. I assured her that we lived far from the World Trade Center, out of the area of danger.

Understandably, on account of the infamous “9/11,” Dr. Chang postponed his visit to New Jersey. And we did not get to see him until December, in a temporary clinic in his motel room in New Providence, New Jersey.

This doctor looked unusual, mainly because he had inordinately long sideburns hanging down beside his left and right ears. But his general manners exuded confidence. His first instruction to Emily was,

"Don't tell *me* anything about your health; let me tell *you* what's wrong with you after I examine you." His examination was incredibly simple; it consisted mainly of placing his fingers over her wrist area, to gauge how her blood was flowing and how her body was functioning. He would first use two fingers, and then three fingers, then two fingers in a different combination and different position to feel how the pulse was going. After just about two or three minutes, he announced his diagnosis in an unequivocal voice. "You have no Alzheimer's disease and no cancer anywhere," he said, "and your lungs are fine, but one of your arteries has a blockage, about 40%. Otherwise, you are healthy." After a sip of water, he added, "That blockage, by the way, needs no surgery. I can successfully treat it with herbal medicine."

I was impressed by his diagnosis of Emily's lungs. It confirmed the pulmonary tests. But the amazing thing was that what took the Western doctor three months to find, Dr. Chang reached the same conclusion within two or three minutes! Not only that, within those same minutes, he also reached a conclusion about Emily's heart condition! Even though the artery diagnosis was yet to be verified by a Western cardiologist, I was confident that it would be.

Dr. Chang's consultation was free of charge, but his medicine carried a high price. Sufficiently impressed with his medical skills, we decided to go with his prescription anyway. The good news was that, because of new technology, we did not have to cook the herbs. He would prepare them into pellets individually wrapped and marked "A" (for Mondays, Wednesdays, and Fridays) or "B" (for Tuesdays, Thursdays, and Saturdays), also marked "Morning," "Noon," and "Evening." That means three pellets every day, except Sundays. The cost came to as much as $40 per day, but I had no hesitation about accepting his treatment.

One More Patient

We were about to leave, when Dr. Chang asked me whether he could give me an examination, too. I had no ailments at the time, but was curious enough to agree to his invitation. Who knew? Maybe I could have some medical problem(s) that I wasn't aware of. He placed his fingers on my wrist briefly. To my great surprise, he not only declared that I was totally healthy, but also added an unexpected comment about my life expectancy. He first asked for my age, and then said with a pleased sigh, "Mr. Chiang, your internal organs are functioning as if you are 20 years younger than your chronological age. To tell the truth, you are only the second person among my patients to display this phenomenon. I am happy to have met you. In fact, I dare say that you will undoubtedly live to a hundred."

That was a nice piece of prediction to hear from a doctor that had already impressed me. But, surely, this kind of prediction should only be taken with several grains of salt. His remarks prompted me to ponder over the possible reasons for my propitious prognosis. Perhaps I have good genes. I also heard that my mother breastfed me for an unusually long time after my birth—three years. But another contributory factor could be the fact that, for a few decades, I have practiced a daily routine of acupressure on many of the acupoints I recognize on my body. Especially important, in my own evaluation, is the massaging of my two ears inside and out every day. I have been told that every organ in the body has nerves extending to the human ears. Regular massaging of the ears should therefore stimulate and benefit the various organs in the human body.

Again, as we were getting ready to leave, the doctor had something more to say—this time with a commercial bent. He said that, if I am interested, he can prescribe herbal medicine to retard my aging process. I thought to myself, "If I am already going to live to a hundred, do I need any more retardation agent?" But, then, in a very positive mood at the time, I answered, "Why not." Maybe it was again the perfectionist in me that urged me to "make it even better."

The medicine was expensive. But it turned out that the cost was well worth it. After the medicine he mailed to me took effect, I could feel my legs stepping on the ground much more solidly than before. We made repeat visits to Dr. Chang a few times, about once every two months. And we stopped seeing him only because he later decided to discontinue his visits to New Jersey.

Angiogram

About two or three months after we saw Dr. Chang, Emily went to see a Western cardiologist as we had planned. In line with our expectations, there were a series of tests, starting with the stress test and the echo test. The cardiologist, Dr. Adina Pascaru, recommended to Emily by her brother Johnny, was a very cautious lady physician. Knowing that Johnny has some heart problem, she probably presumed that Emily might also have it. Thus, she prescribed an angiogram for Emily, which is an invasive procedure involving injecting some dye into the patient's blood stream, and therefore carries some risk. But it has a big advantage: it can render a definitive diagnosis by giving a clearly printed image of the arteries, with blockages, if any, marked in black.

The result from the angiogram procedure was astounding: Emily had one of the arteries blocked, and the blockage was 40%. This result was precisely what our herbal doctor diagnosed! It was at that point we became total believers of Dr. Chang. He has given us instant diagnosis with perfect accuracy, fully supported and verified by definitive tests by Western doctors.

There was a side effect of this angiogram confirmation. Dr. Chang's prediction of my life span now carried more weight. Still, it's only a prediction, and nothing more.

More about Dr. Chang

On our later visits, I learned a bit more about this amazing herbal doctor. He first learned herbal medicine from his brother-in-law in Taiwan, and later attended traditional medical school in Mainland China. But he also studied the basics of Western medicine, and explained things to me using Western anatomical diagrams.

I asked him what specifically does he try to find from his digital examination of the patient's wrist area. His answer related mostly to blood flows: Whether they are rhythmic? How energetic is the flow? Are they intermittently sluggish? With two fingers, or three fingers in different positions, he could access information related to different parts of the patient's body.

I also asked him why he prescribed the pellets for different days and different times of the day. His answer was simple, "I try to target different parts of the body with different pellets at different times."

Another Angiogram

Both Emily and I took Dr. Chang's herbal pellets for quite a few months, until he stopped coming to New Jersey. If he lived somewhat closer to us, we would have taken special trips to see him. But Western Canada was too far for us. Even so, we felt we benefited from his treatment.

Emily had occasion to have a checkup with Dr. Pascaru, the cardiologist, again. The timing was just before we planned to embark on a Mediterranean cruise in October 2008 with eight friends on the new ship Queen Victoria. Overly cautious, the doctor ordered another angiogram for Emily before our trip, about six and half years after the first one. This time, the printed image showed her blockage completely cleared.

We felt relieved. And we also wondered how much of this welcome result was due to Dr. Chang's herbal pellets, and how much it was due to other changes in Emily's self-enforced health habits, such as eating oatmeal breakfast every day. My vote goes to the pellets.

41

Diamond Anniversary

If a golden wedding anniversary (50 years) is worth celebrating, then a diamond wedding anniversary (60 years) must be doubly so. The husband and the wife must not only be both alive, but also still remain married to each other. I am very proud of the fact that I can report in the present chapter not one, but two celebrations of diamond anniversary, one for my parents and one for Emily and me.

Mandarin Ducks: Symbol of Marital Devotion

The exact date of my parents' diamond anniversary was in January 1986, but to coordinate our trip to Hong Kong with our children's school holiday schedule, we had to celebrate the event early, near Christmas time in 1985.

In the meantime, we tried to think of an appropriate present to Mom and Dad. In the Chinese culture, an affectionate married couple is often likened to a pair of mandarin ducks (鴛鴦), because these colorful ducks always appear in a pair, a male and a female, amorously attached to each other. I tried hard to hunt for a pair of artistic mandarin ducks, whether made of wood, porcelain, or metals. But all my search efforts were in vain. The American culture simply does not admit this Chinese concept of mandarin ducks as a symbol of love. I thought of a painting of mandarin ducks, but, unfortunately, my painting training was limited to landscapes.

Imagine my joy when, one day, I spotted one porcelain mandarin duck in a department store. Excitedly, I asked a saleslady, "Where is the other one in the pair?" Her response was a blank stare, and a succinct reply, "This is one of a kind, not a pair."

As a result, I still had no mandarin ducks when our plane landed in Hong Kong. Fortunately, it occurred to me that they might be available at a local arts-and-crafts store, and I did finally find a pair of cloisonné mandarin ducks in time. Though somewhat smaller in size than I had hoped for, this pair was esthetically acceptable, and I purchased it with a relieved sigh without hesitation.

My parents held a religious service at his church, Shanghai Christian Church, on December 23. In addition to the mandarin ducks, our children presented to my parents a pair of pewter cups from Malaysia, inscribed with the four Chinese characters 福祿壽喜 (pronounced as *fu lu shou xi* in Mandarin), all expressing auspicious wishes. Father and Mother both made speeches, followed by me, Emily, Darryl, and Tracey. I was impressed with my parents' speeches for their devotion and humor, Emily's for her sincere admiration of my parents as role models, and the children's speeches delivered entirely in Chinese (Photo 41.1–41.3).

41.1 Mandarin ducks for my parents' 60th anniversary (1986 photo).

41.2 Emily's speech at the church service.

41.3 Darryl and Tracey making their speeches.

Because the church was busy with Christmas season events, the banquet was held a few days later on December 28. My father knew the managers of most of the restaurants because he used to make arrangements for all his church members when they needed to have banquet functions. Hence, he could always assemble a high-quality menu at a reasonable price at social events, including his own diamond anniversary.

Photo 3 in the front of this book captures the moment of our family toast at this 60th anniversary banquet, held in Hong Kong in 1986.

Our Own 60th Anniversary

Emily and I had to wait for almost 30 years after my parents' diamond anniversary before celebrating our own. Ten years before that, for our golden anniversary in 2004, we gave two parties, a dinner–dance and a Chinese opera singing party. Should we do the dual celebration again?

"Tradition" was a good argument for repeating the "two-party system." But Emily had for some time been bothered by a lower back pain. Besides, something terrible had happened to Emily in the meantime, affecting her ability to dance. I therefore decided not to give a dance party this time around, but to limit the celebration to a Chinese opera party alone.

A Broken Patella

What happened to Emily was that she took a hard fall in August 2012 on the sidewalk in Flushing, New York, on our way to a restaurant. As a consequence, she was required to stay in as many as three hospitals, undergo surgery, and live with an unwell knee.

On that fateful day, we were planning to join Johnny and Pearl, Emily's brother and sister-in-law, for dinner. Since Darryl was in town from California, they invited him too, along with Tracey's family. Normally, when walking on streets and sidewalks, especially in crowded Flushing, Emily always held on to my arm for safety. But, on that day, while Darryl and I were talking during the short walk from the parking space to the restaurant, Emily somehow went on ahead by herself, and almost immediately tripped on a piece of cement that had been pushed up by the root of a tree. She fell forward, and injured her right knee, and even broke her patella. With our help, she managed to hop into the restaurant, but the intolerable pain forced us to call an ambulance right away to take her to the nearby New York Hospital, Queens. She, Darryl, and I ended up not having dinner at that restaurant at all.

Despite our wish to go to a hospital in White Plains, the New York Hospital insisted on keeping Emily there for three days. I discovered later that the three-day stay was for the purpose of complying with one of the Medicare regulations. Eventually, Emily was moved to Burke Rehabilitation Hospital in White Plains. This famous rehab facility, conveniently located near where we lived at the time, is where the "Superman" Christopher Reeves did his rehab. For Emily, there was at one time some hope of her knee bone healing by itself. But that hope soon evaporated. And, after a week, she was moved to the Westchester Medical Center for surgery by a Dr. David Asprino. Then, she returned to Burke again, where we spent our 58th wedding anniversary.

In the recovery phase, she needed to use a wheelchair and then a walker, and finally a cane. For nearly four months, she could not operate the automobile, and I had my "Driving Miss Emily" period from August to December in 2012. Having to wear a brace for 10 weeks forced her to walk in an unbalanced manner, producing a bad side effect. Dancing had now become a challenge, because it was not easy to put her weight on her right foot for any length of time.

That period of recuperation was difficult for another reason. We were in the process of selling our White Plains home, for a move to a continuing care retirement community, Cedar Crest, in northern New Jersey.

The Chinese Opera Party

For our Chinese opera party, we invited around 40 guests on September 7 (three days after our anniversary date) for singing in the Catering Room at Cedar Crest, followed by a banquet at Chengdu 23 Restaurant in Wayne, New Jersey.

To minimize possible noise disturbance, I decided not to use any percussion instruments. But our guest list included the top-rank amateur musicians, including James Wang (王正明醫生), Alice Tu (張昭平), Roger Yeu (樂亦平), Peter Lu (盧德先), George Yan (嚴仁安老師), and myself. We took turns to sing our favorite arias, making up a lively musical afternoon. But I could not be sure what the community residents might think, when they heard the unfamiliar music coming from behind the closed doors of the Catering Room.

Of course, we also observed some other usual routines of a celebration. Emily and I cut a 60-anniversary cake. Several guests made speeches. I tried something different about speakers: I invited mostly ladies who normally did not make speeches at parties: Catarina Chi (陳寬泠), a librarian, who rarely sang Chinese opera (she did at my 80th birthday party), and never made a speech at a party before; Mary Chu (高曼琍), a nurse, but a non-singer; Dr. Leepo Yu (鄭麗波), a research scientist at the National Institute Health, for whom I provided musical accompaniment on stage numerous times; Emily's sister Chinyee Sung (何青意) and our daughter Tracey (蔣粹似), who spoke as family members. Each of these lady speakers did a remarkably eloquent job. Finally, Dann Chi (齊家旦), an old-hand public speaker, added a great male touch to the speaking group. And I concluded with my "Reminiscence".

41.4 Cutting the diamond anniversary cake, 2014.

Since my Chinese opera friends did not attend the dance party where I played a magic show, I tried to do an abbreviated version of my magic performance at this singing party. Lack of proper practice, however, resulted in a subpar performance, and I wish I had not attempted it at all.

In contrast to the poor magic show, Mark and Shirley Tou (竇國明曾淑蘭) performed a unique singing treat. They wrote special lyrics to the tune of Teresa Teng's song "Tian Mi Mi" (鄧麗君"甜蜜蜜"), and sang in duet for us at the party. Now, that was a really unique present!

In spite of our sincere pleas for "No gifts, please!" many guests sent roses, wines, and Black Labels. Tracey gave us a bottle of wine named "Red Diamond" to go with the diamond anniversary. And Captain and Mrs. Chia-chin Yang (楊家瑾周芝眉) selected for us a lovely pair of crystal love birds.

Darryl's Speech: "The Four C's of a Diamond"

Our son Darryl, who could not make it to the party, sent a written speech to Tracey, and asked her to read it at our celebration. Tracey yielded the reading job to her 10-year-old son Emmett McGrath. It was thoughtfully composed, and I am proud to reproduce that speech below:

> Today, we celebrate my mom and dad's 60th anniversary. It's aptly called the Diamond Anniversary because of the "four C's." Not "cut, clarity, color, and carats," but four others that came to mind when I was reflecting on their relationship.
>
> (1) The first "C" is for "Children." I wasn't born until they were already married for 14 years. When I finally arrived, I felt that they were deeply grateful to have me, and that they were ready to be wonderful parents.
>
> > (a) For one, they were incredibly unified. Kids always try to divide and conquer their parents, but there was no breaking them apart. They never disagreed in front of me about what

I could or couldn't do, what I should or shouldn't eat, or what was right and wrong. I shared a bedroom wall with them and I never even heard them disagreeing after we went to bed! I realized much later that they share a strong value system and that they showed great respect for each other whenever they made parenting choices.

(b) They also made me understand that although they love children, and although they devoted so much time and energy to enriching our lives with education and the arts, children aren't the center of the world. There is a time for children and a time for adults. They never stopped doing the adult things that they loved—Chinese Opera, spending time with their friends and family in New York, dancing, sewing, and art. Although I wanted the center of the world to revolve around me, it was profoundly helpful for me to see that it didn't—and that the world of grown-ups could be so exciting and full of life.

(2) The second "C" is for "Chinese." Although we grew up in a nearly all-white community, my parents were always proud of, and enriched by, their Chinese roots. They took great pains to teach us Chinese language, history, art, and culture. They fought an uphill battle to instill in me an appreciation of what it is to be Chinese, but today I see how important it was in binding them together. I'm deeply grateful that they shared this language and culture with me. It makes me feel much closer to them.

(3) The third "C" is for "Challenge." Mom and Dad always challenged each other intellectually and morally to be better people—to be as good as they could be. It was okay not to succeed every time, but they never shied away from challenging themselves, and they always instilled in me the same spirit.

(4) The fourth "C" is for "Choices." Mom and Dad had an enormous number of choices to make throughout their marriage—about life, career, our family. But they always made their choices together as a team. At the same time, they also gave me the choice to be my own person—something I'm very grateful for, even though it has taken me so far away from home.

Finally, in thinking again about diamonds, we all know that they symbolize everlasting love. My Mom and Dad have given me that every day of my life. I'm very happy that they've given that love to each other for each of these 60 years as well.

Happy Anniversary, Mom and Dad!

Love,

Darryl

The Blue Danube

To make up for his absence from our 60th anniversary party, Darryl, single at the time, actually invited us to a cruise with him in Europe as an additional celebration. Emily had always wanted to see Prague, whereas I had always wanted to see Budapest. As to Darryl, he would welcome seeing both these places, as well as Vienna. So, we decided on a 12-day riverboat cruise by Tauck, named "The Blue Danube," in the second half of October, 2014.

As a matter of fact, in his early years out of law school, Darryl gave us as a Christmas present an elaborately designed and handwritten gift certificate for "a trip for two, anywhere in the world, any length of time." It was a gift given when he was not quite financially established, and we did not have the heart to cash it. The certificate therefore "slept" in the "Darryl" file in my file cabinet for many years. Emily told Darryl, when we accepted the Danube cruise, that he could consider the trip as "cashing" of that old certificate.

Tauck offers upscale tours of all kinds, land tours, ocean cruises, as well as river cruises. Emily and I had taken their Canyonlands tour (Grand Canyon, Bryce Canyon, and Zion National Park) before, and that qualified us for an extra day's lodging at either the start or the end of the tour. Thus, we could enjoy a three-day stay in Prague, our initial city, and a two-day stay in Budapest. Among the intermediate places during the Danube cruise, we had visited Passau, Salzburg, Dürnstein, and Vienna before. But Prague, Bratislava, and Budapest were new to us. Darryl was at an advantage because, every place being new to him, he had more novel experiences than Emily and I.

The river cruise ship we were on, named "Savor," carried around 130 passengers, served by a large number of staff members. Several competent tour guides not only took us on coaches to the various points of interests, but also gave interesting lectures on board the ship. In view of the small number of passengers, shipboard shows were limited to folklore dances and such. But the small number of passengers was conducive to congeniality among us for a cordial group of travel companions.

Darryl, the youngest passenger on the ship, is fond of dressing up and, throughout this trip, he wore a jacket and tie every day, including on excursions. Even when he climbed up a steep hill one day to see the castle where Richard the Lionheart was kept as a prisoner, he was dressed up. A few days later, a formal night was declared, but Darryl still wore his usual clothing, jacket and tie. A fellow passenger came to him, and said, "Darryl, I am really disappointed in you! Today is formal night, and I was expecting to see you dressed in something spectacular. How can you come tonight just in your hiking outfit?!"

41.5 Breakfast on board the MS Savor.

41.6 On the sun deck of the MS Savor.

His youthful look, gregarious nature, neat dress habit, and especially his consistent attentiveness to his parents, won him praise by many.

Worthy of Memory

Tauck supplied most of the meals. On off nights, Darryl did research and made reservations at several great restaurants. In Prague, we had a multi-meat dinner on the first night at a restaurant called *U Modre Kachricky II*, not far from the Marriott Hotel where we stayed. They served duck, rabbit, veal, and pork, all in one meal.

On the third night, Darryl's Google Map guided us by foot to the Michelin-starred restaurant *La Dégustation Bohême Bourgeoise* in Prague. Its menu shocked me; it showed only two choices, either a 7-course dinner or an 11-course dinner—with or without wine-pairing! I said to Darryl, "Let's take the 7-course dinner." And Emily seconded my motion. But Darryl thought differently, "Mom and Dad, it's unlikely that we'll come here again. We should take advantage of the occasion, and take the 11-course dinner, with wine-pairing."

That was the longest meal we have ever had. It took us four hours. As I write this, I have in my hand a copy of the menu, and I cannot resist the temptation to write it down here (wine in parentheses):

1. snails, garlic, leek (sauvignon blanc barrique)
2. sturgeon caviar, egg, buttermilk (saint-bris 2012)
3. chestnuts, hazelnuts, cracklings, whipped cream (veltlínské zelené 2012)
4. foie gras, pistachio nuts (riesling auslese 2003)
5. european perch, yest, nasturtium (ryzlink vlasský 2013)
6. tomato sauce, mustard (sancerre rosé 2013)
7. potatoes, ash, kefir, prague ham (cuvée petr nejedlík 2004)
8. calf sweetbreads, mushrooms, white truffle (mercurey 1er cru 2010)
9. stepánovsko chicken, corn (ryzlink vlasský 2000)
10. beef tongue, yellow peas, apple (argentiera 2010)
11. boletus mushroom ice cream, marjoram, defrutum (dark beer)

After the 11-course dinner, it is anticlimactic to mention the 6-course dinner Darryl took us to in Budapest, near the end of our tour. The restaurant, *Onyx*, is also Michelin-starred, within walking distance to our hotel. They served many kinds of excellent bread, and we took "one of each." The meal, with wine-pairing, took only a little bit over two hours. Again, I would reproduce the menu (Hungarian Evolution Menu) here:

1. Goose liver, sour cherry, loaf (Nyitnikék 2013)
2. Water buffalo, pickled cucumber, sour cream (Hollóvár Olaszrizling 2013)
3. Brook saibling, kohlrabi, pumpernickel (Tündérek ölén 2013)
4. Goulash soup (Kadarka 2011)

5. Venison, black pudding, endive, beetroot (Vitézföld Kékfrankos 2006)

6. 21st century Somló sponge cake (Kapi Aszú 6 puttonyos 2005)

Aside from the top-notch cuisine onboard the ship, Tauck also arranged two special dinners in palaces. One was in *Lobkowicz* Palace in Prague, with a string quartet playing during dinner. The other was in *Palais Pallavicini* in Vienna, with opera singing and ballet as entertainment. The farewell dinner of our tour took place at the *Akademia Klub* in Budapest. At this event, a wandering band went from table to table to entertain us. Their music was inviting enough to make me want to dance. With Emily's consent, I requested them to play one of my most favorite romantic songs, *Besame Mucho,* and we did an impromptu rumba right there, to the great surprise (maybe horror) of our tour group, Darryl included.

During our three days in Prague, we also took a very interesting day tour of the city: the Hop On Hop Off Tour. This tour company has buses running on a specific route around the city at close intervals. A tourist can buy a ticket, valid for a certain time period, during which the ticket holder can hop on any of their buses, and hop off at any designated tour spot to linger. We three thus had a good opportunity to see various parts of Prague with no transportation problems. And we did our final "hop off" near our hotel.

The most unexpected thing we found in Budapest was that our hotel, *Kempinski,* served congee (soupy rice 粥) at breakfast in the bistro. It even came with some delicious Chinese side dishes, including sweet pickled cucumber (醬瓜). The discovery of that item on the menu delighted me to no end, and I ordered congee every morning there.

Did I find more city pins for my berets on this trip? Yes, three of them – from Prague (Praha), Bratislava, and Budapest.

I took many pictures on the cruise. Here is one taken from my cabin on the ship one morning, when the Danube appeared extra tranquil and dreamlike (Photo 41.7).

41.7 Misty Danube, one morning.

All in all, it was a great trip for all three of us. I would personally rank it as the most nearly "perfect" trip I have ever had. When we thanked Darryl for the big bundle he paid for this cruise, he said, "I am very happy that we could travel together like this. At first I thought Tauck's price was on the high side, but their level of service really makes it worthwhile!"

42

The Treasures of Cedar Crest

As the need for downsizing in our living gradually loomed, and as our energy level palpably waned, Emily started to suggest that we move from our four-bedroom town house to a "continuing care retirement community (CCRC)," to prepare for the days when we could no longer drive, and would even require assistance in our daily living. The basic premise of this idea had merit, and we quickly acted on the idea. The search process for a suitable CCRC, however, was not easy. There were many things to consider: geographical location, initial and maintenance costs, levels of available services, and the general atmosphere of the community.

There are two types of CCRC. One, known as "life care," charges a relatively high (refundable) entrance fee and a relatively high monthly maintenance fee. But when a resident has to move from the "independent living" phase to the "assisted living" or even "memory care" phase of living, the monthly maintenance fee will remain the same. In effect, the higher monthly fee represents a premium payment for the possible future use of more health services. In contrast, in the "fee for service" type of CCRC, the (refundable) entrance fee is lower, and so is the monthly fee. But, when a resident has to move from "independent living" to the "assisted living" or "memory care" phase, the monthly fee will be adjusted upward, depending on the services required.

The community we finally decided on, Cedar Crest, in Pompton Plains, New Jersey, belongs to the "fee for service" type. There are about 1,800 residents, which is considerably more than some other communities with only 200–400 residents. The large size of the community makes possible more group activities and clubs, and a comfortable pool of possible new friends. Unlike some other communities we visited, Cedar Crest permeates with a friendly general atmosphere.

One important feature of Cedar Crest is the sense of security we enjoy. The pull-cord alarms installed in the apartment connect directly to the security personnel. One time, Emily pulled such a chord by accident, and just as I was calling the Security Office to apologize, a security guard was already at our door. Every day at night, the security people engage a special latch on the apartment door, which will be automatically disengaged when the resident opens the door the next morning. If the latch is found to remain engaged by 11:00 in the morning, the security personnel will knock on the door to make sure that the residents inside are safe and sound.

Cedar Crest provides meal plans, either 30 means or 20 means per month. For the first few months at Cedar Crest, Emily and I sat with random dining companions in either of three main dining rooms. I tried to check off their names in the directory, and tried to match their faces with their names so that I could address them by their first names. Out of curiosity, I counted the checked names after a few months; it came to 96! Some of them I could not carry on conversations with, because of their hearing problem or lack of subjects of mutual interest, but most of them shared with us the stories of their lives, making mealtime a fun time.

Off the Mainstream

Aside from doctors, professors, and engineers, I have met several people in professions off the mainstream that I normally would not have met. Bill Mack, a corporate jet pilot, had a generous employer. On some flights to business meetings in foreign countries, the CEO of the company invited the wives of the two pilots (one for the outbound flight and the other for the inbound flight) to accompany them for a free vacation. Once, in Taiwan, the CEO requested the local business host to serve them authentic Chinese food, and the host ordered a banquet with, among other expensive delicacies, sharks' fins (魚翅) and sea cucumber (holothurian, 海參). These are indeed expensive delicacies. But, while Bill and his wife Marylou found the sharks' fins tolerable, they were completely turned off by the shape and the texture of the sea cucumber. The upscale dinner was rated a black spot of their Taiwan vacation. How cultural differences could spoil things!

Another Bill we dined with was a handsome lawyer Bill Santoro. His wife specifically and proudly pointed out that Bill was a defense lawyer for the Mafia. Since I have always been a big fan of courtroom scenes in movies and TV shows, I could not resist asking Bill whether he would tell me some of his best courtroom stories—without revealing names and places, of course. He responded positively with a smile, and said, "Sure." But when he started to describe a case, he paused, scratched his head, and said, "I don't remember." I was of course greatly disappointed. Was he promising me to tell me stories, only to renege? Or, . . . It turned out that he really was a victim of Alzheimer's disease. He even had to rely on his wife to order his dinner. It was my lost opportunity to hear firsthand details of court trials.

Ed Jannicelli was a bit vague about his line of business. He said, "I was in the foundation business." "Foundation business?" I asked, "building and construction?" "No," he said. I switched my guess to a different occupation, "So, you ran a charitable organization?" He chuckled, and replied, "Neither of these; I designed bras." Emily and I laughed at his interesting euphemism. He obviously impressed his boss; his boss' daughter became his wife.

Some years later, we had dinner with David and Norma Gridinsky. David was also a little vague about his line of business. "I was in the 'meatpacking' business," he said. What does "meatpacking" mean? Only upon further clarification did it become clear that he worked for a manufacturer of bras. I couldn't believe how prominently bras figured at Cedar Crest.

Then I also discovered that several residents here were publishers of specialty magazines. One Donald Bender, usually wearing Western-like (cowboy) garb, used to publish a calendar of country music performances, listing the time and venue of their bookings. Fans of country music subscribed to it in large numbers. Jerry Steinman, on the other hand, published a magazine or bulletin for beer breweries, reporting news and developments in the beer industry. And Frank Nothaft was actually a publisher of a variety of magazines, one for hair salon owners, one for professional barber stylists, one for vegetarians, and one for candy lovers. He and his wife even managed the publication of NASA's technical briefs, although the technical contents were supplied by NASA, so they did not have research or editing responsibilities.

Degrees of Separation

Bernard Goldberg is our friendly next-door neighbor. Because he is badly hard of hearing, he and I could not engage in long conversations. One time, he introduced us to his visiting granddaughter, Julia Goldberg, who was studying for her PhD at Harvard in the field of public health. At dinner, Julia made known that her major advisor is a Chinese professor named William Hsiao. "William Hsiao? Really?" I couldn't hide my surprise. William (蕭慶倫), a professor of economics teaching at the School of Public Health at Harvard, has been a good friend of mine for decades. "You and he are good friends? I have to tell him I met you," Julia could not hide her surprise either. So, here at Cedar Crest, the granddaughter of my next-door neighbor happens to be a PhD student of my good friend at Harvard. Isn't that surreal? A case study of "degrees of separation"?

Photo 38 is an early picture of the Hsiao family. William (Bill) is the second from the right. First from the left is his wife Ruth (俞毓慶), who had kindly served as a reader for this book, giving me many excellent suggestions, until she had to stop for ill health and death. I owe her much, and miss her a great deal in the writing of the later chapters.

With Richard and Barbara Armstrong at our first or second dinner together, our conversation touched upon our children. They told us that one of their sons, Jim, went to Princeton, majored in history, lived in the dorm named Rockefeller College, and graduated in 1990. "Are you kidding me?" I almost yelled out, "our son Darryl also went to Princeton, majored in history, lived in Rockefeller College, and graduated in 1990!" Subsequently, we independently checked with our respective sons, and, sure enough, they knew each other. How can there be such an incredible coincidence here at Cedar Crest?

Robert and Sophie Murray distinguished themselves by earning their respective doctorates late in their lives. For that reason, I always address them as "Dr. Murray, and Dr. Murray." In return, they always address me as "Dr. Chiang." Normally, a dinner engagement for us two families would involve a table for four. But one time, Sophie called for a dinner with us for six persons, to include their daughter Therese ("Tessie") Faessler and grandson Marcus Faessler, who were coming from Switzerland to visit. They wanted to meet me. "Of course," I said, "It would be a pleasure to meet them. But why do they want to meet me specifically?" Sophie's explanation gave me a surprise: "When Tessie was studying at Rutgers University, she had become a big fan of the book you wrote, and when she learned that Alpha Chiang is living at Cedar Crest, she was eager to have dinner with you." It turned out that Marcus is studying my book, too. Wow, another interesting case of "degrees of separation"!

"If it's good enough for Emily and Alpha, . . ."

Half a year after we moved to Cedar Crest, our old opera friends Herbert and Mary Chu decided to move here, too. Mary's reasoning went like this: "If that place is good enough for Emily and Alpha, it's good enough for us." Hearing this caused me much apprehension. This kind of move is a major change, and even though it was their own decision, we would bear moral responsibility for it. Luckily, Herbert and Mary found Cedar Crest to their liking, and we felt relieved. (See Photo 52 for an early likeness of Herbert and Mary.)

Having spent many years of her youth in Rome as a daughter of a diplomat, Mary is fluent in Italian. Thus she naturally joined the Italian Roundtable right after she moved to Cedar Crest. After her mastery of Italian became known, however, she was asked to become the group's teacher.

Two years later, Roger and Lilian Yeu, another couple that we have known for 60 years, moved here. Their move was the result of the persuasive power of Mary Chu, so I felt less apprehension this time. It turned out that Roger and Lilian like Cedar Crest as well. These two couples, with long friendship with us through Chinese opera, further solidified our own liking of this community. In them, we have a "treasure" of mature friendship. (See Photo 69 for a group picture with Roger and Lilian.)

Herbert, an excellent singer of the hero role, regularly came to our apartment to practice opera with me as accompanist. Our apartment, an end unit on the sixth floor in a seven-story building, could accommodate singing, because Bernard Goldberg next door is hard of hearing, and Phyllis Gutwetter across the hall had kindly told us that she does not mind my piano practices, or even if we do Chinese opera singing. Roger, my longtime musical partner, also came to my apartment to play with me, for Emily's singing. This continued until it became difficult for Herbert and Roger to walk over from their building to ours, which forced us to suspend our opera sessions.

Inventions of China

I have always been extremely proud of my Chinese ancestry, on account of the colorful history and culture of the country. Even as a school boy, for example, I learned about the four great inventions of ancient China: the compass, gun powder, papermaking, and printing. All of these produced far-and-wide effects on mankind. When Eliot Steinberg, a chemist in the pharmaceutical field, had dinner with us one day, he said, "Alpha, here is a book on Chinese inventions that you ought to read." I thought its subject would be the "four great inventions" that I am already familiar with. But, no, it is a book dealing with hundreds of inventions that Chinese people have made in our long history, systematically collected and reported by Joseph Needham (1900–1995), a British biochemist, historian, and Sinologist.

Joseph Needham's interest in China began after he fell in love with a Chinese girl, Lu Gwei-djen (魯桂珍), who went to Cambridge to study, and who later became his second wife. He learned Chinese from her, and initiated research for a project "Science and Civilization in China," with ever expanding volumes. The Chinese inventions he and his assistants unearthed beyond the "four great inventions," all from recorded Chinese sources, ranged from civil engineering, roads and bridges, astronomy, physiological alchemy, military technology, ferrous metallurgy, ceramic technology, mining, botany, agriculture, forestry, food science, medicine, and language and logic. I could not believe what I read. Unfortunately, I neglected to jot down the name of the book before I returned it to Eliot, no longer with us.

Lu, Joseph Needham's wife, gave him a Chinese name: 李約瑟. While 約瑟 is a standard translation of Joseph, the last name 李 (pronounced Li), a common name in China, was ill-chosen in my opinion, because it has no phonic or other relation to the name Needham. I suspect that Lu had come from a part of China where the local dialects make no distinction between the "el" and "en" sounds, which could have led to confusing Needham with Leedham, leading to the choice of the choice of Li for the L sound. An alternative Chinese last name, 倪 (pronounced Ni), would have been a more appropriate choice from the phonic point of view.

The Learned Professor Silver

A fellow resident from whom I learned much was Arnold Silver, a retired professor of English literature at the University of Massachusetts. One of the "treasures" of Cedar Crest is the Elderhostel courses, all taught by residents, many of whom are retired professors, doctors, engineers, and other professional people. We tried to take all the courses Professor Silver offered, including Aphorisms, Philosophers, Shakespeare's *Hamlet*, *King Lear*, and *Tempest*. He was an erudite and fascinating teacher.

And we also arranged to have dinner with him often. As expected, he was a wide-ranging conversationalist. Instead of small talks, he would regularly raise thought-provoking topics at the dinner table. Once, his question was: How would you have chosen to live your life, had it been possible for you to redirect it? That called for some mental search beyond the ready answer I normally gave, and a revision of my old thoughts—a stimulating exercise.

He was a liberal-turned-conservative. Having thought through the beliefs of the two camps, his final espousal of the conservative cause was based on tight logic, not blind faith. Interestingly, his lady companion, Mildred Kaye, a vocal, dedicated liberal, often differed with him openly and they would engage in vociferous arguments, our presence notwithstanding. It became our frequent job to intervene and force a change of subject.

At the memorial service for Arnold, we told Arnold's daughter how much we enjoyed Arnold's courses, and our dinners together, and how much we missed him. She said, "My father always enjoyed having dinner with you two also. Every time he finished dining with you, he would call me to tell me that he just had a delightful dinner with the Chiangs."

Medical Doctors

One unavoidable headache after moving to a new residence is to form a new network of medical doctors. The foremost difficulty is the lack of any clue as to where to begin. At Cedar Crest, I was lucky to have had dinner with Fred Palace and his wife Ruth. Fred, a retired physician, is thoroughly familiar with the medical scene in the Morristown area. When I asked him for recommendations, he gave me the names of his own doctors. They worked out well. Some years later, however, we gradually switched, for convenience, to physicians that either work full time at the medical center at Cedar Crest, or visit Cedar Crest on a regular basis. Since Ruth used to be a competitive ballroom dancer, we also had a topic of common interest with her.

Lingual Resources

Living a relatively sedentary life, and fully aware of the benefits of walking exercise, I had sincere intentions to make walking a part of my daily routine. But, unlike dancing, plain walking can be painfully monotonous. To enliven this boring activity, I tried to inject some musical element into it. Humming tunes would be fine, but too simple for me since, with fairly good ears, I have always found musical scores easy to memorize. For greater mental challenge, I decided to learn and memorize the lyrics of old songs whose tunes I am already familiar with but whose lyrics I never paid attention to.

My repertoire started with songs like "To Each His Own," a song I fell in love with while at the University of Colorado, although my fascination was mostly with the tune, and I neglected its lyrics altogether. Now I could also savor its verses:

A rose must remain

In the sun and the rain

Or its lovely promise won't come true

To each his own, to each his own

And my own is you . . .

"You Belong to My Heart," is a song I used to dance to, way back in Shanghai. Gradually, I added "Moonlight and Shadow," a song I once sang on a radio broadcast when I was a young boy in Shanghai; "As Time Goes By," from the movie *Casablanca*; and "Memory" from the Broadway musical *Cats*, and others. The song lyrics, now readily obtainable on the internet, contain simple but cute rhymes. In the song "It's All in the Game," for example, we find

Many a tear has to fall

But it's all

In the game . . .

Once in a while he won't call

But it's all

In the game . . .

I love the rhyming that uses very simple words like *fall, all,* and *call.*

Songs in English posed little problem. But for lyrics in foreign languages, I needed help. Schubert's "*Ave Maria*" is in Latin, and I never studied Latin. Fortunately, a fellow resident, John Devine, knows Latin well and kindly taught me the words in "*Ave Maria.*" John was a Jesuit priest who left the priesthood after he fell in love with a divorced lady with children. The children collectively adopted him as their father. Thus, in an instant, he turned from a religious "Father" into a familial "father." While a priest, he taught theology and served as Dean of Students at Georgetown University. Later, after earning a doctorate at New York University, he taught sociological anthropology there.

The French song "*La Vie en Rose*" is, to me, a must-learn. But Edith Piaf sang it from the female point of view, and I needed to change it to the male voice. Unfortunately, my knowledge of French was not up to the task. This time, help came from Audrey Zubkoff, who majored in French and Spanish in college, and lived in Paris where she met her husband Seymour Zubkoff, an engineer who worked abroad a lot. Audrey also helped me with the Spanish in my favorite song "*Besame Mucho*." I might actually have tried to learn more French and Spanish songs if Audrey had not passed away so early.

A Third Piano Teacher

I first saw Elaine Thomas when she (a pianist), her husband Leo Thomas (a violinist), and another resident Cathy Charles (a cellist) played a concert as a trio at Cedar Crest. She impressed me not only as a pianist, but as an outstanding speaker. Before each piece of music was played, she would give a succinct introduction about the salient features of the piece, some tidbits about the composer, and an alert to what specific things to look for in that piece. That brief but lucid introduction raised the listening enjoyment to a much higher level, and she immediately won my ardent admiration. Later, for physical problems, Cathy had to quit playing, and Leo soon followed suit. Then Elaine switched to four-hand piano concerts with Fred Knapp, a mechanical engineer and pianist. The trios and four-hand piano concerts were all good, and Elaine's introductions remained an outstanding feature of those musical events.

Little did I expect that Elaine would consent to be my third piano teacher. I had to warn her, as I did my previous teachers, that I am an "oddball student," and that I only want to review some old pieces. But she did not mind it. By this time though, almost three decades after I first ventured into piano playing, my learning ability had immeasurably deteriorated. So, she had to be even more patient than Sue DeWolf and Tammy Lum in working with me. Elaine and her husband Leo can be seen in Photo 87.

At one time, Elaine made an intriguing suggestion. "You like 'Moonlight' and '*Clare de Lune*,'" she said, "maybe you can consider learning another moon piece, to form a Moon Trilogy." After discussing some possibilities, I said, "I would like to try Mancini's 'Moon River.'" Elaine liked the idea, and was kind enough to get me a copy of the sheet music. On paper, the score looked simple enough, but the actual playing was something else. I found it hard to proceed. Another piece that I thought might be easy to learn, Schumann's "*Träumerei*," also proved to be much more difficult than I imagined. I memorized the first part, but have been stuck midway through it.

With many other commitments, I found it necessary to suspend the piano lessons. It is a pity, because Elaine is such a good teacher. Cedar Crest is lucky in that Elaine enthusiastically shares her talent at many events, concerts, and community functions.

Even without piano lessons, we often have dinner together with Elaine and Leo Thomas, and Fred and Ruth Knapp—a highly musical group. Ruth plays the relatively rare musical instrument, the Q Chord. She is also an artist (drawing, painting, photography), specializing in flowers.

The Memoir Group

The idea of memoir writing had been floating in my mind for some time, even before I moved to Cedar Crest. Whenever certain themes hit me, I wrote them down, all random, unorganized, some in English, and some in Chinese. When I learned about the Memoir Group at Cedar Crest, I naturally tried to attend.

The leader of the group is Helene Zablocki, a lady who does not live here, but who has kindly led the group as a volunteer for many years. Meeting on Monday evenings twice a month, the group of from 6 to 20 writers gather to take turns reading their stories. Depending on the size of attendance, sometimes each person only has a five-minute allotment to read. My pieces are usually too long, yet breaking a piece into smaller segments would lose the intended flow of thoughts. The time limitation is probably also the reason for lack of critiques from the fellow writers. It was consecutive readings, without the benefit of discussion and constructive criticism. This format is not what I hoped for.

In my case, since I usually submitted my piece to Helene in advance with a request for comments, I did get the benefits of critique and suggestions from the leader. But when I firmed up my plan to write a complete book instead of random chapters, I stopped going to the group meetings, and just concentrated on writing. Nevertheless, I owe to the Memoir Group, and especially to Helene Zablocki, for the initial spark for my project.

The fact that several residents here have published their memoirs, including Werner Neuburger and Loren Schmidtberger, also provided encouragement for me. Werner's book is called *Dark Clouds Don't Stay Forever: Memoirs of a Jewish German Boy in the 1930's and 1940's*. Loren's book has the title *The Beginner's Cow: Memories of a Volga German from Kansas.* (Loren Schmidtberger was a professor of English.) More recently, Betsy Burr published her book *Dancing with Whales: A Book of Encounters.* All of these books have given me reading pleasure.

The CC Villager

David Greenwood, a woodworker, actor, and writer, decided one day to start a quarterly magazine, The *CC Villager* (CC for Cedar Crest). There are enough local writers and artists to supply the contents of such a publication, with the inaugural issue coming out marked "Fall, 2016." It is to the credit of David Greenwood, as the Editor-in-Chief, to see to the smooth flow of successive issues, with ever improving quality.

I had had three pieces published in the magazine, which, with the magazine's permission, now appear in a revised form in this book.

In the Dining Room

Cedar Crest supplies one meal a day, and residents have a choice of three dining rooms, plus a café and a bistro. It's always such a pleasure to go to dinner in the evening, even with the usual long waiting in line we have to endure. Dining with, or even just seeing, some resident friends is nice. But the opportunity to interact with the young dining room staff provides a welcome relief from, and counterbalance to, conversing only with our similarly aged fellow diners. Their youngish faces and display of energy truly add another dimension to our dining experience.

One of the managers of the Overlook dining room, Mohammad Bayan, has known us for a few years, and he always stops by to chat a bit. Allysa Post is also always friendly and helpful. And Karen Meyer, another managerial staff member, never permits her smile to leave her face for a single minute. For her extraordinary services, she has received multiple awards, including a prize of "reserved parking" for a month. *Brava*, Karen! Personally, I think she deserves a permanent reserved parking space.

The waiting staff, all high-school or college students, are mostly energetic, conscientious youngsters trying hard to serve us oldsters, some of whom could be grumpy because of bodily discomforts or other personal problems. Emily and I try our best to be polite to the servers to show our appreciation of their services. And we have formed meaningful friendships with them.

Ashley and Ethan Logan, brother and sister, so efficient and courteous, are two of our favorites. We once had dinner with their maternal grandmother, Janyce Hoogmoed, who is also a resident here. Actually, Janyce has four other grandchildren serving us in the dining room right now.

Breanna Freideman, an exotic beauty with a charming personality to match, is one of the most delightful servers one could ask for. With a genuine smile, she treats the diners as friends. Studying to be a nurse, she is sure to become a sought-after one. And I predict that her caring

42.1 With Breanna Freideman in the Overlook dining room, 2017.

attitude and endearing personality would prove helpful in speeding up the recovery of her patients.

Michael Dambra, a friendly tall young man, received a "Hero" award for volunteering to cut food for a lady who found it difficult to do it by herself. I am glad that Cedar Crest has this personnel system to commend good people. Michael did not talk to us much, but Kait Tenhoeve always came over to say hello like an old friend, even if she was not assigned to our table. And Tracey ("Ace") Webb, who has the same first name as my daughter, routinely greets us with warmth.

Djellza "De De" Kica, is a funny server who sometimes jokes around with me. One day, when she asked me about dessert, I said, "De De, I really shouldn't eat dessert tonight." But when I jokingly added, "Unless you insist," she replied in a matter-of-fact manner, "Oh, I do insist; what would you like to have?" I thought for a while, and, still in a jolly mood, said, "Surprise me." What do you think she came up with? Four different kinds of desserts on a single plate! It was more than I could eat, but, in her honor, I did clean up the plate that night.

42.2 At dinner on my 90th birthday, with dining-room staff (from left) De De Kica, Sara Gustavsen, Christine Wasiuk, and Karen Meyer, July 2017.

42.3 A wider view of my 90th birthday dinner table at Cedar Crest, July 2017. Sitting at the table (from left): Mary Chu, me, Emily, Roger, and Lilian Yeu.

With no party planned for my 90th birthday, I just had dinner in our Overlook dining room. Roger and Lilian Yeu joined Emily and me. Mary Chu also came, but Herbert could not make it. That gave me an opportunity to take some more pictures in our dining room.

For the most extraordinary service we have ever received in the dining room, we have to thank Veronica Campbell. With an inexplicable kindness toward Emily and me, Veronica would habitually rush over to our table to fill our tea cups with hot water (with a bit of honey for me), even if our table was outside of her jurisdiction. That made us feel very, very special. She is in college, preparing herself to become a clinical psychologist. She certainly has our very best wishes, always.

42.4 With Veronica Campbell, 2017.

Dining Partners

We have had many dining companions over the years, too numerous to mention here. One of them, Debby Greenberg, surprised Emily and me greatly, when she confided to us that she had her (ultramodern) haircut done in Chinatown, Manhattan. An American customer in a Chinese hair salon? What a sight that would be!

Florence Mehl always brings fancy appetizers when we dine together. With great knowledge about cheeses, she introduces us to many that we never tasted before. For some reason, she just loves our baby-grandson, Julian. She admits to an addiction: a daily dose of Julian photographs.

One of the topics at dinner with Jim Gallagher was college baseball. He took as much pride in the men's basketball at Villanova, his undergraduate alma mater, as we have in the achievements of the women's basketball teams at University of Connecticut (UConn). Bill McConnell, who lived in Connecticut before moving to Cedar Crest, shared our interest in UConn women's basketball, and his wife Sue is, like me, a student in the playwriting class here at Cedar Crest conducted by Joan Ludwig, the subject of the next chapter (Chapter 43).

Arthur Lewis, after hearing about my varied interests in new ventures, made up a list of ten Mission-Impossible-type of assignments for me to work on. Phyllis Hassard has interesting stories, including those about his grandson in show business. And Neal and Bette Monda never fail to ask me about the progress I am making on the present book.

Better Bones

There are fitness centers at Cedar Crest, plus exercise classes led either by professional trainers or fellow residents. We have taken advantage of some of these, but not as much as we should.

Recently, Emily and I joined an excellent "Better Bones" class led by resident Joan Kelly, that exercises all parts of the body, using weights. The fact that every movement is done in slow motion made me think at first that it might compromise the effectiveness of the exercises. But then it became clear to me that the slowness feature is actually the key to its effectiveness, because it takes more strength to execute a slow movement than a fast one. It made me recall what my Tai Chi teachers frequently repeated: "Do it slowly; the slower, the better."

Our Own Contributions to Cedar Crest

On our part, we also made attempts to contribute to the community. When we first arrived here, we naturally joined the Social Dance Group. Since we were more experienced with many years of lessons, the fellow members asked us to be their teachers. We gladly did. But when one lady fell to the floor while dancing, I came to the realization that several of the members have balance problems, and dancing could be a source of accidents. To avoid legal and moral responsibility, we decided to quit teaching after four months.

Emily soon found other ways to make a contribution. She joined a knitting group that knitted baby clothing and blankets for sale, with the proceeds going to our Resident Care Fund, to help those residents who, through no fault of their own, have become unable to pay their monthly maintenance fees.

She has also volunteered for two hours every month to attend to the little Corner Shop that sells such daily-use items as milk, eggs, juice, toilet paper, and candy bars.

As for me, I offered an Elderhostel course titled "A Glimpse of Chinese Culture" three semesters in a row. The course touches on the Chinese language system, Chinese art (calligraphy and painting), Chinese opera (music and costumes), customs and etiquette, religions, and cuisine. It ran for six weeks, 90 minutes per week. For the session on Chinese opera, I enlisted the help of Herbert Chu and Emily to demonstrate singing, with me accompanying. Those arias and the costume display enthralled the audience.

There was enough interest for me to repeat the course three times. Emily co-taught with me the last two times. But after three semesters,

I began to feel the strain of teaching, and decided to suspend further offerings.

Attendance at the class sessions tended to be erratic; some residents could not remember the class schedule, and some others had medical appointments to keep. It was heartening, therefore, to find in the audience one couple, Seymour and Audrey Zubkoff, that always came early and sat in the front row center, and listened to me with intense interest. Actually, when someone not attending the class asked Seymour, "What's the highlight of the Chinese-culture course?" he paid us a high compliment by replying, "There is no highlight–every class session is a highlight."

The View from Our Windows

Our apartment being a corner unit, I could play the piano and do Chinese opera in it without disturbing too many neighbors. But that wasn't the main reason we chose it.

The main reason was that, the minute the marketing staff of Cedar Crest showed us this apartment, both Emily and I were struck by the view from our kitchen and living-room windows. As we looked far into the distance, we saw a vista of several layers of mountains that were separated from one another by mists and clouds. It was a beautiful picture of nature, but better than a masterpiece painting because it was alive. Almost instantly, we said in one voice, "We'll take this unit."

Now, every morning, we can always enjoy the view of distant mountains, with or without mists, sometimes with lots of sunshine on them, but sometimes diluted in color by rain. In the foreground is a parking lot. But the lot is nicely landscaped, with curvy designs and a good number of strategically placed trees. At the far end of the parking lot, stands the Interfaith Chapel to add an element of serenity to the whole attractive scene. I could not have expected any lovelier window view than that to start my daily life. It gives me great pleasure to share this view with you in Photo 89 in the front of the book.

43

The Fortuitous Playwright

In Chapter 42, I mentioned a playwriting class conducted by Joan Ludwig. That is another activity at Cedar Crest I could have elaborated in that chapter. I purposely left it out, so that I can elaborate on it with more details here.

CC Players

Cedar Crest Players, a drama group, periodically puts on plays at our Performing Arts Center (PAC), with around 300 seats. Of course, senior residents who participate can hardly be expected to memorize lines. Instead of acting, they did "readings," that is, the actors can bring the scripts on stage and read from them. There are actions, too, of course. But the physical conditions of the players place natural limits on what they can do on the stage. We are happy to support this activity. Admission charges, usually at $5.00, are affordable, and the profits become contributions to the Resident Care Fund.

CC Players were an ongoing group. But when Jay and Joan Ludwig, a couple with long theatrical background, moved here a few years ago, they brought new vitality to the group. Jay was Dean of Arts and Communication, and professor of theater and communications at William Paterson University, and Joan was a playwriting teacher with Playwrights Theatre of New Jersey (fourth grade through college). Both of them act on stage. And Joan has also been active in producing and directing. This couple is shown in Photo 83.

The Playwriting Class

Of particular relevance to me is Joan Ludwig's offering of a playwriting class at Cedar Crest. Up to that time, I had never seen a script before, and did not even know how a script would look like. I had written two short stories in the Chinese language while in college, one of which was published in the literary supplement of a newspaper, and the other, in a magazine. But never could I imagine ever writing stage plays, either in Chinese or in English. The announcement of a playwriting class naturally attracted my attention, and, ever eager to try something new, I enrolled in Joan's class.

She started with the very basics. The standard format of a script requires a listing of the characters, a description of the setting, and a synopsis of the story. Each time a character speaks, the character's name is indicated on a separate line, centered on the page, with the speech written on the next line(s). The playwright can also write down, in parentheses, the actions or movements the characters are supposed to make. But, as Joan warns, the playwright's parenthetical directions are often ignored by the director of the play when it's produced on stage. On the other hand, the director of the play is supposed to respect to the letter the text written by the playwright.

There are two main types of stage plays: drama and comedy. In either case, though, Joan emphatically pointed out, the play must have one or more conflicts to be explored, and to be finally resolved at the end of the play. And these conflicts must occur on stage, not off stage.

Members of the playwriting class were assigned short scenes to write, right there in class. They also played the game of group story-making, with everyone offering a sentence or two as part of a continuing story. Then, she assigned homework, at first a "monologue," then two-character plays, . . .

A Monologue

For my monologue, I had difficulty finding suitable material, until I hit upon an actual incident that my good friend Tom Tang (湯永謙) told me. Tom was my contemporary at Columbia University, studying for a doctorate in chemical engineering. But as a graduate student, he enjoyed working for a company that designed packaging for various products, such as the outer cellophane wrappings for cigarette packs that could be opened by pulling a tiny tab, and boxes for hamburgers and such. When the owner of the company decided to retire, Tom gave up his studies and took over the company. A very generous and kind person, he treated his employees extremely well. And years later, for example, when Tom sold this business, his terms of sale included a stipulation that the new owner must not lay off any current employees for a period of one year.

The particular incident I planned to use for my monologue, however, involved an employee caught stealing company products. Normally, such an employee would certainly face dismissal. But since this worker was actually among the most productive, Tom just wanted to find out why he would steal. When it was determined that gambling was the problem, Tom offered to forgive this employee on condition that he would never gamble again. The story ended well.

My monologue was set in a church. The character, a repentant thief, is offering a prayer for his forgiving employer, recounting his sin that he promises not to repeat in the future. I carefully polished my writing, in order to make a heartwarming story as moving as I could make it.

Shockingly, Joan the teacher said, "This monologue is not acceptable." In a mildly protesting tone, I asked, "Why?" Joan's explanation was understandable: "The stealing crime is already forgiven by the employer. There is no conflict, and there is no play!"

"Crime and Punishment"

In spite of the failure of the monologue, I considered Tom's story to be too good to be scrapped. It should be used, somehow, in some way. And I did it in the next assignment, a one-act play with two characters.

Of course, I must first create the requisite CONFLICT out of a forgiven crime. How? A lot of thinking finally led me to a solution. Anthony, the financial officer of a company, embezzled large sums of company funds to finance his constant desire to give expensive gifts to his lovely new bride, Dora. A play-by-the-rules kind of person, he acknowledges his wrongdoing, and is not only willing to receive due punishment, but also insists on it. But for various considerations of his own, the CEO, Tom Hanson, wants to lend money to Anthony to make restitution and sweep the crime under the carpet. Not because Anthony is a cousin of Tom's wife, but because he is an excellent financial officer who is very much needed by the company. More importantly, the CEO is afraid that the publicity of the crime would cause a scandal, and adversely affect the company and its stock price.

Still, Anthony's sense of morality and conscience keeps him stubbornly resistant to Tom's offer of a bailout. He even argues that if the company keeps him in his original position, it can set a bad precedent for other employees. On and on, he did not yield until Tom finally reminds him how his new wife, Dora, will react to the news of his dismissal from his position and, even worse, an arrest. Bringing Dora into the picture does the trick. Anthony then accepts Tom's loan. Tom makes Anthony promise to change his gifting habits, and even suggests to him a less expensive but equally effective substitute: Don't send her expensive gifts, but write her tender, surprise love notes.

I gave this one-act play the title "Crime and Punishment." Joan the teacher seemed to like the play—at least it does contain a conflict, nicely resolved at the end. But she said, "Alpha, I really don't care for the title. Why do you have to borrow the title of a famous Russian novel?" Well, my reason was simple: That title perfectly fits the story. In a teasing mood, I jokingly retorted, "I am sorry you don't like the title. Wait till you see my next play. It will be called 'War and Peace!'"

No, I had no such play in mind. I was only joking.

"Crime and Punishment" was presented as a stage reading in October 2015, with Jay Ludwig playing the CEO and David Greenwood (Editor-in-Chief of the *CC Villager* magazine) playing the employee Anthony.

Rhino Theatre

Rhino Theatre, a community theater in Pompton Lakes, New Jersey, is located so close to Cedar Crest that we soon discovered it after we moved here. Established in 2000, it has a main stage and also a small studio theater nearby called Studio 237. With Carmela Wolosz (Artistic Director and Executive Producer) and Jo Ann Ventor (Managing Director and Executive Producer) in charge, the theater puts on many different shows throughout the year.

I entered my email address on their mailing list after seeing a show there, and that fact later sprouted an altogether different relationship between Rhino and me from that of a theater and an attendee.

In the spring of 2016, I received a notification, not of new shows, but of their initiation of an Annual One-Act Jamboree. They were calling for submission of scripts. Since I have a ready-made one-act play lying in my drawer, it did not take much thinking on my part to decide to submit it. Luckily, in a blind selection process, the panel of judges picked my "Crime and Punishment" as one of the 10 accepted.

Rhino produced the 10 selected one-act plays in four shows in August 2016, but to avoid the show being too long, each play was only staged three times. I was thrilled enough to take time to attend their auditions and rehearsals, besides the stage performance at Studio 237.

Rob Nicholson, the director of my play, did an excellent job. An experienced actor, Brad Bebout, portrayed the CEO Tom Hanson to good effect, but the actor who played Anthony was a first-timer, who (I was later told) nervously decided to back out from the show right before curtain time. My salute to the director Nicholson who had to use all his persuasive power to prevent this last-minute cancellation from happening.

Needless to say, I was filled with thrill while listening to the words I wrote spoken by live persons on the stage.

"War and Peace"

When I first mentioned the title "War and Peace" to Joan, there was no thought of such a play in my mind. But when the time came to write another assignment, I thought, "Why not write a piece with just that title?" It took a while to search for a suitable conflict to fit the title. But I finally settled on the theme of daily lifestyle frictions in the lives of a married couple. Take the bathroom first. What is the correct way to insert a roll of toilet paper into the holder in the wall? With the free end of the paper hanging down in front facing you or the opposite way with the free end going toward the wall? Should the man leave the toilet seat up after use or put it down afterward every time? Should you flush the toilet with the seat cover open or closed? Where do you squeeze the tube of toothpaste: at the middle or near the end of the tube? Little problems can cause big conflicts.

To work this theme into a comedy, I created a couple, Victor and Victoria, who seek the advice of Dr. Albright, owner of the Happily Ever After Marriage Counselors. Paying more attention to characterization this time around, I made Victor a dominating, fastidious husband, and Victoria an easygoing, unstructured lady. The major comic lines, however, are given to Dr. Albright, who loves to use high-sounding words and pseudo-scientific terms. In expounding the importance of flushing the toilet with the cover closed, for example, Dr. Albright points out its "hygiene" aspect thus:

> Well, it involves a potential peril which I call the *Specter of the Airborne Micro Water Particles.* You see, every time you flush the toilet, the centrifugal force of the whirling water causes tiny water particles to fly up into the air, carrying germs plus whatever other substance happens to be present in the water. Unless the cover is closed during flushing, the micro particles might reach up far and wide, and in fact colonize all the things lying nearby. That would of course include your towels, your soap dish, and your cups. Even worse, the tiny particles are likely to stampede out of the toilet bowl, merrily dancing in the air, and determinedly targeting your toothbrushes!

Also, when Victor complains about his wife putting all the bottles and cans in the pantry in a disorderly manner, not with the labels facing the front to be clearly visible, Dr. Albright refers to this habit of Victoria as "playing the Label Hide-and-Seek Game," causing Victor to experience a "Container Cognizance Problem." And a controversy between the couple about the way clothes hangers are arranged in the closet, some facing left while others facing right, the pretentious counselor calls it the age-old "Directional Homogeneity versus Diversity Controversy." I thought these pseudo-scientific terms are quite funny, and Joan agrees.

There are other points of controversy between the husband and wife, and Victor seems to win on most of these. In other words, he wins the war. But, when Victoria excuses herself to go to the restroom, Dr. Albright alerts Victor to the fact that Victoria is ostensibly resentful, and now, to win the peace, he must apologize and make a peace offering to her. All ends in both parties agreeing to a compromise.

The pseudo-scientific terms I made up are unfamiliar words, and they may very well prove difficult for the audience to digest upon first hearing. For this reason, when I read the script to the playwriting class, I deliberately slowed down in pronouncing these terms, so they will not sound just like a lot of meaningless gibberish. I was able to get the laughs I expected.

Rhino Theatre Again

Just around the time, another call for scripts came from Rhino Theatre. I submitted "War and Peace" for the Second Annual One-Act Jamboree and, luckily, it was again accepted by the panel of judges. As before, I excitedly attended the auditions and rehearsals, and the actual performance in August 2017 at Rhino's Studio 237.

This time, only seven plays were staged. Each play was presented in four shows. Denise MacLean directed my play, with Levi Aray, Paul Diverio, and Theresa Lyons acting the three parts. In theater tradition, once the playwright is done with the script, he is not supposed to be involved with the staging of the play. And the director will have complete control. Nevertheless, because of my strong feelings about the need for the audience to digest and chew the flavor of those pseudo-scientific terms, plus the perfectionist propensity in me, I volunteered to alert the director to have the actor playing the marriage counselor pronounce them slowly and distinctly, for the intended comic effect. But I guess I did not impress the director, or she might have felt offended. In the actual performance, my wish was not fulfilled, and the audience was not given sufficient time to appreciate those comic phrases in the dialogue. The waves of laughter I expected did not materialize.

Once More about My 90th Birthday

At this point, I am going to have a sudden reversion to the subject of my 90th birthday in 2017. This may seem out of place for two reasons. First, I have already explained in Chapter 42 that, instead of giving two parties as I used to on big occasions, I decided to have a simple dinner party at Overlook, our regular dining room, on my 90th birthday (see Photos 42.2 and 42.3). I perhaps should add that, on that day, I did ask Emily to take a formal picture of me with balloons and birthday cards, which is printed as Photo 80 in the front of the book. But why bring back the subject? Second, why do this in a chapter on playwriting?

The reasons are really quite simple. In spite of my decision not to have any elaborate celebration, my children thought that such a "milestone" should not be allowed to pass without doing something to remember it by. So, I yielded to their opinions, and, borrowing a great idea from a fellow resident at Cedar Crest, agreed to take the whole family on a one-week family cruise to Bermuda. The ship Celebrity Summit was my first choice, primarily because the cruise was a round trip from Bayonne, New Jersey, to Bermuda, and back to Bayonne, totally obviating the fuss and aggravation of air travel. Conveniently, the very first embarkation date I proposed to the family happened to fit the schedules of everyone, including son Darryl and daughter-in-law Andrea; daughter Tracey and son-in-law Jonathan; grandsons Emmett McGrath and Kieran McGrath.

43.1 A decadent dinner at Qsine, on board the Celebrity Summit.

We had a smooth cruise from July 23 through 30, 2017. Besides shipboard activities, there was a daily magnificent dinner. But our most memorable meal was at a special restaurant on board, Qsine, where we partook a decadent multicultural dinner.

I had declared to everyone in no uncertain terms that this cruise was a thanksgiving gift from me to them, but I did not want any gifts in return. Nevertheless, against my admonition, a surprise present did come my way during one dinner on the ship.

The contents of the nicely wrapped package looked like books—maybe mystery novels that I have always enjoyed reading? Wait. There seemed to be multiple copies of the same book! Wouldn't that be superfluous and silly? Then I saw on the cover the title "Two One-Act Plays, by Alpha C. Chiang." My goodness! They had secretly published "Crime and Punishment" and "War and Peace" as a book, and printed 20 copies as a surprise present for my 90th birthday! That indeed was THE biggest surprise of my lifetime! And this explains why I am digressing to the story of my birthday cruise in a chapter on playwriting.

The Secret Publication

The original idea of the secret publication was Emily's (bless her), but everyone in the family supported it. She contacted Joan Ludwig, my playwriting teacher, for copies of the scripts. A minor regret was that I had made some revisions without sending them to Joan, so what Emily got from Joan was not the latest version.

The actual work of arranging the publication fell on Tracey, our graphic-designer daughter. She had to design the cover, choose the font, and plan the general layout. The cover has a striking red background, with black letters on white in the middle part for the title. For the lovely cover of that book, see Photo 65 in the front of the book.

The most time-consuming part of the job, however, involved converting my plays from the original script form to the book form. She did a perfect job (bless her). To my great delight, she also designed a book mark to go with the book. On it, she wrote a description as follows: "Alpha C. Chiang's 'Two One-Act Plays' is published by his wife and children as a surprise gift for his 90th birthday. Crime and Punishment, a boss's dilemma with a trusted employee, is a dialogue on love, mistakes, and morals. War and Peace depicts a couple's farcical first session with a marriage counselor. Both plays emphasize the importance of interpersonal communication and simple but meaningful gestures that can be better than anything money can buy." I could not have written a more succinct and well-worded summary.

When you publish a book with Amazon, or with any other publisher, you are asked to set a price for the book. Expecting no market sales, Emily felt completely free to choose a price out of the thin air. She showed her sense of humor by choosing "$8.88" as the official price. It is a humorous choice, because the numeral "8" is considered a lucky number in Chinese superstition, especially in Hong Kong. This is why most of the telephone numbers of Chinese restaurants usually are full of figures like 8988, 8818, 2838. In Hong Kong, auto license plates with multiple 8s are auctioned off for huge sums of money. The "8.88" price for my book was chosen, jokingly, for good luck. Did I get any good luck so far? I'll let you guess.

Bermuda: Two Visits 50 Years Apart

The 90th birthday visit to Bermuda was not my first. Half a century ago, right after I finished writing and sending the manuscript of *Fundamental Methods of Mathematical Economics* to McGraw-Hill in August 1966, I took Emily to Bermuda for a vacation before starting my visiting professorship year at Cornell University. Both of us deserved a period of relaxed life after two solid (really solid) years of serious work, during which we swore off moves, TV, and weekend entertainments of any description. Besides, we were celebrating our 12th wedding anniversary in 1966. The resort hotel we stayed at boasted a cozy private bay and a beach, which even we, non-water-sport people, found eminently enjoyable.

Among the adventures on our first visit to Bermuda, the one thing that stood out in our memory was the "Underwater Wonderland" tour. Advertised as "a walk on the bottom of the ocean," it involved "helmet diving." On that fine day, the tour guide took the six or seven participants on a motor boat out to the ocean, and anchored it at a particular spot in the Atlantic where the water was suitably shallow. Each of us, in swimming wear, was given a glass helmet with an open bottom to wear, but with proper pressurization, no water could enter into the helmet as we descended into the water. He had lights installed in the water, so that we could see our way while walking on the bottom of the ocean. It was exciting to mingle with different varieties of colorful tropical fish, which would approach us and eat mussels from our hands. They also danced around some metal hoops on the site at the tour guide's command. I have earlier introduced a picture of our underwater walk in Photo 28.4.

But other things about our first visit to Bermuda had become hazy in our minds, and I could not even quite recall the name of our hotel. All I remembered was the first word: Carleton. When I mentioned this to the tour guide who was driving our whole family in his spacious van on a tour of the island, he said, "You must be thinking of the Carleton Beach Hotel. That hotel has been demolished, but I can take you to see the abandoned site." Perhaps because the abandoned site is no longer easily accessible by car, he just took us to a high point overlooking the site from above. Sure enough, there was the cozy private bay and a beach. But there were no people and no buildings.

43.2 Above the old site of the Carleton Beach Hotel, Bermuda.

I looked at the altered scene with some measure of sadness. But it is inevitable for things to change as time marches on—often at supersonic speed. The Carleton is no more, but at least the bay is still there after 50 years. In contrast, when I tried, in 2004, to look for things relating to my childhood in my native village Baoshan, some 70 years after I moved away, not even a single trace of my early days there could be found.

44

The Kitchen and I

In the era when I grew up in China, children in middle-class and well-to-do families were never required to do any housework. Education was the main focus of their lives. No housework assignment did not mean leisure; it was their duty to devote much time to study hard, to excel academically. I enjoyed good food, but knew absolutely nothing about cooking.

As a graduate student in the United States, I had most of my meals in local restaurants, with friends or alone. Some of my fellow students from China rented living quarters with cooking privileges and learned to cook. But I never did. Marriage was the first event in my life that could change things.

Career Considerations

After I married Emily in 1954, we immediately moved from New York City to Granville, Ohio, to start my full-time teaching. As newlyweds, we naturally discussed the matter of division of labor in our home life. I would do all the driving, of course, because Emily had not yet learned to operate a car. Emily preferred not to handle financing, so that was left to me, too. Neither of us possessed cooking skills, and it looked like that we would both learn by experimenting with the help of cookbooks. But when I declared that I harbor a serious wish to study and work the hardest, to develop into a best professor, Emily showed her enthusiastic support by exempting me from all kitchen chores. "You work towards becoming the best professor. I will do all of the house work." What a great life partner!

Such understanding support from my bride served to spurt me on in my academic career. Suffering from a bookworm's misconception of academics, I thought that a professor has to know everything. That misconception forced me into an obsessive desire to get the answers to all the questions the students could possibly ask. As a result, I grossly overprepared for my classes. This took so much time that I had no leisure hours at all, at least not during my first year as a full-time assistant professor. Not until a couple of years later, did I realize that a professor does not have to know everything, and it is not shameful to say, "I do not have the answer to that, but will find out."

The reward for my efforts came in the form of good end-of-semester student evaluations of my courses. I quickly gained confidence and learned how to teach. But I learned nothing about cooking. Meanwhile, Emily became a constantly improving chef, feeding me tasty and artistically presented dishes. It soon became pointless for me to try to compete with her in culinary art.

And there arose more legitimate reasons for me to stay out of the kitchen. My academic work now demanded more than diligent teaching. I must also extend my efforts to research and writing papers for publication in professional journals, and administrative work as well.

A Turning Point

Something did happen to draw me to the estranged part of the dwelling known as the kitchen, but this occurred much later—decades later.

Around the late 2000s, Emily developed a lower back pain. She refused to seek medical help for fear of receiving a possible verdict that she needed spinal surgery. Spinal procedure was then generally considered very risky, and we had actually heard of friends who had become paralyzed as a result of unsuccessful surgery, notably the Musketeer George Hsu. On our travels in those years, she had to tolerate severe pain during the inevitable walks between points of interest. In Pompeii and Ephesus, which we visited in 2008, she often lagged behind fellow tourists by a substantial distance.

She did agree to try acupuncture. It proved ineffective. Chiropractic did help, and after numerous sessions, her pain dramatically receded. Unfortunately, she fell on the street pavement in 2012, breaking the patella in her right knee, and the resulting surgery and the need to wear a cast on her right leg, forced her to walk in an unbalanced way, exacerbating her spinal alignment again. The pain returned.

By that time, however, success stories regarding spinal surgery cropped up, and she became more amenable to medical consultations. One spinal specialist we talked to confirmed that Emily had spinal stenosis, with the nerves irritated by narrowing spinal channels where they are located. Operation is indicated, but in view of Emily's age, the doctor advised against surgery. We then consulted Dr. Russel Huang, the Director of Spinal Surgery at the Hospital for Special Surgeries in Manhattan. He confirmed the diagnosis, but highly recommended surgery. Emily became his patient.

The procedure, a minimally invasive one involving only a three-inch incision, could be done on the outpatient basis. In view of Emily's age, however, Dr. Huang kept Emily overnight at that hospital for observation and discharged her the next day. That was in January, 2017.

During her recuperation, I naturally served as a caregiver/nurse/household help. It was not easy work, since I had so much to learn. In the process, I felt that I was growing as a person, in more ways than one. I also became much more keenly aware and heartily appreciative of Emily's contribution to our home life via her daily housework over the decades.

Wanting to do something for Emily, I made a surprise announcement one day, "From this day forward, I volunteer to take responsibility for our daily breakfast." Strangely, or not so strangely, she raised no objection at all. Thus, in a flash, I fell into the tenured job of "breakfast chef." To mark this new milestone, I looked for a toque blanche, chef's white hat. When I asked the head chef in our dining room where I could buy one, he just fetched one from the kitchen and offered it to me with a wink.

44.1 Chef Alpha, 2017.

A Prior Experience

As I embarked on what I thought was my inaugural kitchen duty, I suddenly recalled a prior kitchen experience, a temporary assignment way back in 1968.

Emily's sister Chinyee, then a simultaneous interpreter for the United Nations, had to go on a mission to Vienna for a month. As a single mother at the time, she asked us whether we could take care of her 11-year-old son, David Kwo, during her absence. We gladly picked David up for a short stay in Connecticut. We enrolled him in our local school, and every morning I prepared breakfast for him before seeing him off on the school bus.

But why was I, not Emily, doing the breakfast? Because Emily had to obey doctor's order to have bed rest throughout that period. Before David came to our house on Southwood Road, Emily went to shop for a new chest, vacuumed and cleaned the entire basement, and overstrained herself for a few days—without realizing that she was pregnant and should avoid heavy-duty housework. She was actually in danger of losing the baby. When the doctor discovered her condition, her order was a stern warning: "total bed rest!" Accordingly, I drove the three of us gingerly (to avoid bumps) to the nearest restaurant for dinner every night, and had simple breakfasts and lunches at home. The "total bed rest" saved our first child, Darryl.

David's month at our home was my first one-on-one relationship with a little boy. I learned from that experience, and became very fond of David. I still remember a couple of little things about David. I gave him a haircut, but, at his request to "not take too much off," I merely trimmed his hair a bit. When I let him have a look in the mirror, he declared me a "great barber." I laughed, because it gave me a convincing example of the motto "Less is more."

I had an even greater laugh when I tried to get him a playmate since we did not yet have children of our own. Our neighbors across the street have a daughter, Allison, about the same age as David, and I suggested to introduce them to each other. David's answer was a thunderous, "What?! Play with a girl? Over my dead body!" His show of determination, with a resolute hand gesture, impressed both Emily and me. With laughter, we promised, "Okay, okay, no girl." Time, of course, would soon cure him.

A grown-up version of David can be seen in Photo 25.4 (extreme right). He now lives near London with his English wife Kate and has two grown-up daughters. Rebecca is a licensed commercial pilot in the United Kingdom; Elizabeth is a handbag designer in Sweden.

My Specialty?

Now that I am known as a breakfast chef, some people tend to ask: "What are your specialties?" My answer, a laugh-getter, is "cold cereals." But I always hasten to clarify that my "cold cereals" are not just pouring something out of a box and adding milk. It bears the name of "Ten-treasure Breakfast (十珍早餐)," containing two kinds of cereals, augmented by strawberries, blueberries, walnuts, sliced almonds, pistachios, banana, black sesame powder, and even Chinese goji berries (枸杞子), topped by a spray of pine nuts.

The cold cereal idea was not initiated by me for the purpose of work minimization. I simply inherited the pattern from Emily. And even for Emily, that was a relatively new practice. She used to serve a variety of things, like eggs, bacon, English muffins, pancakes. But one time, in a phone conversation with Steve and Mildred Ying, our old friends who are living in a retirement community near Boston, the subject of breakfast came up, and Mildred said that she was confining breakfast to cold cereals. This somewhat shocked us, because Mildred used to be the Food Editor for Good Housekeeping and, in that capacity, she edited several cook books for that well-known company. And she was only serving cold cereals for breakfast! From that point on, Emily switched to cold cereals as the breakfast staple: "if cold cereals are good enough for Mildred Ying, then they are good enough for us."

In order not to be labeled a "one-item chef," I did serve oatmeal, too. And the menu may even undergo further growth. Truthfully, though, I am fully aware that my talent clearly does not lie in the culinary field.

A Dad Joke

When a father tells jokes to his children, the children quite often tend to turn their thumbs down and declare the jokes to be corny, either because the jokes are truly bad, or because the children just want to enjoy teasing their otherwise omnipotent dad.

For Christmas 2019, my daughter-in-law Andrea gave me a book of "Dad Jokes" among other presents. I read the whole book that night, and laughed hard at many of the simple but clever jokes. I was even inspired to adapt some of them, and emailed them the next morning to entertain my children and grandchildren. They all expressed delight after receiving my emails. They especially like this little one:

Question: What do you call a so-called "Breakfast Chef" that we know when he murders his food?

Answer: A cereal killer.

As I have long found out, self-mocking or self-deprecation is usually well-received in humor.

45

A Life Foretold

I have reported on many events in my life that may be considered incredible, uncanny, or altogether surreal. During a visit to my native village in my youth, for example, I had a stupid backward fall from a cliff down to the ground below, but I turned out to be 100% injury-free. Even less believable was my mother's miraculous healing overnight, which brought her back from imminent demise. In another case, I was somehow granted a second encounter with a swindler that cheated me out of the then-handsome sum of $5, and succeeded in recouping the full amount plus interest. In Paris, I searched for my friend Patrick for days in vain, but then ran into him in a small antique shop, which Emily and I hurriedly entered by chance, to escape from the penetratingly cold evening air on the street. Also, much to my own surprise, a piece of piano music came into being just because a couple of musical phrases happened to float their way into my dream at night. And a Chinese herbal doctor examined Emily by feeling her pulse area for only a couple of minutes and announced his perfectly accurate diagnosis, which took many Western medical tests to confirm. Almost impossible to believe, but they were all true.

It is only fitting that, in this concluding chapter, I add another uncanny story of my life: When I was about 10 years old, I was foretold a sketch of my future life, which proved to have an unbelievable degree of accuracy.

Fortune-Telling via "The Eight Words"

Fortune-telling is generally considered a superstitious practice. And I am certain that many forms of fortune-telling are indeed nothing but scams. But I am equally certain that the classic Chinese fortune-telling based on "the eight characters" or "the eight words" (八字) stands out as a mysterious but valid predictive system. Its predictions tend to parallel real facts and actual happenings to such a degree that I find it difficult to discredit it.

This form of fortune-telling is said to be based on the ancient Chinese classic called *I Ching, or Yi Jing* (易經, The Book of Changes). Only four pieces of information are used as the basis of all predictions of a person's life path: (1) the year of birth, (2) the month of birth, (3) the day of birth, and (4) the time of birth. Each of these four is represented by two Chinese words (or characters), giving a total of eight words. In the Chinese culture, chronological sequences are traditionally grouped into repeatable cycles of 60; thus 60 years constitute one yearly cycle, 60 months constitute a monthly cycle, and so on, and each member of the 60 in a cycle is designated by a pair of words. The four pairs of words relating to a person's birth year, month, day, and time together form an array—a 2 x 4 matrix—from which a trained fortune-teller can decipher a great deal of life information.

My "Life-Book"

The "life-book (命書)" my father commissioned for me, when I was around 10, came as a booklet with a red cover—red being the most auspicious color in the Chinese culture. It showed my "eight words" in an array on the first page, followed by the description of my life pattern implied by those eight words. I paid little attention to the name of the author, but did notice his good calligraphy. The description was written in an older, semi-literary style that I was too young to comprehend fully, but I did attempt to read it through. Afterward, Father put the book away, and I never had an opportunity to review it again. Still, I could recall the major points that I could and did understand. I would have liked to re-read it now, but my father had burned it following his conversion to Christianity.

What are the major points I still recall from that life-book?

For one thing, the book says that I am destined not to have many siblings, actually not even a few. In actual life, I am an only child. There was almost a brother coming to the family when I was already out of college, but he was stillborn.

My life is to be characterized by a smooth progression throughout, without ups and downs, in my schooling as well as in my career. In actual life, from the 1930s through 1946, through the Sino-Japanese War (into WWII) even under Japanese occupation of Shanghai, I never experienced a day of stoppage in my education. There was indeed a dark period after I skipped from the first grade to the third, and fell hopelessly behind in class, but schooling still went on uninterrupted. Later, studying for my MA and PhD degrees in the United States also followed a continuous path. And similarly, my teaching career, helped by several "uplifting hands," also stayed on a smooth course, without bumps and stoppage.

Regarding the field of study, the life-book specifically mentions economics. Despite the study of economics, though, the likely career for me is to be on the scholarly rather than the business side of the field. Again, this prediction conforms to the reality that played out.

One prediction I considered as strange, even wild, is that my career will take place far away from Shanghai! "Wait a minute," I thought, "Shanghai has long been the principal metropolis in China, a place rich in career opportunities, where enterprising people all over China would flock to. I am already living in Shanghai, and yet I am supposed to leave home for my career?!" That wild prediction almost made me doubt the whole book. I discussed this matter with my cousin Ellen Chiang (蔣懿然), two years my junior and my close pen pal even though she lived only five minutes away, and she also considered that prediction to be too wild to be believable. But look at what happened in reality. Circumstances that developed resulted in my settling in a land far away from Shanghai, thus completely validating the career prediction of the book. And, incidentally, Ellen herself later came to the United States, married Hsi-lung Pan (潘錫龍), and settled in Seattle. Ellen and I both enjoy writing, and we remained pen pals for years. Ellen can be seen in Photo 60.

In a somewhat related point, the book says that I am destined not to be living close to my parents for the greater part of my life.

That again struck me as a very strange prediction, because, as an only son, I am supposed is to stay close to my parents. Yet, in reality, the prediction again proved correct. Even after my parents moved from Shanghai to Hong Kong, and in spite of our several attempts to invite them to come to live with us in the United States, my father always put his church ministry above family considerations and decided in favor of staying in Hong Kong.

What about offspring? The prediction in the book is two-fold: the number will be small; the timing will be late. Emily and I actually had to wait for 14 years after our marriage before our son Darryl arrived in 1968, followed by our daughter Tracey in 1970. We only have two children.

The book supplies no details of the uncanny and surreal events that happened in my life. And it does not enumerate the many hobbies—the spices of my life—that I have developed over the years. Neither does it hint at how long I shall live. But, to this day, I marvel at the degree of accuracy of the predictions it does proclaim.

Other Cases

My life-book is not the only example of accurate predictions from "the eight words." Emily's father had the fortunes of all of his children told, and mailed us a one-page predictive description for Emily's life. Remarkably, it predicts the exact year Emily will bear our first child: age 36.

In 1973, on one of our summer visits to Hong Kong and Taiwan to visit my parents and Emily's parents, respectively, I was introduced to an amateur fortune-teller in Taipei, Mr. Pin-Yuan Chen (陳炳元), Chairman of two commercial firms, but also the President of The Chinese Association of I Ching (中華易經學會理事長). At one time, I was curious enough to find out what the classic *I Ching* is all about. But I found the ancient writing in it grossly unintelligible to me. Now, I was going to talk to the president of an organization devoted to the study of that classic; awesome. In a face-to-face session with him, we discussed not only my life pattern, but that of Emily.

For me, many of his remarks were similar to the contents of my life-book. The new remark that struck me was his description of my sibling situation. "You are the first-born," he said, "and you have a brother, but on the other hand, you don't," he said. This perfectly described the case of my stillborn brother.

For Emily, who did not accompany me, Mr. Chen noted that she was born into a family in government service rather than business. Accurate. Her schooling was as disrupted as could be. Accurate again. On account of the Sino-Japanese War, her family retreated many times from Nanking into the interior provinces of China with the government. Repeatedly yanked from one school to be placed into another, Emily attended as many as 12 different schools from grade 1 through grade 12. Disruption to the extreme!

When Mr. Chen announced that Emily has two elder sisters and one younger sister, however, I immediately corrected him: "No, she only has TWO ELDER sisters!" I was very assertive; I have always known that my wife is the youngest child in her family, with two elder brothers and two elder sisters. Not perturbed by my denial, however, Mr. Chen was equally assertive. "It can't be," he said, "because if she has no younger sister, then all the other information will become out of synch." I continued to insist. And so did he. It came to a dead impasse!

After a couple of minutes of silence, I thought he would be backing off his position any second. But he did not, and just calmly added, "By the way, you should know that a half-sister also counts as a sister." It then dawned on me that there is indeed a half-sister in the picture. I had to apologize to Mr. Chen for my failure of recollection. At the same time, I became even more respectful to the power of "the eight words."

Three Questions

To take advantage of the face-to-face contact with Mr. Chen, I asked three questions that had always bothered me over the years regarding "the eight words." He answered them all to my satisfaction.

First, my life-book classified my eight-word array to fall under a specific category known as "the double-butterfly pattern." I wanted him to verify it, and explain to me what that pattern implies. Yes, my pattern indeed is the double-butterfly (蝴蝶雙飛格), with auspicious implications. "What are the specific benefits to me?" I asked. "The benefits do not come to you"; he replied, "they go to your children."

My second question relates to the use of the admonition frequently given by fortune-tellers to their clients that goes like: "That particular month or year is ill-boding. You should exercise extra care." For one thing, the unpropitious situation is never clearly specified. How could one guard against an unknown mishap or danger? Besides, if taking extra care does succeed in avoiding the mishap or danger, then won't that invalidate the prediction? Mr. Chen's answer was that exercising extra care will not negate the prediction, but will ameliorate the damage. A prediction of bleeding, for instance, may involve a car accident, but it might be fulfilled by a minor cut during shaving.

For the third question, I asked Mr. Chen, "How come the predictions of past events are usually very definite and specific, especially in matters of family relationships, but predictions about the future tend to be vague and general?" His explanation introduced the concept of "mutability" of the future. A person's future fortune can be modified, within limits, by the way he/she conducts his/her life. It can improve or it can worsen. For that reason, predictions about the future have to be less definite.

A Cousin's Story

One of my cousins, Kuo-tao Yui (余國燾), is among the closest to me, because he lived with my family during the Sino-Japanese War, and later also studied and taught economics. He migrated to Vancouver, Canada, after retirement, and has maintained an ongoing email chat with me on all kinds of topics. One of our communications related to a fortune-telling experience his wife, Kung Juan Liu (劉公娟), had before the two of them even met. Kung Juan asked a fortune-teller about her matrimonial prospect, and the fortune-teller answered, "Your future husband is currently studying in England." Kuo-tao was indeed studying at that time at Cambridge University, England, for his MA degree on a government scholarship.

See Photo 57 for the group image of the Yui family.

A Multifaceted Life

My life-book foretold a smooth life, but my actual life has been more than smooth. I have been blessed with an abundance of curiosity, which propelled me into a wide range of interesting avocations, from Chinese opera to ballroom dancing, from Chinese classical calligraphy and painting to photography, from piano to music composition, and from short story writing in college to playwriting in old age. Many things happened to me that can be considered incredible or surreal. It has been a most colorful life.

I have also been blessed in generational relationships. My caring parents provided well for my living and their attention to my education proved priceless. One regret of mine is that even though my mother was amenable to coming to live with us, my father was never sold on the idea of leaving his church in Hong Kong. As a result, they mostly lived far away from me. I have learned to accept this as something predestined, as clearly foretold in my life-book.

My spouse, Emily, has a fully supportive attitude toward our joint life. By shouldering a lot of household work, she allowed me to devote myself to my career of teaching and writing. Yet we have also shared strong common interests in ballroom-dancing and Chinese opera singing and performing.

My son Darryl and daughter Tracey are both well-educated. They hold good jobs, and are making their fair share of contributions to society. More importantly, they are good, sincere, compassionate persons. Emily and I are genuinely proud of them, and equally proud of their respective spouses, Andrea and Jonathan, and their children, Julian, Emmett and Kieran.

It is in the cordial spirit of sharing that I have written down some of the stories in my life. No, I have not told you everything. For example, I am purposely omitting any mention of my venture into

Chinese lyrical poetry (填詞), because I do not possess the necessary skill to translate Chinese poems into English. That topic is reserved for a memoir in Chinese that I plan to write. Certain other stories I deem improper to tell here on account of privacy issues. But most of the ones with entertainment value I have shared with you.

Farewell, Dear Reader

Dear reader: If you have kept reading this volume faithfully to this point, I owe you my sincere thanks—for your time, patience, as well as forbearance. And if you like what I have written, I also congratulate you for your good taste. If you do not, then please accept my apologies for having wasted your time. Sorry, sorry, sorry.

Either way, I bid you a fond, grateful farewell.

Before you leave the book, however, allow me to take you once more to the title of this book, *Tales from My First 90 Years*. It is obvious that the word "First" does not properly belong there. Its insertion, merely a feeble attempt at humor, in no way implies that I expect to live a "second" 90 years. Although the ancient Chinese medical classic, *Huang Di Nei Jing* (黃帝內經), had long proclaimed that a person's original expected life is 120 years, deductions must be made for injuries, diseases, worries, and bad living habits, thereby cutting down the realizable life span to 100, 90, 80, or lower. I have read somewhere recently that there is also talk in the Western medical circles of the 120-year-life-span thesis. The upshot is that, with an acknowledged maximum life expectancy of 120, I surely won't reach 180. So, please do not hold your breath for a sequel to this book.